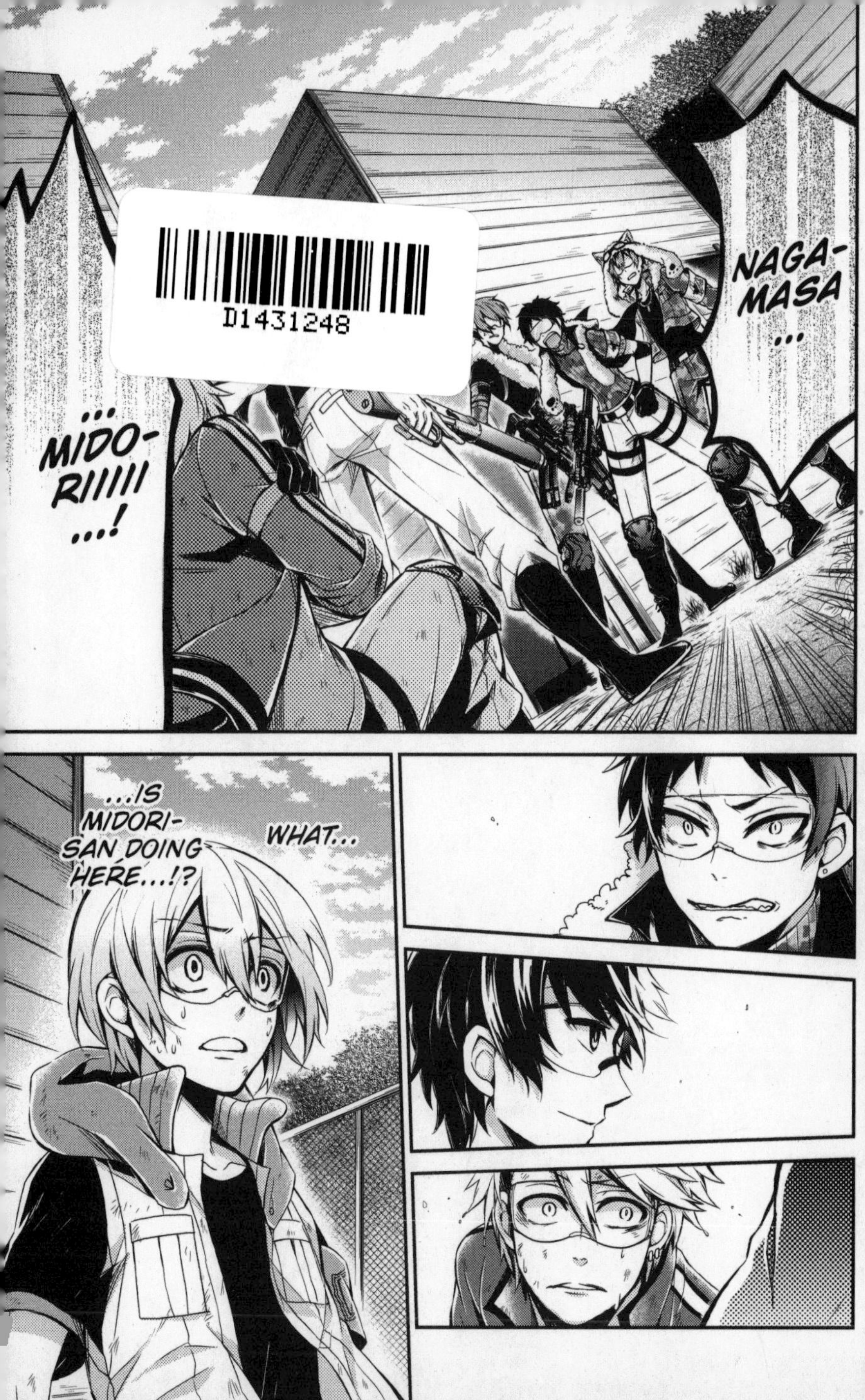
NAGA-MASA...
...MIDO-RI!!!!!! ...!
WHAT...
...IS MIDORI-SAN DOING HERE...!?

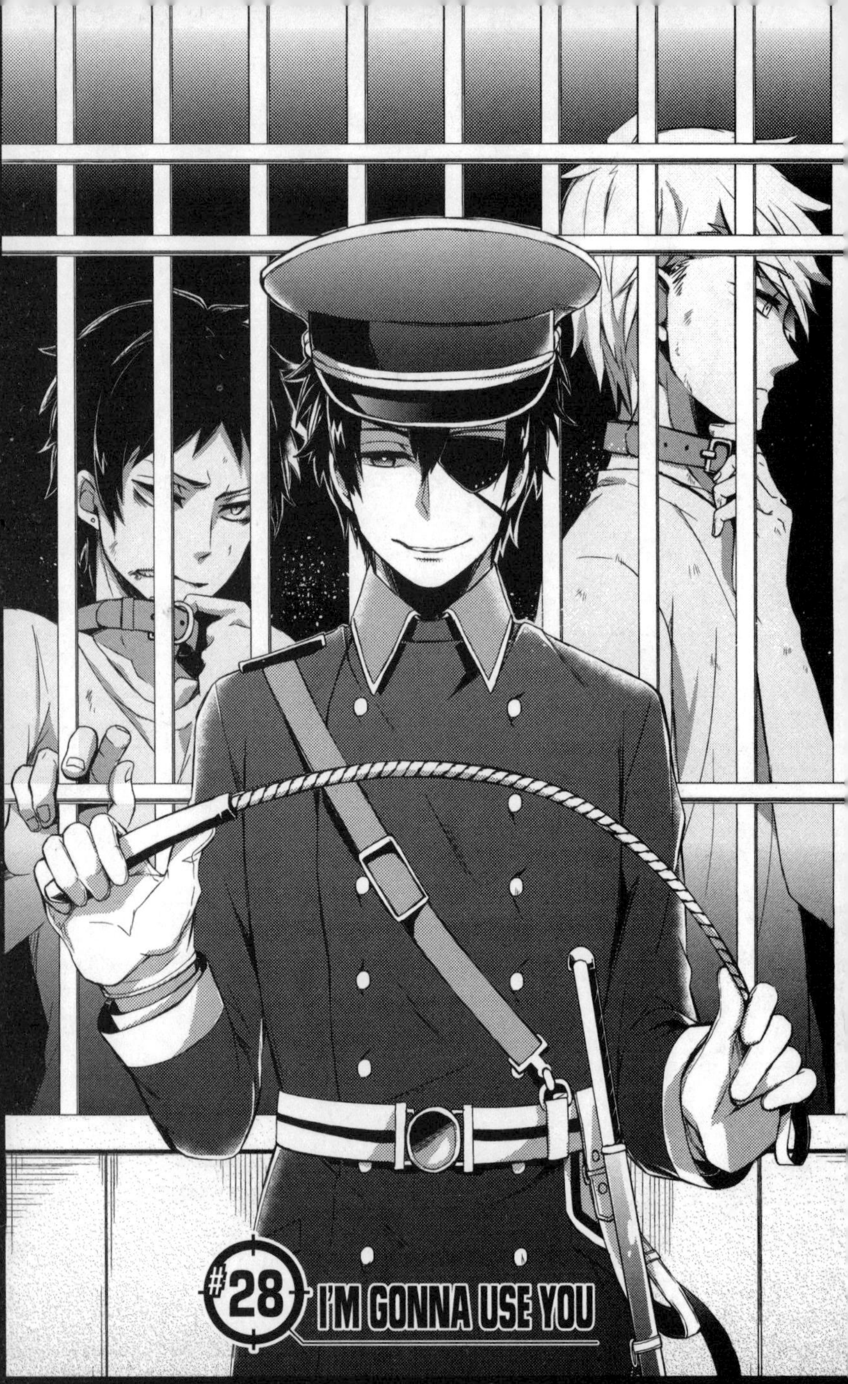
#28
I'M GONNA USE YOU

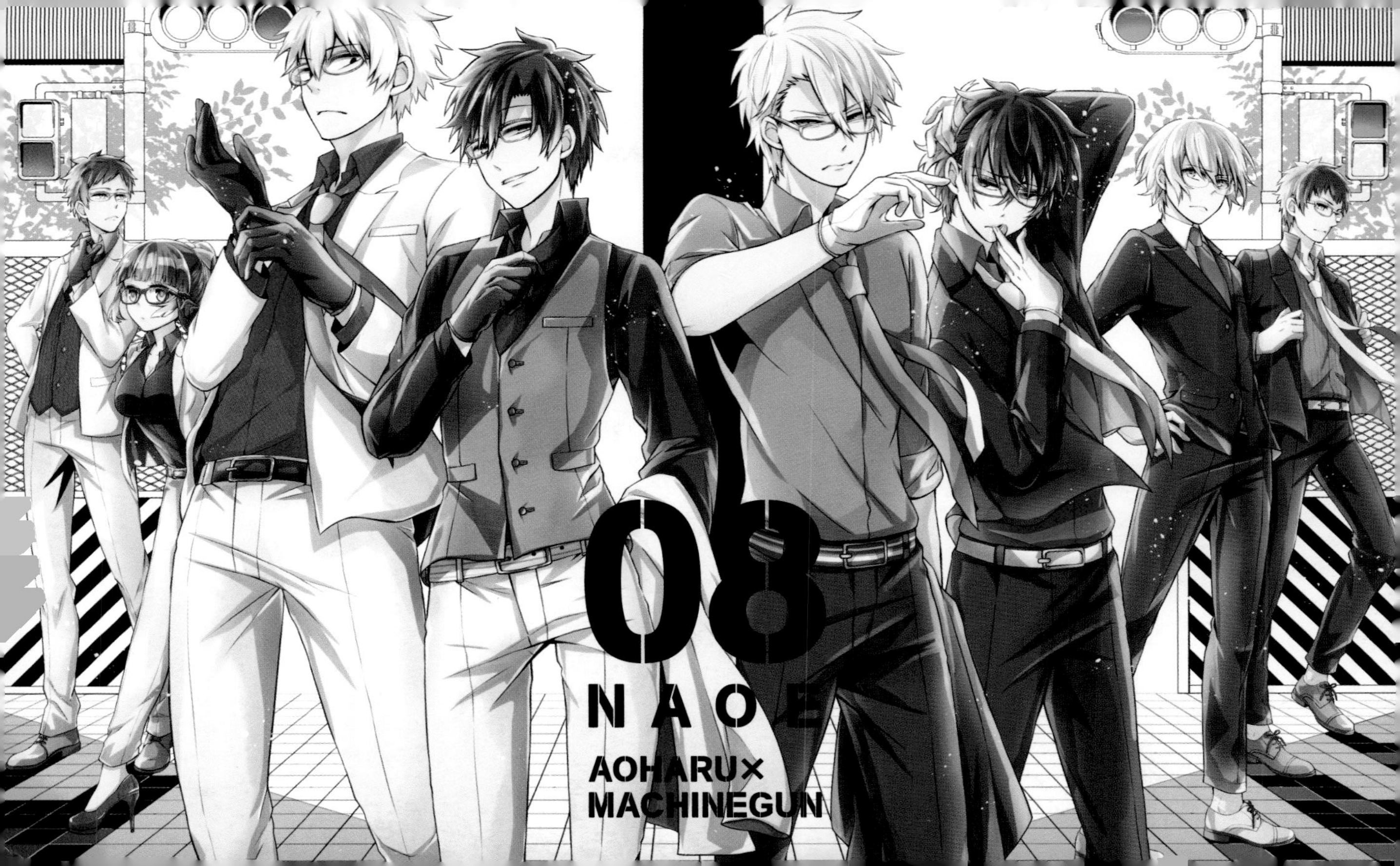
08
NAOE
AOHARU×
MACHINEGUN

CONTENTS

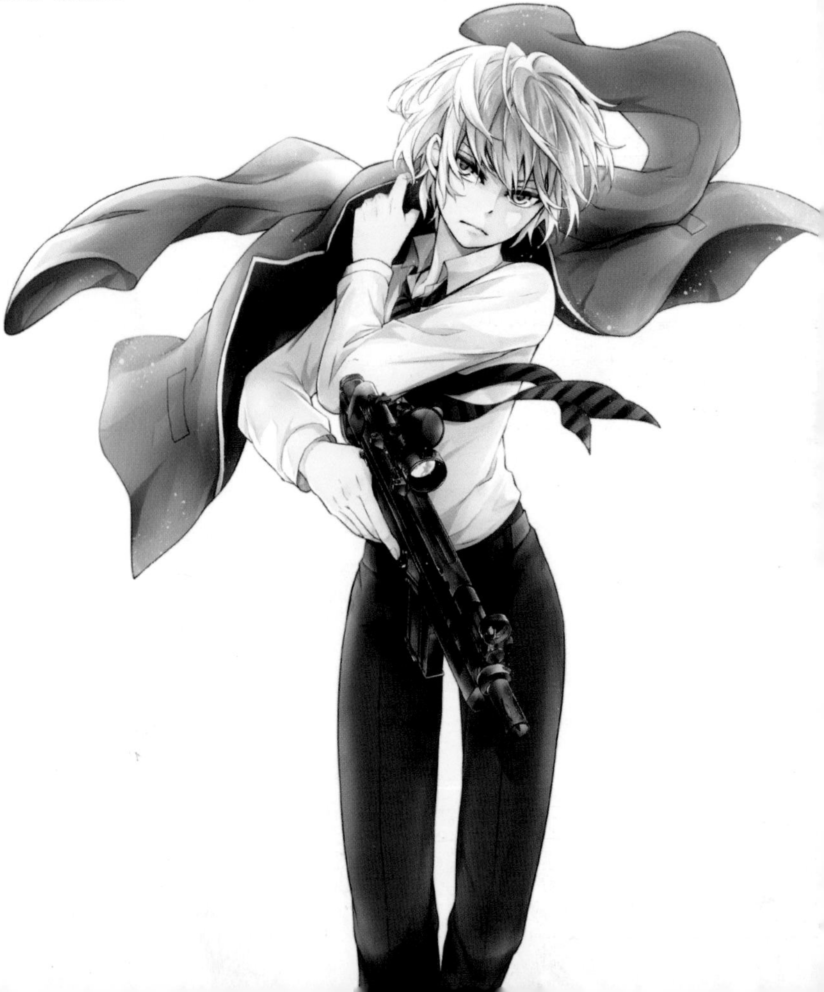

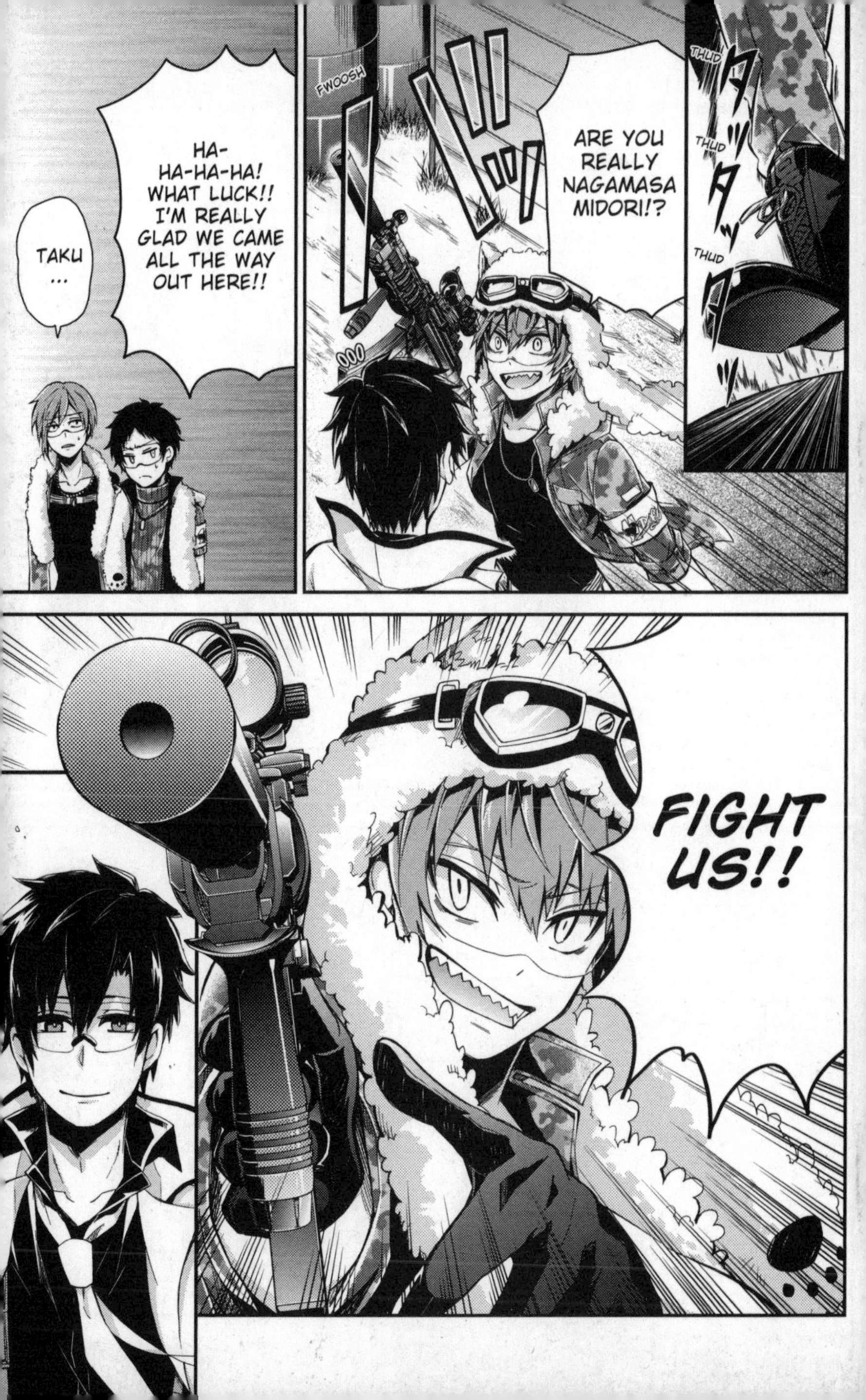
THUD
THUD
THUD
FWOOSH
ARE YOU REALLY NAGAMASA MIDORI!?
HA-HA-HA-HA! WHAT LUCK!! I'M REALLY GLAD WE CAME ALL THE WAY OUT HERE!!
TAKU ...
FIGHT US!!

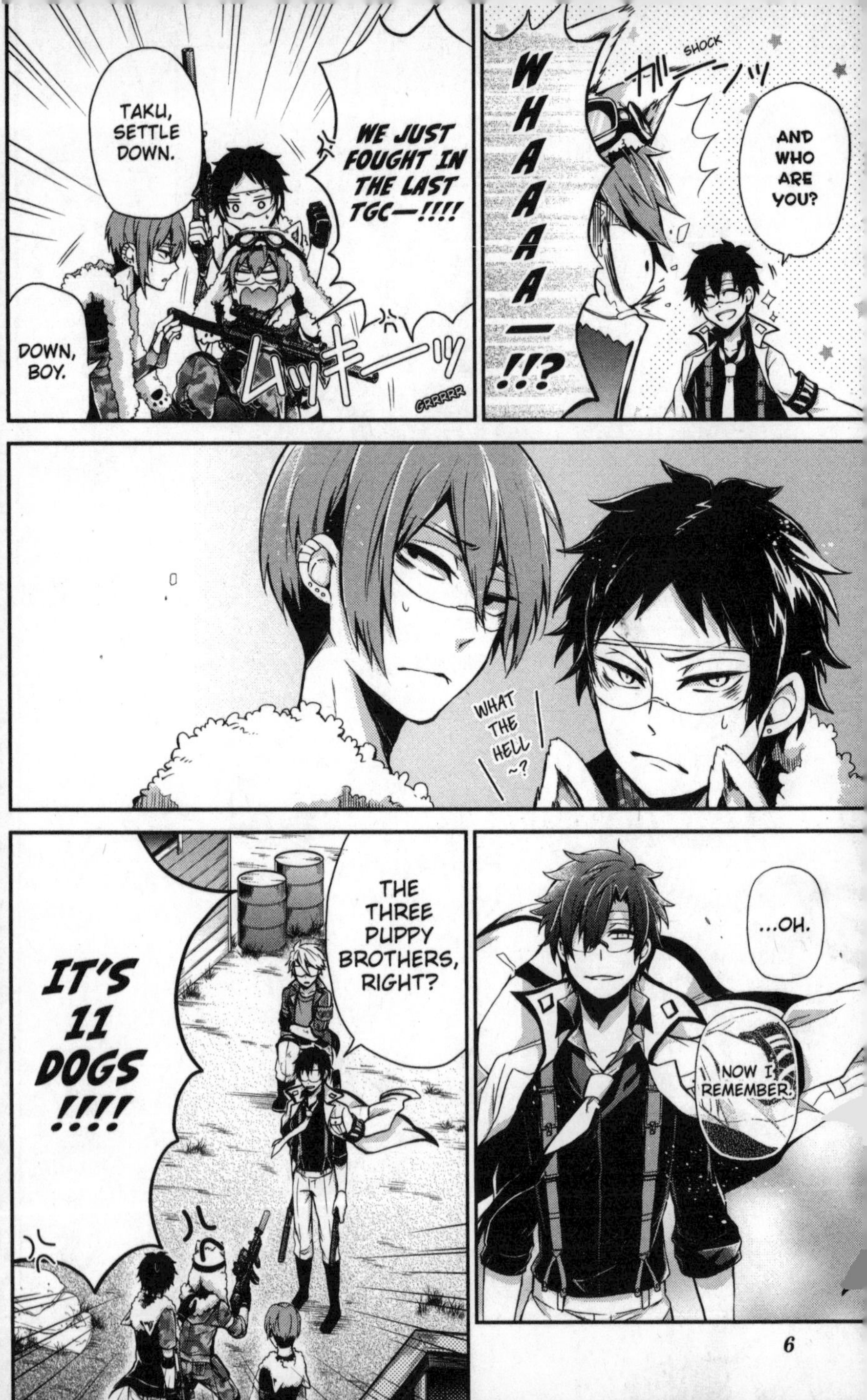
SHOCK
AND WHO ARE YOU?
WHAAAAA—!!?
WE JUST FOUGHT IN THE LAST TGC—!!!!
TAKU, SETTLE DOWN.
DOWN, BOY.
GRRRRR
WHAT THE HELL ~?
...OH.
NOW I REMEMBER.
THE THREE PUPPY BROTHERS, RIGHT?
IT'S 11 DOGS !!!!

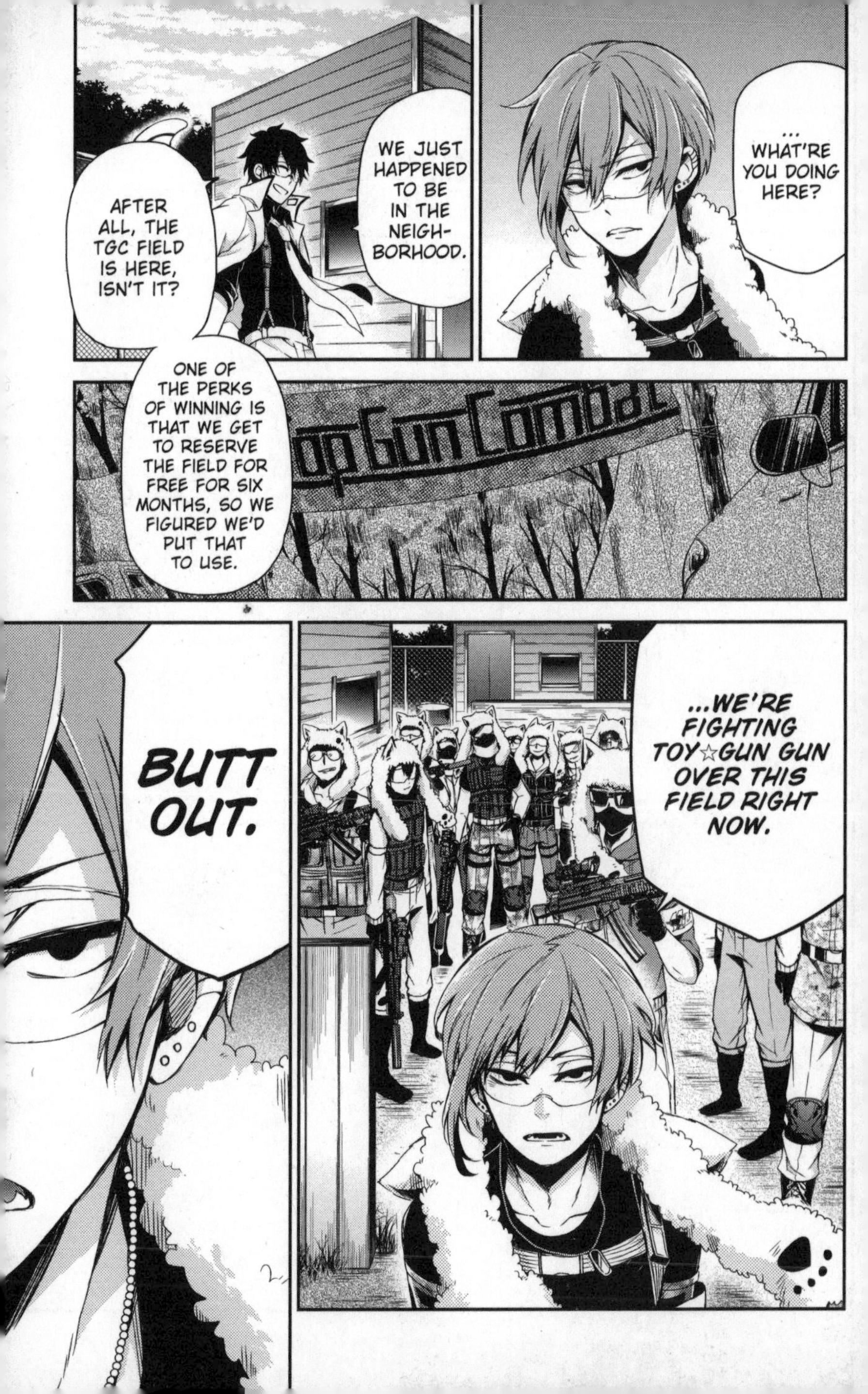
...WHAT'RE YOU DOING HERE?
WE JUST HAPPENED TO BE IN THE NEIGHBORHOOD.
AFTER ALL, THE TGC FIELD IS HERE, ISN'T IT?
ONE OF THE PERKS OF WINNING IS THAT WE GET TO RESERVE THE FIELD FOR FREE FOR SIX MONTHS, SO WE FIGURED WE'D PUT THAT TO USE.
...WE'RE FIGHTING TOY☆GUN GUN OVER THIS FIELD RIGHT NOW.
BUTT OUT.

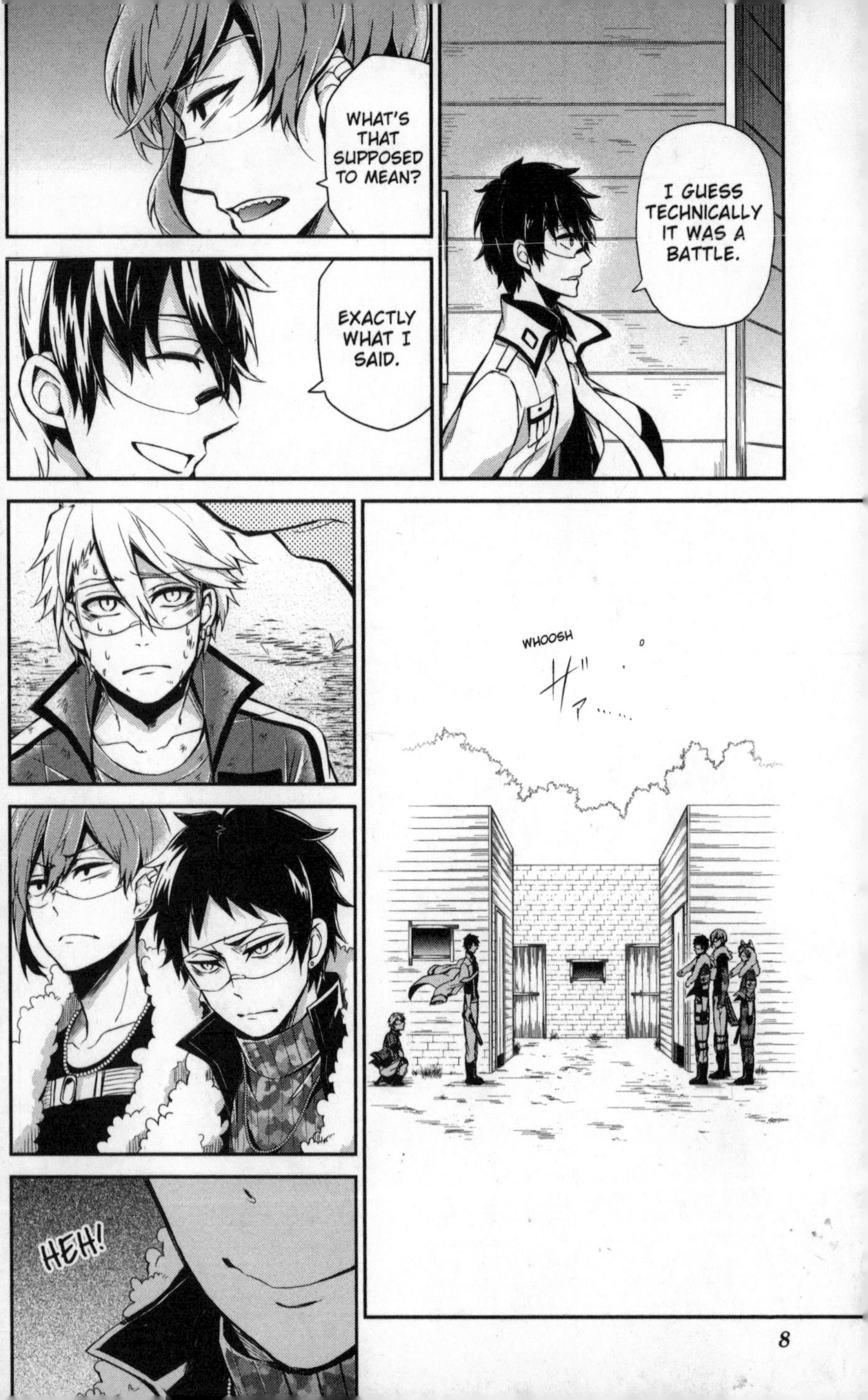
I GUESS TECHNICALLY IT WAS A BATTLE.
WHAT'S THAT SUPPOSED TO MEAN?
EXACTLY WHAT I SAID.
WHOOSH
ザァ……
HEH!

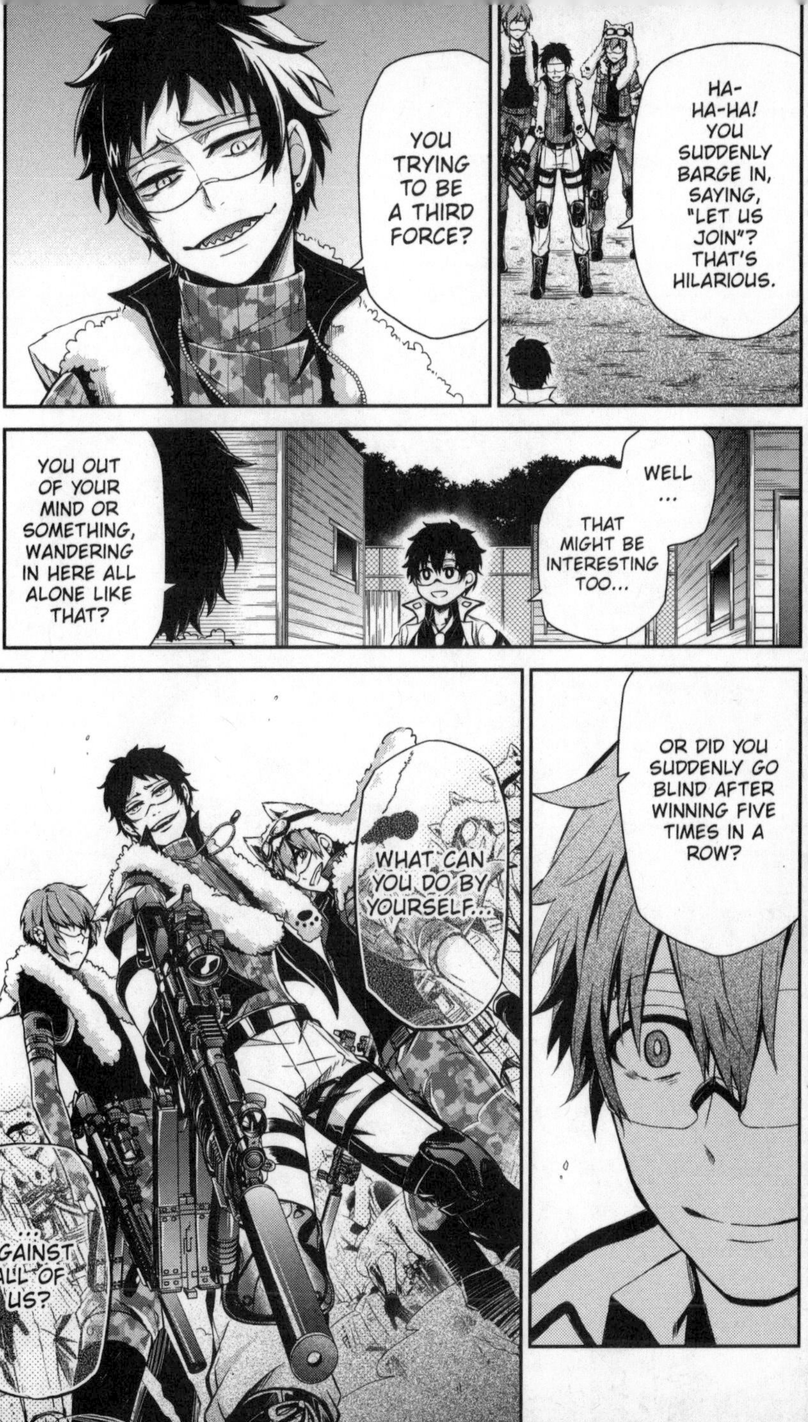
HA-HA-HA! YOU SUDDENLY BARGE IN, SAYING, "LET US JOIN"? THAT'S HILARIOUS.
YOU TRYING TO BE A THIRD FORCE?
WELL ... THAT MIGHT BE INTERESTING TOO...
YOU OUT OF YOUR MIND OR SOMETHING, WANDERING IN HERE ALL ALONE LIKE THAT?
OR DID YOU SUDDENLY GO BLIND AFTER WINNING FIVE TIMES IN A ROW?
WHAT CAN YOU DO BY YOURSELF...
...AGAINST ALL OF US?

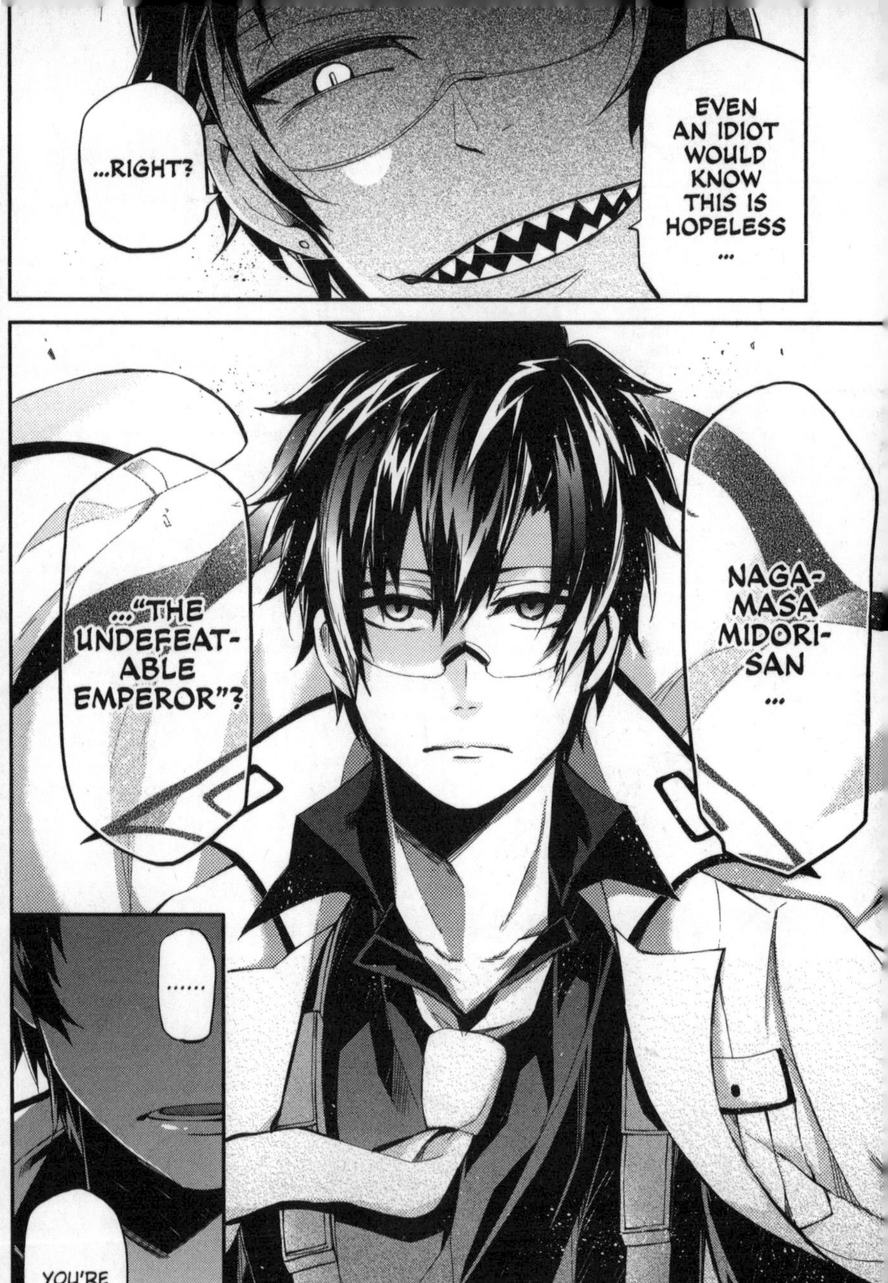
EVEN AN IDIOT WOULD KNOW THIS IS HOPELESS ...
...RIGHT?
NAGA-MASA MIDORI-SAN ...
..."THE UNDEFEAT-ABLE EMPEROR"?
......
YOU'RE RIGHT.

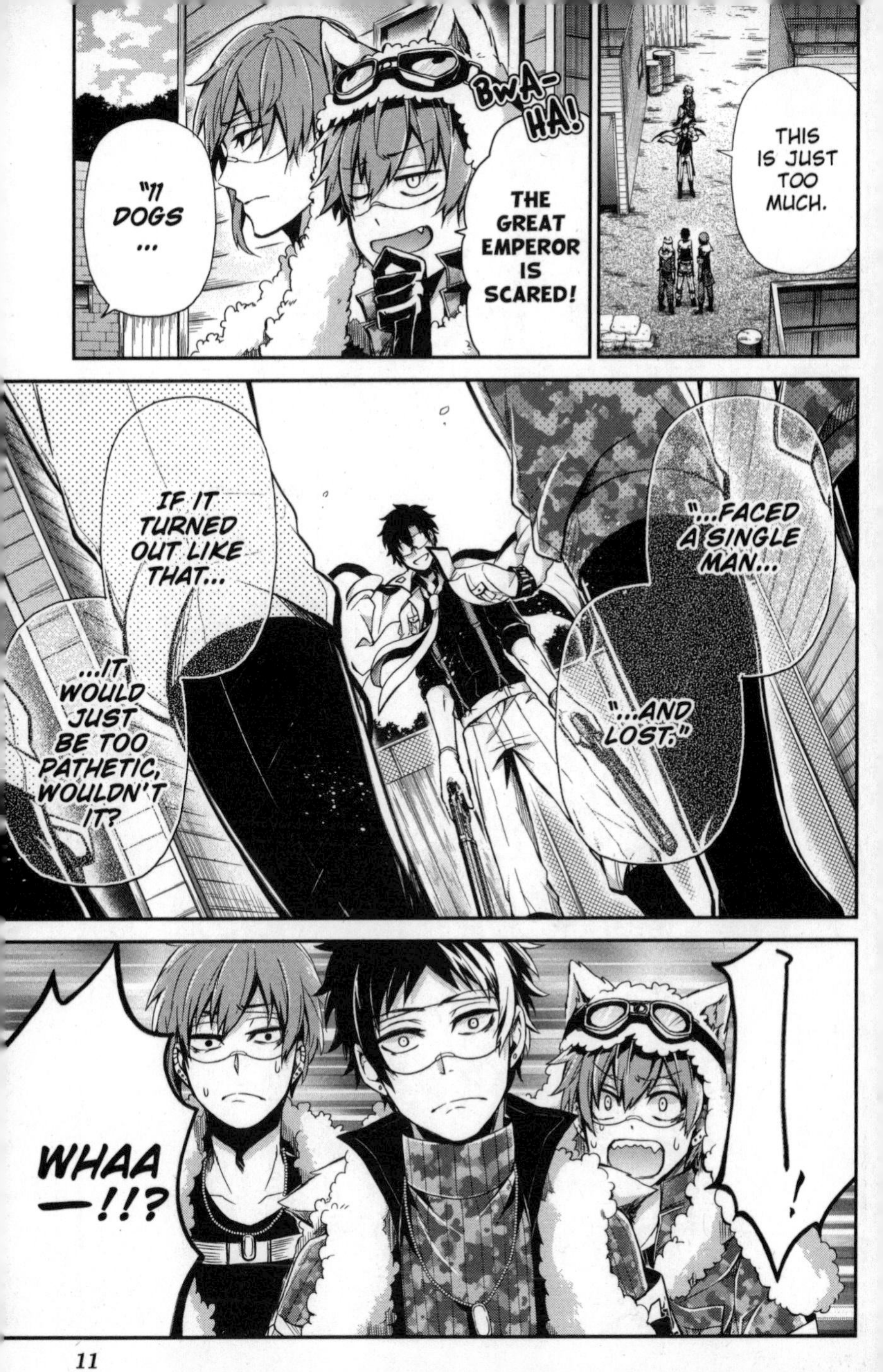
THIS IS JUST TOO MUCH.
BWA-HA!
THE GREAT EMPEROR IS SCARED!
"11 DOGS ...
"...FACED A SINGLE MAN...
"...AND LOST."
IF IT TURNED OUT LIKE THAT...
...IT WOULD JUST BE TOO PATHETIC, WOULDN'T IT?
!
WHAA—!!?

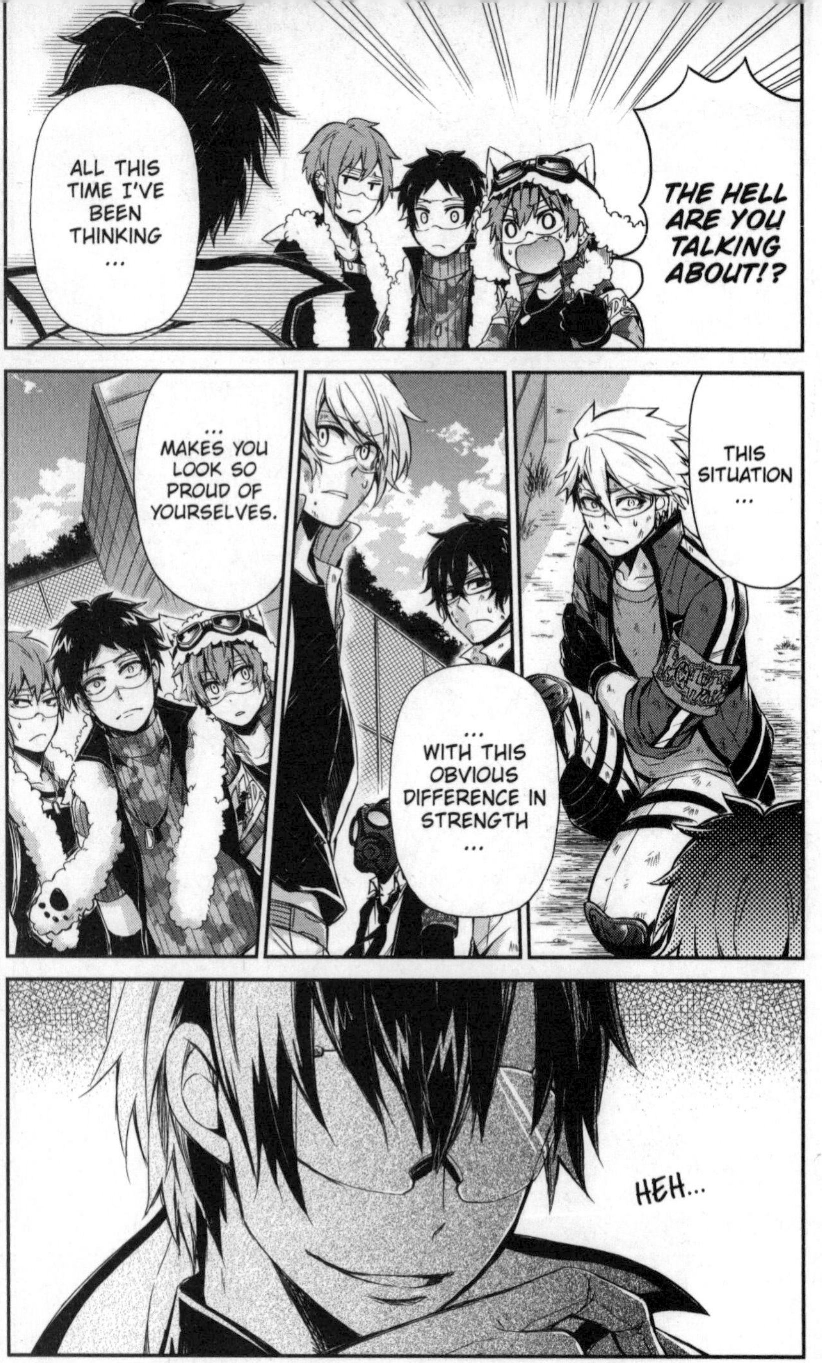
THE HELL ARE YOU TALKING ABOUT!?
ALL THIS TIME I'VE BEEN THINKING ...
THIS SITUATION ...
... WITH THIS OBVIOUS DIFFERENCE IN STRENGTH ...
... MAKES YOU LOOK SO PROUD OF YOURSELVES.
HEH...

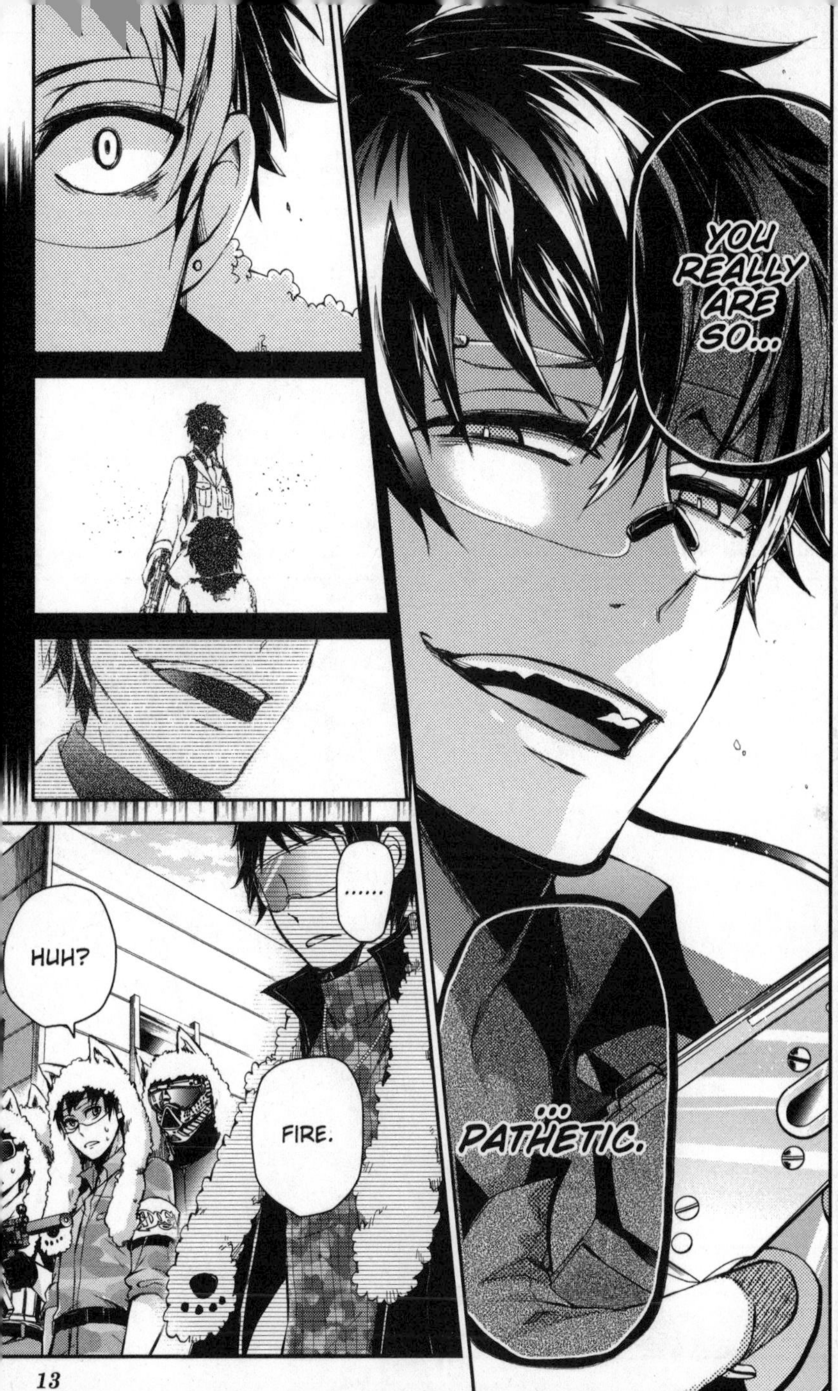
YOU REALLY ARE SO...
...PATHETIC.
......
HUH?
FIRE.

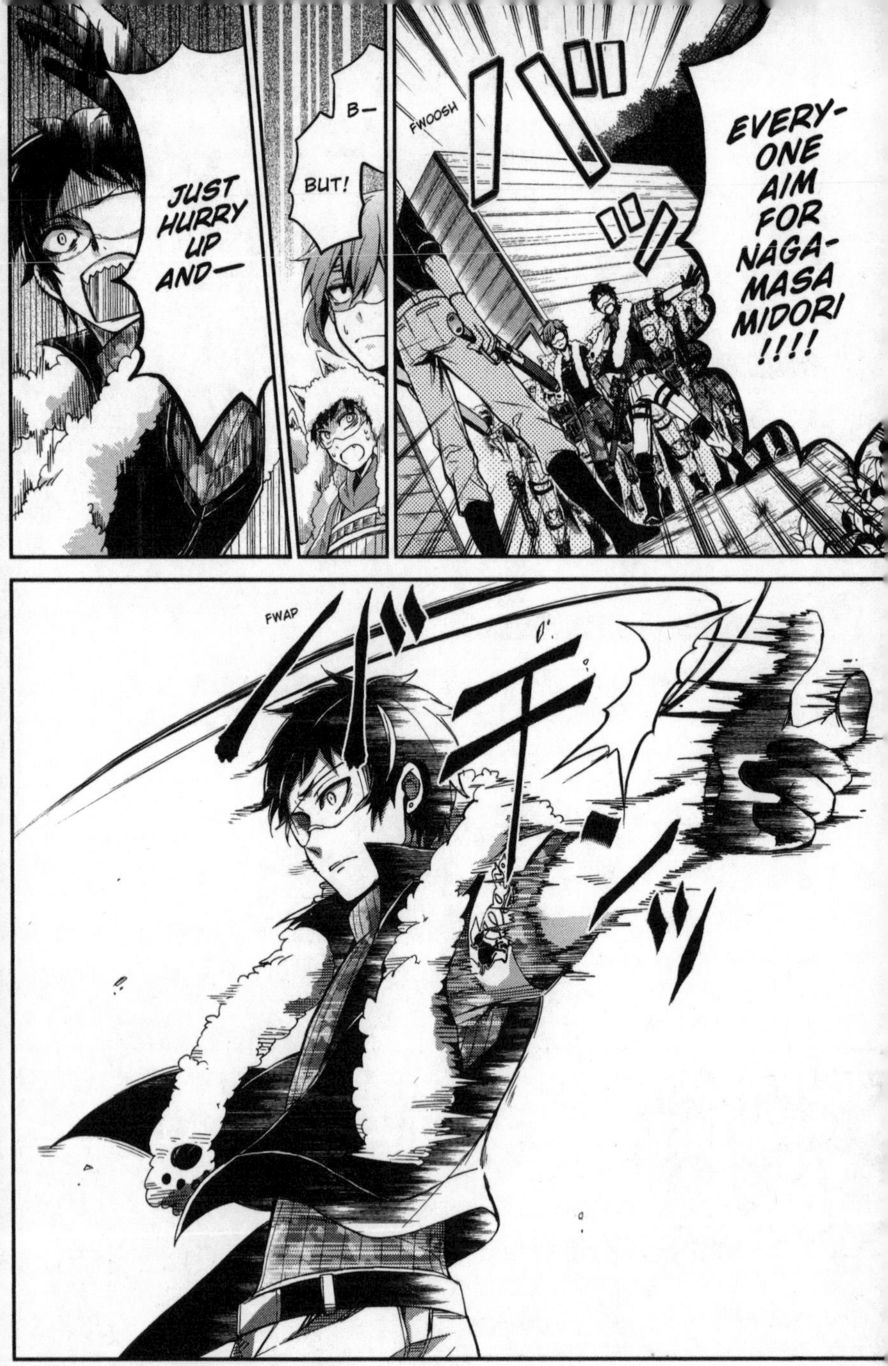
EVERYONE AIM FOR NAGAMASA MIDORI!!!!
FWOOSH
B—
BUT!
JUST HURRY UP AND—
FWAP

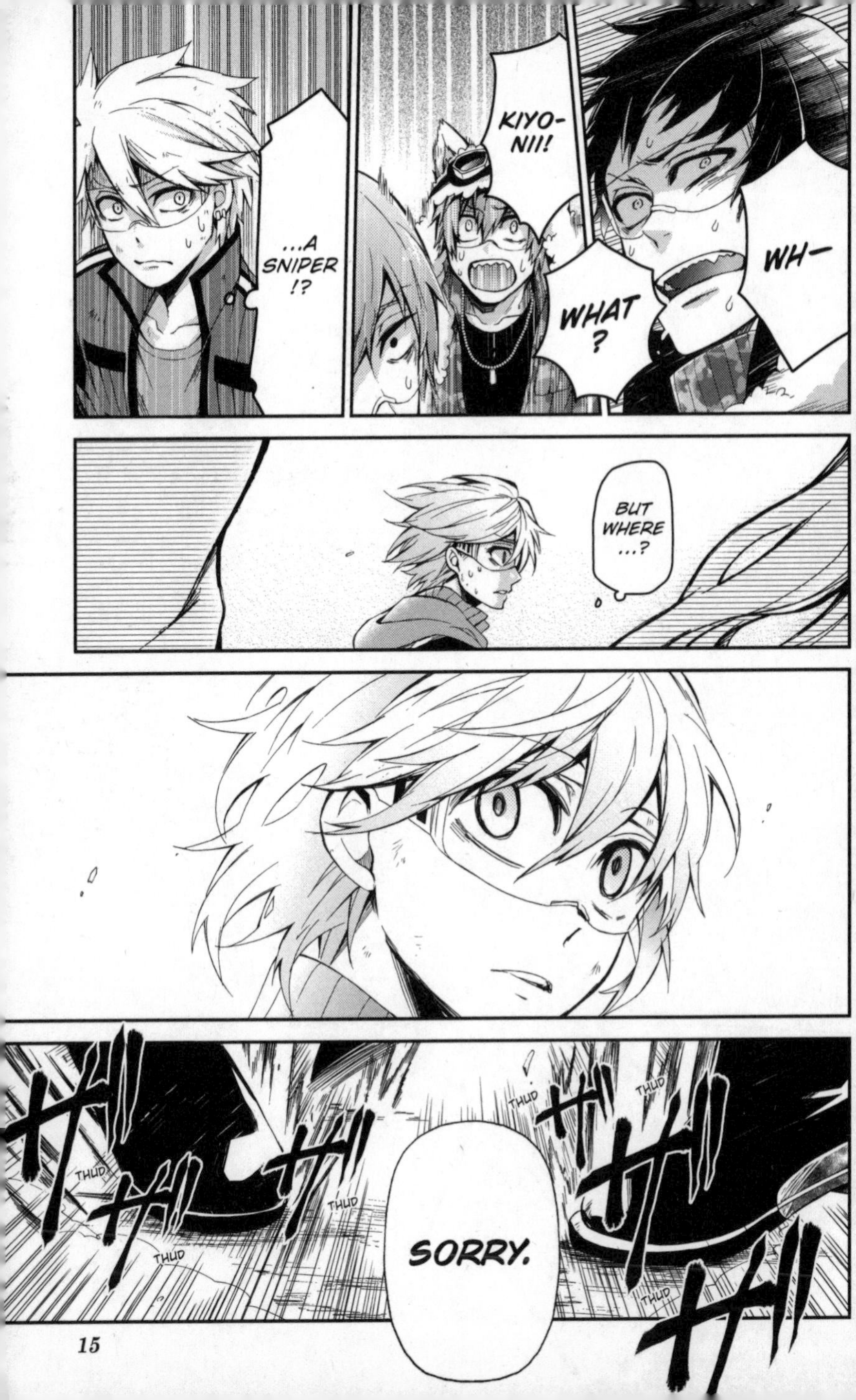
WH-
WHAT?
KIYO-NII!
...A SNIPER!?
BUT WHERE...?
THUD
THUD
SORRY.
THUD
THUD
THUD
THUD

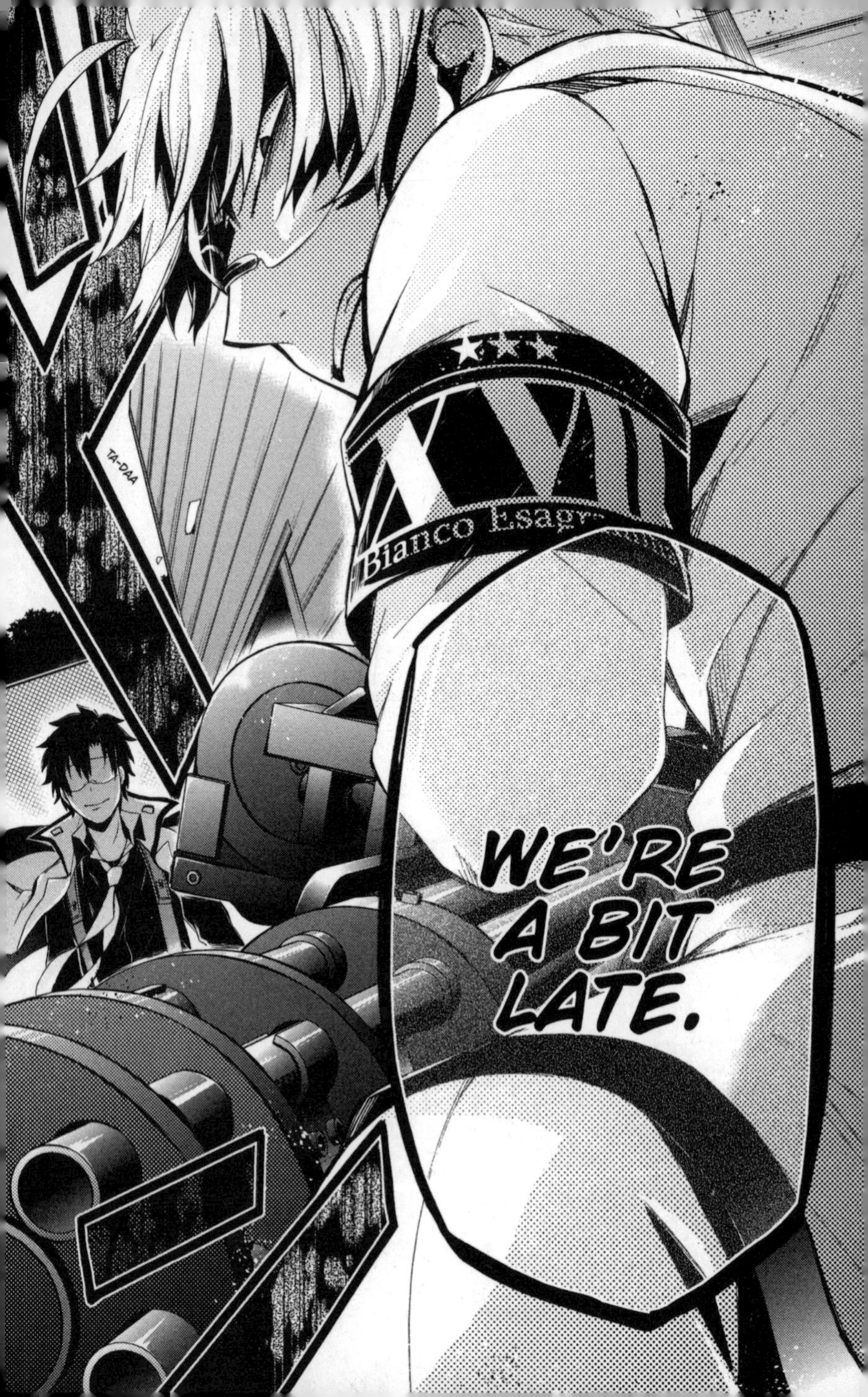
Bianco
WE'RE A BIT LATE.
TA-DAA

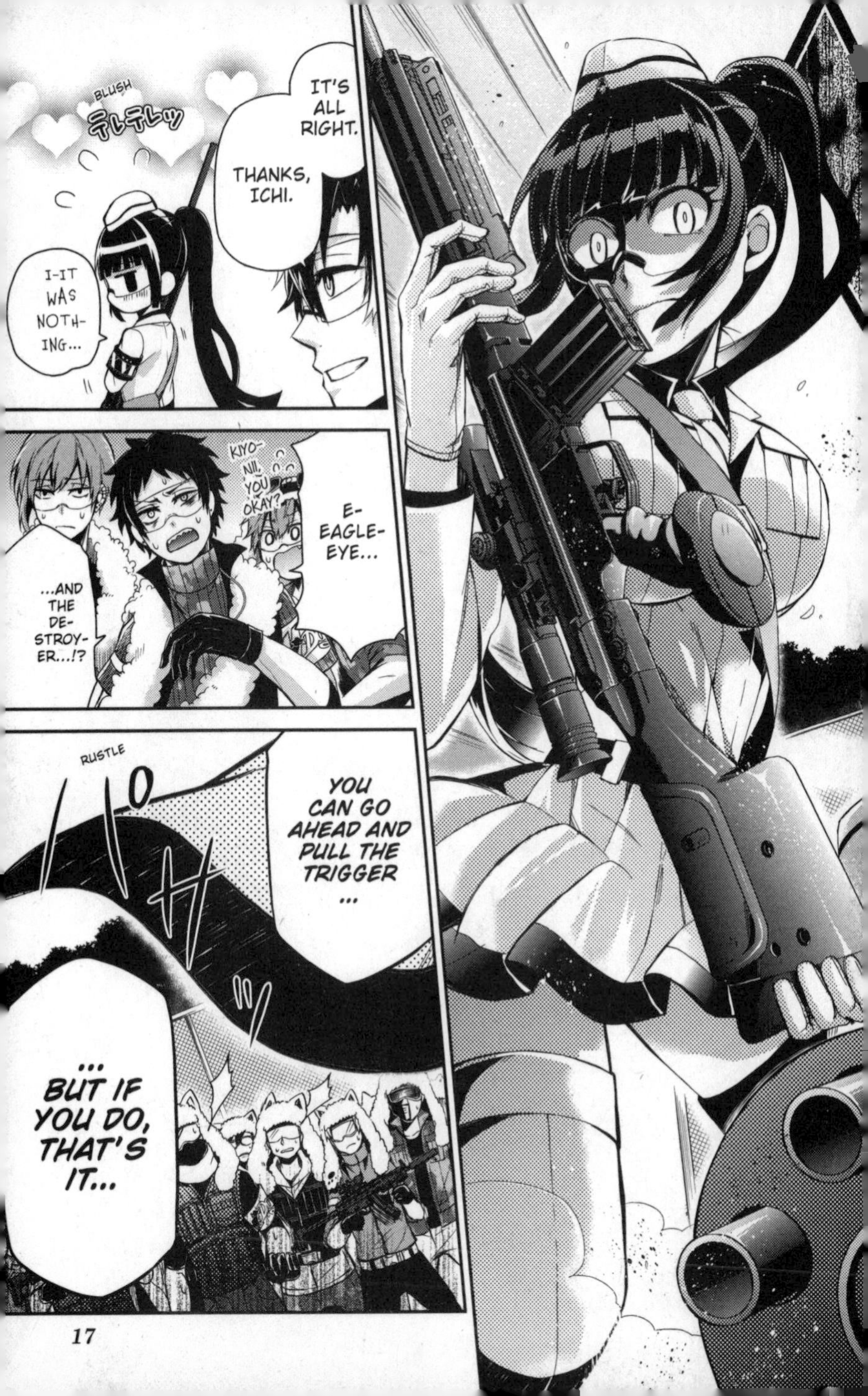
IT'S ALL RIGHT.
THANKS, ICHI.
BLUSH
テレテレッ
I-IT WAS NOTHING...
E-EAGLE-EYE...
KIYO-NII, YOU OKAY?
...AND THE DESTROYER...!?
YOU CAN GO AHEAD AND PULL THE TRIGGER ...
RUSTLE
... BUT IF YOU DO, THAT'S IT...

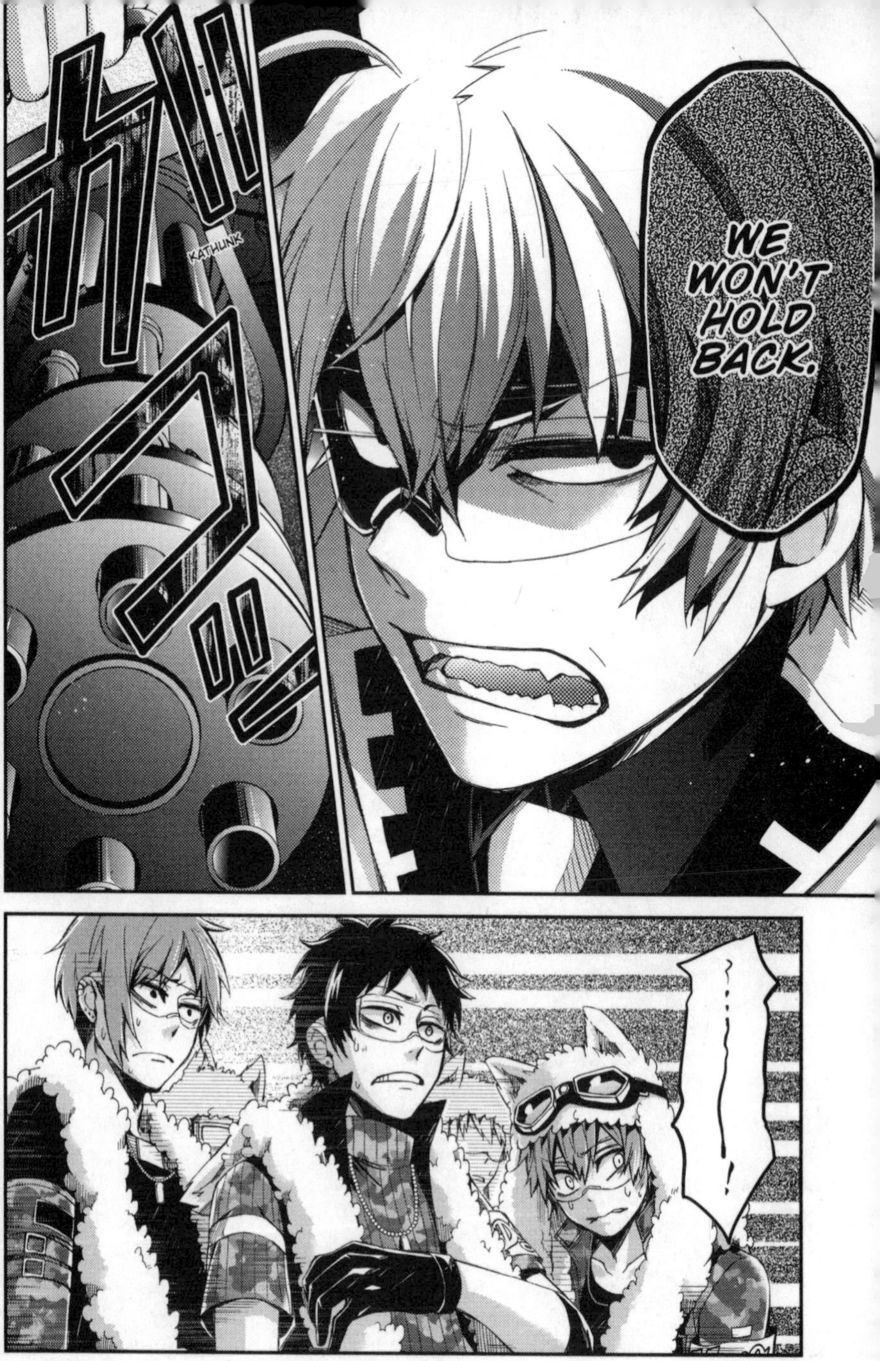
WE WON'T HOLD BACK.
KATHUNK
......!

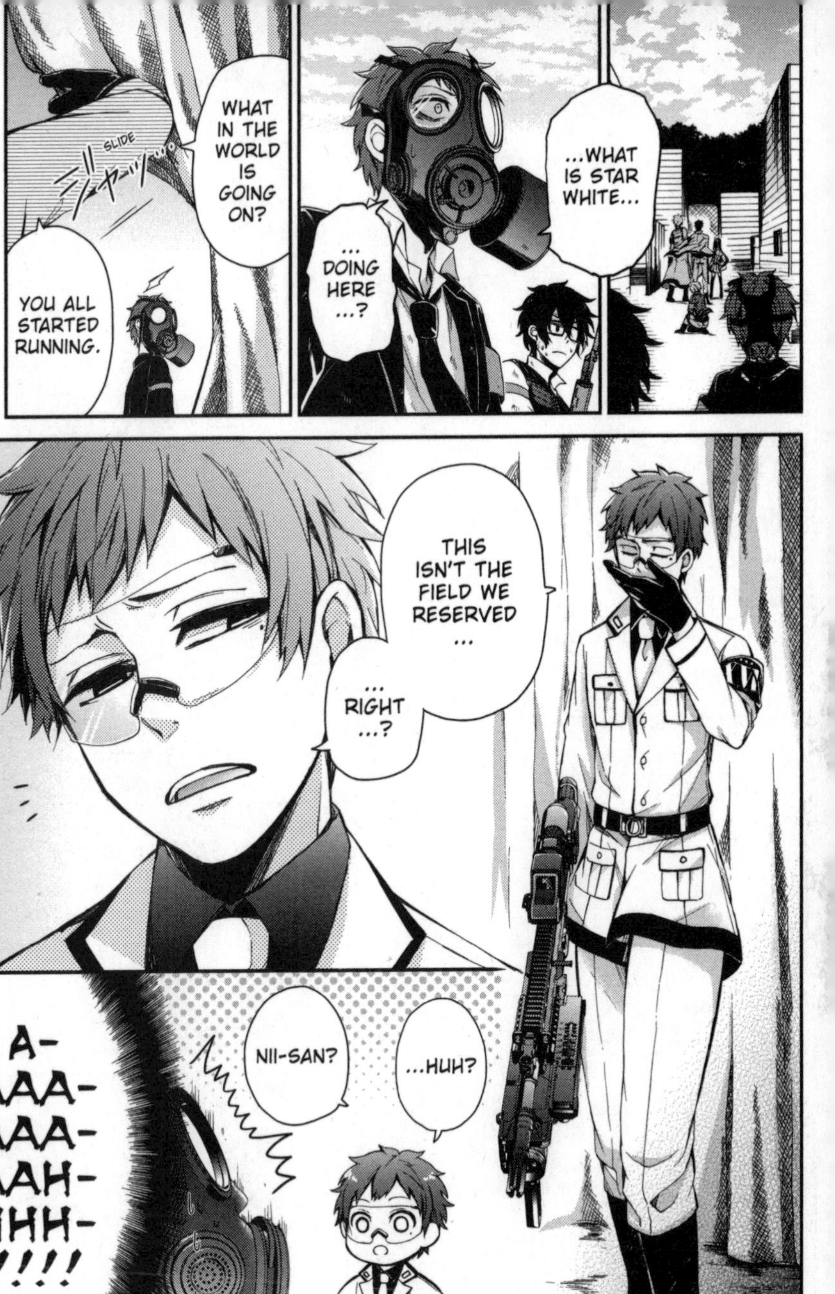
...WHAT IS STAR WHITE...
... DOING HERE ...?
WHAT IN THE WORLD IS GOING ON?
SLIDE
YOU ALL STARTED RUNNING.
THIS ISN'T THE FIELD WE RESERVED ...
... RIGHT ...?
...HUH?
NII-SAN?
A-AAA-AAA-AAH-HHH-!!!!

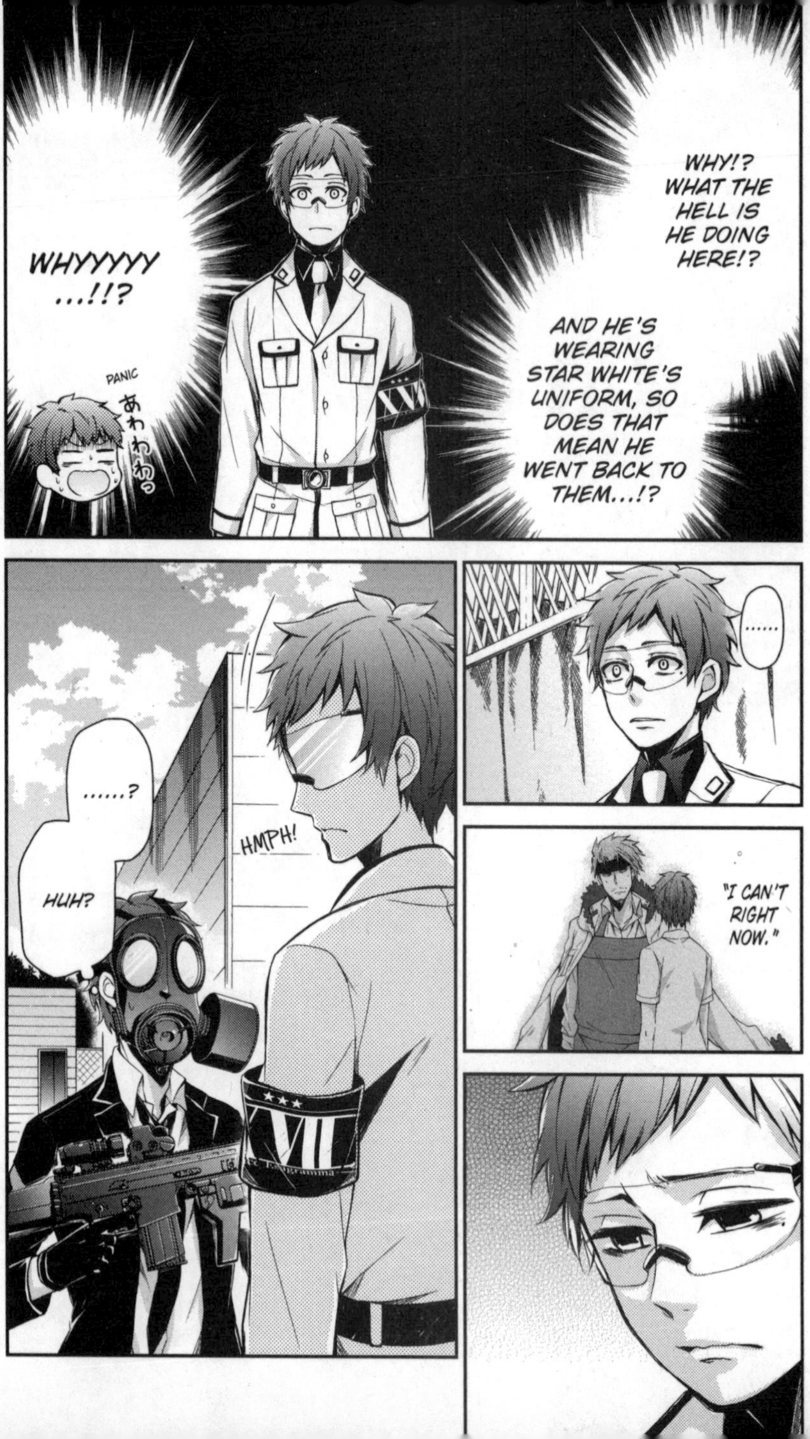
WHY!? WHAT THE HELL IS HE DOING HERE!?
AND HE'S WEARING STAR WHITE'S UNIFORM, SO DOES THAT MEAN HE WENT BACK TO THEM...!?
WHYYYYY ...!!?
PANIC
あわわわっ
......
"I CAN'T RIGHT NOW."
HMPH!
......?
HUH?

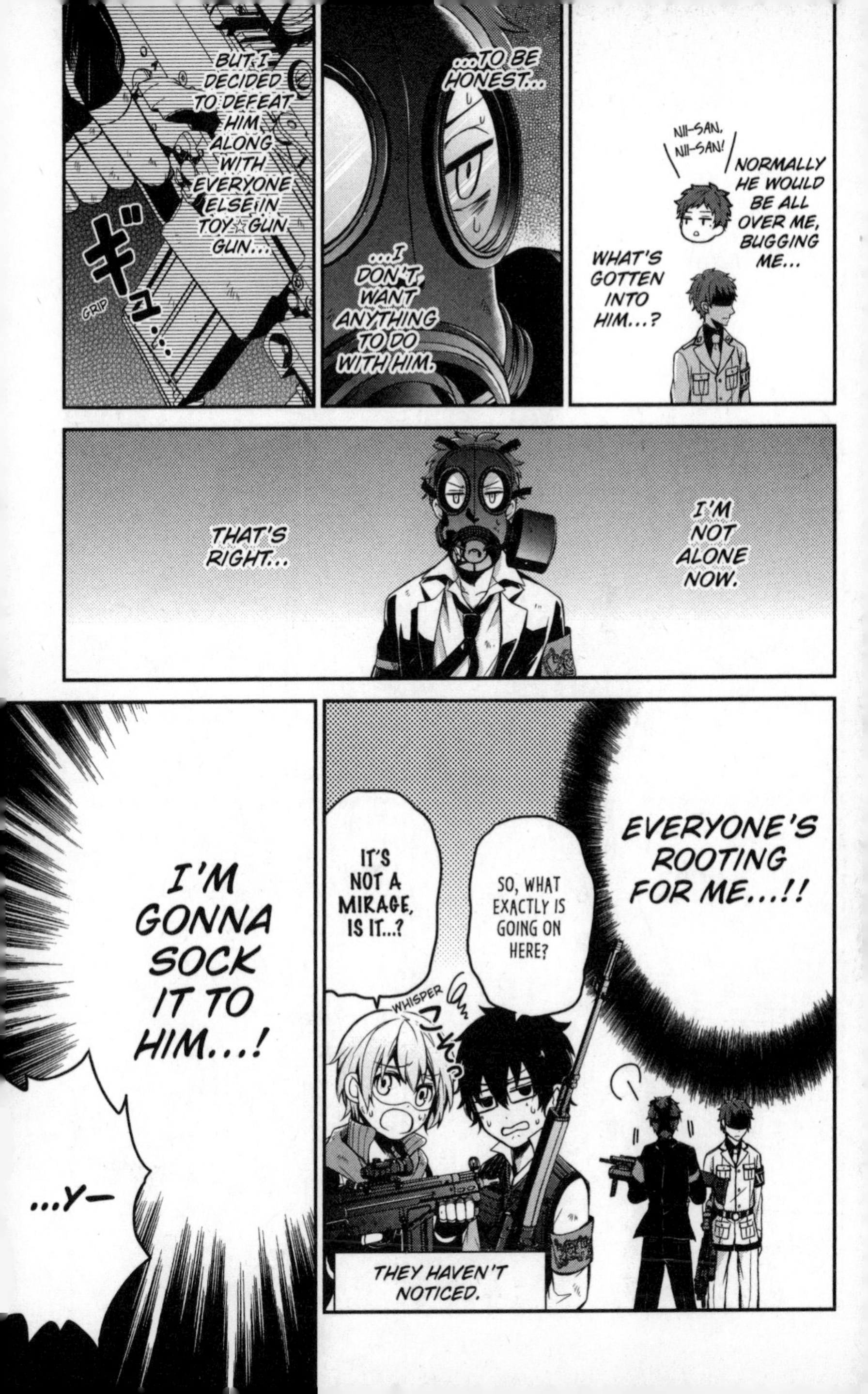
NII-SAN, NII-SAN!
NORMALLY HE WOULD BE ALL OVER ME, BUGGING ME...
WHAT'S GOTTEN INTO HIM...?
...TO BE HONEST...
...I DON'T WANT ANYTHING TO DO WITH HIM.
BUT I DECIDED TO DEFEAT HIM ALONG WITH EVERYONE ELSE IN TOY☆GUN GUN...
ギュ
GRIP
I'M NOT ALONE NOW.
THAT'S RIGHT...
EVERYONE'S ROOTING FOR ME...!!
SO, WHAT EXACTLY IS GOING ON HERE?
IT'S NOT A MIRAGE, IS IT...?
WHISPER
THEY HAVEN'T NOTICED.
I'M GONNA SOCK IT TO HIM...!
...Y—

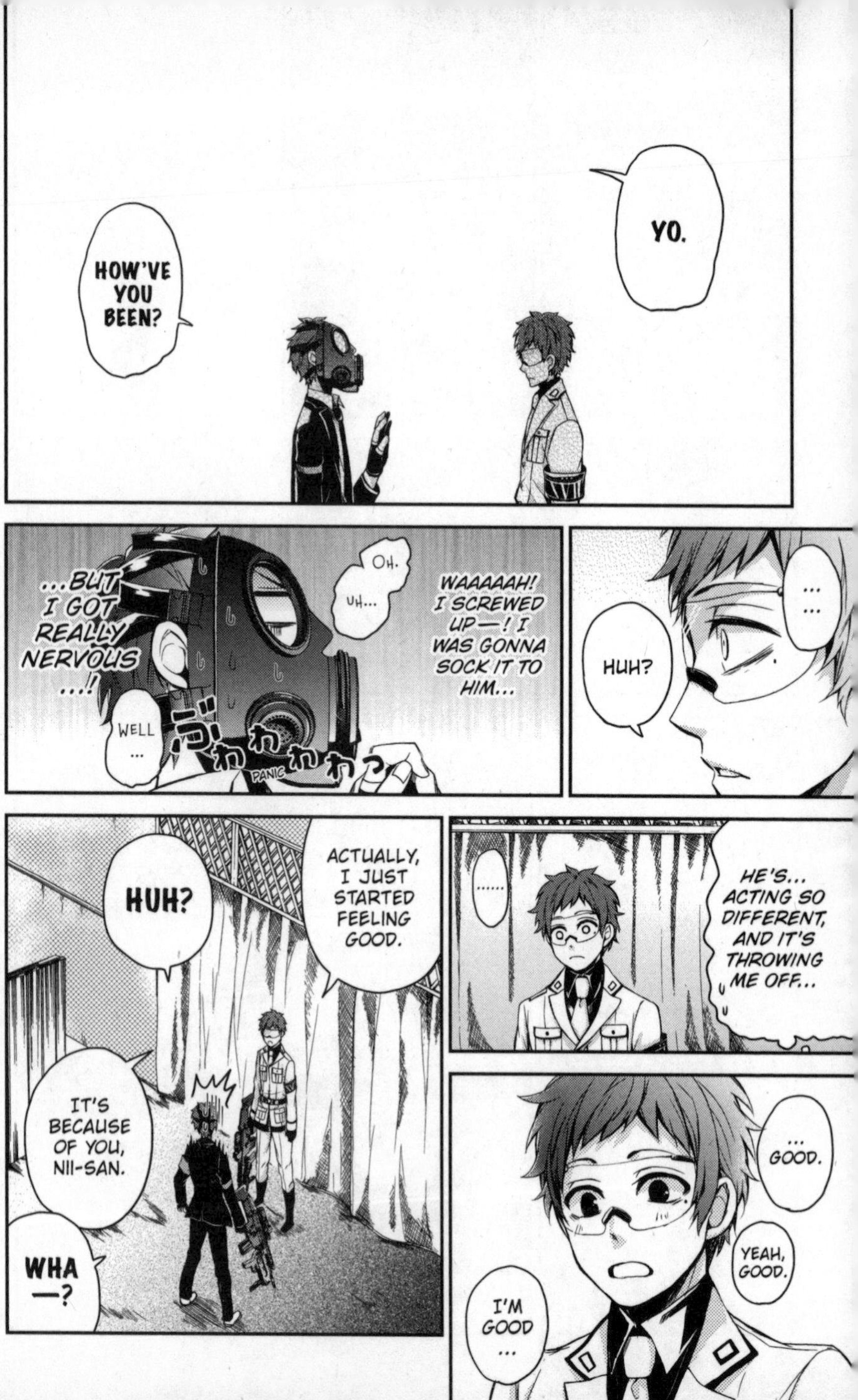
YO.
HOW'VE YOU BEEN?
... ...
HUH?
WAAAAAH! I SCREWED UP—! I WAS GONNA SOCK IT TO HIM...
OH.
UH...
...BUT I GOT REALLY NERVOUS ...!
WELL ...
ぶわわわわっ
PANIC
HE'S... ACTING SO DIFFERENT, AND IT'S THROWING ME OFF...
......
...GOOD.
YEAH, GOOD.
I'M GOOD ...
ACTUALLY, I JUST STARTED FEELING GOOD.
HUH?
IT'S BECAUSE OF YOU, NII-SAN.
WHA —?

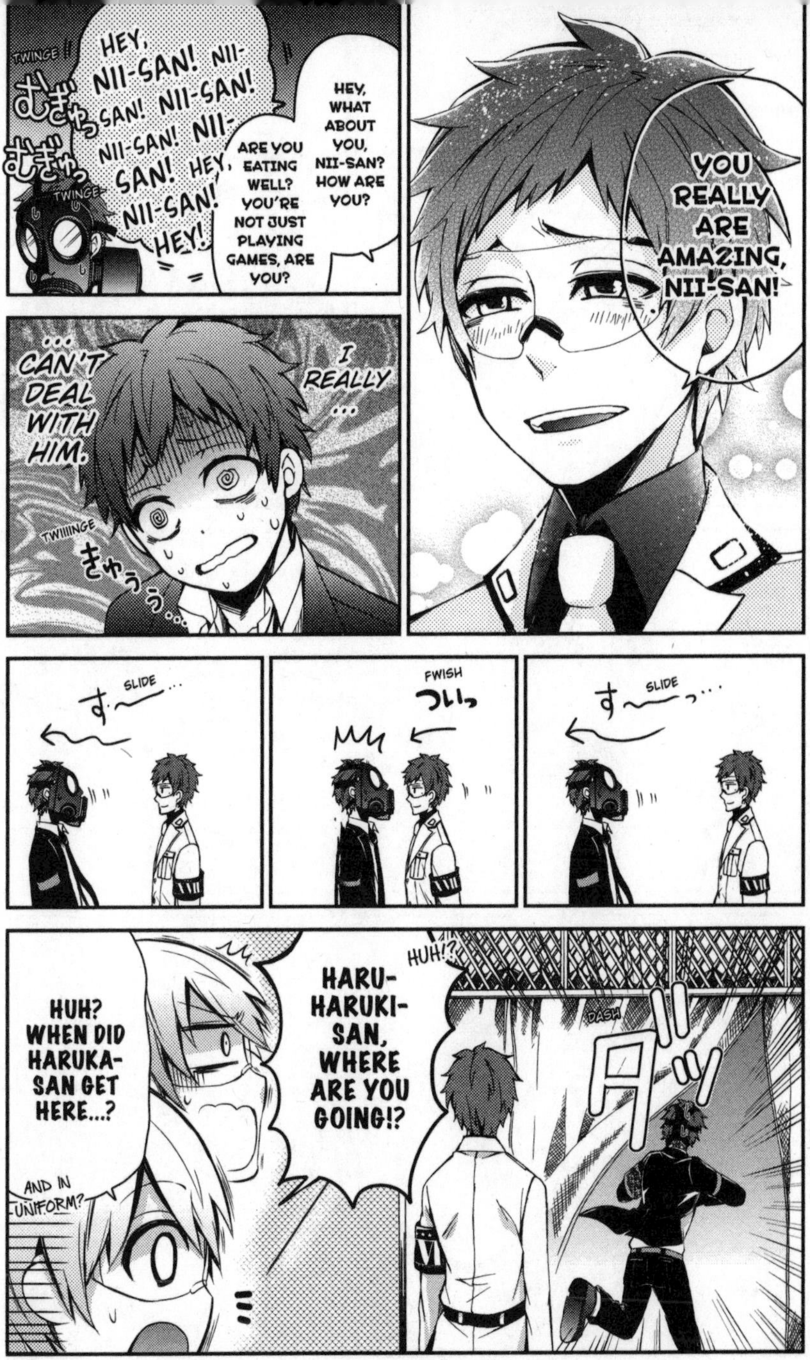
YOU REALLY ARE AMAZING, NII-SAN!
HEY, WHAT ABOUT YOU, NII-SAN? HOW ARE YOU?
ARE YOU EATING WELL? YOU'RE NOT JUST PLAYING GAMES, ARE YOU?
HEY, NII-SAN! NII-SAN! NII-SAN! NII-SAN! NII-SAN! HEY, NII-SAN! HEY!
TWINGE むぎゅっ
TWINGE むぎゅっ
I REALLY...
...CAN'T DEAL WITH HIM.
TWIIINGE きゅううう...
SLIDE すー...
FWISH ついっ
SLIDE すーっ...
HUH!?
DASH ダッ
HARU-HARUKI-SAN, WHERE ARE YOU GOING!?
HUH? WHEN DID HARUKA-SAN GET HERE...?
AND IN UNIFORM?

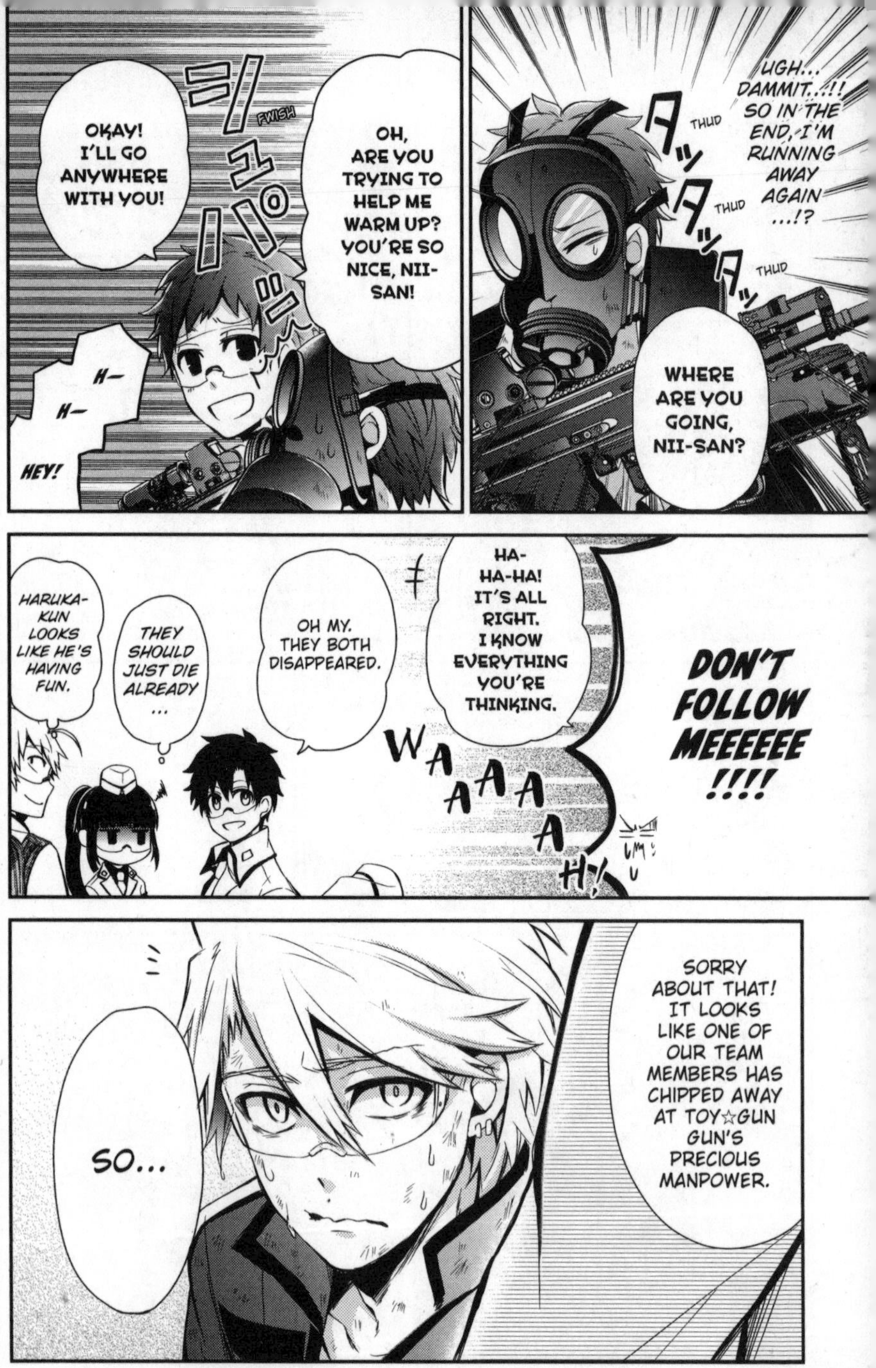
UGH... DAMMIT...!! SO IN THE END, I'M RUNNING AWAY AGAIN...!?
THUD
THUD
THUD
WHERE ARE YOU GOING, NII-SAN?
OH, ARE YOU TRYING TO HELP ME WARM UP? YOU'RE SO NICE, NII-SAN!
FWISH
OKAY! I'LL GO ANYWHERE WITH YOU!
H— H— HEY!
DON'T FOLLOW MEEEEEE !!!!
WAAAAAAH!
HA-HA-HA! IT'S ALL RIGHT. I KNOW EVERYTHING YOU'RE THINKING.
OH MY. THEY BOTH DISAPPEARED.
THEY SHOULD JUST DIE ALREADY...
HARUKA-KUN LOOKS LIKE HE'S HAVING FUN.
SORRY ABOUT THAT! IT LOOKS LIKE ONE OF OUR TEAM MEMBERS HAS CHIPPED AWAY AT TOY☆GUN GUN'S PRECIOUS MANPOWER.
SO...

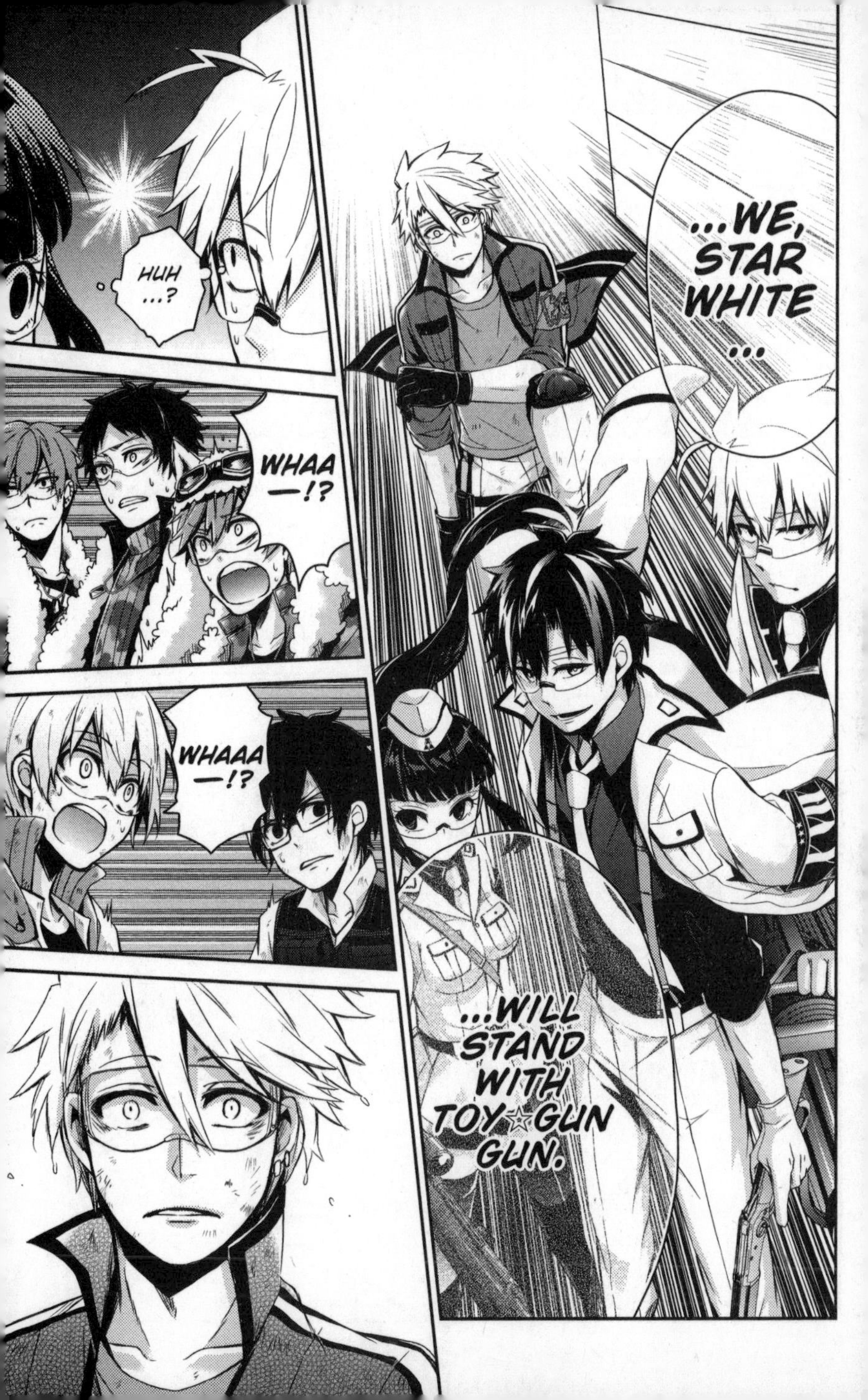
...WE, STAR WHITE ...
...WILL STAND WITH TOY☆GUN GUN.
HUH ...?
WHAA —!?
WHAAA —!?

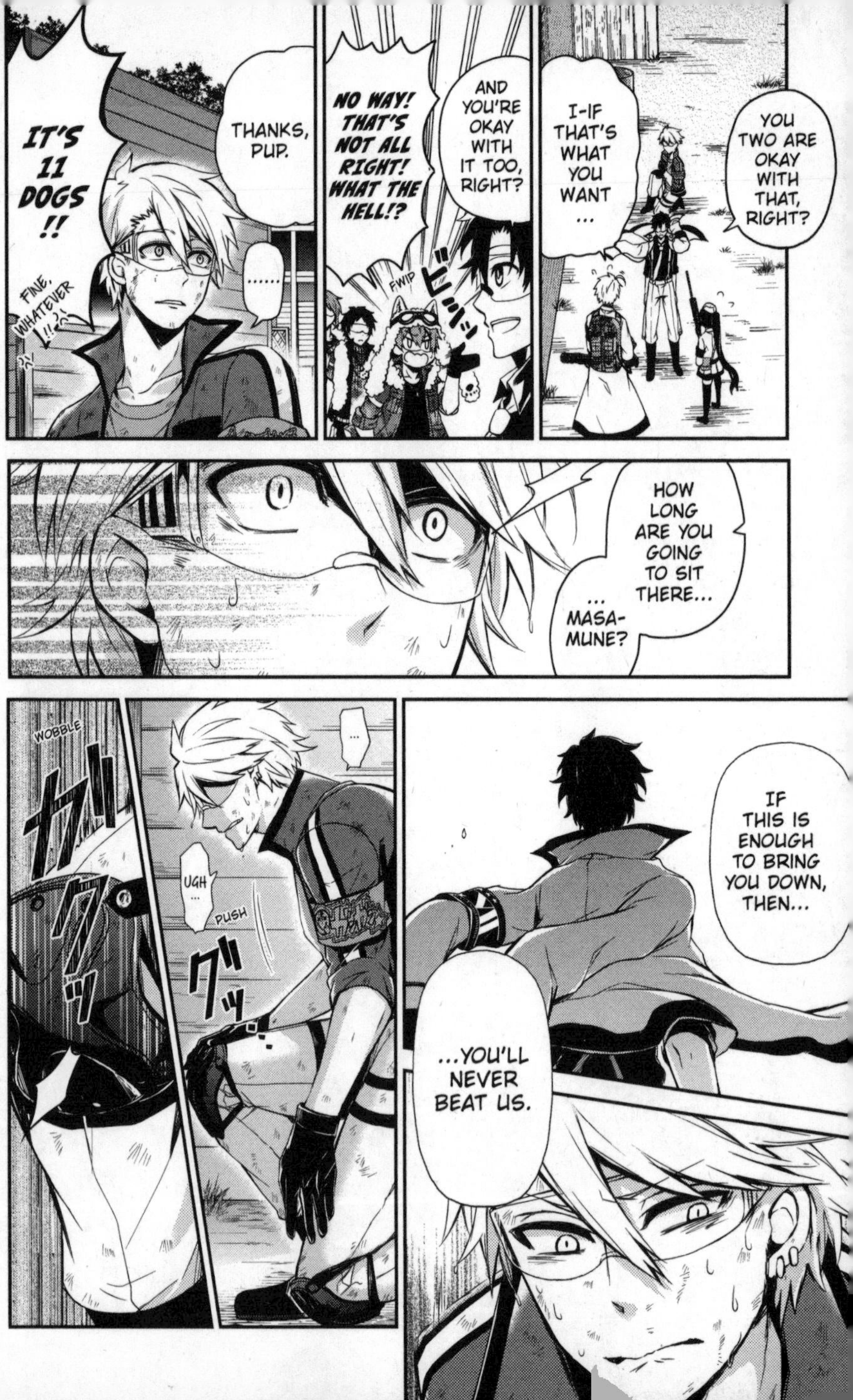
YOU TWO ARE OKAY WITH THAT, RIGHT?
I-IF THAT'S WHAT YOU WANT...
AND YOU'RE OKAY WITH IT TOO, RIGHT?
FWIP
NO WAY! THAT'S NOT ALL RIGHT! WHAT THE HELL!?
THANKS, PUP.
IT'S 11 DOGS!!
......
FINE, WHATEVER!!
HOW LONG ARE YOU GOING TO SIT THERE...
...MASAMUNE?
IF THIS IS ENOUGH TO BRING YOU DOWN, THEN...
...YOU'LL NEVER BEAT US.
...
UGH...
PUSH
WOBBLE

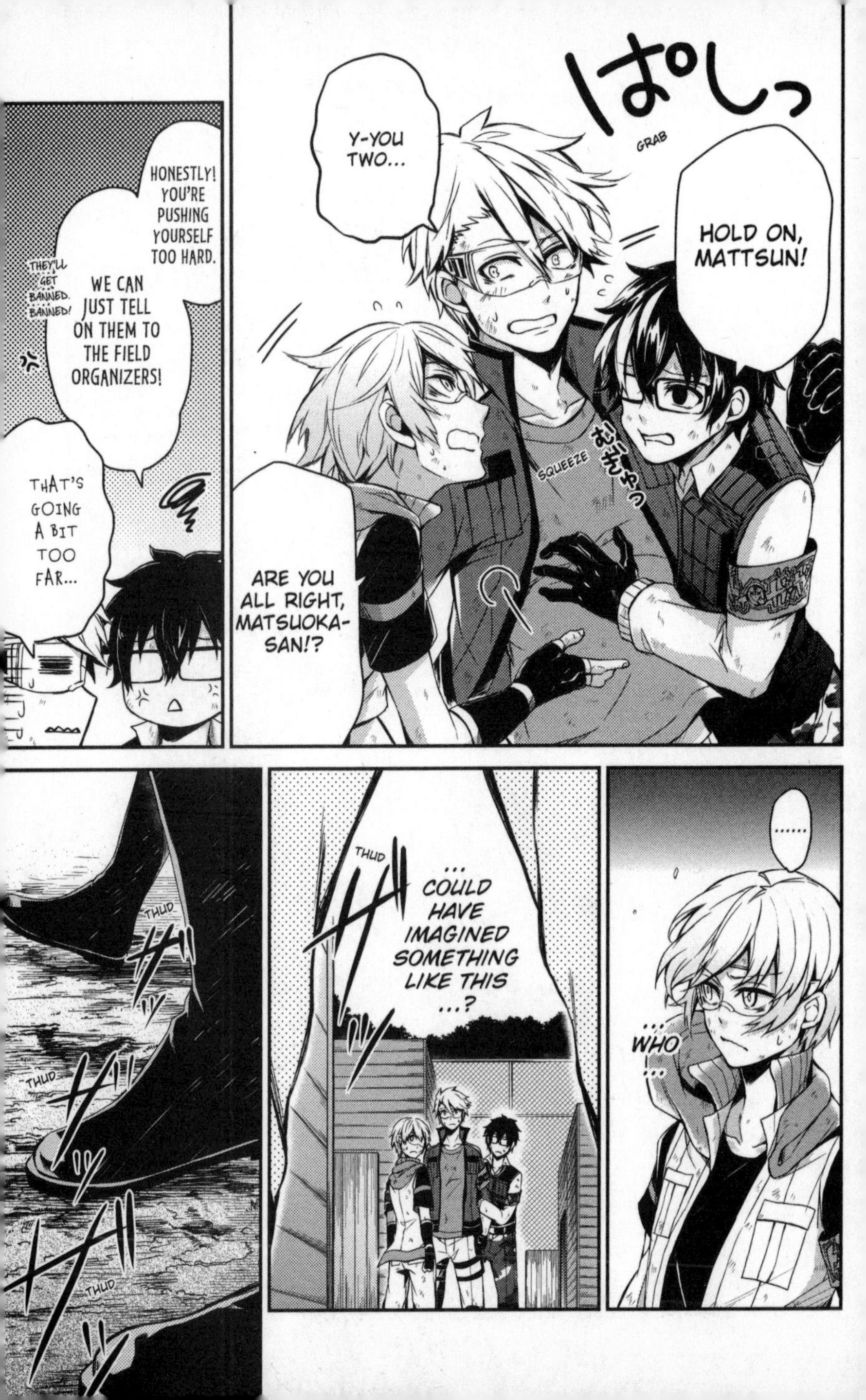
ぱしっ
GRAB
Y-YOU TWO...
HOLD ON, MATTSUN!
むぎゅっ
SQUEEZE
ARE YOU ALL RIGHT, MATSUOKA-SAN!?
HONESTLY! YOU'RE PUSHING YOURSELF TOO HARD.
WE CAN JUST TELL ON THEM TO THE FIELD ORGANIZERS!
THEY'LL GET BANNED. BANNED!
THAT'S GOING A BIT TOO FAR...
......
...WHO...
...COULD HAVE IMAGINED SOMETHING LIKE THIS...?
THUD
THUD
THUD
THUD

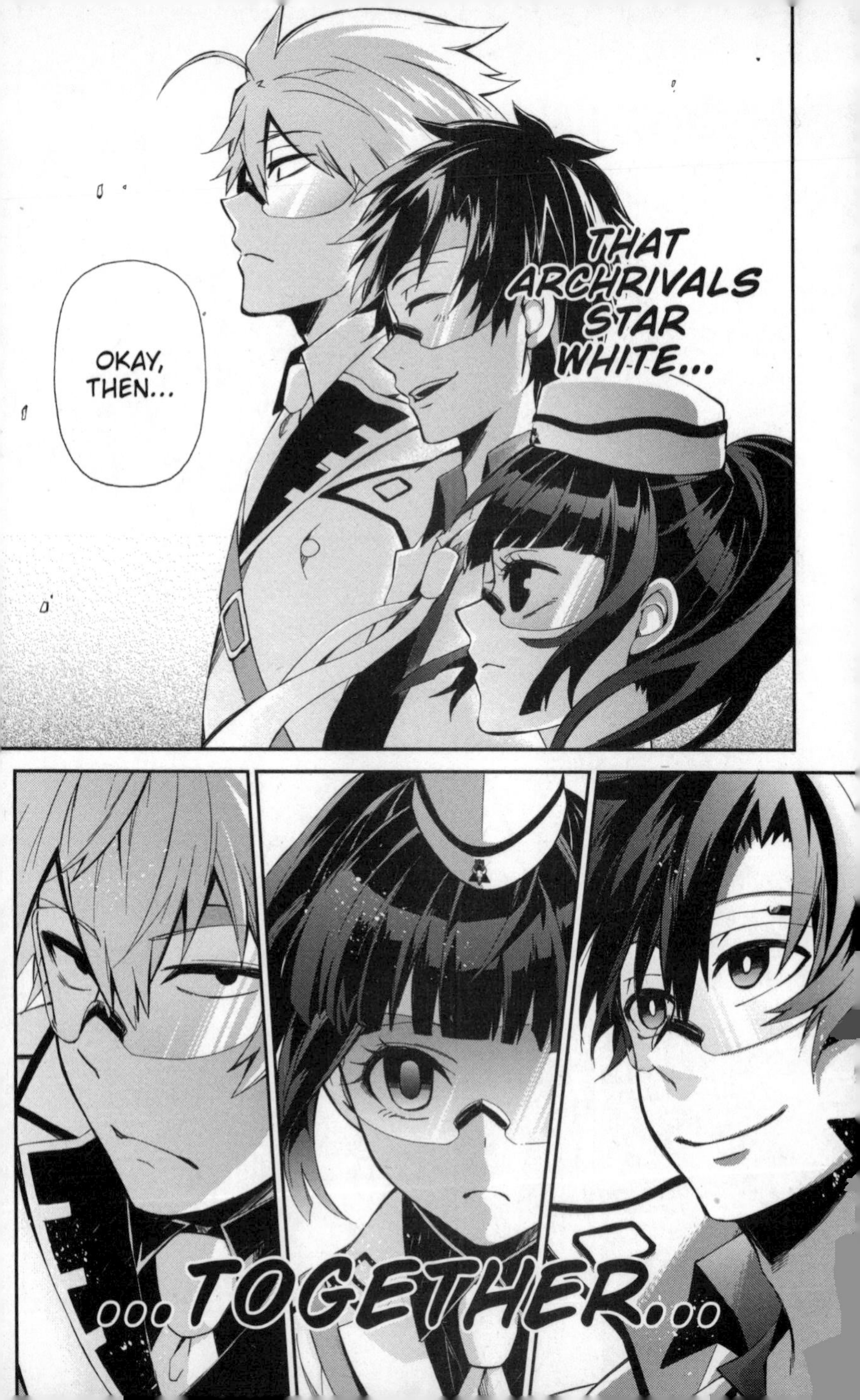
THAT ARCHRIVALS STAR WHITE...
OKAY, THEN...
...TOGETHER...

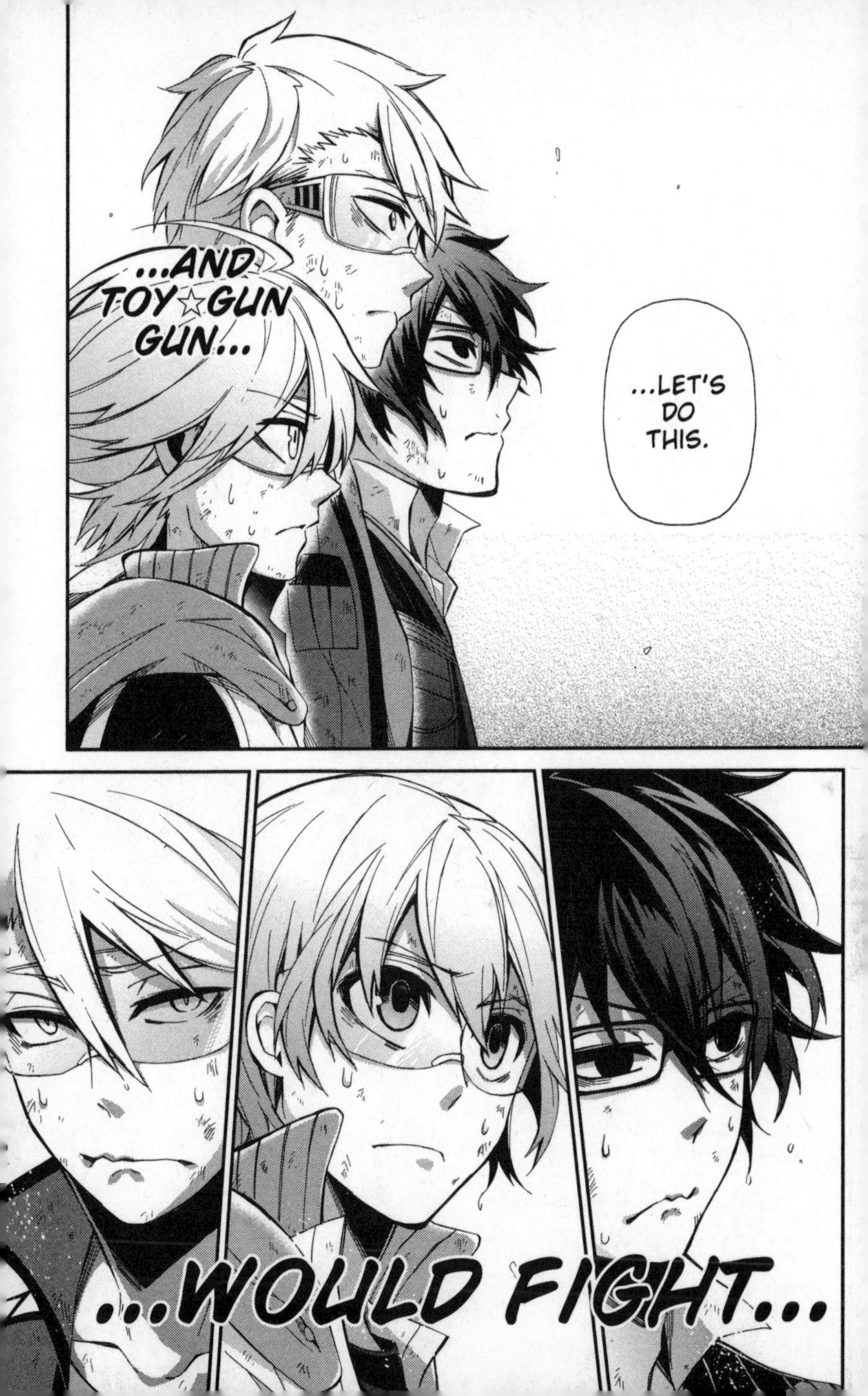
...LET'S DO THIS.
...AND TOY☆GUN GUN...
...WOULD FIGHT...

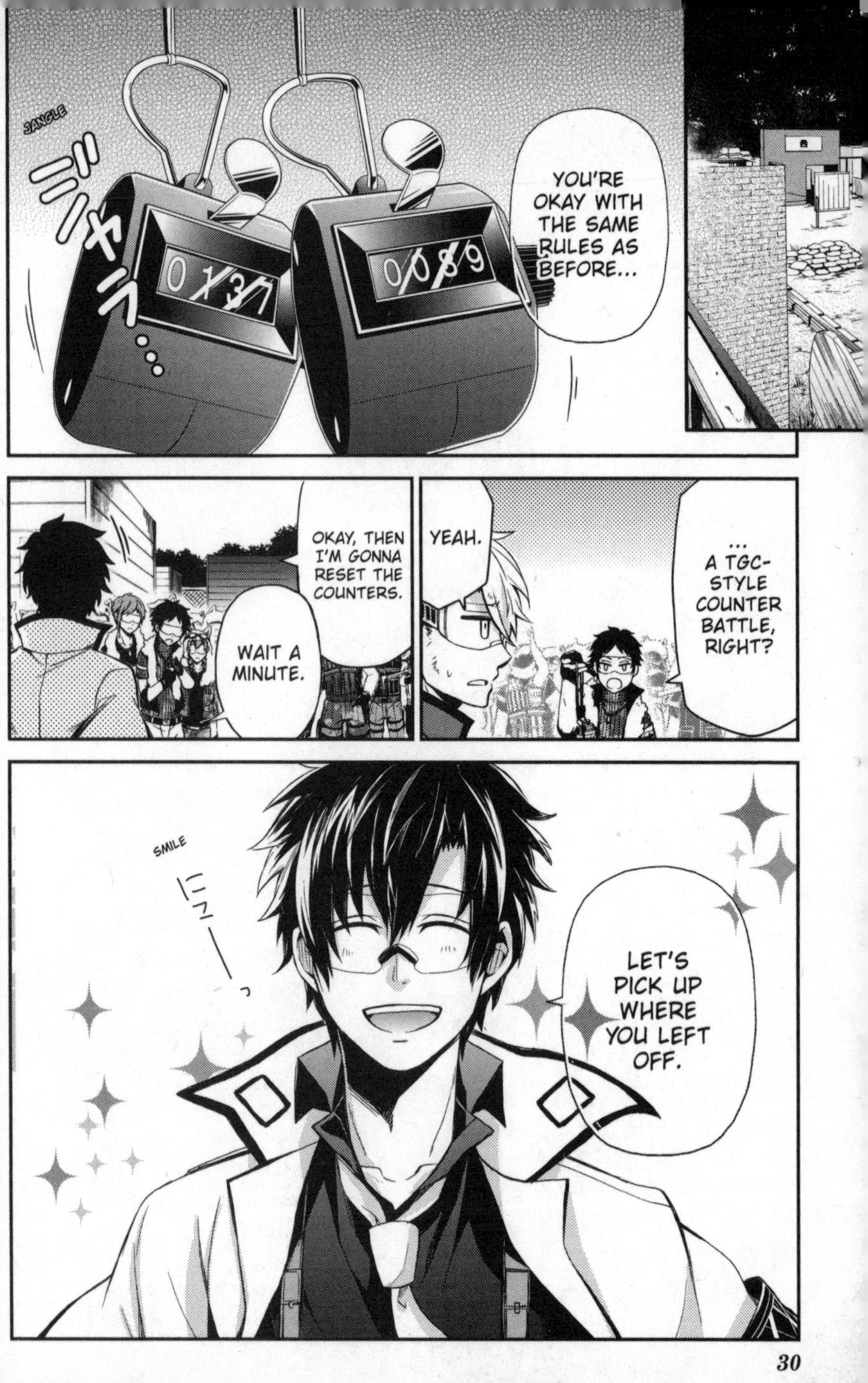
YOU'RE OKAY WITH THE SAME RULES AS BEFORE...
JANGLE
... A TGC-STYLE COUNTER BATTLE, RIGHT?
YEAH.
OKAY, THEN I'M GONNA RESET THE COUNTERS.
WAIT A MINUTE.
LET'S PICK UP WHERE YOU LEFT OFF.
SMILE

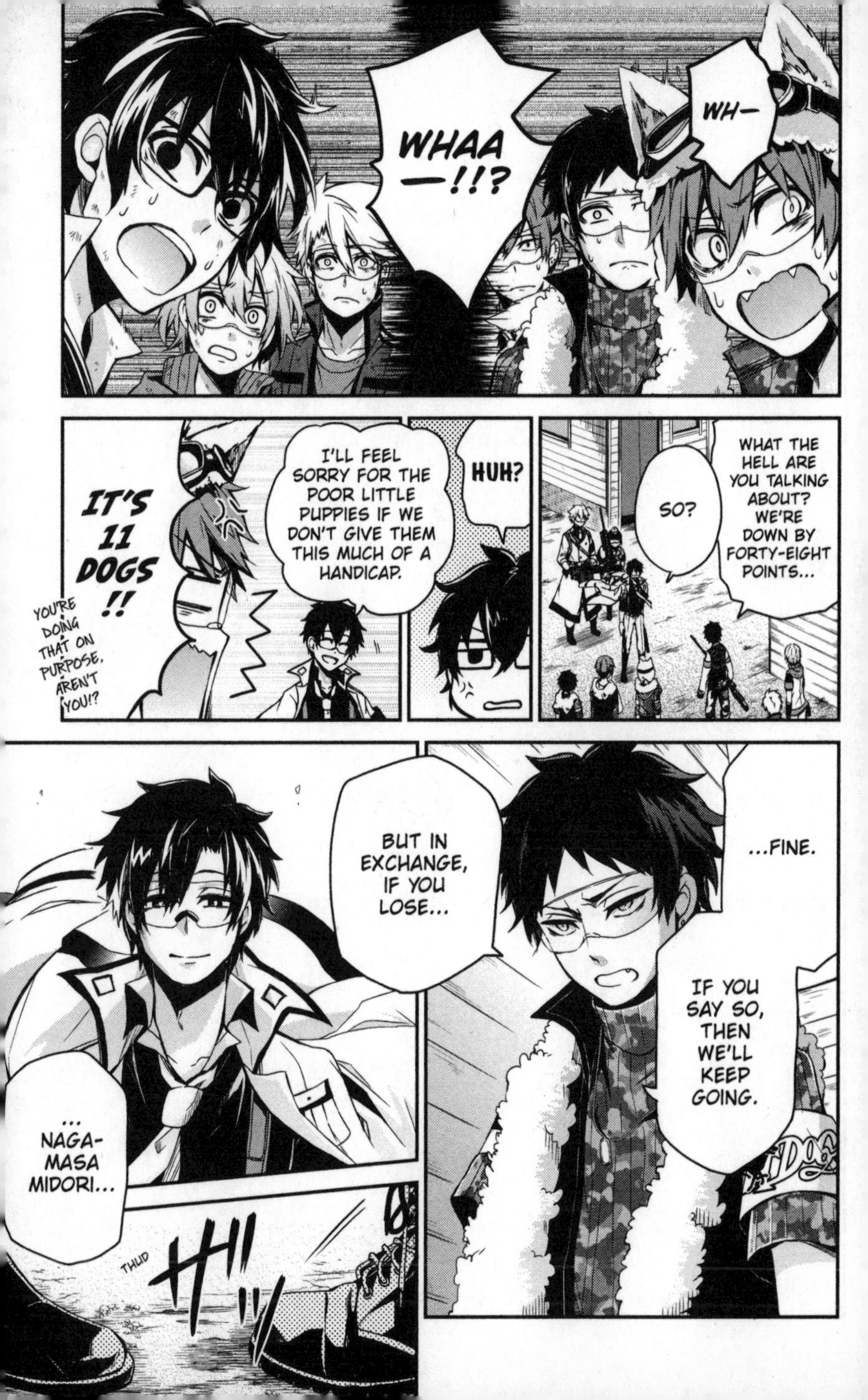
WH—
WHAA—!!?
WHAT THE HELL ARE YOU TALKING ABOUT? WE'RE DOWN BY FORTY-EIGHT POINTS...
SO?
HUH?
I'LL FEEL SORRY FOR THE POOR LITTLE PUPPIES IF WE DON'T GIVE THEM THIS MUCH OF A HANDICAP.
IT'S 11 DOGS!!
YOU'RE DOING THAT ON PURPOSE, AREN'T YOU!?
...FINE.
IF YOU SAY SO, THEN WE'LL KEEP GOING.
BUT IN EXCHANGE, IF YOU LOSE...
...NAGA-MASA MIDORI...
THUD

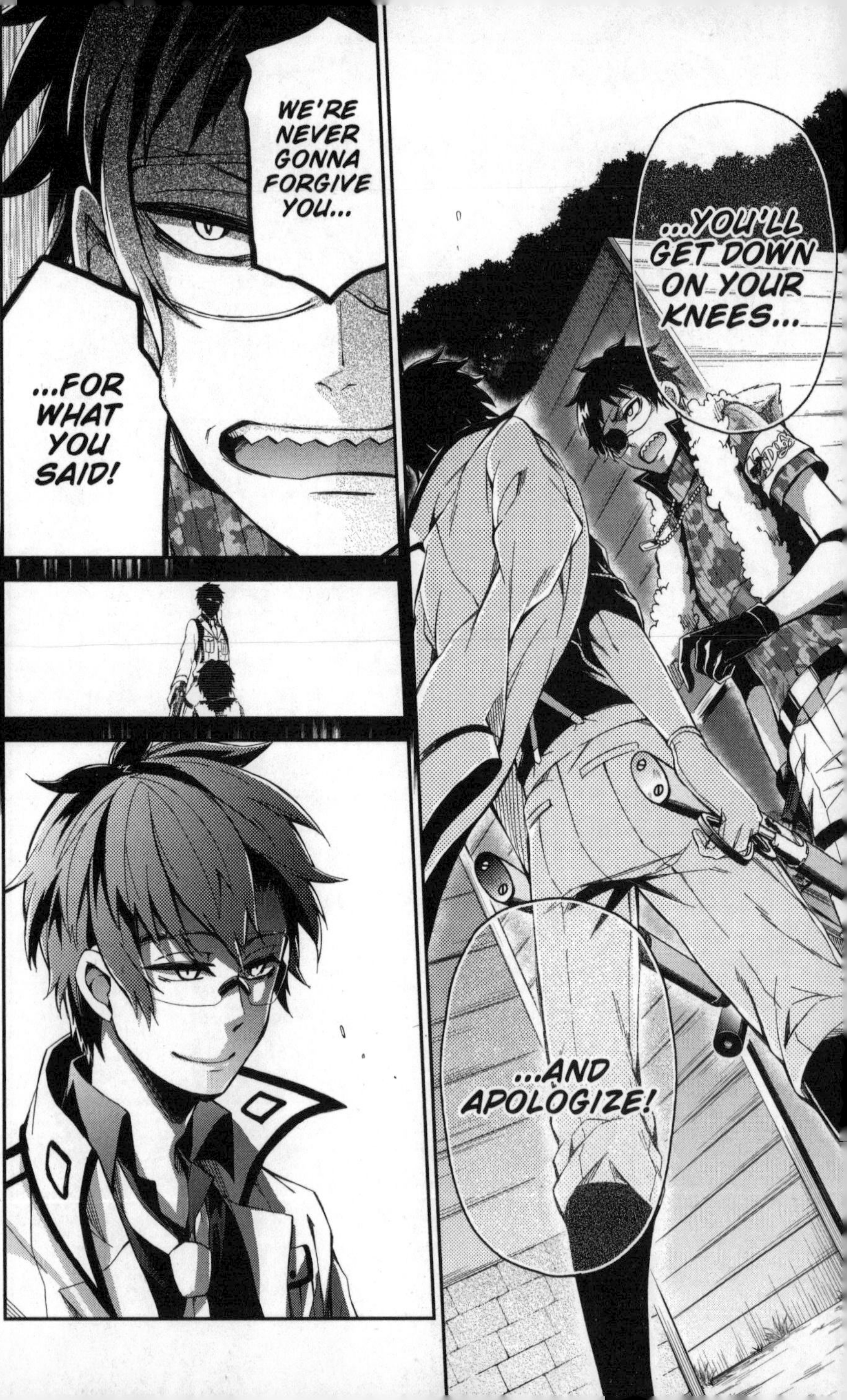
...YOU'LL GET DOWN ON YOUR KNEES...
...AND APOLOGIZE!
WE'RE NEVER GONNA FORGIVE YOU...
...FOR WHAT YOU SAID!

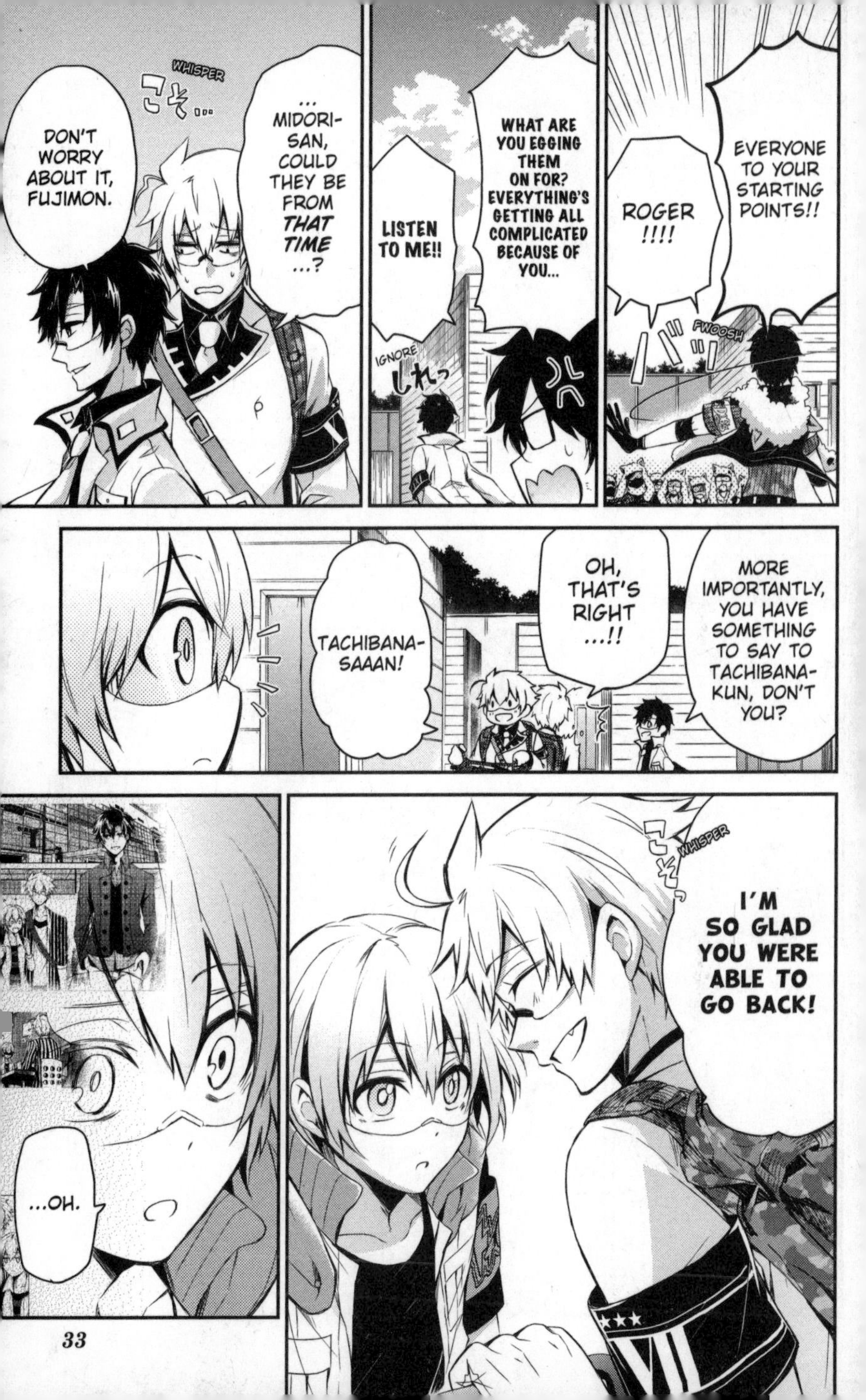
EVERYONE TO YOUR STARTING POINTS!!
ROGER!!!!
FWOOSH
WHAT ARE YOU EGGING THEM ON FOR? EVERYTHING'S GETTING ALL COMPLICATED BECAUSE OF YOU...
LISTEN TO ME!!
IGNORE
...MIDORI-SAN, COULD THEY BE FROM *THAT TIME*...?
WHISPER
DON'T WORRY ABOUT IT, FUJIMON.
MORE IMPORTANTLY, YOU HAVE SOMETHING TO SAY TO TACHIBANA-KUN, DON'T YOU?
OH, THAT'S RIGHT...!!
TACHIBANA-SAAAN!
WHISPER
I'M SO GLAD YOU WERE ABLE TO GO BACK!
...OH.

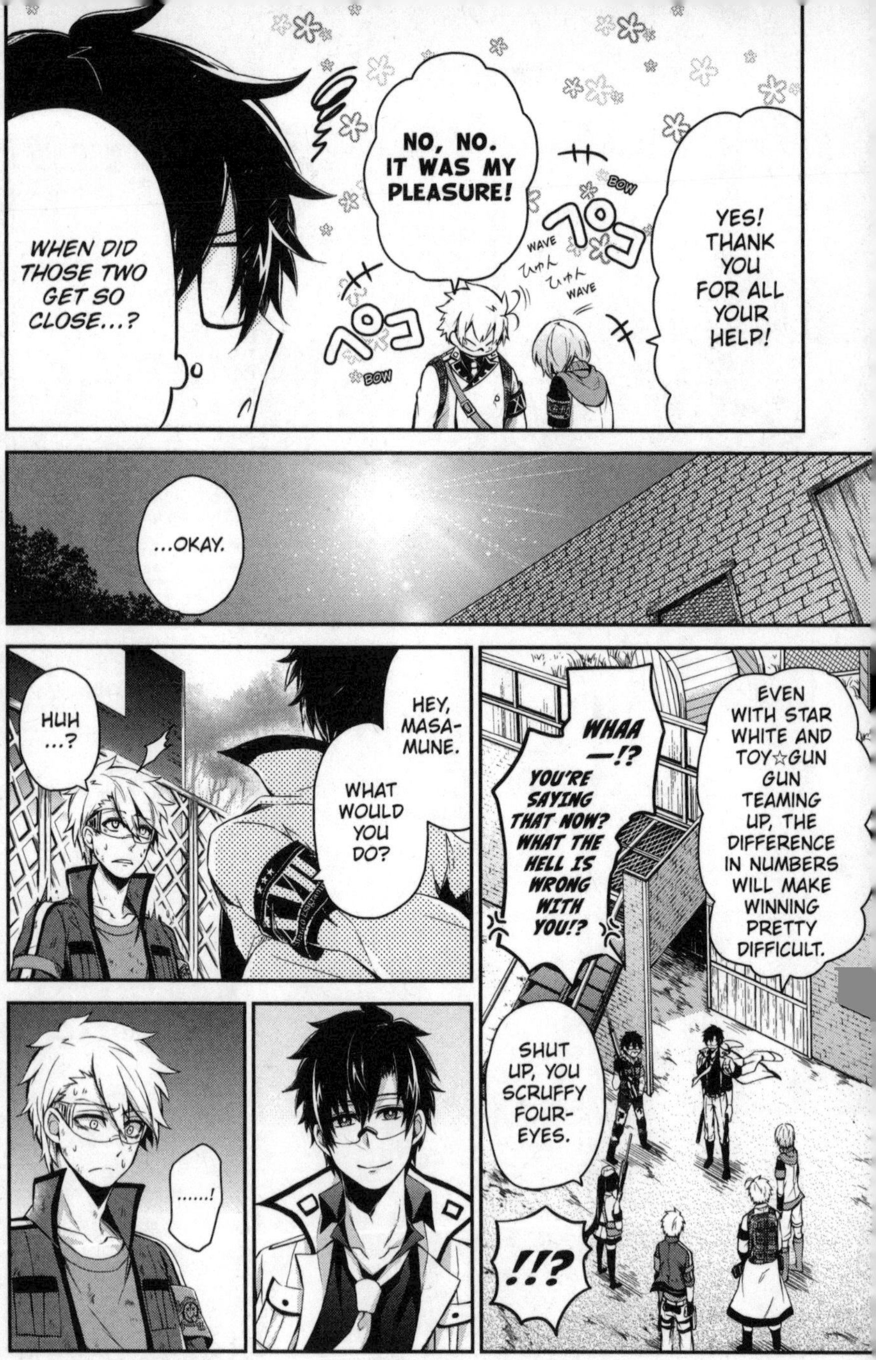
YES! THANK YOU FOR ALL YOUR HELP!
BOW
NO, NO. IT WAS MY PLEASURE!
WAVE
ひゅん
ひゅん
WAVE
BOW
WHEN DID THOSE TWO GET SO CLOSE...?
...OKAY.
EVEN WITH STAR WHITE AND TOY☆GUN GUN TEAMING UP, THE DIFFERENCE IN NUMBERS WILL MAKE WINNING PRETTY DIFFICULT.
WHAA—!?
YOU'RE SAYING THAT NOW? WHAT THE HELL IS WRONG WITH YOU!?
SHUT UP, YOU SCRUFFY FOUR-EYES.
!!?
HEY, MASAMUNE.
WHAT WOULD YOU DO?
HUH...?
......!

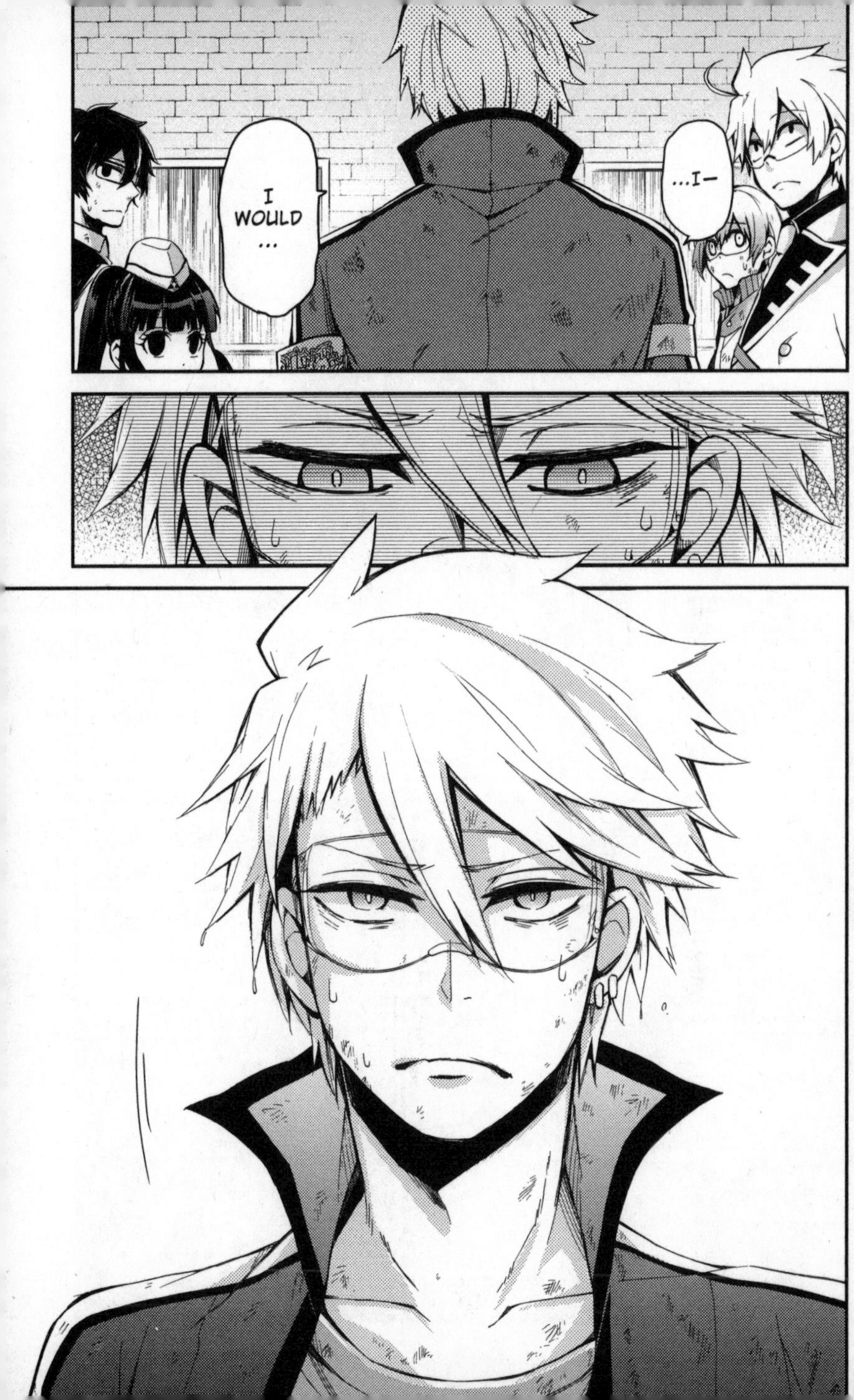
...I—
I WOULD ...

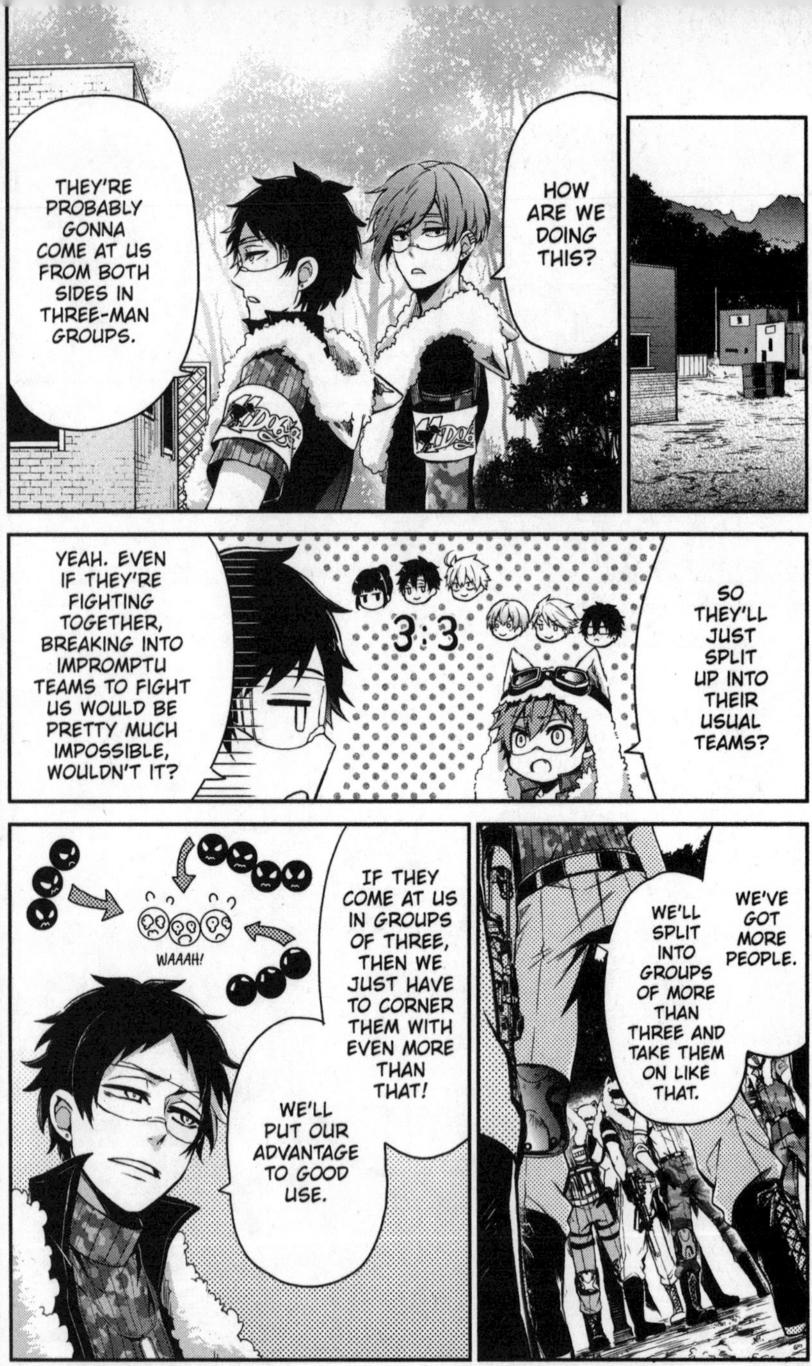
HOW ARE WE DOING THIS?
THEY'RE PROBABLY GONNA COME AT US FROM BOTH SIDES IN THREE-MAN GROUPS.
SO THEY'LL JUST SPLIT UP INTO THEIR USUAL TEAMS?
3:3
YEAH. EVEN IF THEY'RE FIGHTING TOGETHER, BREAKING INTO IMPROMPTU TEAMS TO FIGHT US WOULD BE PRETTY MUCH IMPOSSIBLE, WOULDN'T IT?
WE'VE GOT MORE PEOPLE.
WE'LL SPLIT INTO GROUPS OF MORE THAN THREE AND TAKE THEM ON LIKE THAT.
IF THEY COME AT US IN GROUPS OF THREE, THEN WE JUST HAVE TO CORNER THEM WITH EVEN MORE THAN THAT!
WAAAH!
WE'LL PUT OUR ADVANTAGE TO GOOD USE.

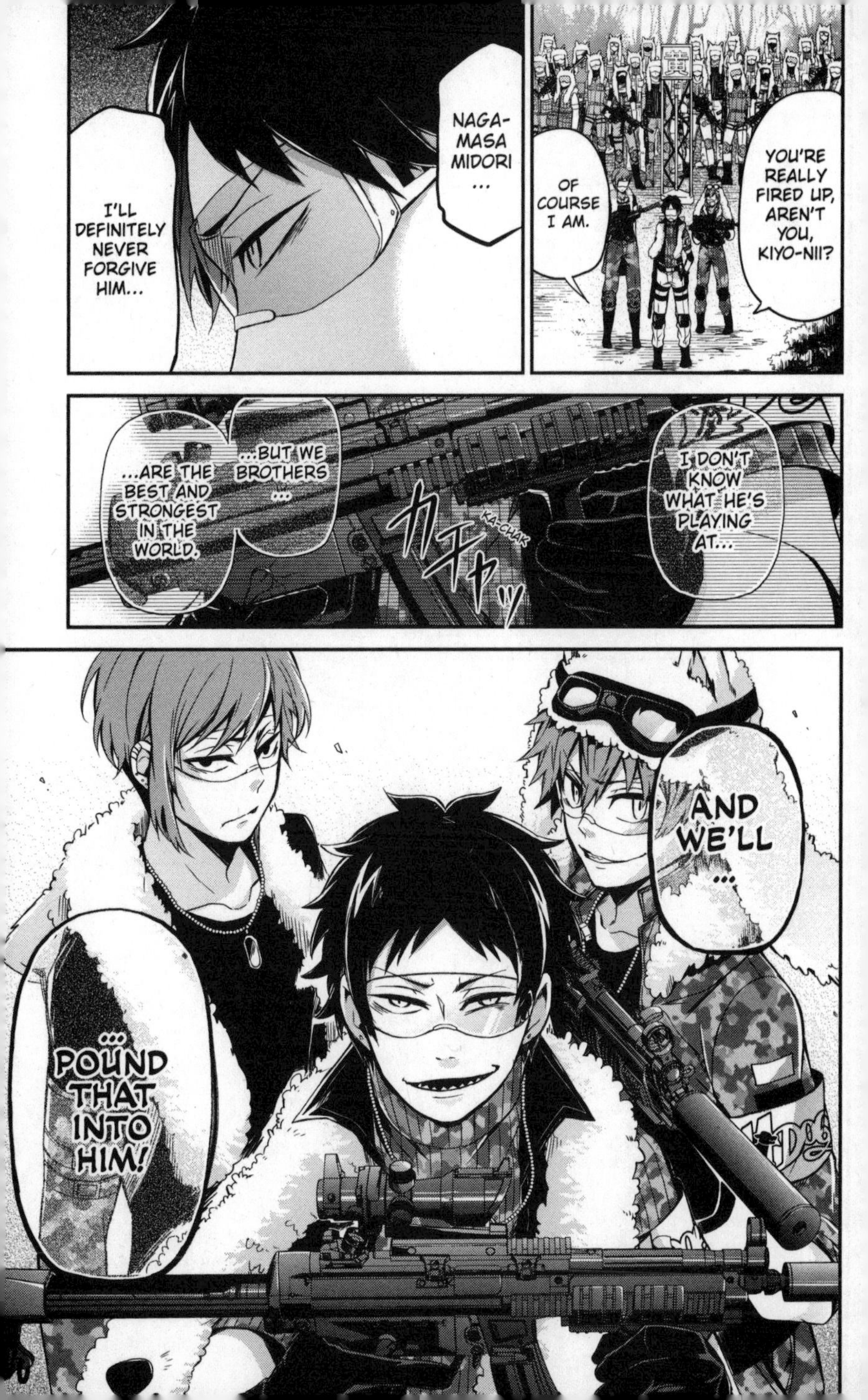
YOU'RE REALLY FIRED UP, AREN'T YOU, KIYO-NII?
OF COURSE I AM.
NAGA-MASA MIDORI...
I'LL DEFINITELY NEVER FORGIVE HIM...
I DON'T KNOW WHAT HE'S PLAYING AT...
KA-CHAK
...BUT WE BROTHERS...
...ARE THE BEST AND STRONGEST IN THE WORLD.
AND WE'LL...
...POUND THAT INTO HIM!

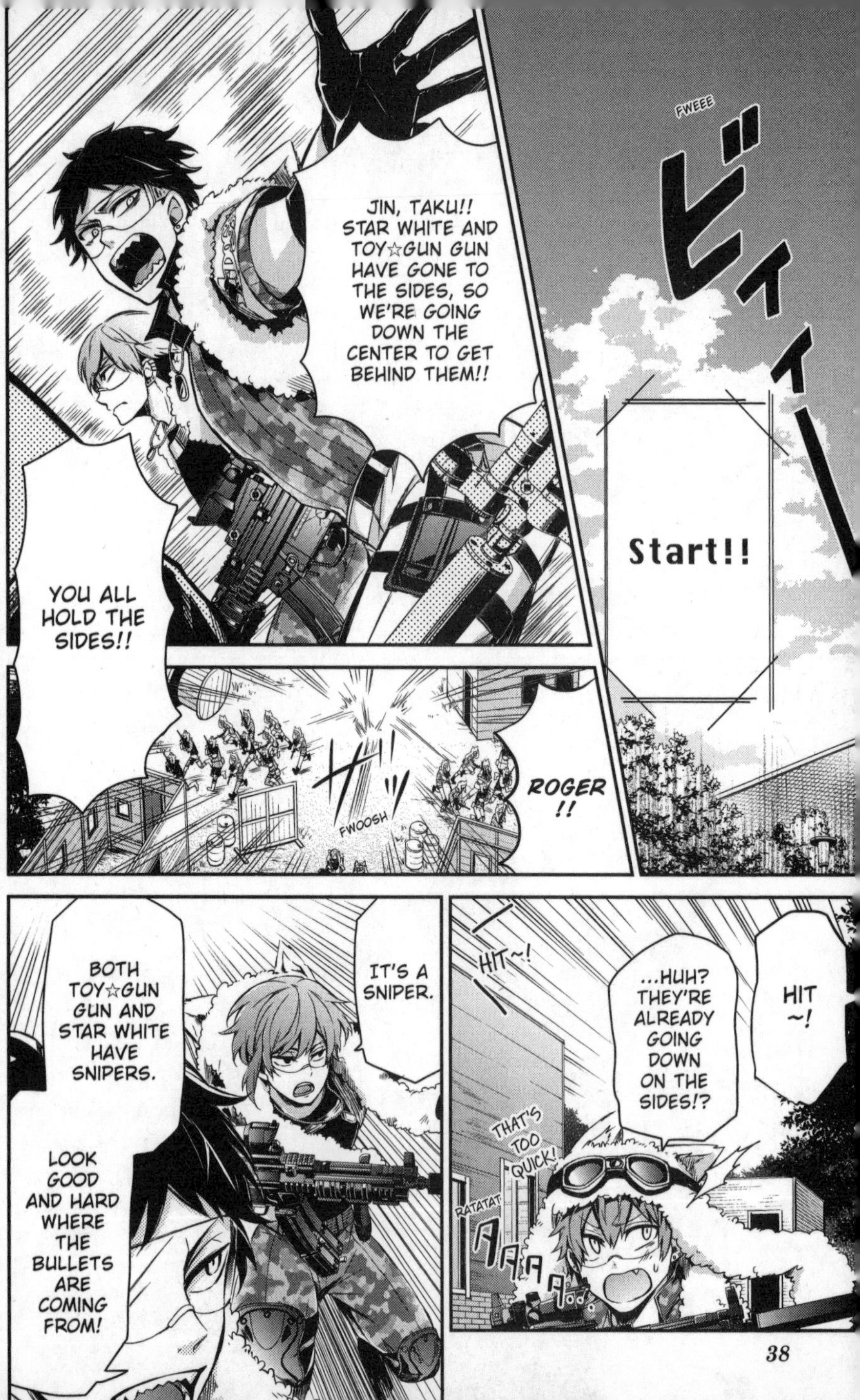
FWEEE
Start!!
JIN, TAKU!! STAR WHITE AND TOY☆GUN GUN HAVE GONE TO THE SIDES, SO WE'RE GOING DOWN THE CENTER TO GET BEHIND THEM!!
YOU ALL HOLD THE SIDES!!
ROGER !!
FWOOSH
HIT ~!
HIT~!
...HUH? THEY'RE ALREADY GOING DOWN ON THE SIDES!?
THAT'S TOO QUICK!
RATATAT
IT'S A SNIPER.
BOTH TOY☆GUN GUN AND STAR WHITE HAVE SNIPERS.
LOOK GOOD AND HARD WHERE THE BULLETS ARE COMING FROM!

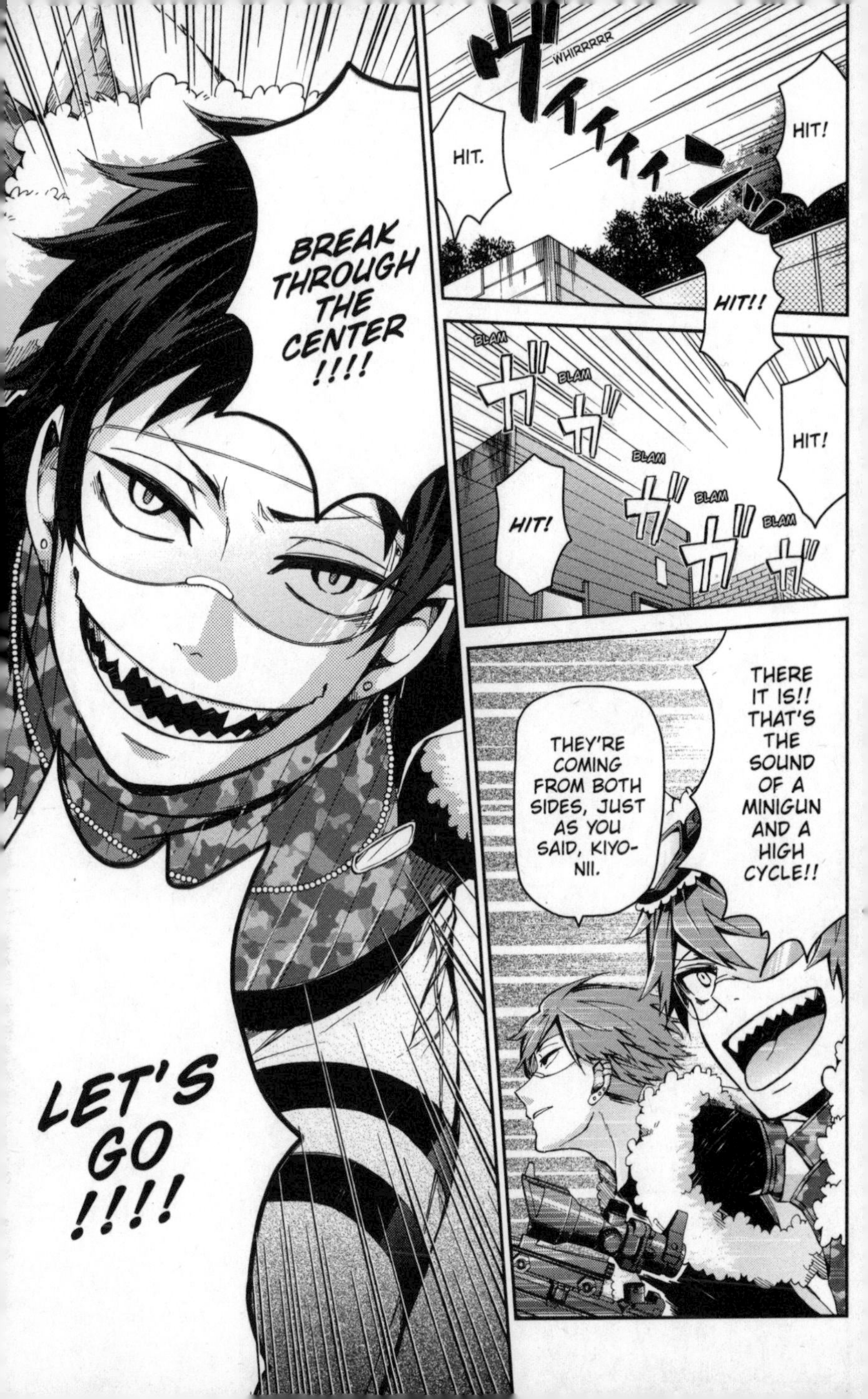
HIT!
WHIRRRRR
HIT.
HIT!!
HIT!
BLAM
BLAM
BLAM
BLAM
BLAM
HIT!
THERE IT IS!! THAT'S THE SOUND OF A MINIGUN AND A HIGH CYCLE!!
THEY'RE COMING FROM BOTH SIDES, JUST AS YOU SAID, KIYO-NII.
BREAK THROUGH THE CENTER!!!!
LET'S GO!!!!

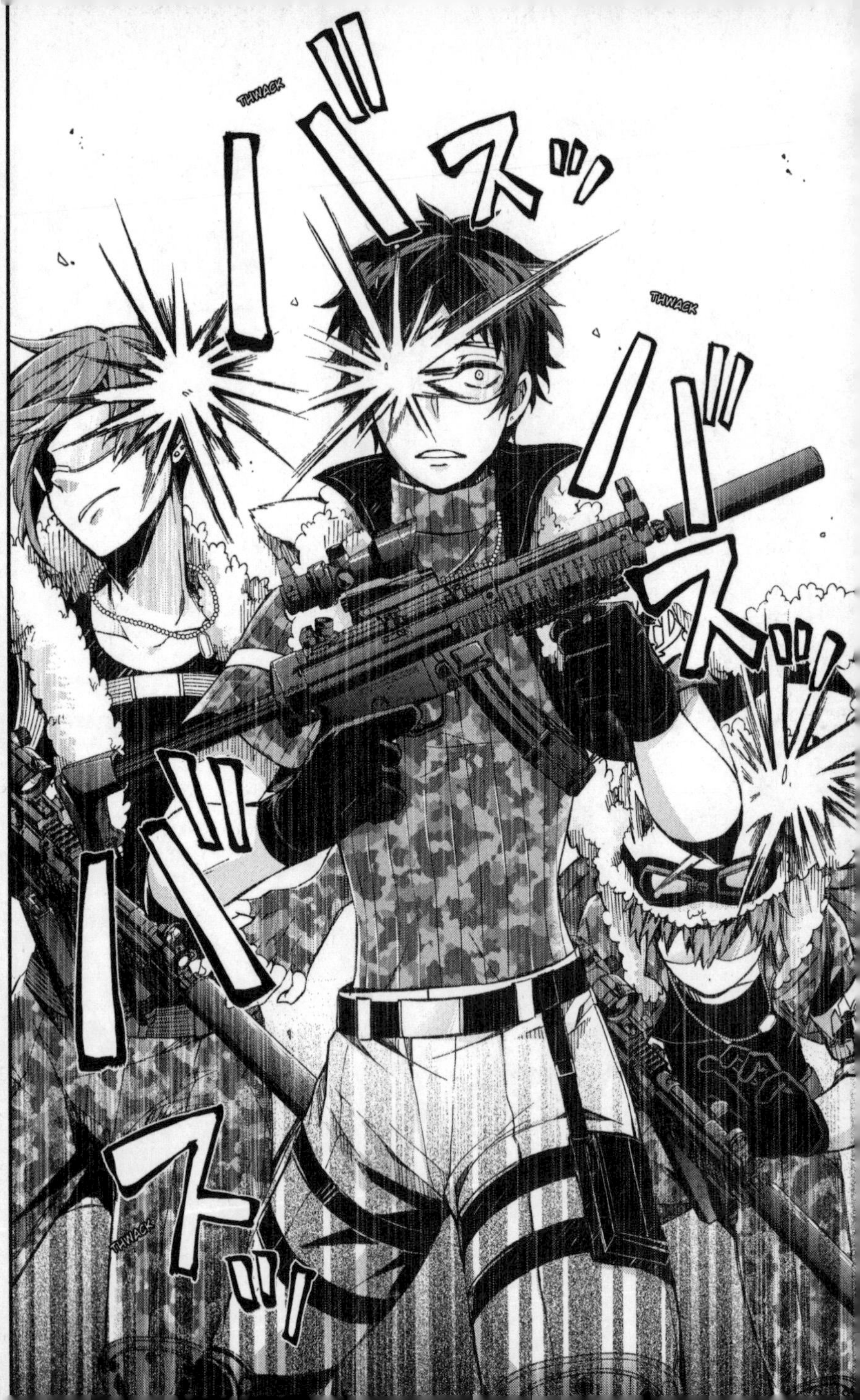
THWACK
ドバスッ
THWACK
ドバスッ
THWACK
ドスッ

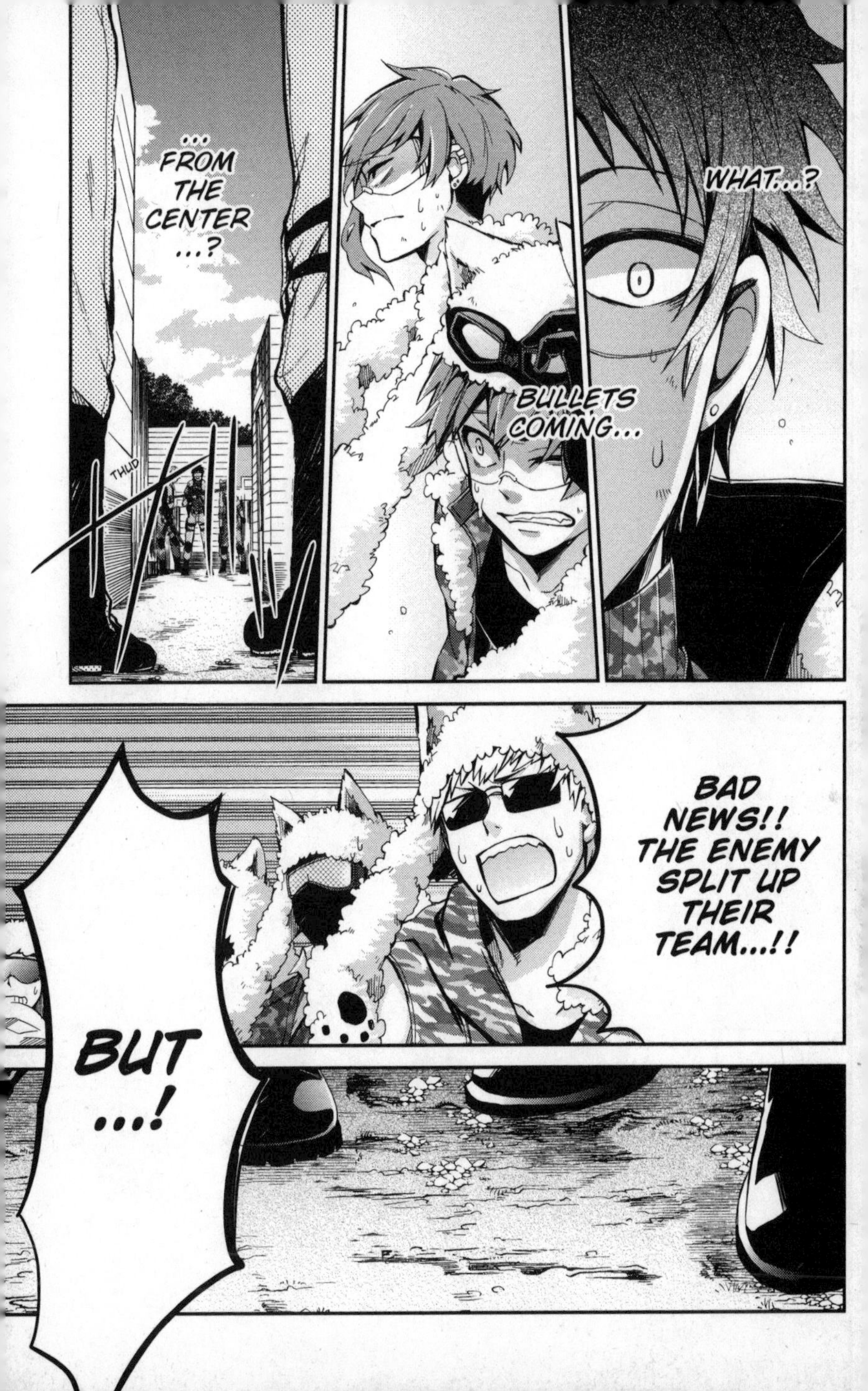
WHAT...?
BULLETS COMING...
...FROM THE CENTER...?
THUD
BAD NEWS!! THE ENEMY SPLIT UP THEIR TEAM...!!
BUT...!

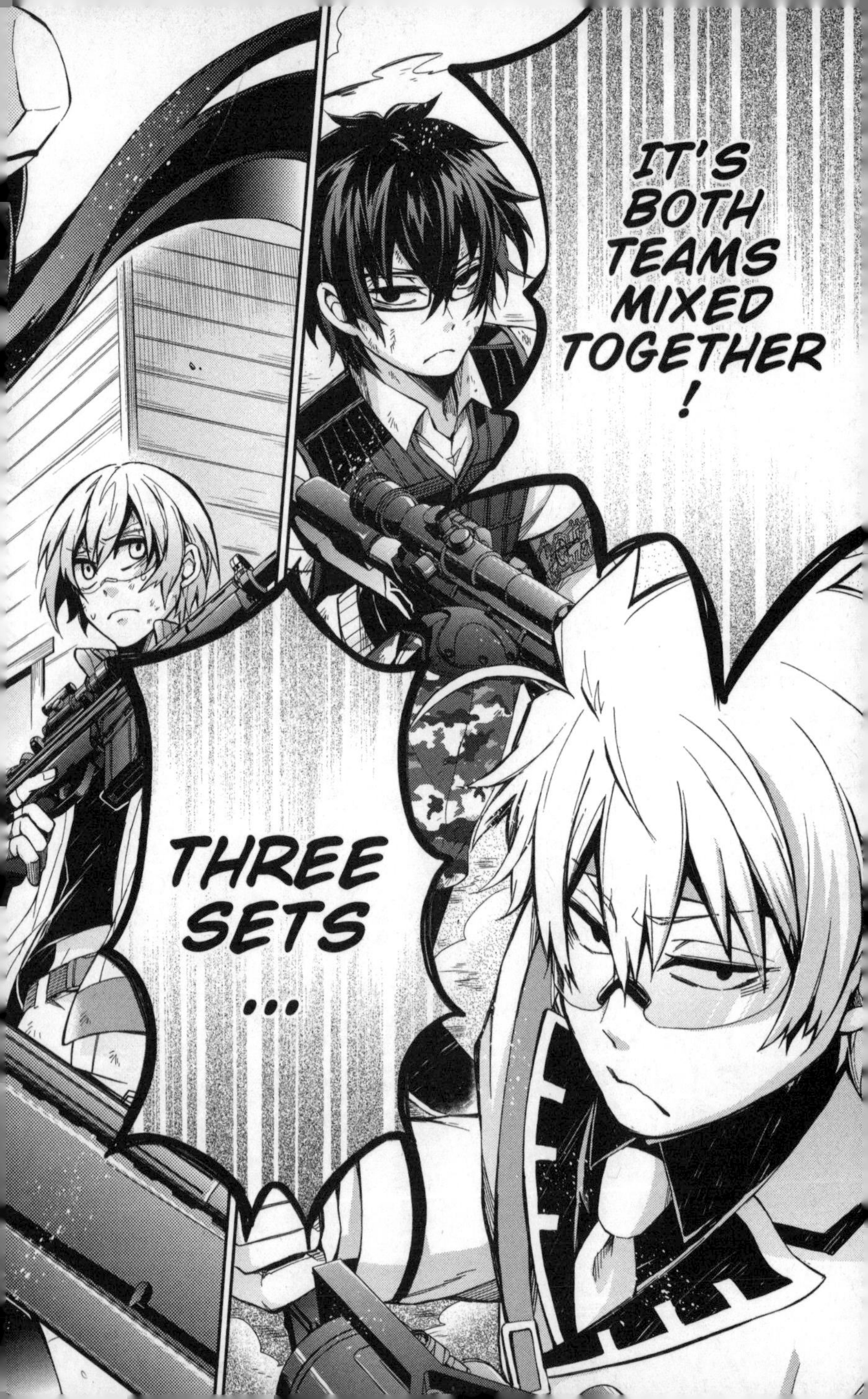
IT'S BOTH TEAMS MIXED TOGETHER!
THREE SETS...

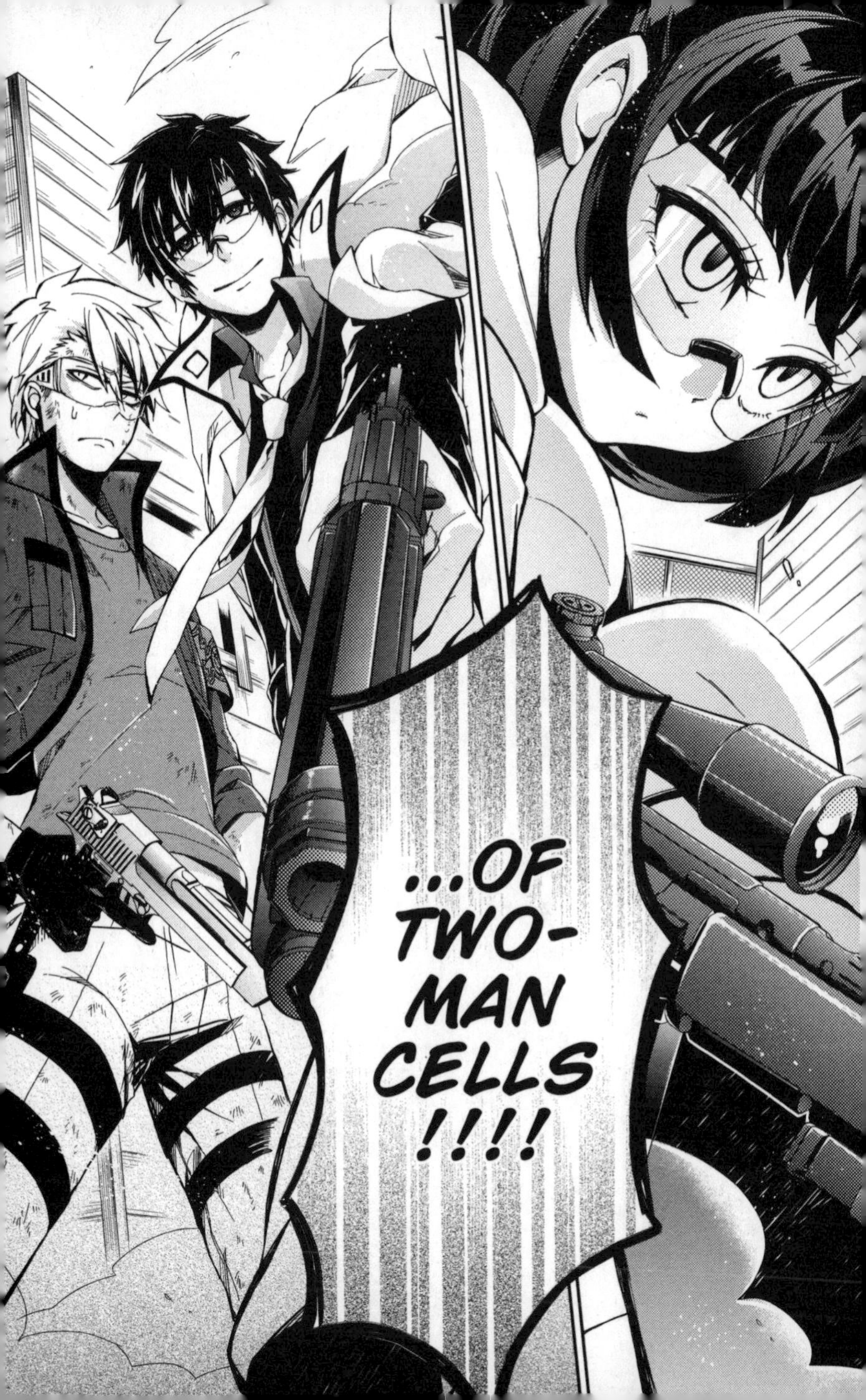
...OF TWO-MAN CELLS !!!!

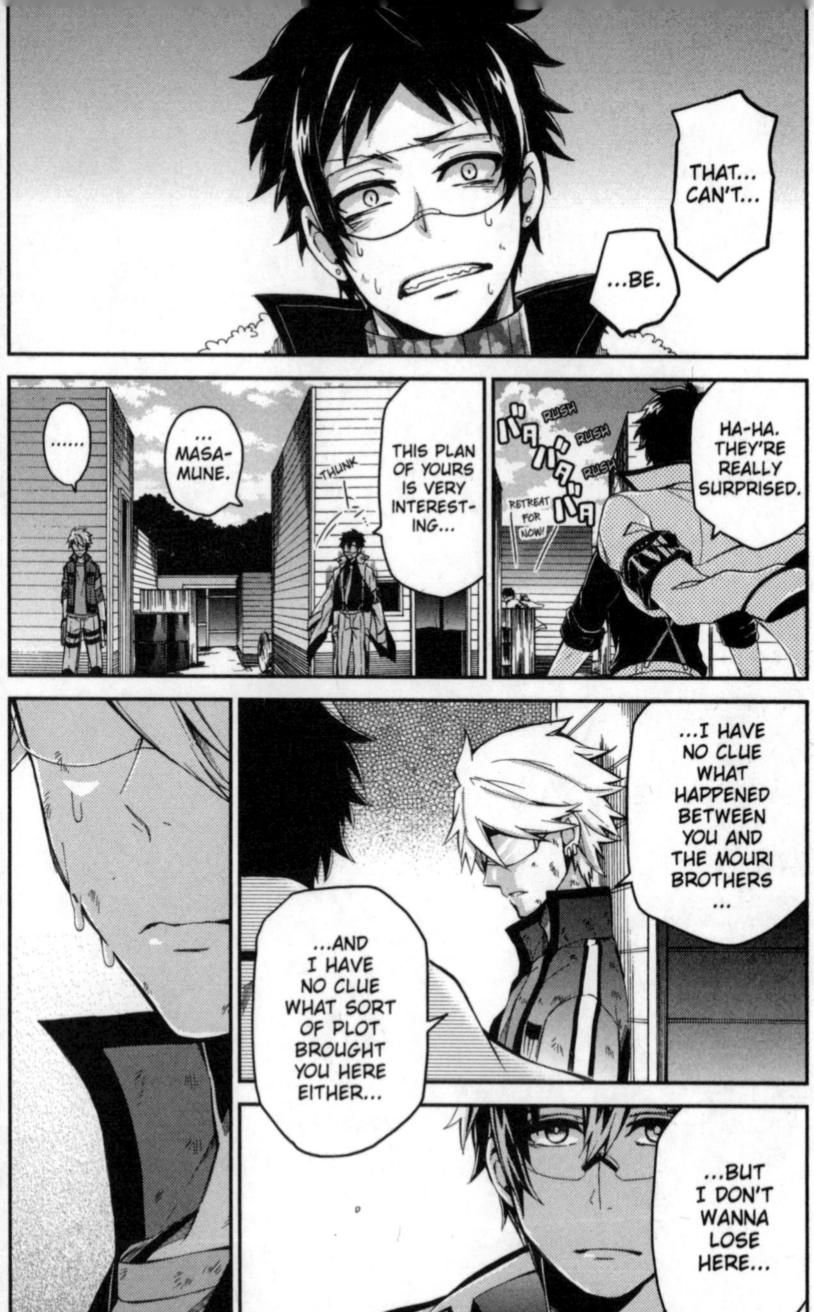
THAT... CAN'T...
...BE.
RUSH
RUSH
RUSH
RETREAT FOR NOW!
HA-HA. THEY'RE REALLY SURPRISED.
THUNK
THIS PLAN OF YOURS IS VERY INTERESTING...
... MASAMUNE.
......
...I HAVE NO CLUE WHAT HAPPENED BETWEEN YOU AND THE MOURI BROTHERS ...
...AND I HAVE NO CLUE WHAT SORT OF PLOT BROUGHT YOU HERE EITHER...
...BUT I DON'T WANNA LOSE HERE...

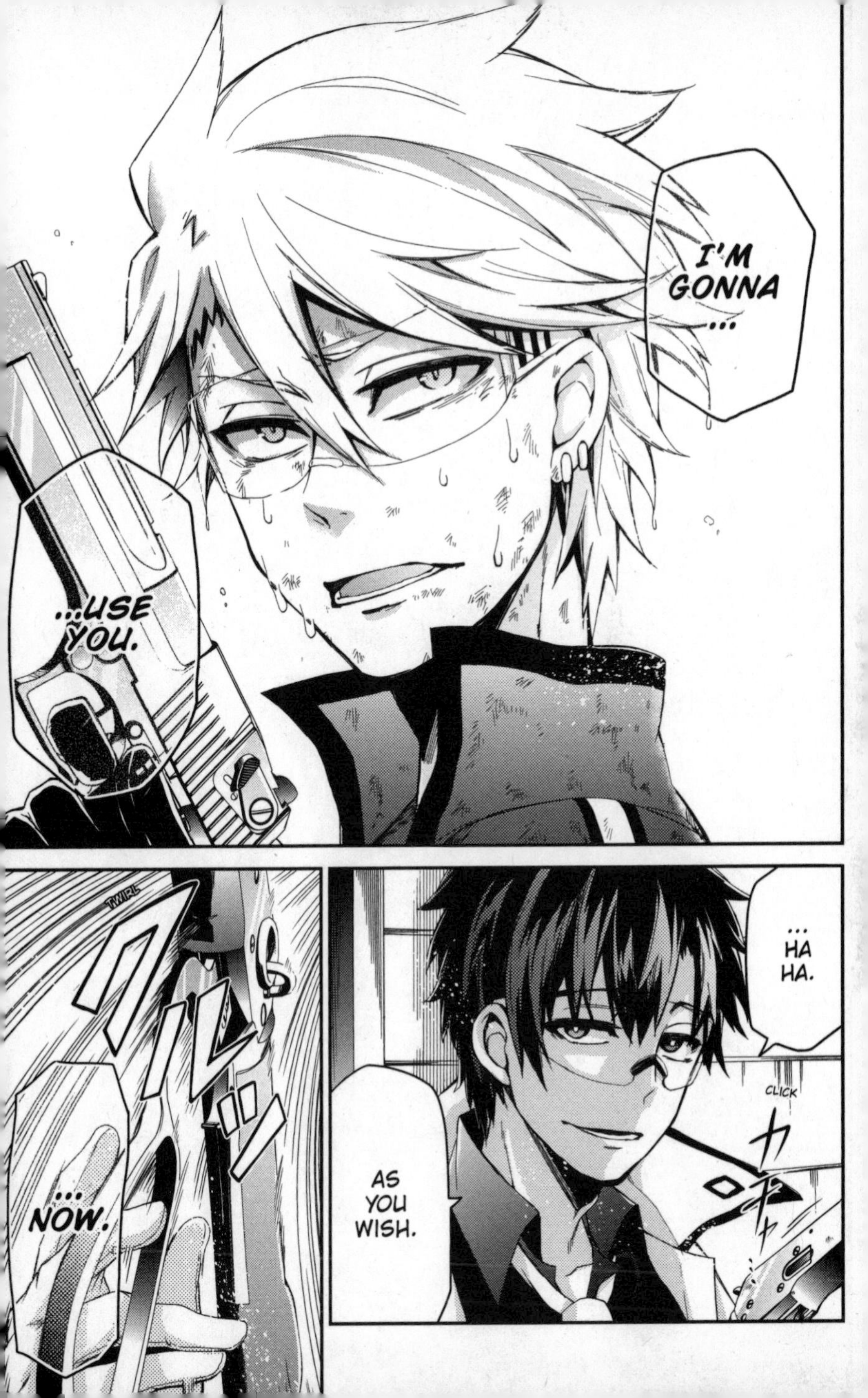
I'M GONNA
...
...USE YOU.
...
HA HA.
AS YOU WISH.
CLICK
TWIRL
...
NOW.

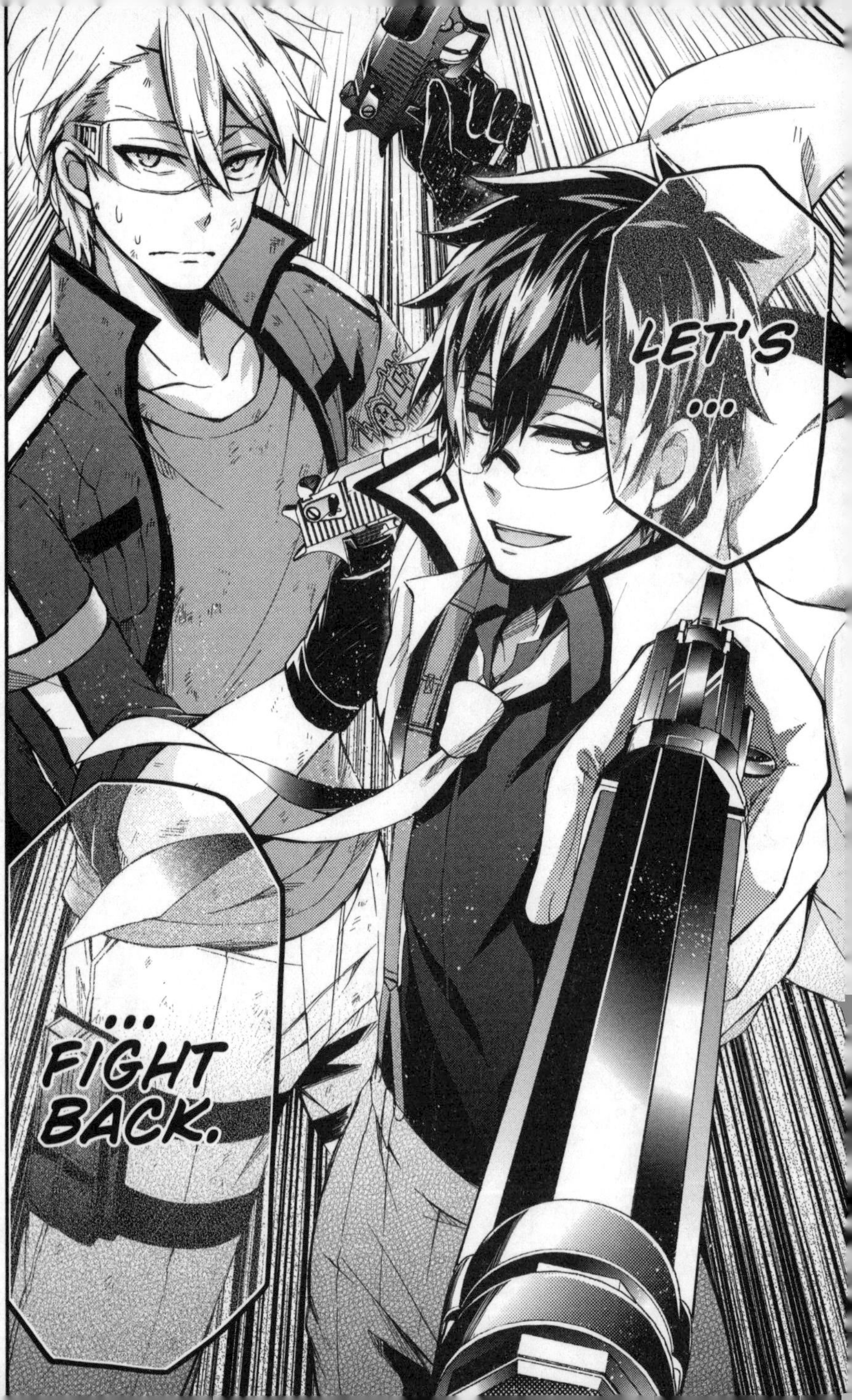
LET'S
...
...FIGHT BACK.

AOHARU×MACHINEGUN

AT THAT TIME, THE HOSOKAWA BROTHERS ...
EEEEEEEEEK!
NII-SAN.
NII-SAN.
NII-SAN.
NII-SAN.
NII-SAN.
NII-SAN.
NII-SAN.
NII-SAN.
NII-SAN.
NII-SAN.
...WERE RUNNING.

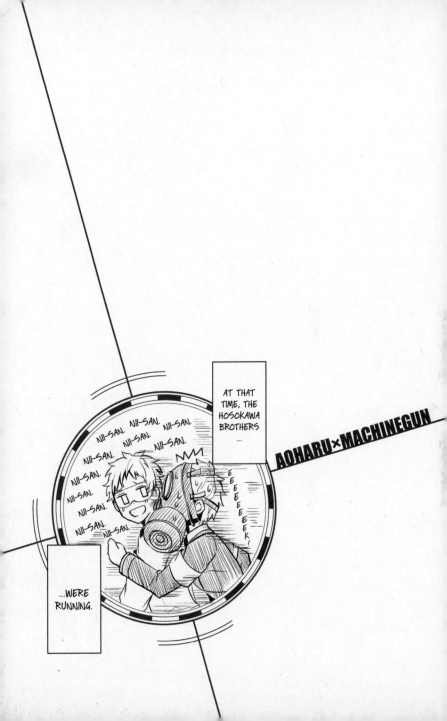

AOHARU
MACHINE
GUN

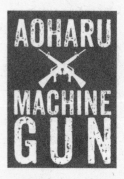

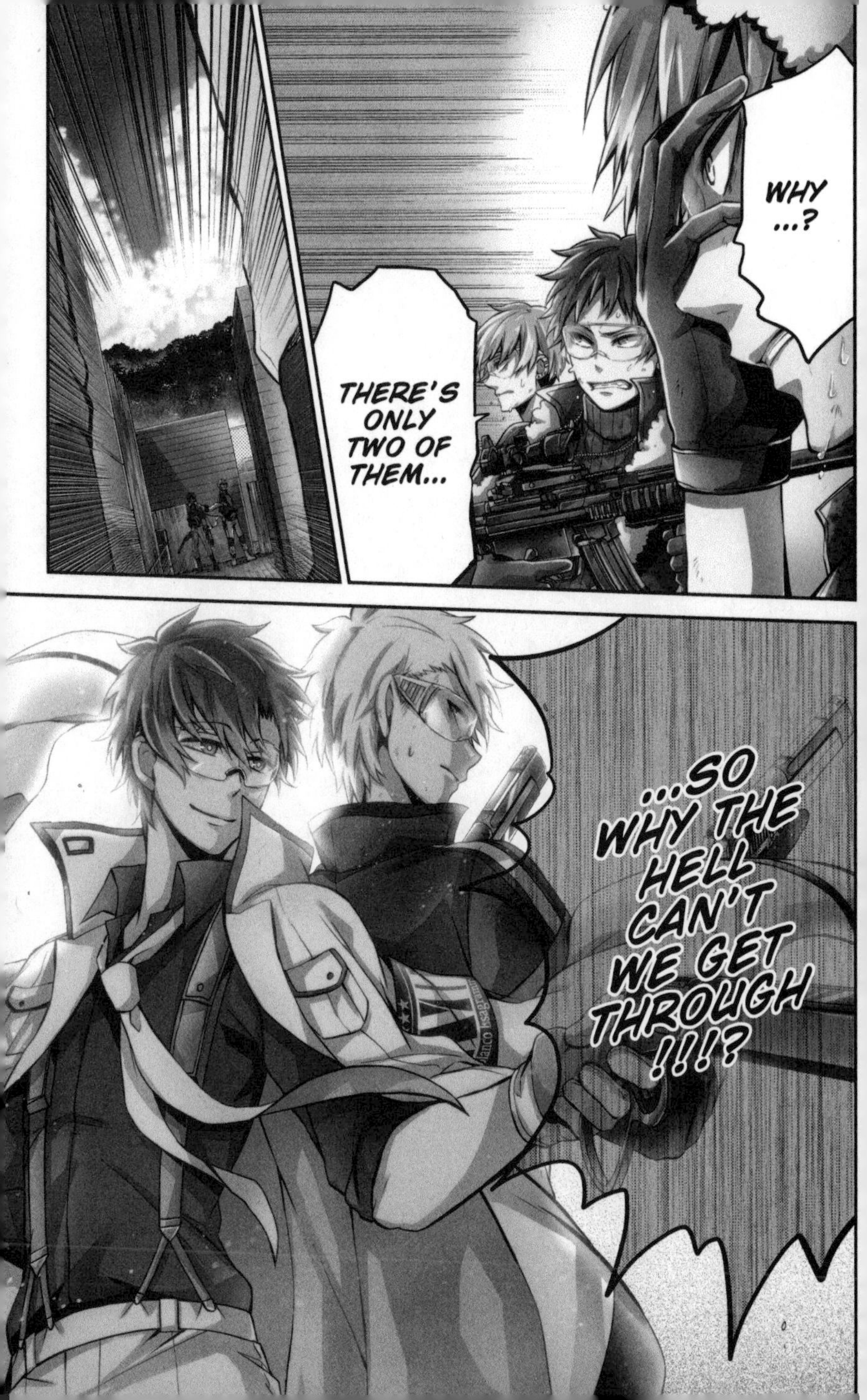
WHY ...?
THERE'S ONLY TWO OF THEM...
...SO WHY THE HELL CAN'T WE GET THROUGH !!!?

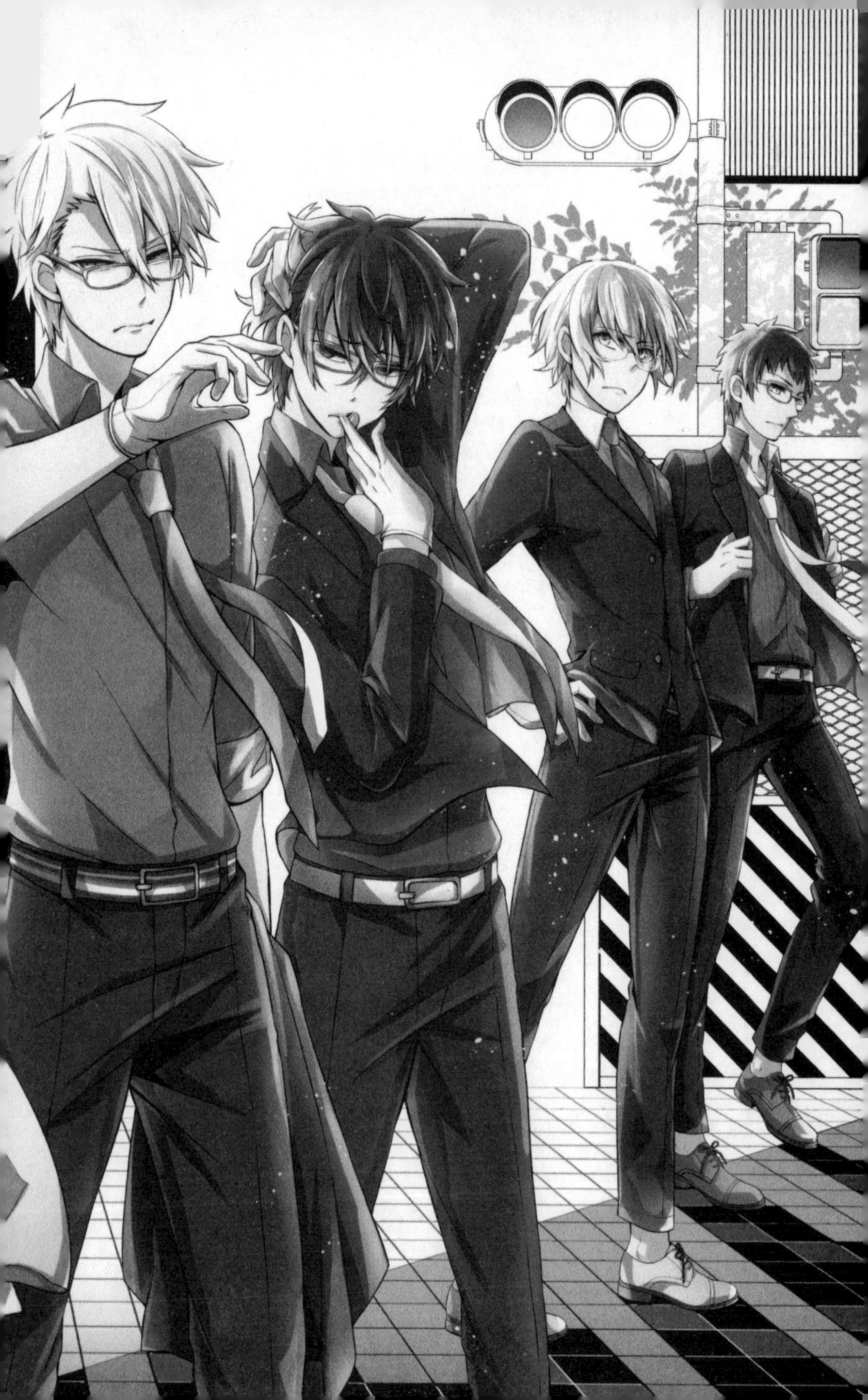

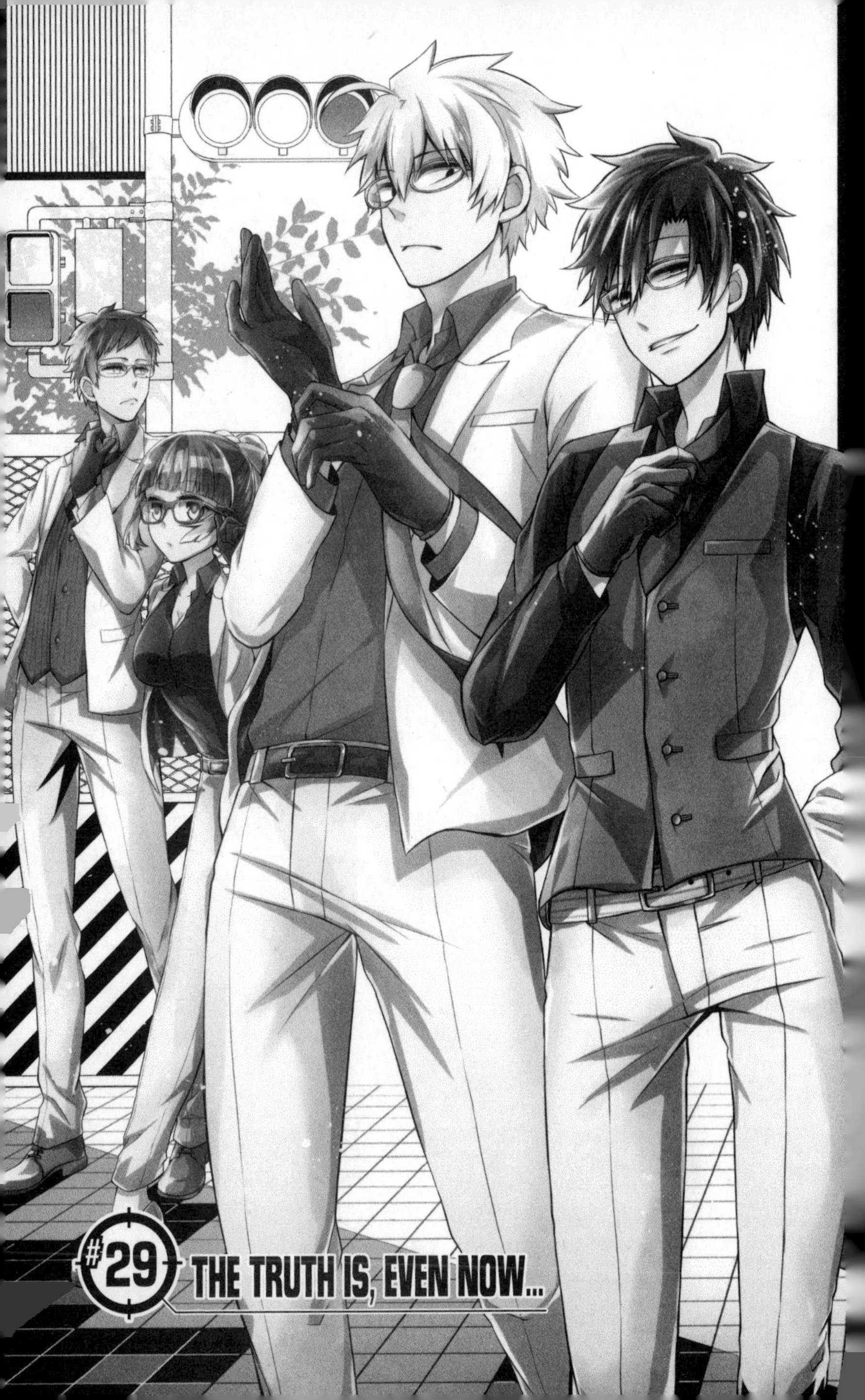
#29
THE TRUTH IS, EVEN NOW...

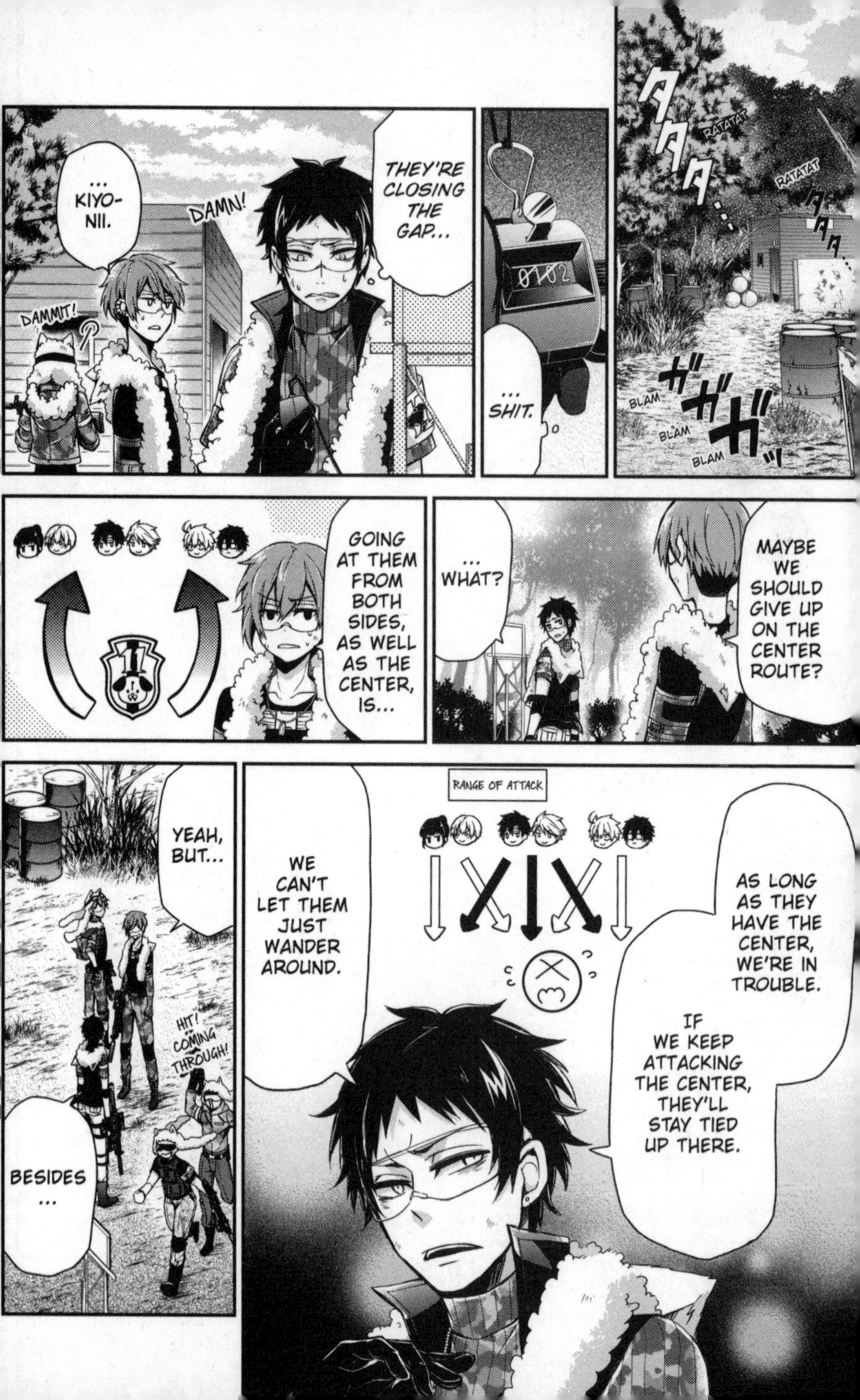
タタタ…
RATATAT
RATATAT
タタ…
ガガガッ
BLAM
BLAM
BLAM
... SHIT.
THEY'RE CLOSING THE GAP...
DAMN!
... KIYO-NII.
DAMMIT!
MAYBE WE SHOULD GIVE UP ON THE CENTER ROUTE?
... WHAT?
GOING AT THEM FROM BOTH SIDES, AS WELL AS THE CENTER, IS...
RANGE OF ATTACK
AS LONG AS THEY HAVE THE CENTER, WE'RE IN TROUBLE.
IF WE KEEP ATTACKING THE CENTER, THEY'LL STAY TIED UP THERE.
WE CAN'T LET THEM JUST WANDER AROUND.
YEAH, BUT...
HIT! COMING THROUGH!
BESIDES ...

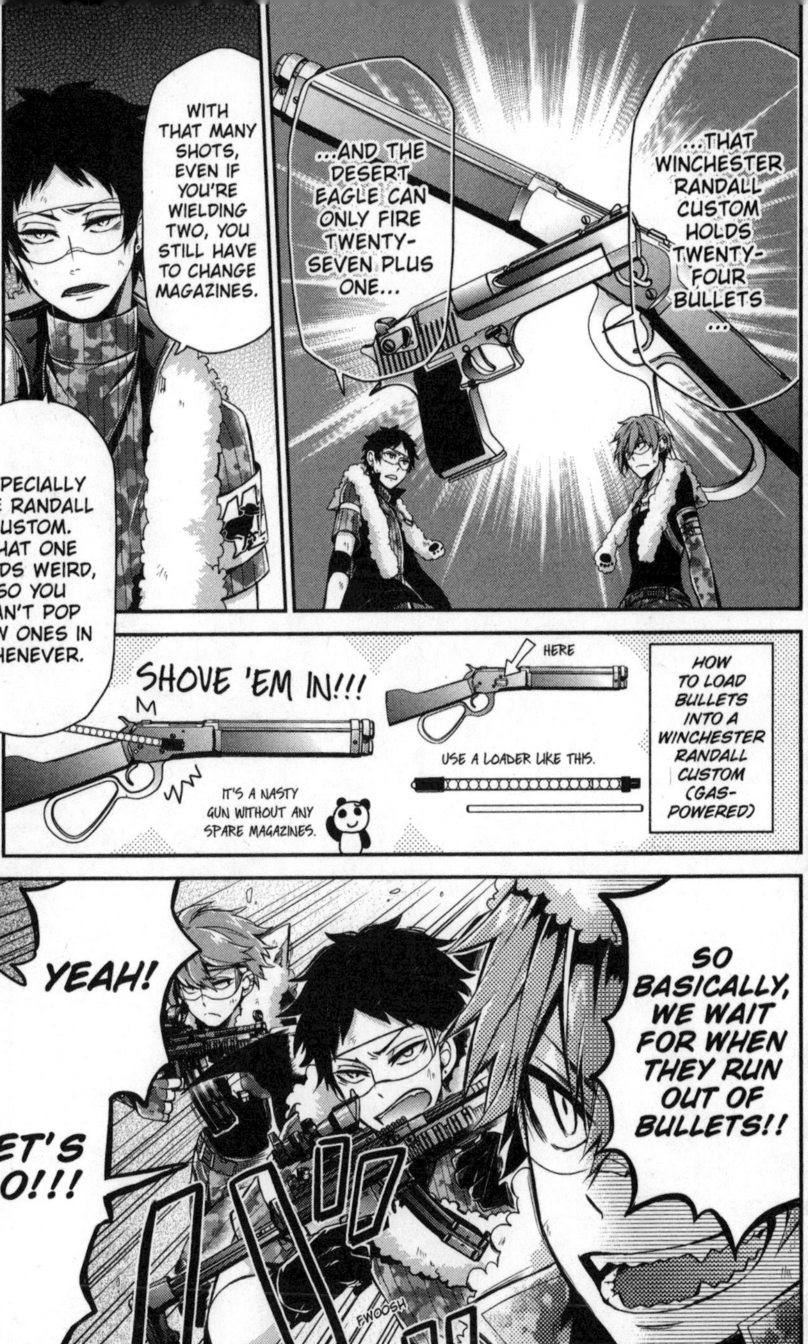
...THAT WINCHESTER RANDALL CUSTOM HOLDS TWENTY-FOUR BULLETS ...
...AND THE DESERT EAGLE CAN ONLY FIRE TWENTY-SEVEN PLUS ONE...
WITH THAT MANY SHOTS, EVEN IF YOU'RE WIELDING TWO, YOU STILL HAVE TO CHANGE MAGAZINES.
ESPECIALLY THE RANDALL CUSTOM. THAT ONE LOADS WEIRD, SO YOU CAN'T POP NEW ONES IN WHENEVER.
HOW TO LOAD BULLETS INTO A WINCHESTER RANDALL CUSTOM (GAS-POWERED)
HERE
USE A LOADER LIKE THIS.
SHOVE 'EM IN!!!
IT'S A NASTY GUN WITHOUT ANY SPARE MAGAZINES.
SO BASICALLY, WE WAIT FOR WHEN THEY RUN OUT OF BULLETS!!
FWOOSH
YEAH!
LET'S GO!!!

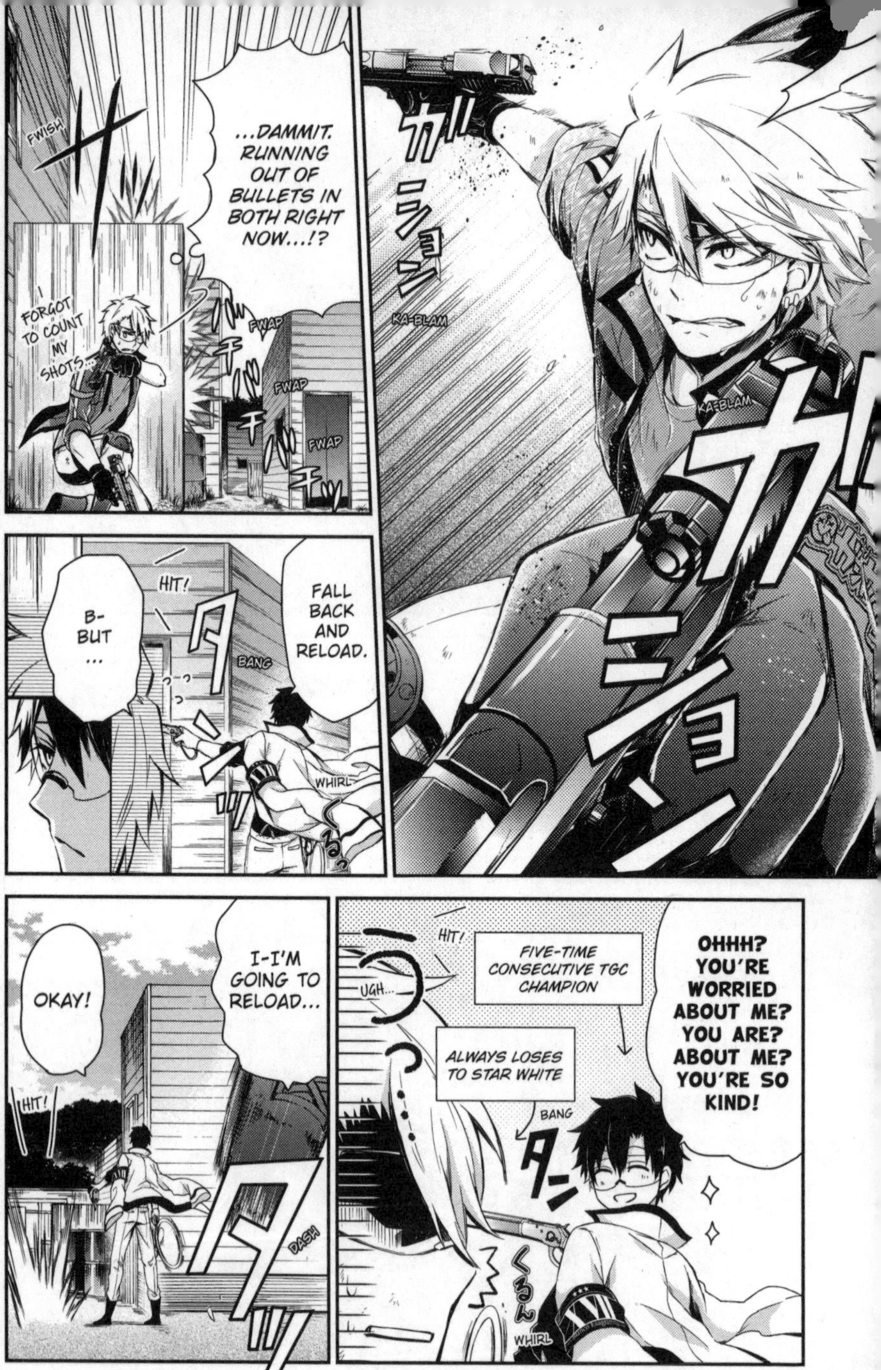
KA-BLAM
KA-BLAM
...DAMMIT. RUNNING OUT OF BULLETS IN BOTH RIGHT NOW...!?
FWISH
I FORGOT TO COUNT MY SHOTS...
FWAP
FWAP
FWAP
FALL BACK AND RELOAD.
HIT!
BANG
B- BUT ...
WHIRL
OHHH? YOU'RE WORRIED ABOUT ME? YOU ARE? ABOUT ME? YOU'RE SO KIND!
HIT!
FIVE-TIME CONSECUTIVE TGC CHAMPION
UGH...
ALWAYS LOSES TO STAR WHITE
BANG
WHIRL
I-I'M GOING TO RELOAD...
OKAY!
HIT!
DASH

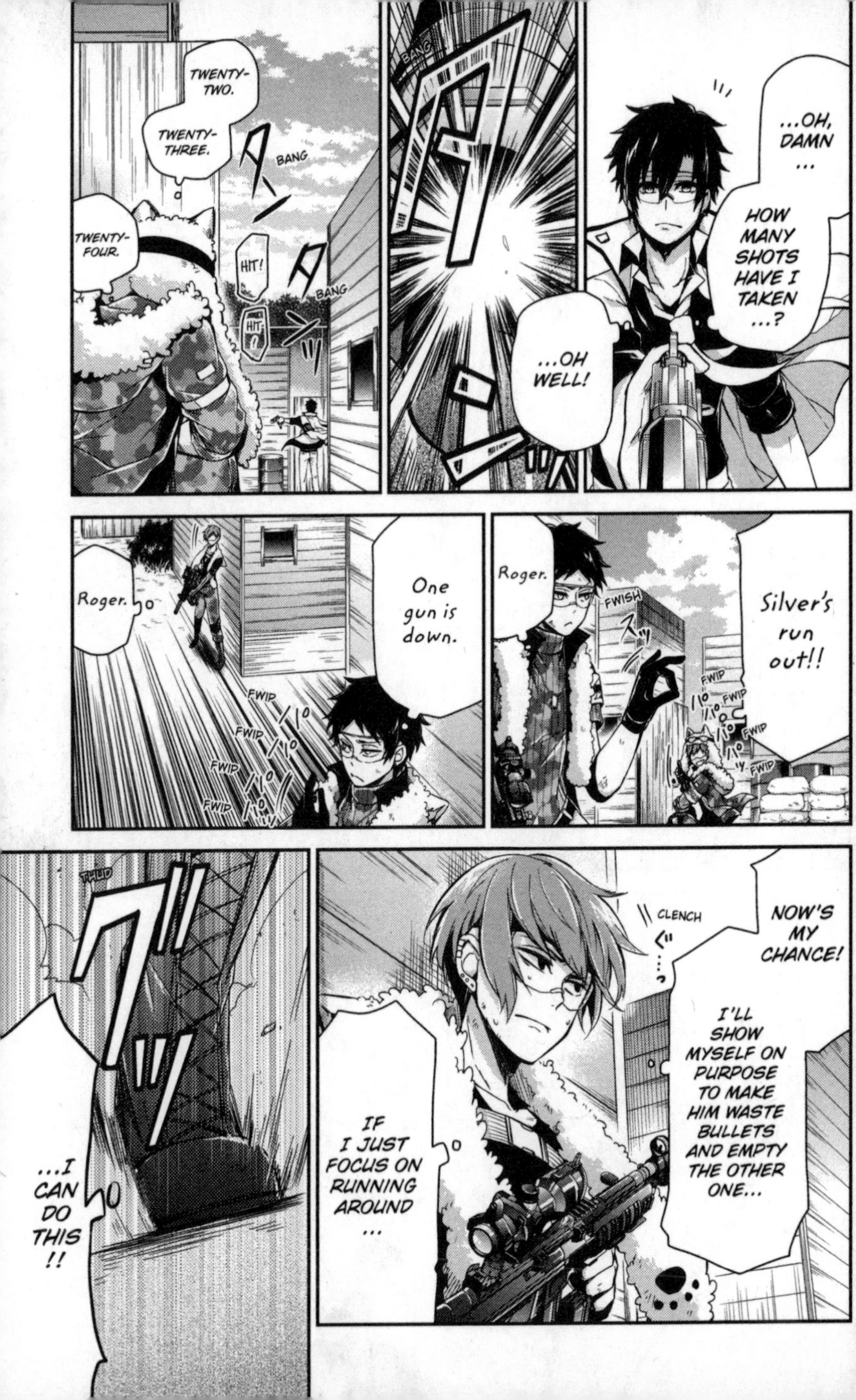
...OH, DAMN...
HOW MANY SHOTS HAVE I TAKEN...?
...OH WELL!
BANG
TWENTY-TWO.
TWENTY-THREE.
BANG
TWENTY-FOUR.
HIT!
BANG
HIT!
Silver's run out!!
Roger.
FWISH
FWIP
FWIP
FWIP
FWIP
One gun is down.
Roger.
FWIP
FWIP
FWIP
FWIP
NOW'S MY CHANCE!
CLENCH
I'LL SHOW MYSELF ON PURPOSE TO MAKE HIM WASTE BULLETS AND EMPTY THE OTHER ONE...
IF I JUST FOCUS ON RUNNING AROUND...
THUD
...I CAN DO THIS!!

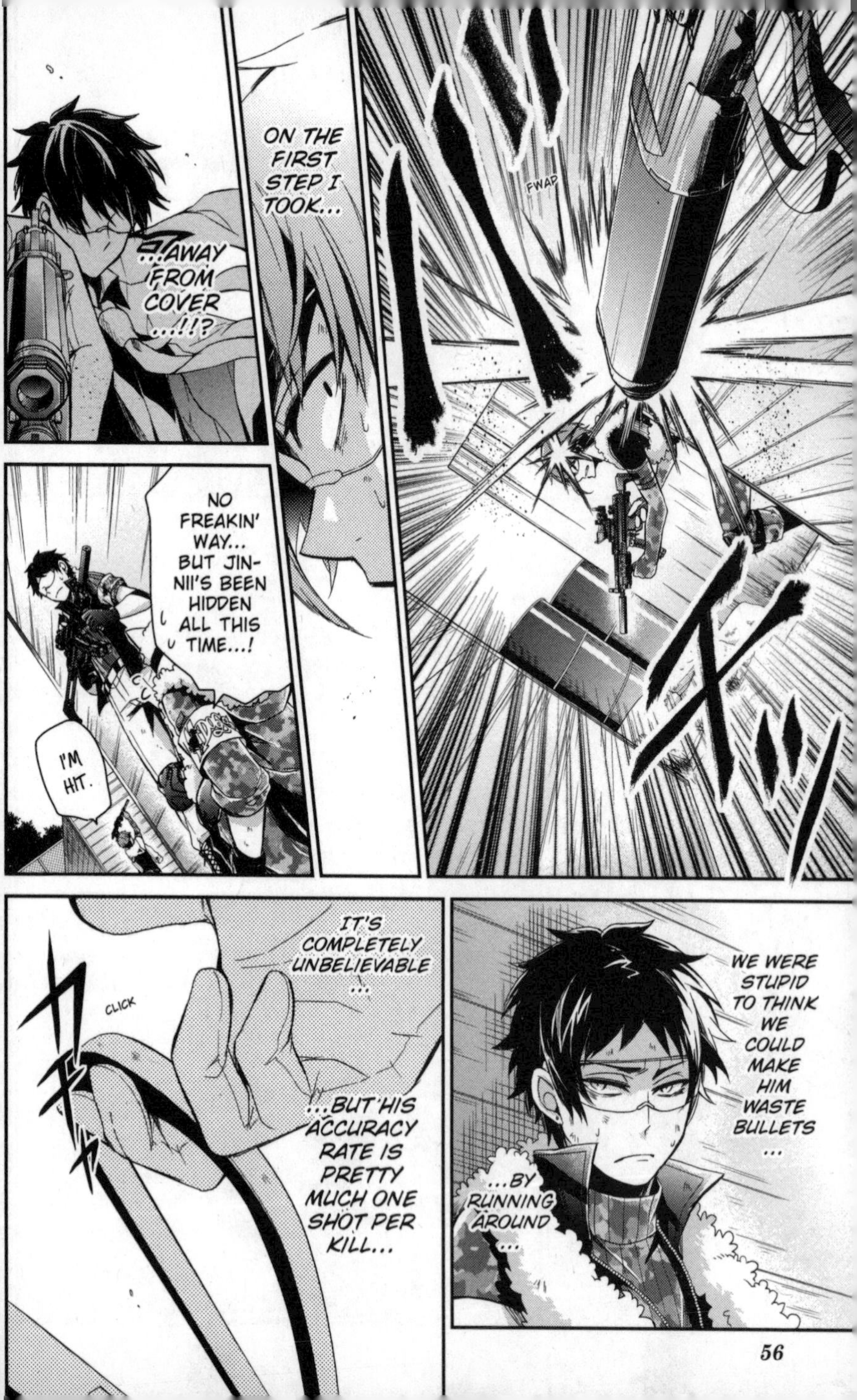
FWAP
ON THE FIRST STEP I TOOK...
...AWAY FROM COVER...!!?
NO FREAKIN' WAY... BUT JIN-NII'S BEEN HIDDEN ALL THIS TIME...!
I'M HIT.
WE WERE STUPID TO THINK WE COULD MAKE HIM WASTE BULLETS...
...BY RUNNING AROUND...
IT'S COMPLETELY UNBELIEVABLE...
...BUT HIS ACCURACY RATE IS PRETTY MUCH ONE SHOT PER KILL...
CLICK

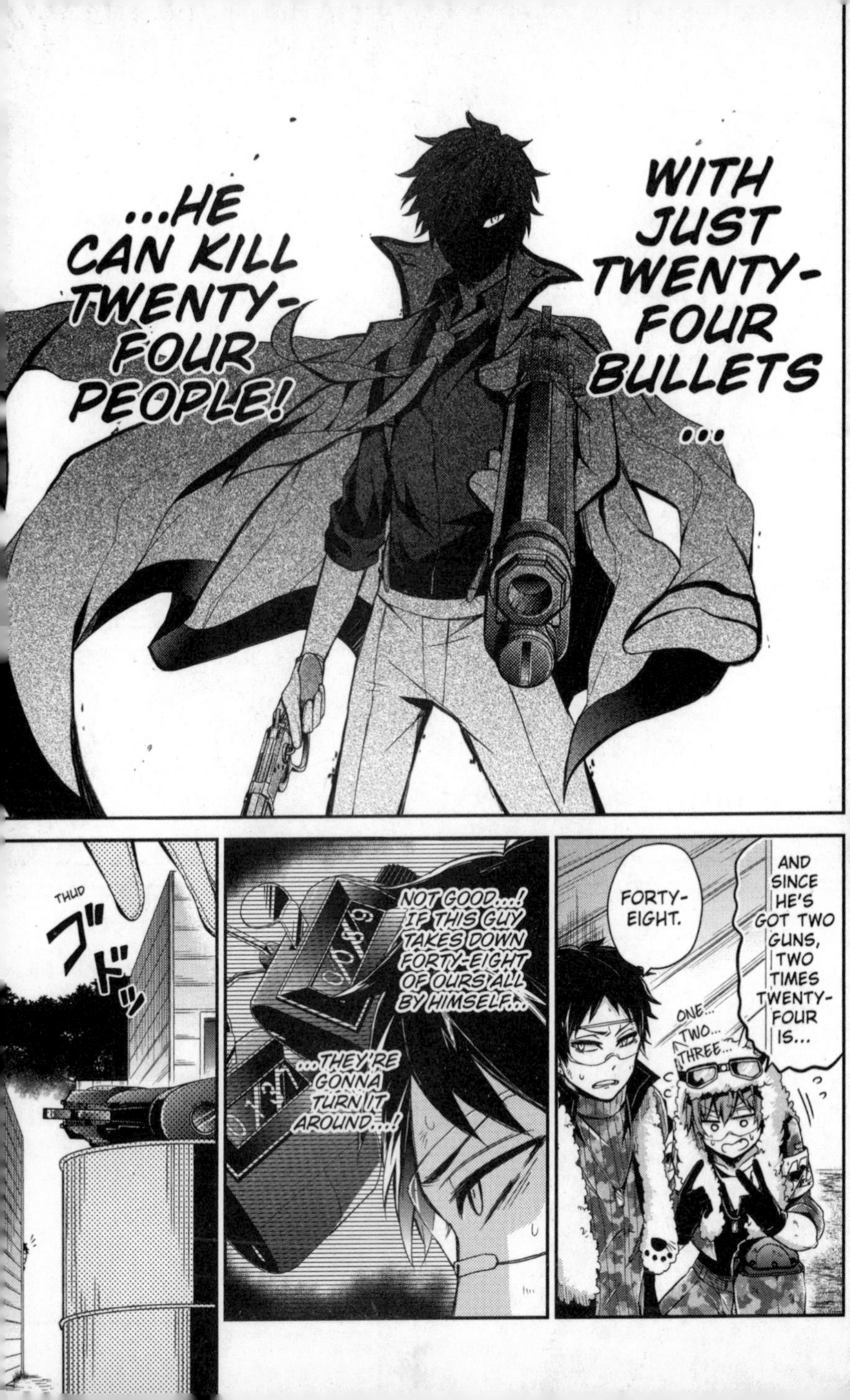
WITH JUST TWENTY-FOUR BULLETS...
...HE CAN KILL TWENTY-FOUR PEOPLE!
AND SINCE HE'S GOT TWO GUNS, TWO TIMES TWENTY-FOUR IS...
FORTY-EIGHT.
ONE... TWO... THREE...
NOT GOOD...! IF THIS GUY TAKES DOWN FORTY-EIGHT OF OURS ALL BY HIMSELF...
...THEY'RE GONNA TURN IT AROUND...!
THUD
ゴドッ

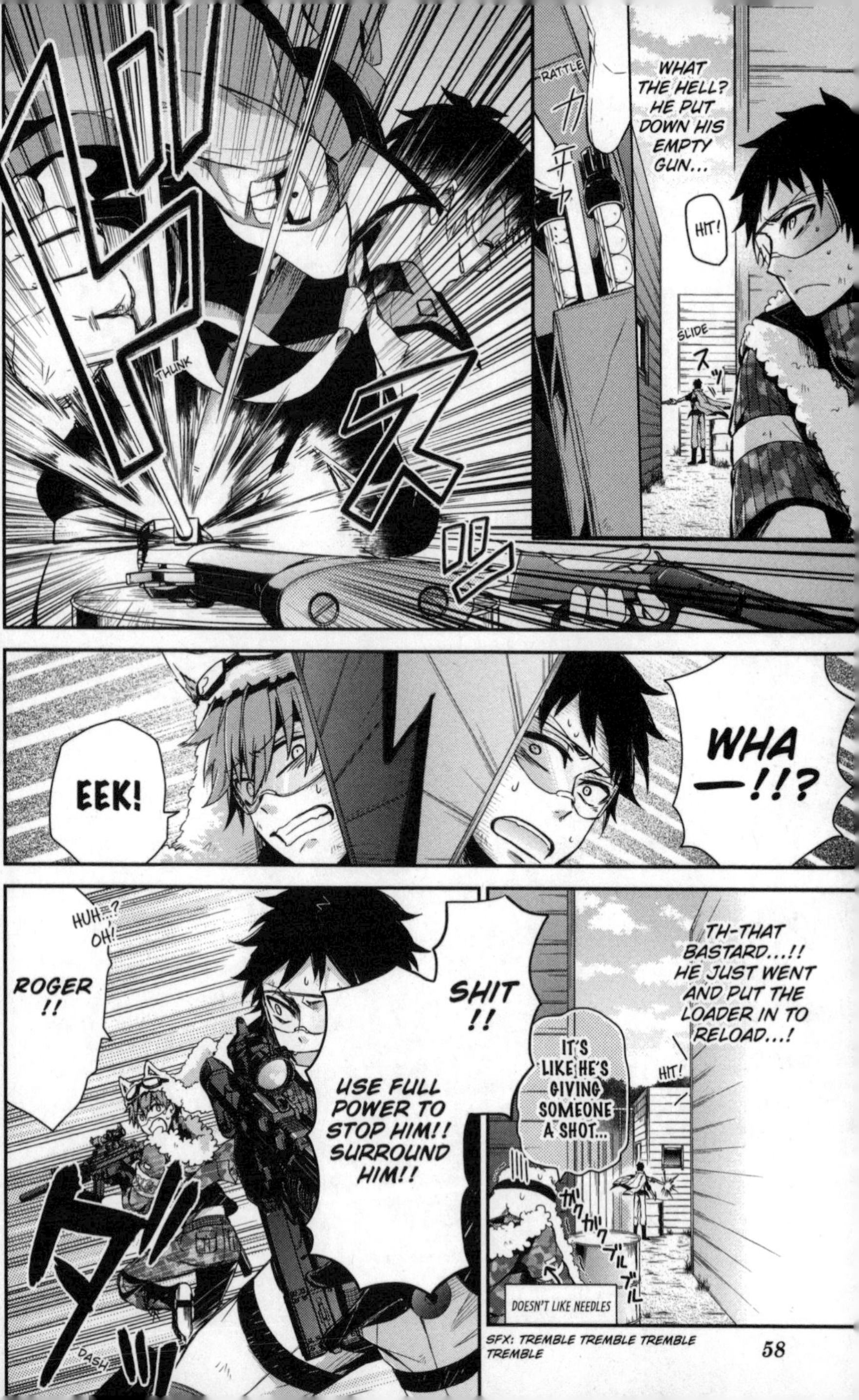
RATTLE
WHAT THE HELL? HE PUT DOWN HIS EMPTY GUN...
HIT!
SLIDE
THUNK
WHA—!!?
EEK!
TH-THAT BASTARD...!! HE JUST WENT AND PUT THE LOADER IN TO RELOAD...!
HIT!
IT'S LIKE HE'S GIVING SOMEONE A SHOT...
DOESN'T LIKE NEEDLES
SHIT!!
USE FULL POWER TO STOP HIM!! SURROUND HIM!!
HUH...? OH!
ROGER!!
DASH

SFX: TREMBLE TREMBLE TREMBLE TREMBLE

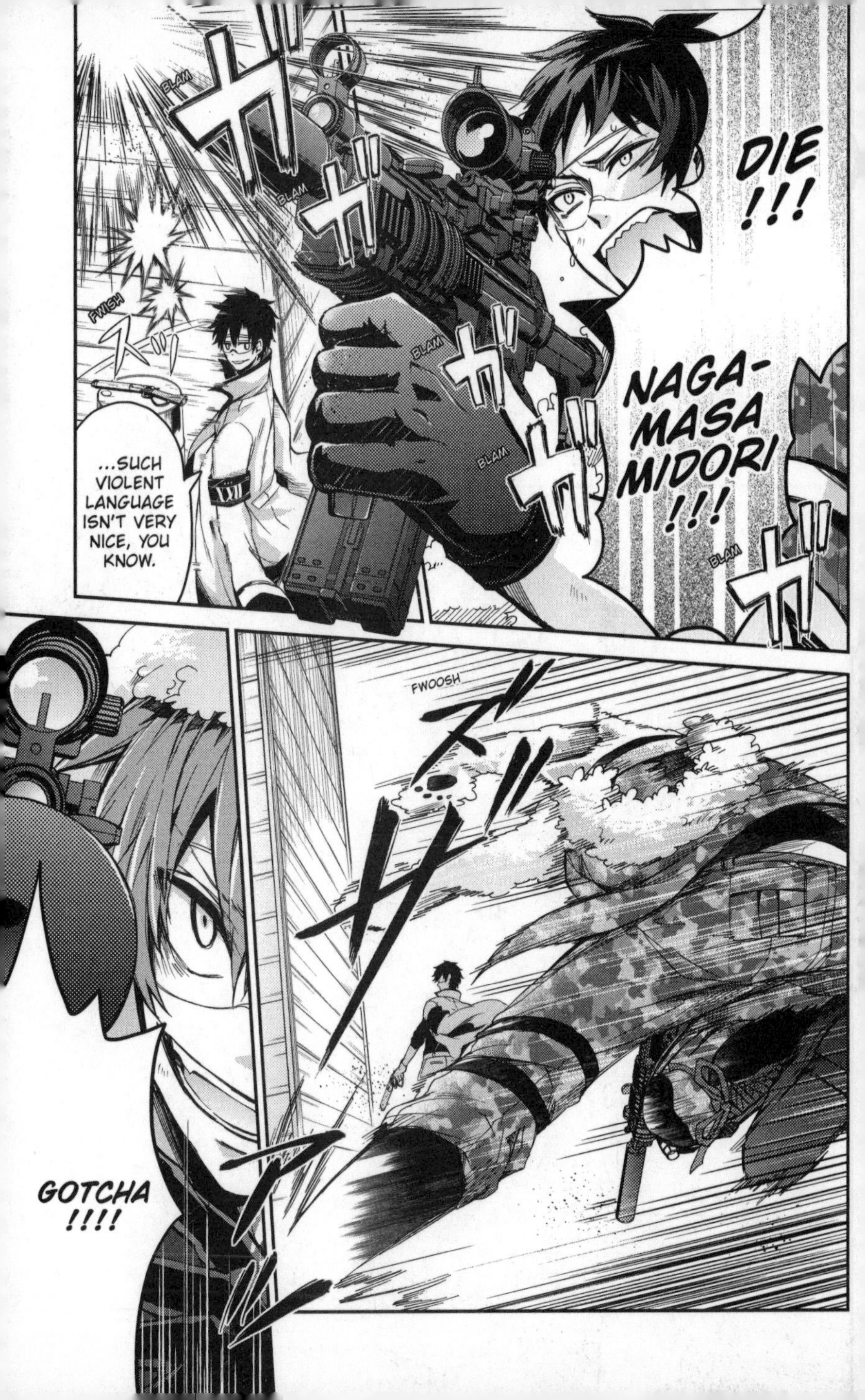
DIE !!!
NAGA-MASA MIDORI !!!
BLAM
BLAM
BLAM
BLAM
BLAM
FWISH
...SUCH VIOLENT LANGUAGE ISN'T VERY NICE, YOU KNOW.
FWOOSH
GOTCHA !!!!

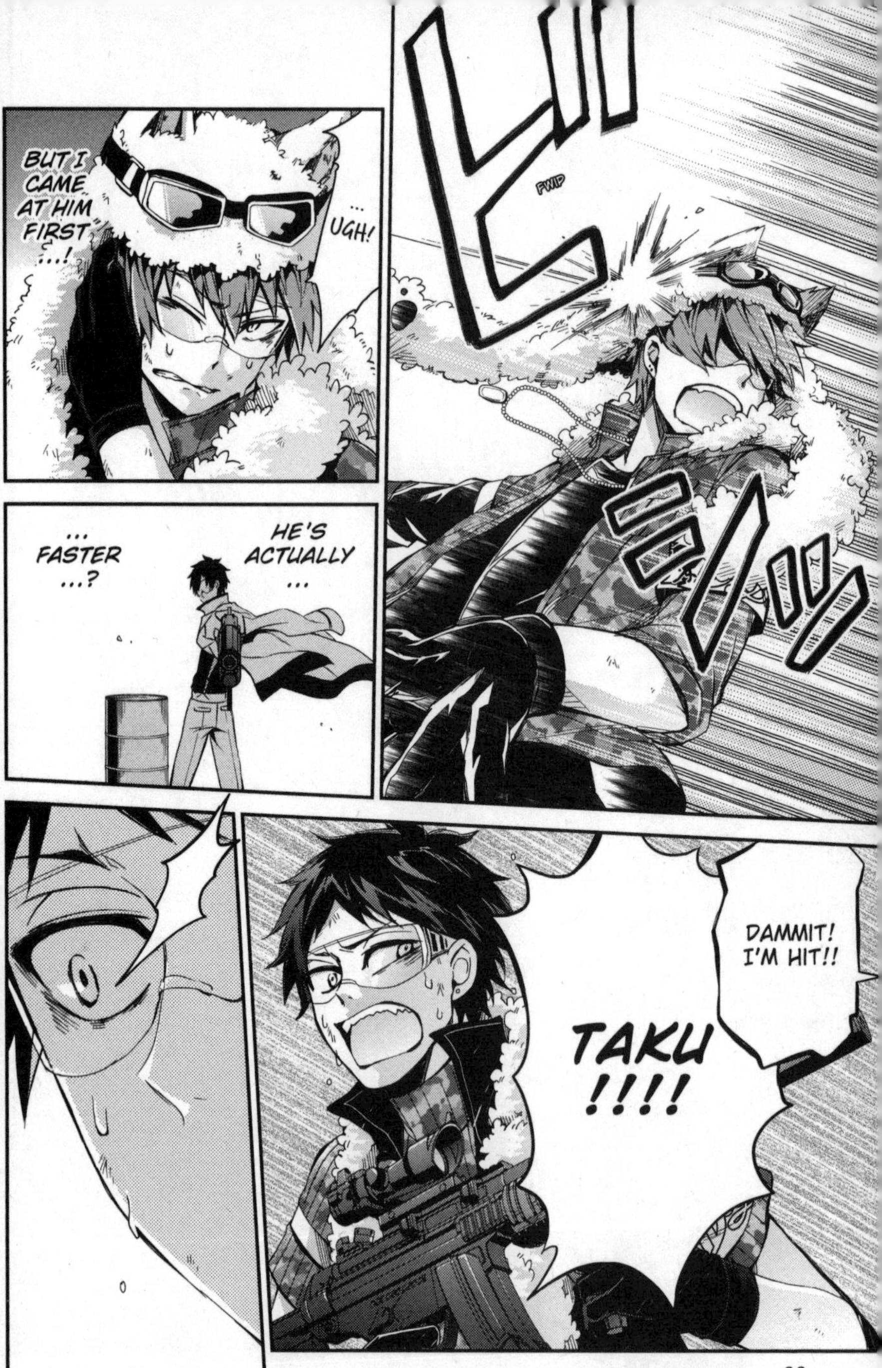
FWIP
...UGH!
BUT I CAME AT HIM FIRST...!
HE'S ACTUALLY...
...FASTER...?
DAMMIT! I'M HIT!!
TAKU!!!!

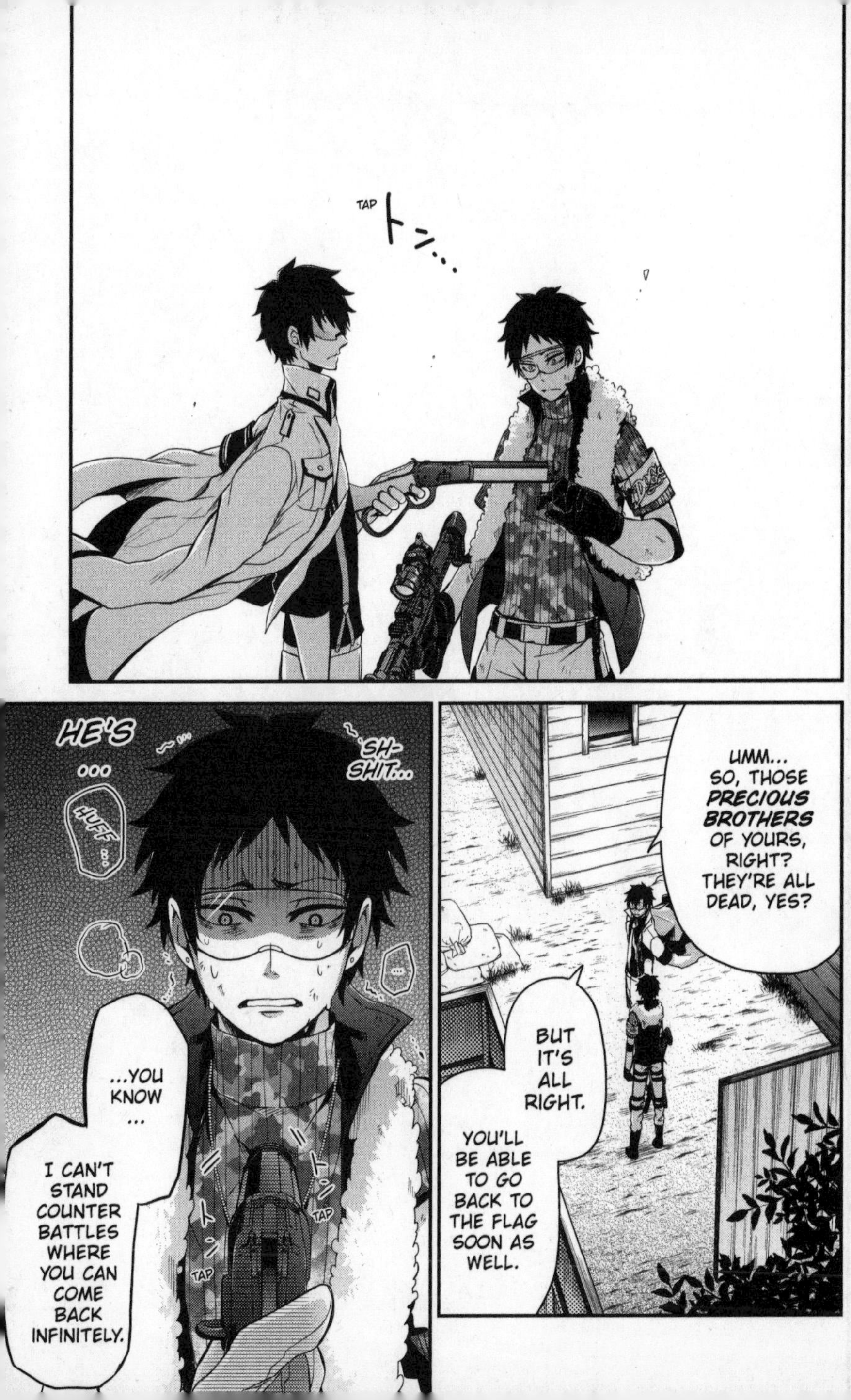
TAP
UMM... SO, THOSE PRECIOUS BROTHERS OF YOURS, RIGHT? THEY'RE ALL DEAD, YES?
BUT IT'S ALL RIGHT.
YOU'LL BE ABLE TO GO BACK TO THE FLAG SOON AS WELL.
SH-SHIT...
HE'S
HUFF
...YOU KNOW ...
TAP
I CAN'T STAND COUNTER BATTLES WHERE YOU CAN COME BACK INFINITELY.
TAP

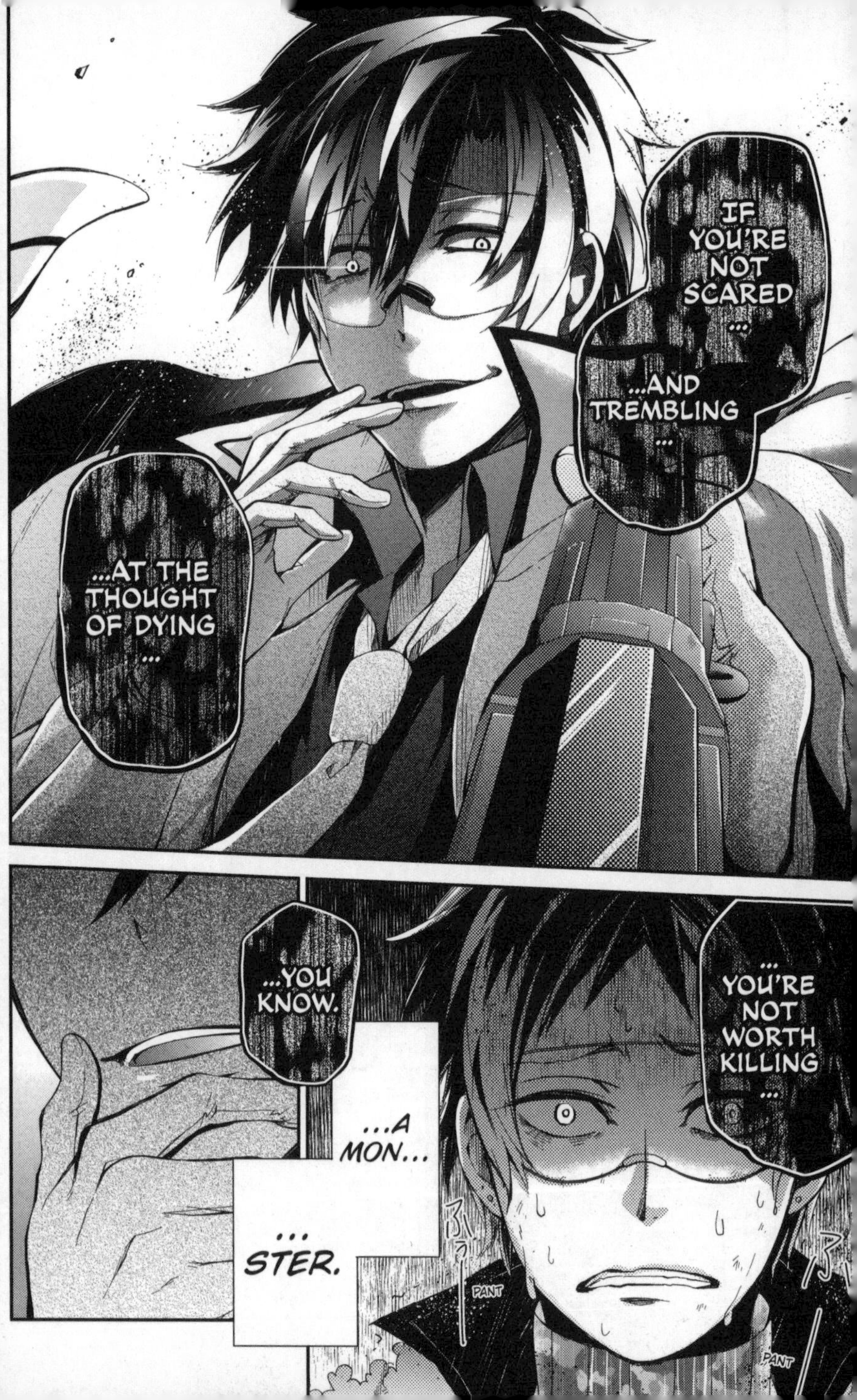
IF YOU'RE NOT SCARED...
...AND TREMBLING...
...AT THE THOUGHT OF DYING...
... YOU'RE NOT WORTH KILLING...
...YOU KNOW.
PANT
PANT
...A MON...
... STER.

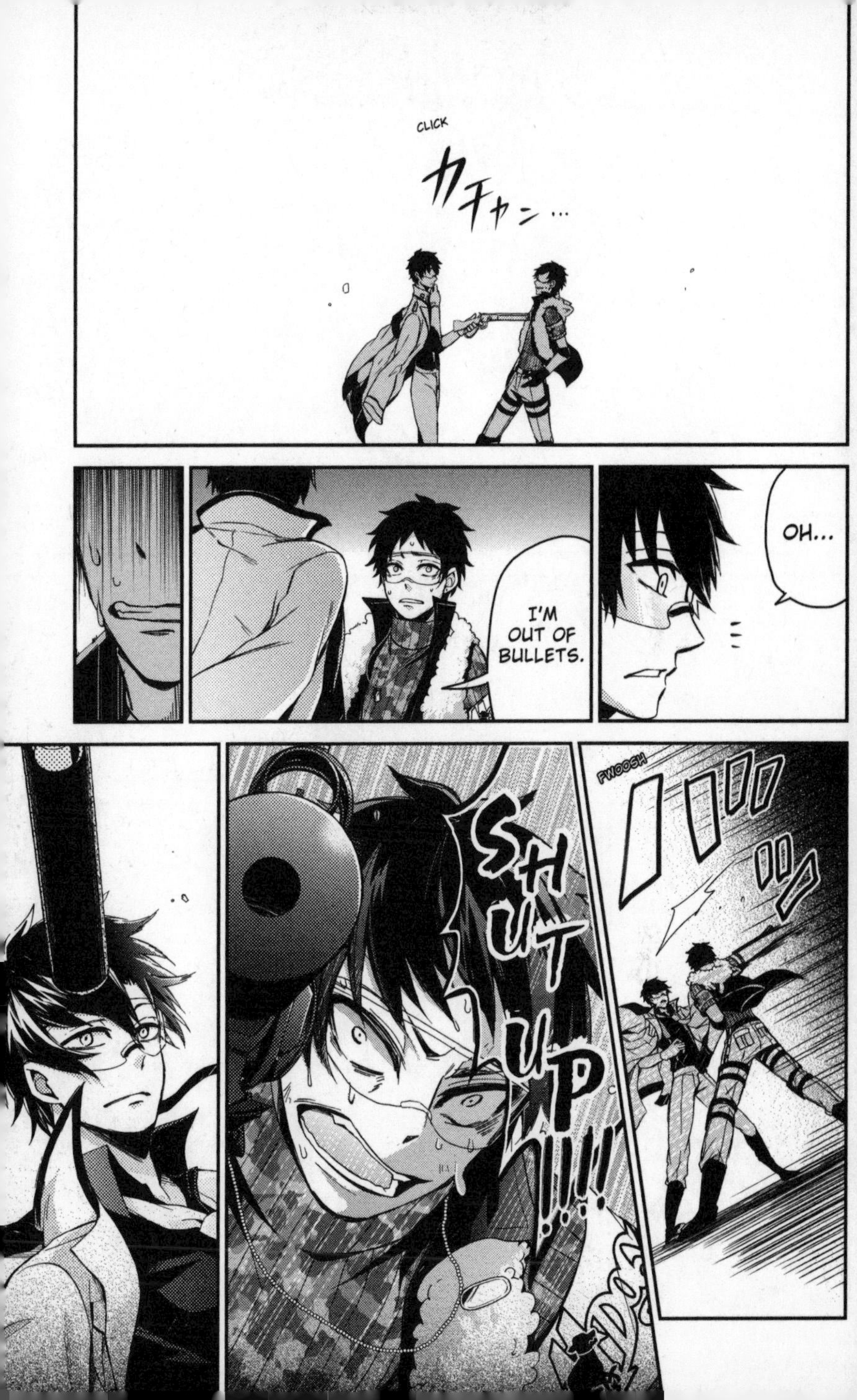
CLICK
カチャン…
OH…
I'M OUT OF BULLETS.
FWOOSH
SHUT UP!!!!!

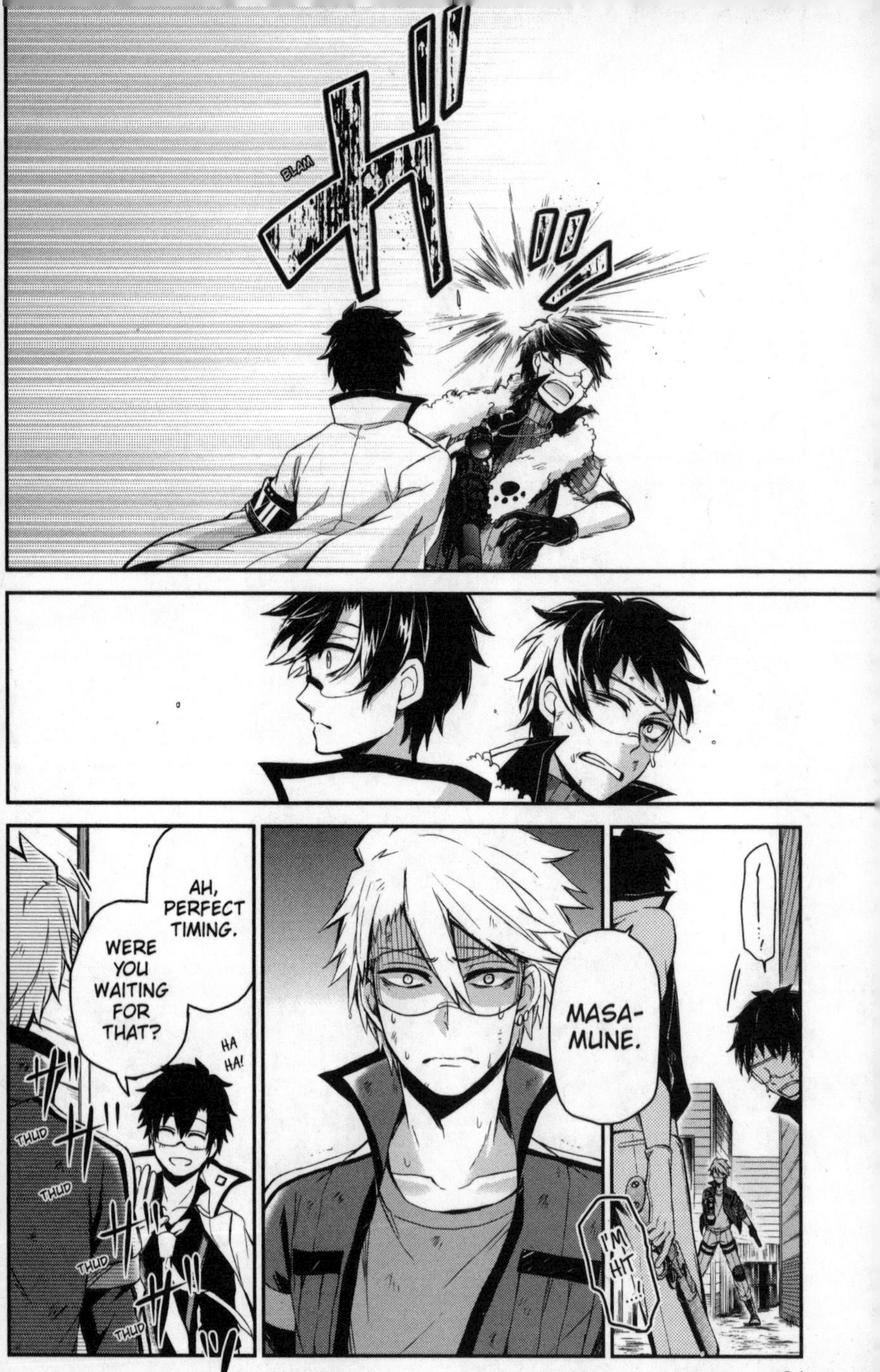
BLAM
!
...!
I'M HIT...!
MASA-MUNE.
AH, PERFECT TIMING.
WERE YOU WAITING FOR THAT?
HA HA!
THUD
THUD
THUD
THUD

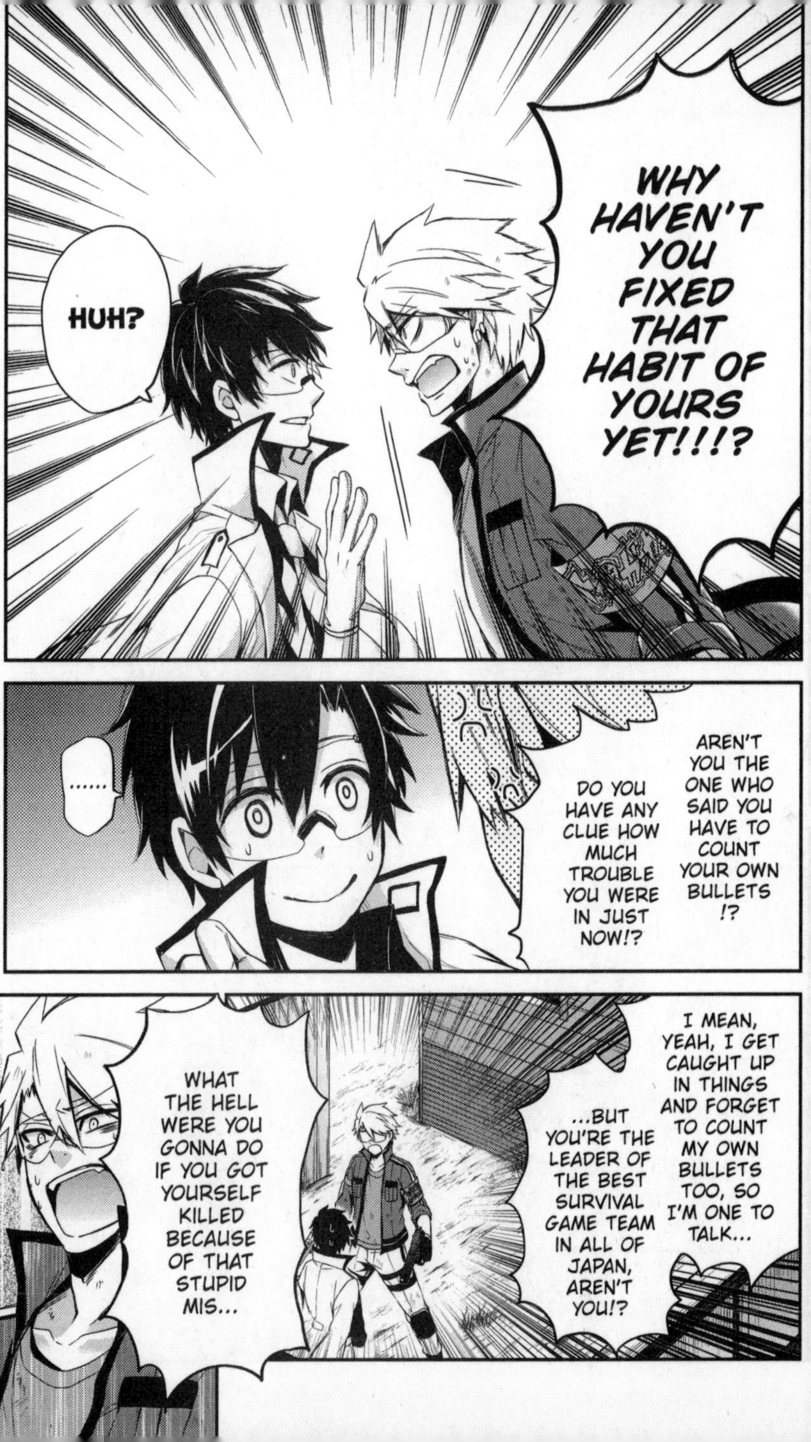
WHY HAVEN'T YOU FIXED THAT HABIT OF YOURS YET!!!?
HUH?
AREN'T YOU THE ONE WHO SAID YOU HAVE TO COUNT YOUR OWN BULLETS !?
DO YOU HAVE ANY CLUE HOW MUCH TROUBLE YOU WERE IN JUST NOW!?
......
I MEAN, YEAH, I GET CAUGHT UP IN THINGS AND FORGET TO COUNT MY OWN BULLETS TOO, SO I'M ONE TO TALK...
...BUT YOU'RE THE LEADER OF THE BEST SURVIVAL GAME TEAM IN ALL OF JAPAN, AREN'T YOU!?
WHAT THE HELL WERE YOU GONNA DO IF YOU GOT YOURSELF KILLED BECAUSE OF THAT STUPID MIS...

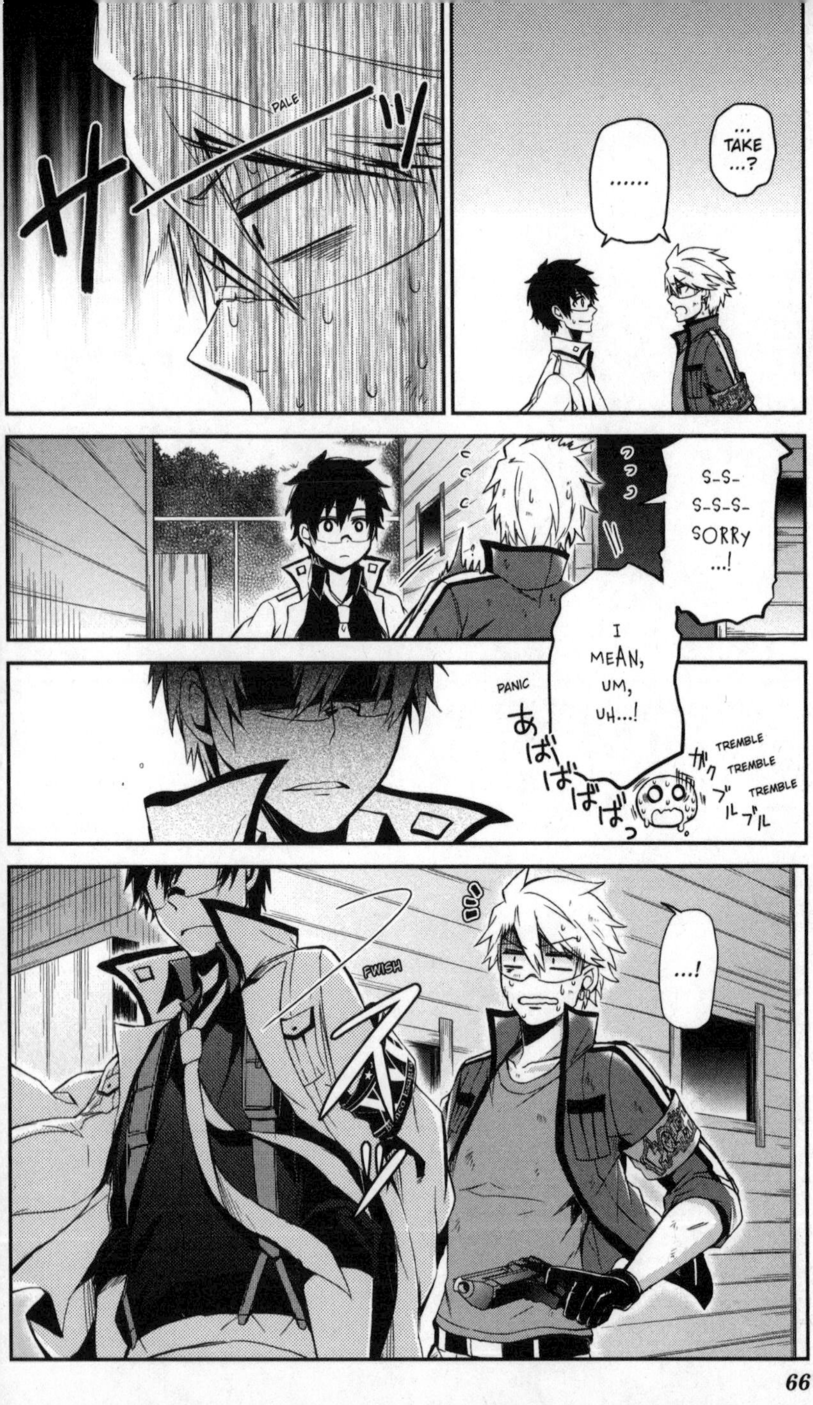
...TAKE...?
......
PALE
ザッ
S-S-S-S-S-SORRY...!
I MEAN, UM, UH...!
PANIC
あばばばっ
TREMBLE TREMBLE TREMBLE
ガクブルブル
...!
FWISH

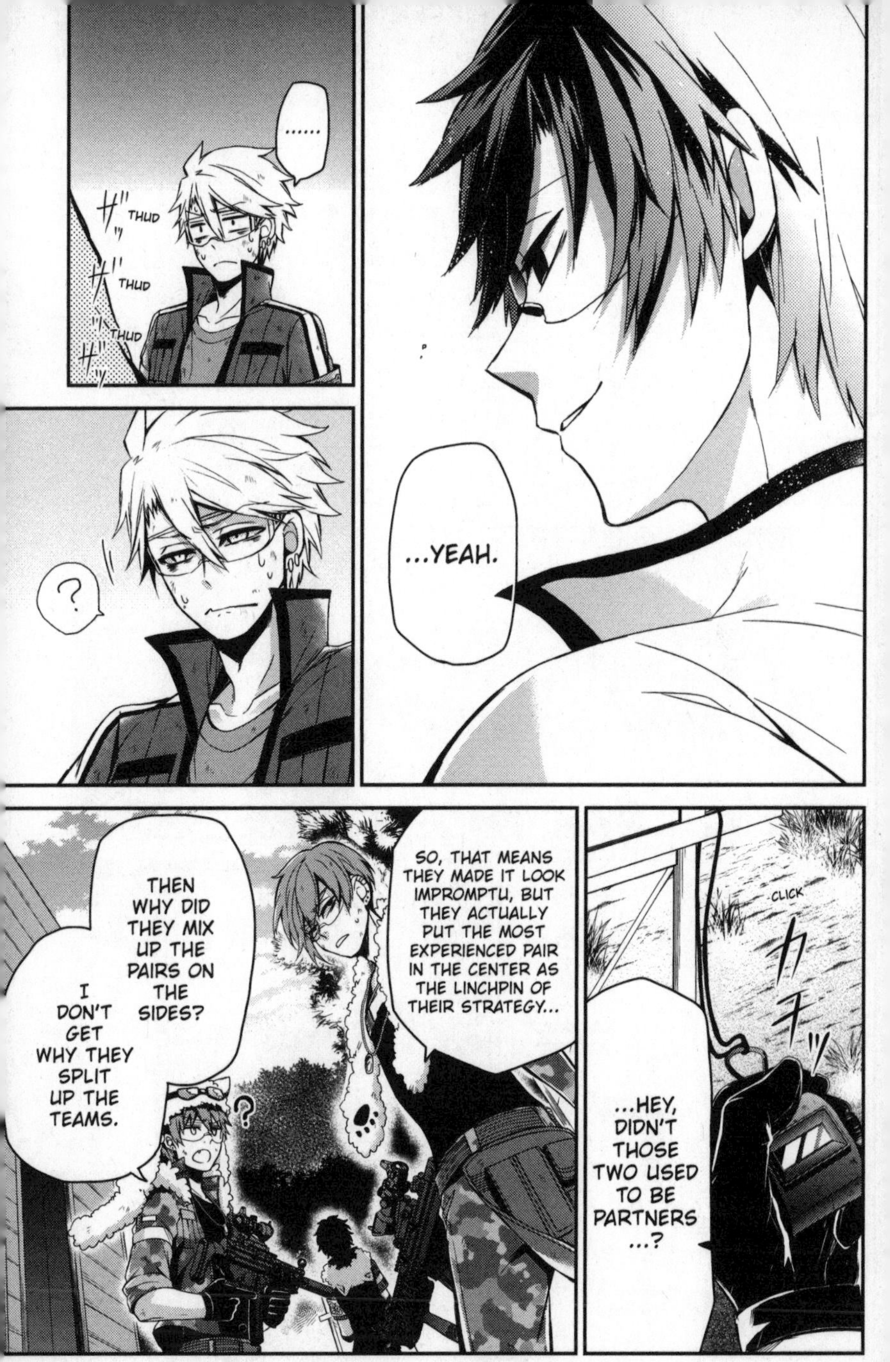
...YEAH.
......
THUD
THUD
THUD
?
CLICK
...HEY, DIDN'T THOSE TWO USED TO BE PARTNERS ...?
SO, THAT MEANS THEY MADE IT LOOK IMPROMPTU, BUT THEY ACTUALLY PUT THE MOST EXPERIENCED PAIR IN THE CENTER AS THE LINCHPIN OF THEIR STRATEGY...
THEN WHY DID THEY MIX UP THE PAIRS ON THE SIDES?
I DON'T GET WHY THEY SPLIT UP THE TEAMS.
?

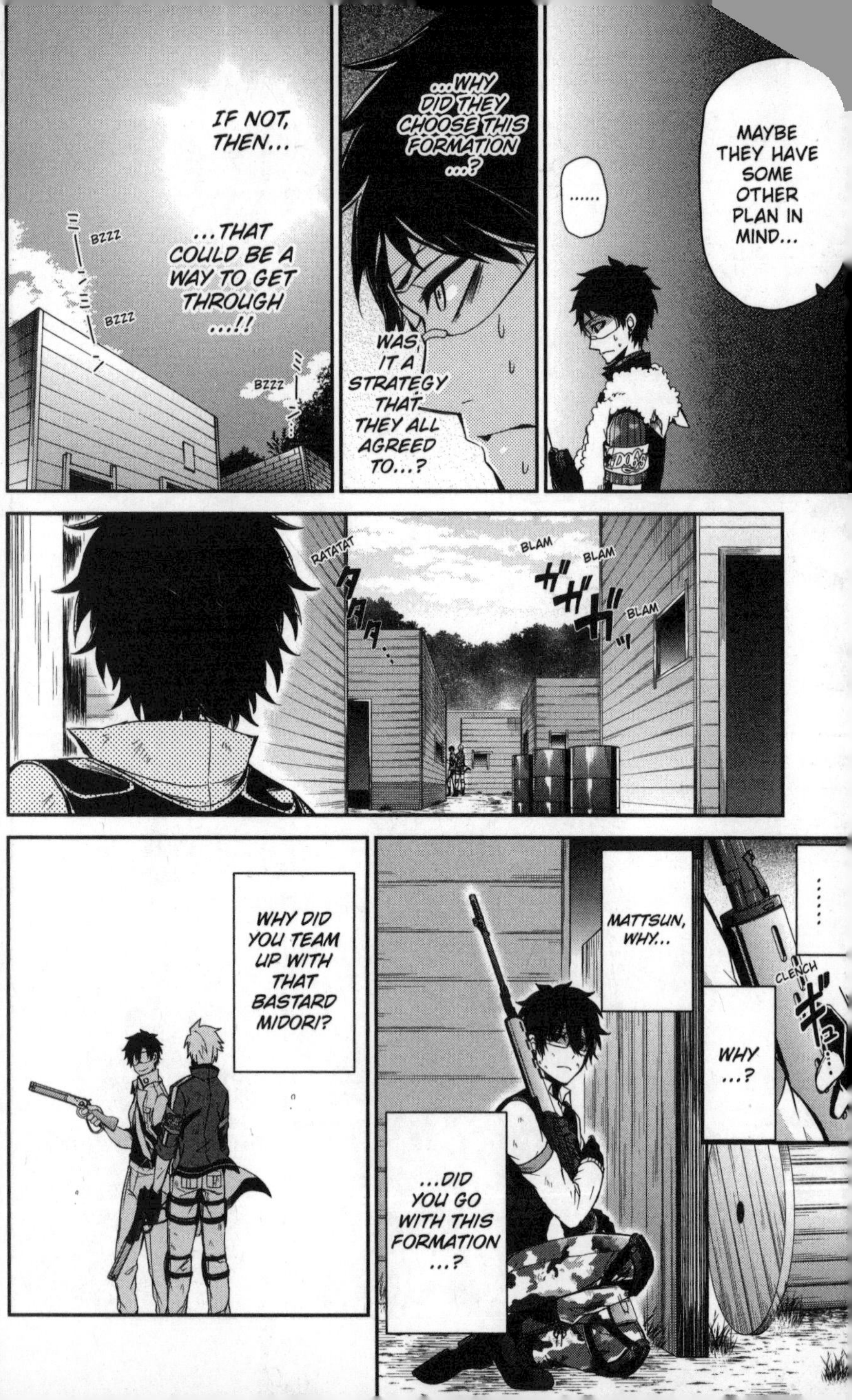
MAYBE THEY HAVE SOME OTHER PLAN IN MIND...
......
...WHY DID THEY CHOOSE THIS FORMATION ...?
WAS IT A STRATEGY THAT THEY ALL AGREED TO...?
IF NOT, THEN...
...THAT COULD BE A WAY TO GET THROUGH ...!!
BZZZ
BZZZ
BZZZ
BLAM
BLAM
BLAM
RATATAT
......
CLENCH
WHY ...?
MATTSUN, WHY...
...DID YOU GO WITH THIS FORMATION ...?
WHY DID YOU TEAM UP WITH THAT BASTARD MIDORI?

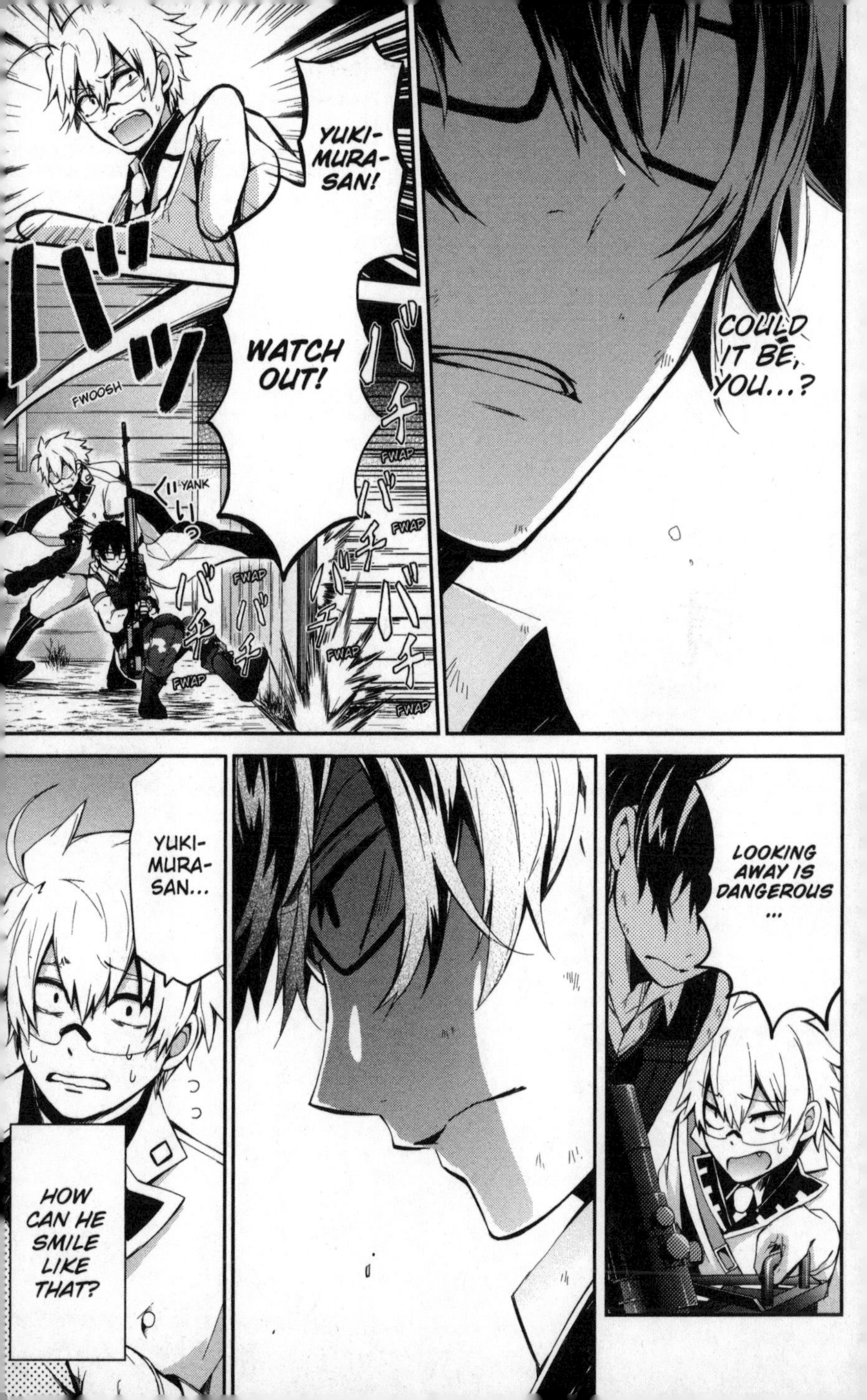
COULD IT BE, YOU...?
YUKI-MURA-SAN!
WATCH OUT!
FWOOSH
YANK
FWAP
FWAP
FWAP
FWAP
FWAP
FWAP
LOOKING AWAY IS DANGEROUS...
YUKI-MURA-SAN...
HOW CAN HE SMILE LIKE THAT?

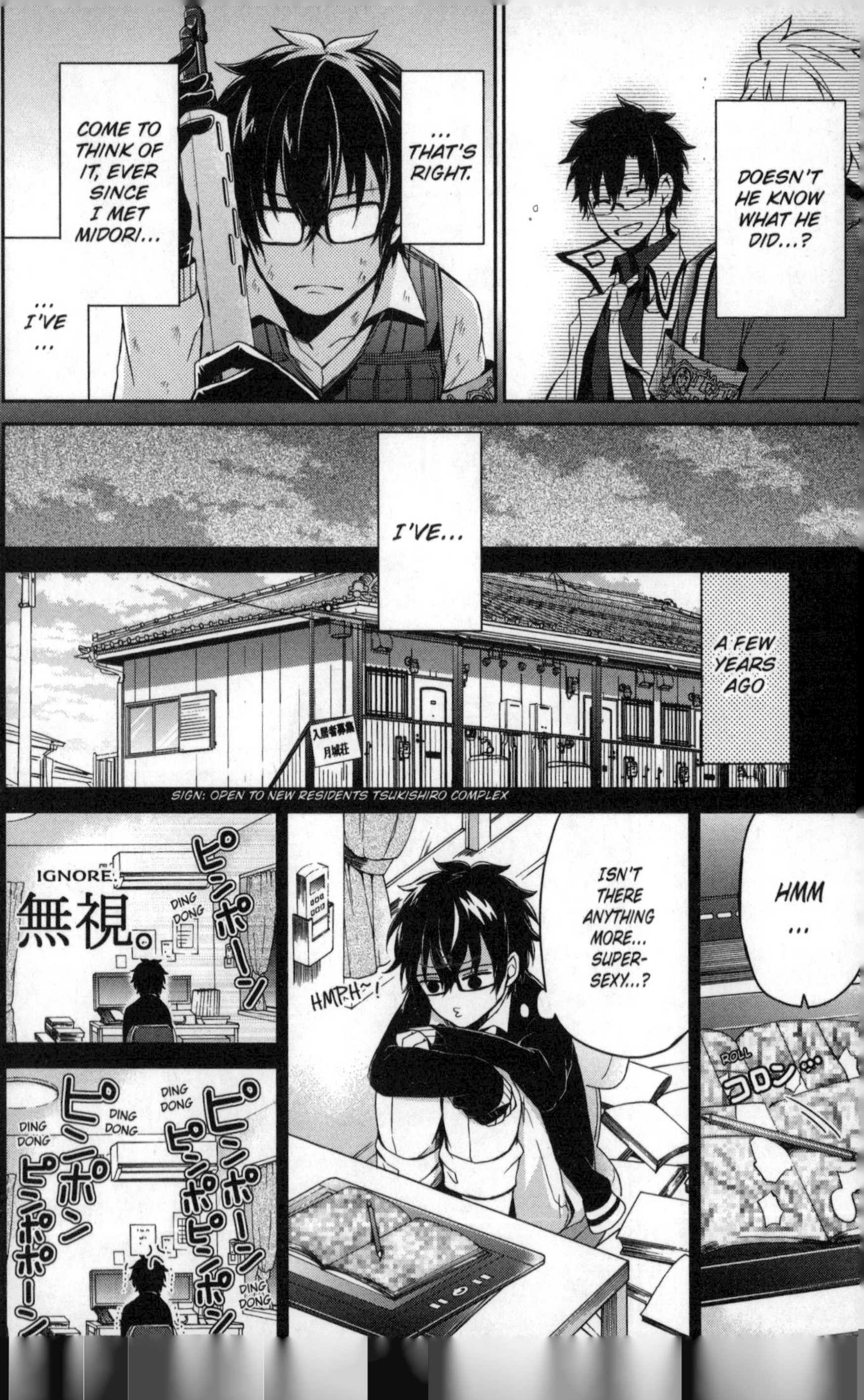
DOESN'T HE KNOW WHAT HE DID...?
...THAT'S RIGHT.
COME TO THINK OF IT, EVER SINCE I MET MIDORI...
...I'VE...
I'VE...
A FEW YEARS AGO
入居者募集
月城荘
SIGN: OPEN TO NEW RESIDENTS TSUKISHIRO COMPLEX
HMM...
ROLL
コロン...
ISN'T THERE ANYTHING MORE... SUPER-SEXY...?
HMPH~!
ピンポーン
DING DONG
無視。
IGNORE
ピンポーン
ピンポピンポン
ピンポン
ピンポーン
DING DONG
DING DONG
DING DONG
DING DONG

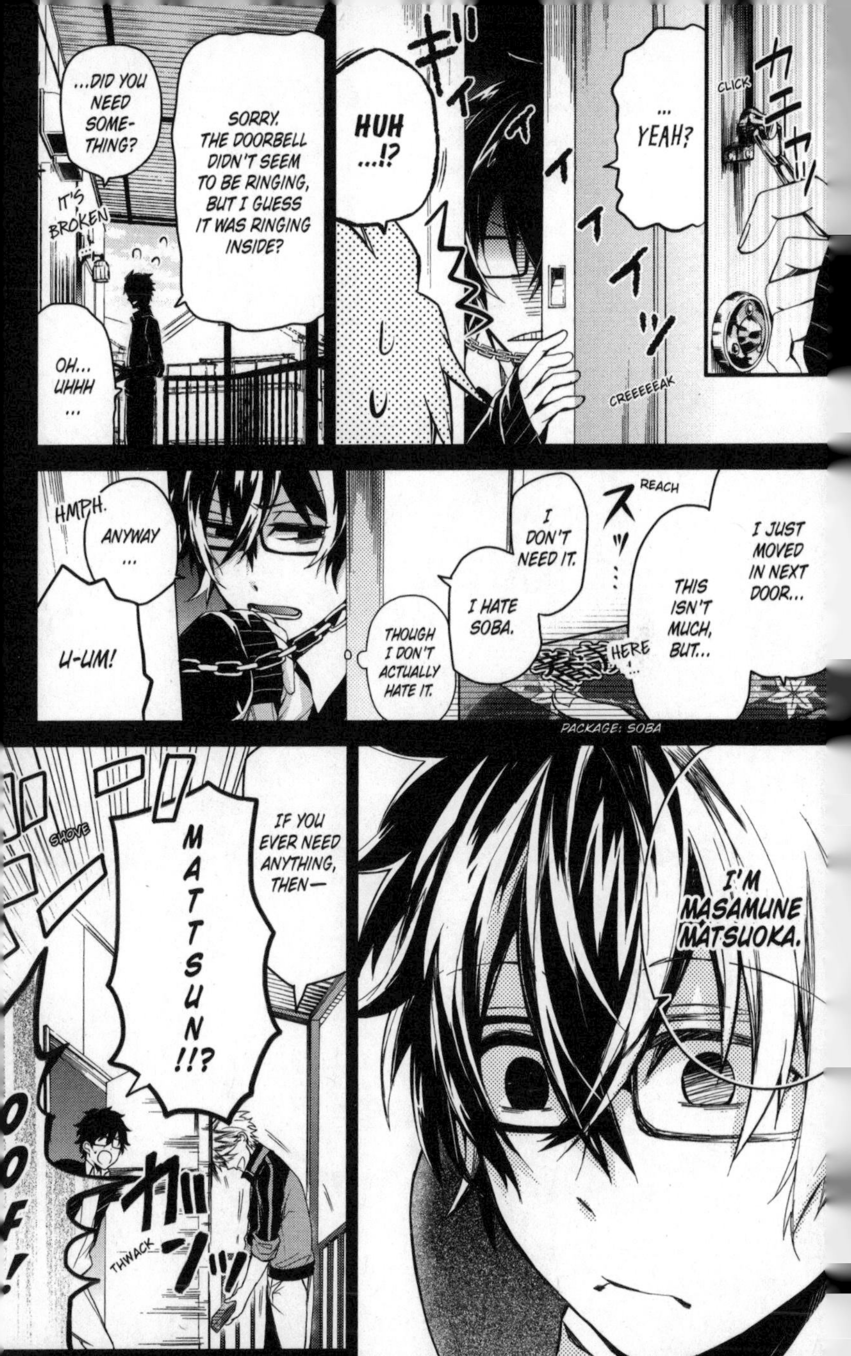
CLICK
... YEAH?
CREEEEEAK
HUH ...!?
...DID YOU NEED SOME-THING?
SORRY. THE DOORBELL DIDN'T SEEM TO BE RINGING, BUT I GUESS IT WAS RINGING INSIDE?
IT'S BROKEN
OH... UHHH ...
REACH
I JUST MOVED IN NEXT DOOR...
THIS ISN'T MUCH, BUT...
HERE...
I DON'T NEED IT.
I HATE SOBA.
THOUGH I DON'T ACTUALLY HATE IT.
PACKAGE: SOBA
HMPH.
ANYWAY ...
U-UM!
I'M MASAMUNE MATSUOKA.
IF YOU EVER NEED ANYTHING, THEN—
MATTSUN!!?
SHOVE
THWACK
OOF!

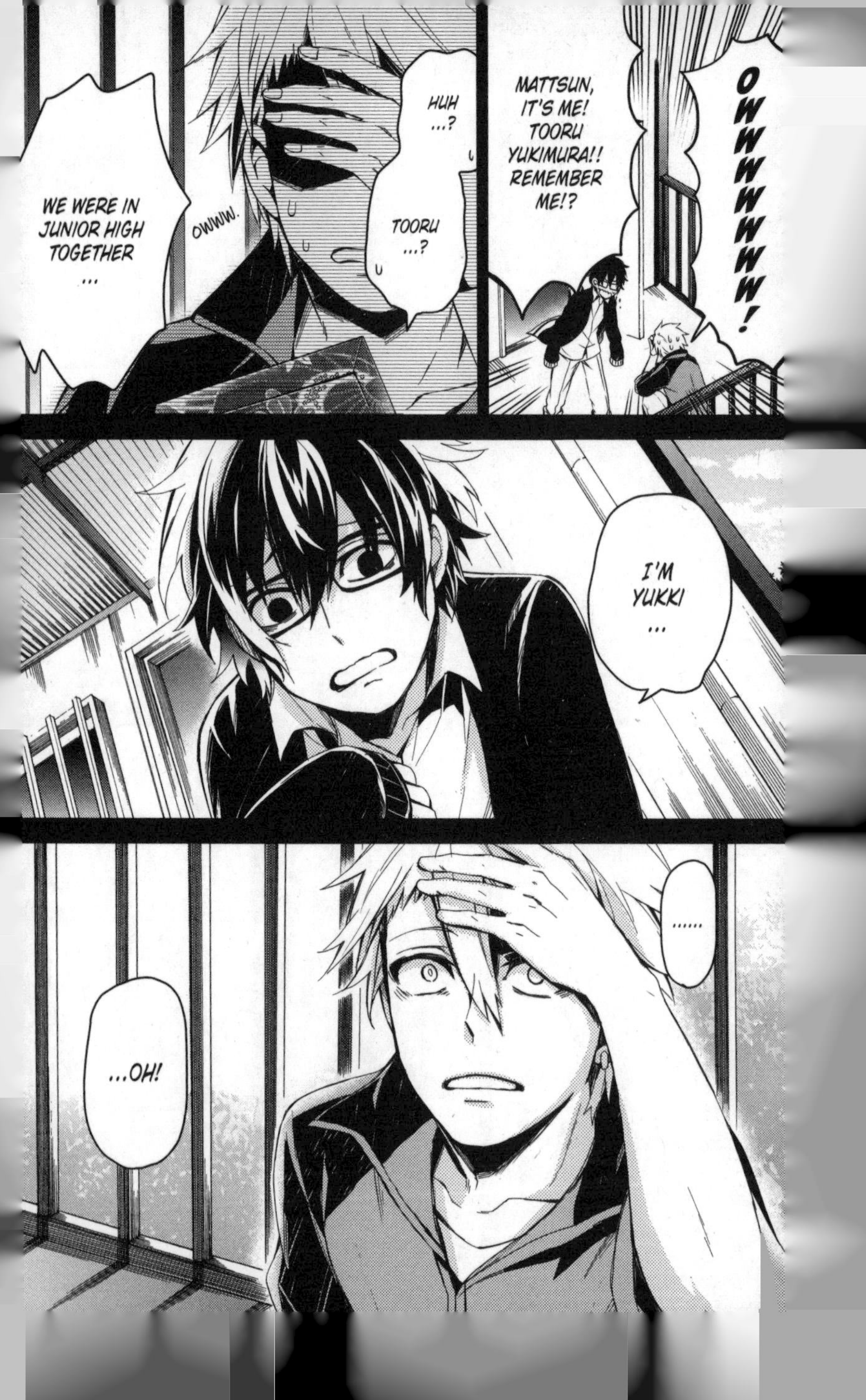
OWWWWWWW!
MATTSUN, IT'S ME! TOORU YUKIMURA!! REMEMBER ME!?
HUH ...?
TOORU ...?
OWWW.
WE WERE IN JUNIOR HIGH TOGETHER ...
I'M YUKKI ...
......
...OH!

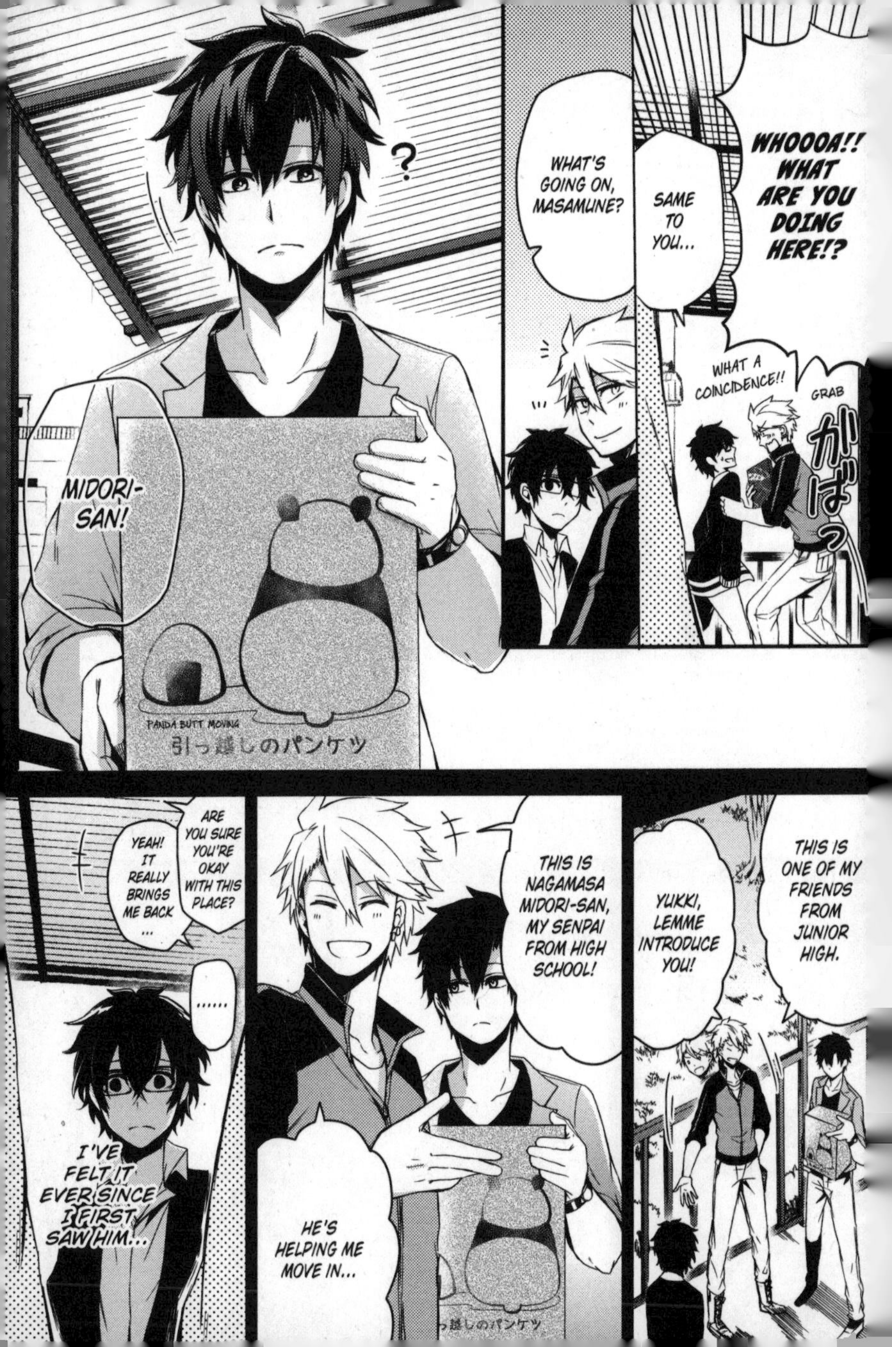
WHOOOA!! WHAT ARE YOU DOING HERE!?
SAME TO YOU...
WHAT A COINCIDENCE!!
GRAB
がばっ
WHAT'S GOING ON, MASAMUNE?
?
MIDORI-SAN!
PANDA BUTT MOVING
引っ越しのパンケツ
THIS IS ONE OF MY FRIENDS FROM JUNIOR HIGH.
YUKKI, LEMME INTRODUCE YOU!
THIS IS NAGAMASA MIDORI-SAN, MY SENPAI FROM HIGH SCHOOL!
HE'S HELPING ME MOVE IN...
っ越しのパンケツ
ARE YOU SURE YOU'RE OKAY WITH THIS PLACE?
YEAH! IT REALLY BRINGS ME BACK ...
......
I'VE FELT IT EVER SINCE I FIRST SAW HIM...

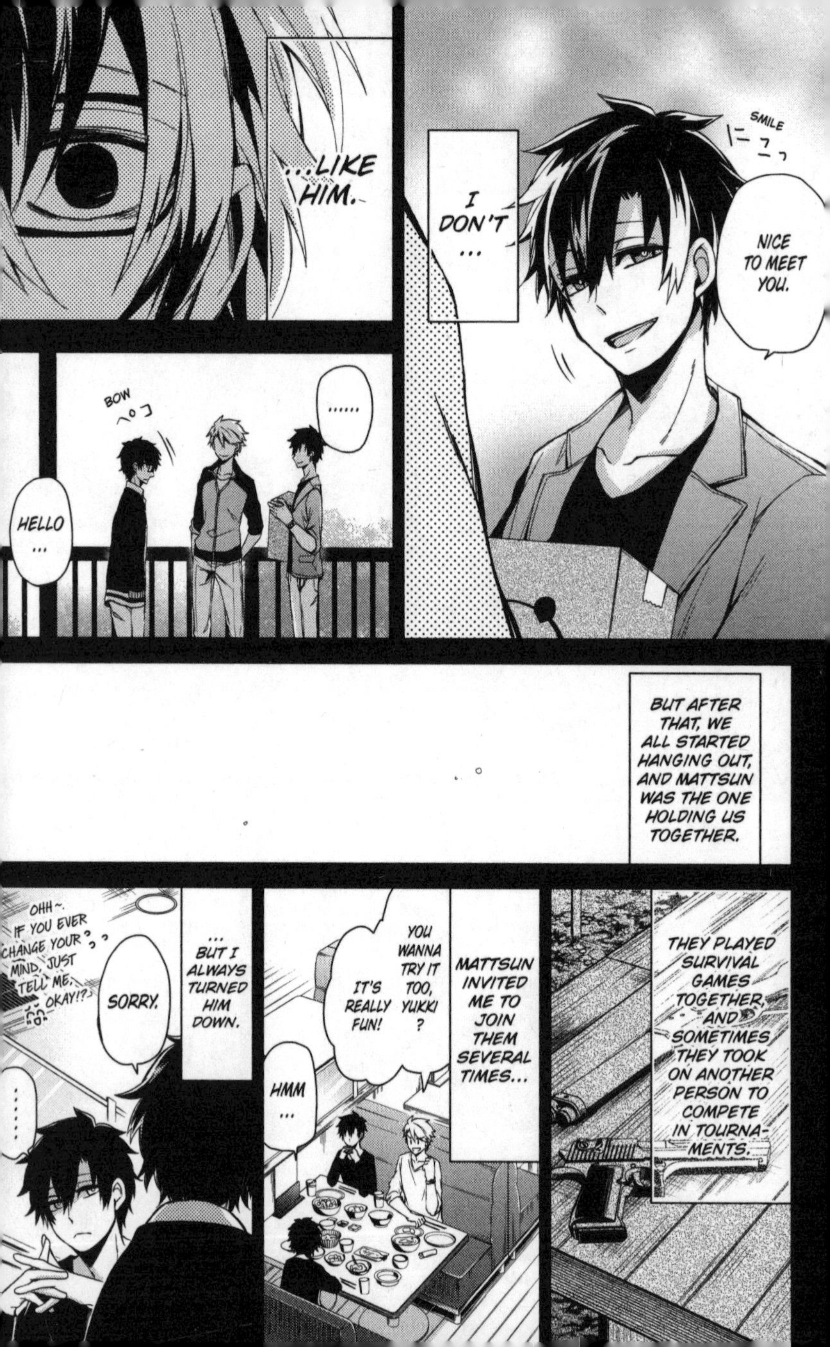
SMILE
NICE TO MEET YOU.
I DON'T ...
...LIKE HIM.
......
BOW
HELLO ...
BUT AFTER THAT, WE ALL STARTED HANGING OUT, AND MATTSUN WAS THE ONE HOLDING US TOGETHER.
THEY PLAYED SURVIVAL GAMES TOGETHER, AND SOMETIMES THEY TOOK ON ANOTHER PERSON TO COMPETE IN TOURNAMENTS.
MATTSUN INVITED ME TO JOIN THEM SEVERAL TIMES...
YOU WANNA TRY IT TOO, YUKKI?
IT'S REALLY FUN!
HMM ...
... BUT I ALWAYS TURNED HIM DOWN.
OHH~. IF YOU EVER CHANGE YOUR MIND, JUST TELL ME, OKAY!?
SORRY.
......

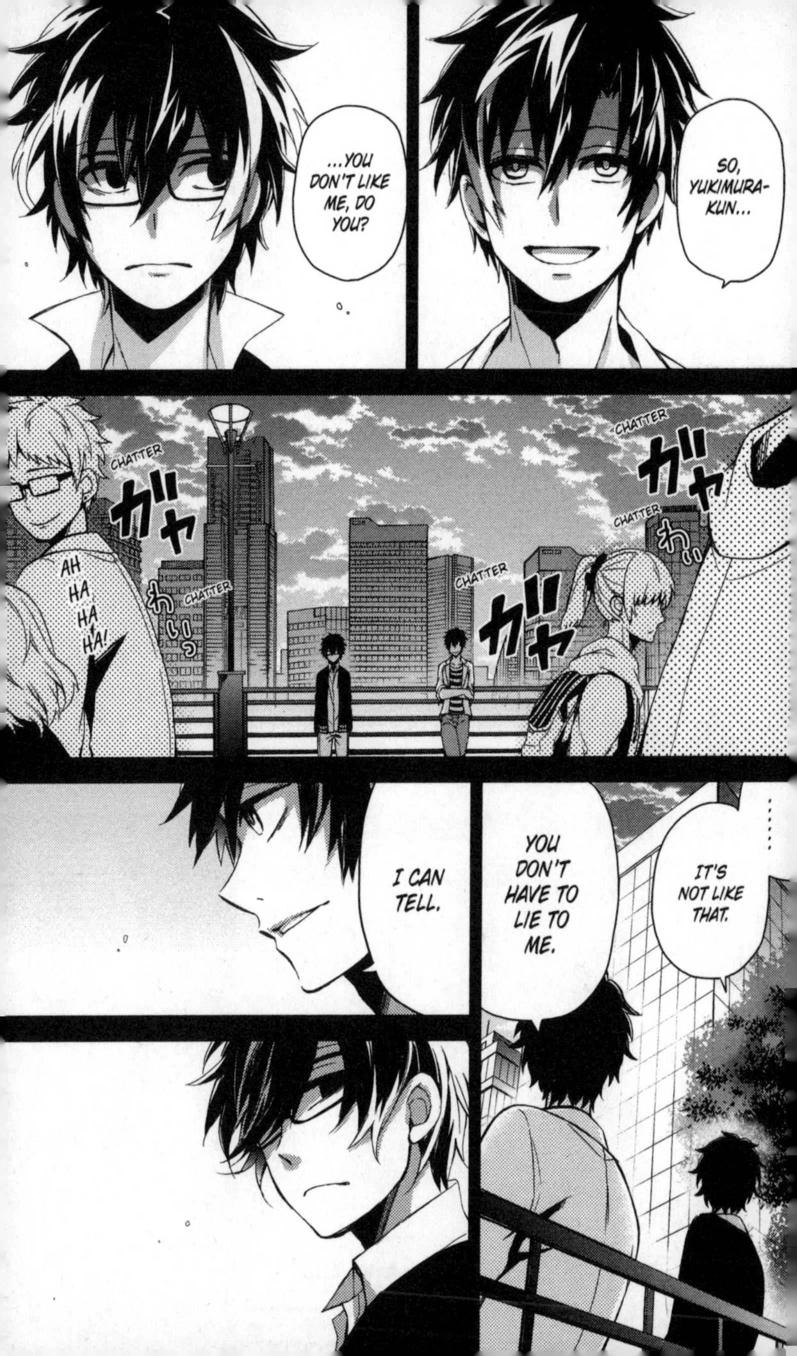
SO, YUKIMURA-KUN...
...YOU DON'T LIKE ME, DO YOU?
CHATTER
ガヤ
CHATTER
わい
CHATTER
ガヤ
CHATTER
ガヤ
AH HA HA HA!
CHATTER
わいっ
IT'S NOT LIKE THAT.
YOU DON'T HAVE TO LIE TO ME.
I CAN TELL.

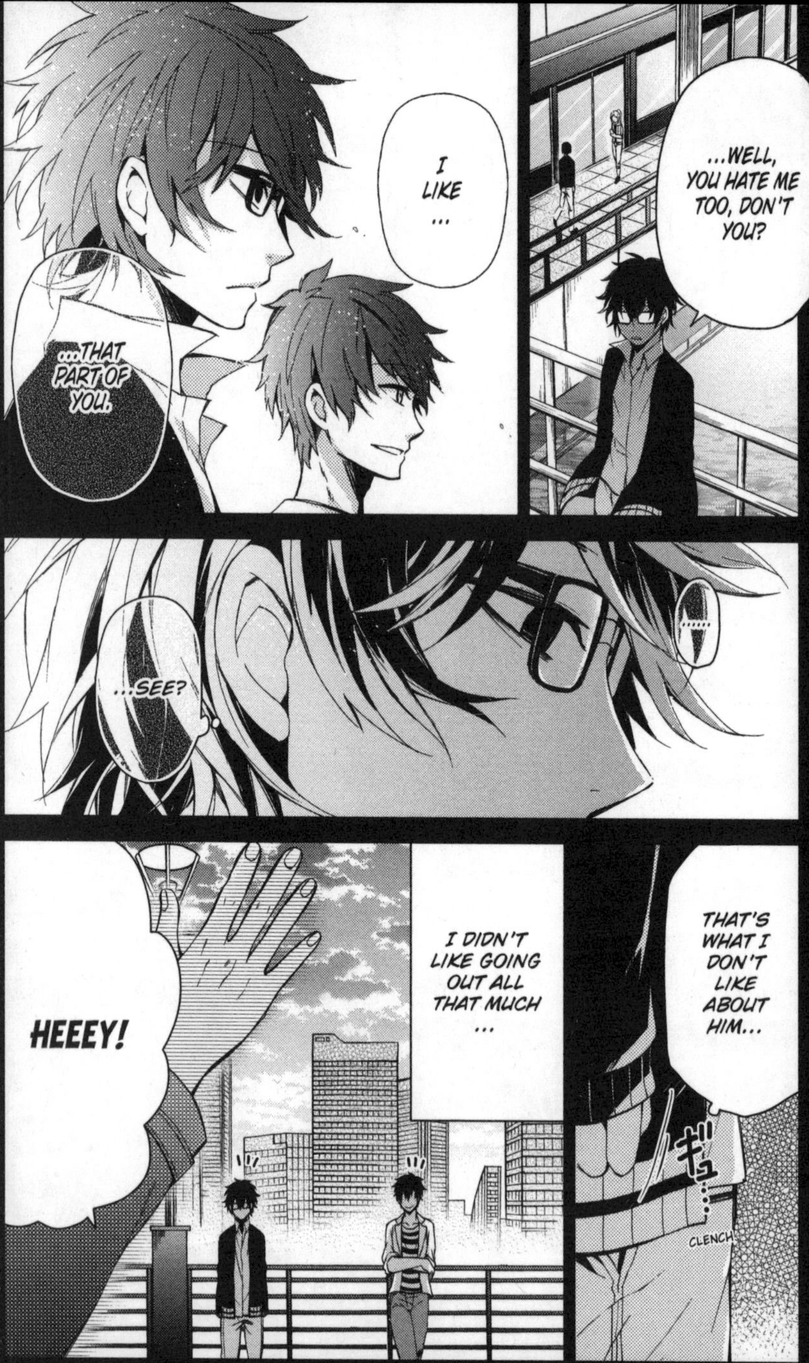
...WELL, YOU HATE ME TOO, DON'T YOU?
I LIKE ...
...THAT PART OF YOU.
......
...SEE?
THAT'S WHAT I DON'T LIKE ABOUT HIM...
ギュ…
CLENCH
I DIDN'T LIKE GOING OUT ALL THAT MUCH ...
HEEEY!

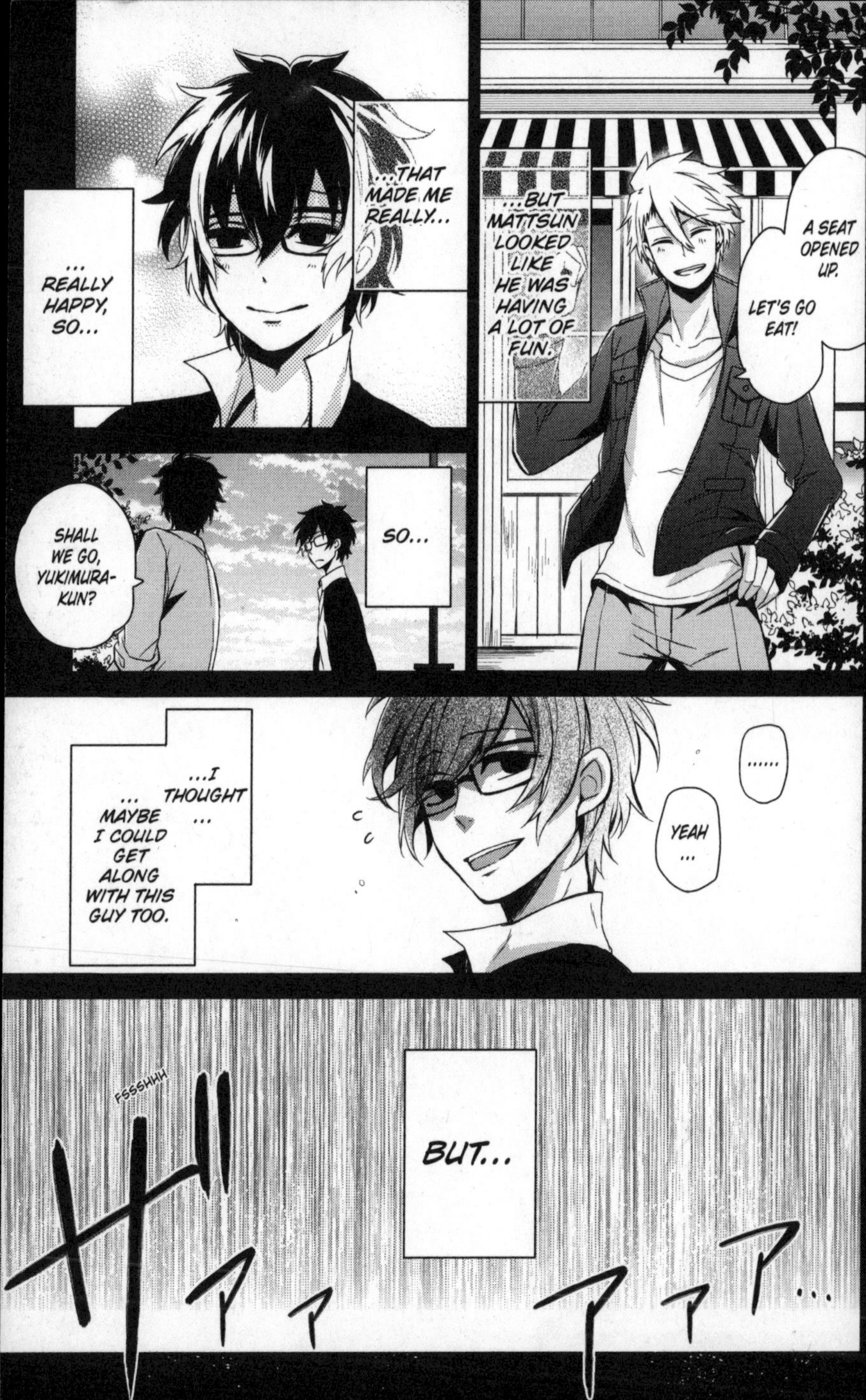
A SEAT OPENED UP.
LET'S GO EAT!
...BUT MATTSUN LOOKED LIKE HE WAS HAVING A LOT OF FUN.
...THAT MADE ME REALLY...
...REALLY HAPPY, SO...
SO...
SHALL WE GO, YUKIMURA-KUN?
......
YEAH...
...I THOUGHT...
...MAYBE I COULD GET ALONG WITH THIS GUY TOO.
BUT...
FSSSHHH

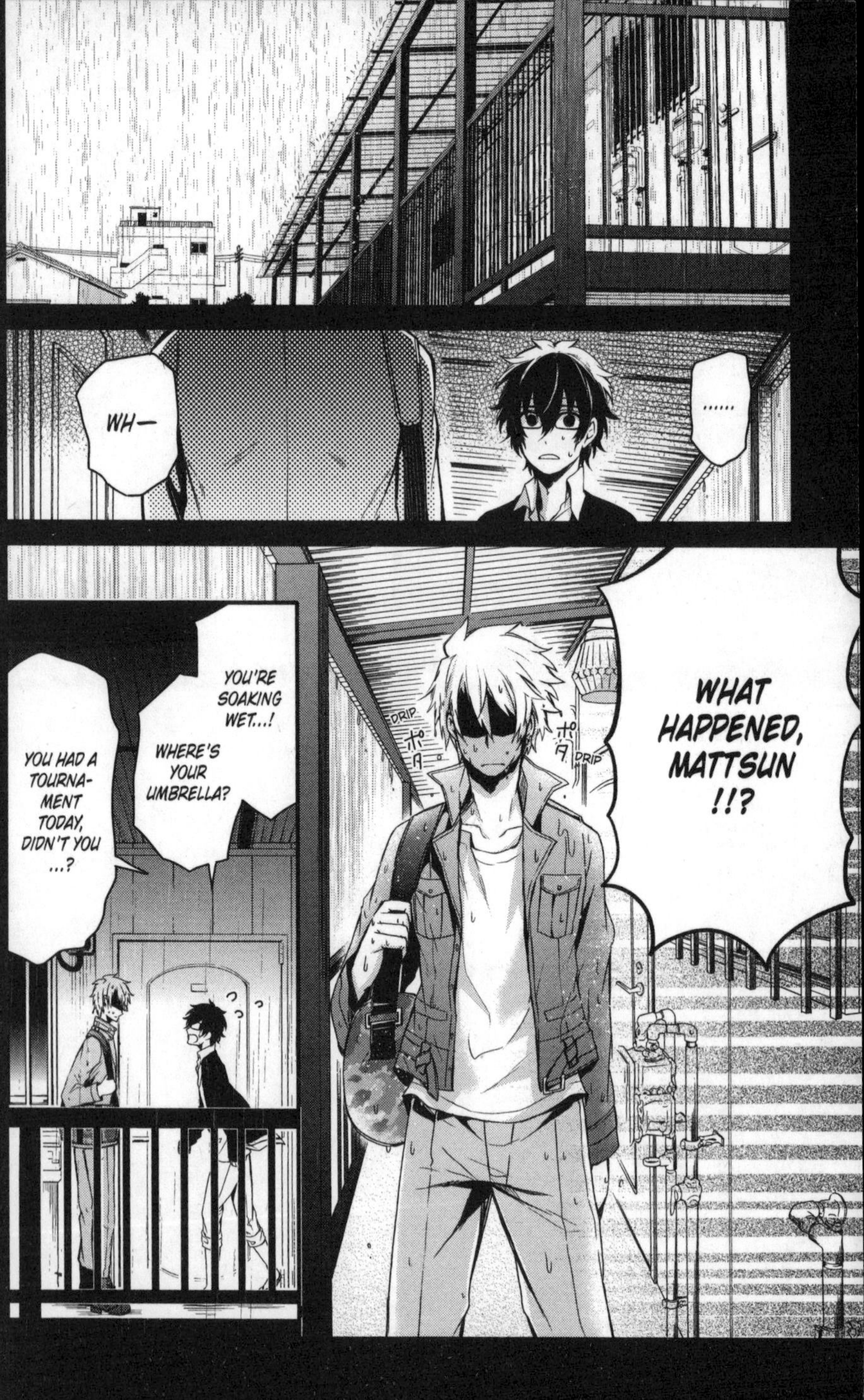
......
WH—
WHAT HAPPENED, MATTSUN!!?
DRIP
DRIP
YOU'RE SOAKING WET...!
WHERE'S YOUR UMBRELLA?
YOU HAD A TOURNAMENT TODAY, DIDN'T YOU...?

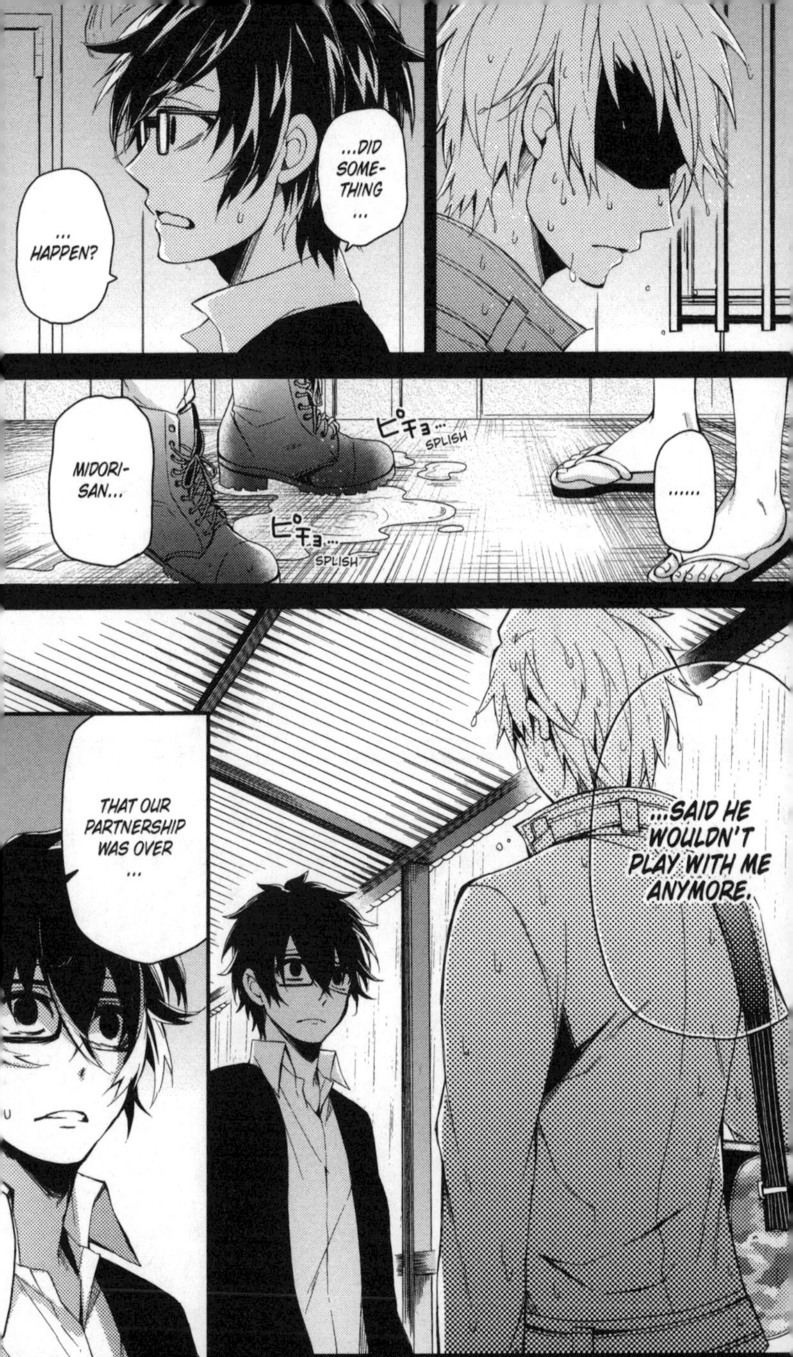
...DID SOME-THING ...
... HAPPEN?
......
ピチョ... SPLISH
ピチョ... SPLISH
MIDORI-SAN...
...SAID HE WOULDN'T PLAY WITH ME ANYMORE.
THAT OUR PARTNERSHIP WAS OVER ...

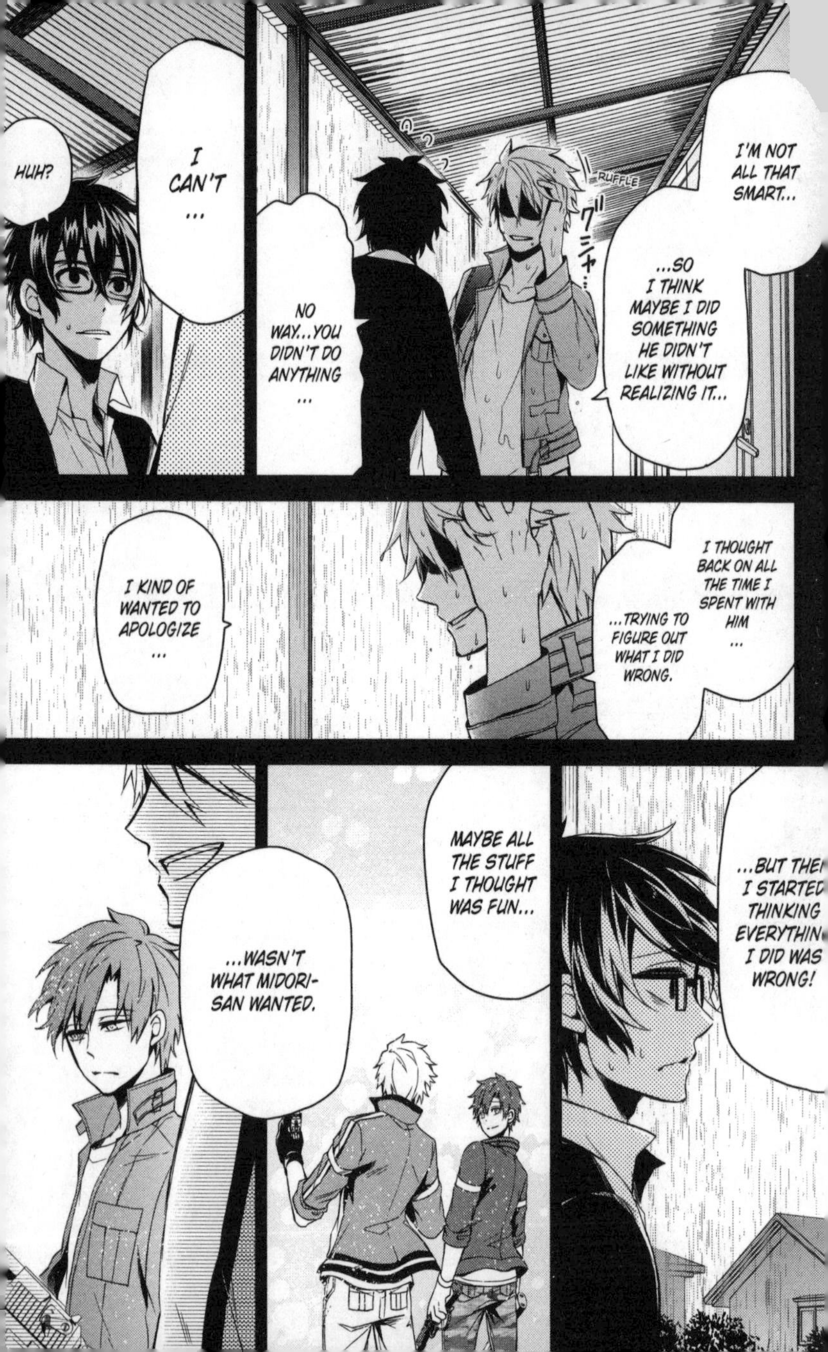
I'M NOT ALL THAT SMART...
...SO I THINK MAYBE I DID SOMETHING HE DIDN'T LIKE WITHOUT REALIZING IT...
RUFFLE
グシャ…
NO WAY...YOU DIDN'T DO ANYTHING ...
I CAN'T ...
HUH?
I THOUGHT BACK ON ALL THE TIME I SPENT WITH HIM ...
...TRYING TO FIGURE OUT WHAT I DID WRONG.
I KIND OF WANTED TO APOLOGIZE ...
...BUT THE I STARTE THINKING EVERYTHIN I DID WAS WRONG!
MAYBE ALL THE STUFF I THOUGHT WAS FUN...
...WASN'T WHAT MIDORI-SAN WANTED.

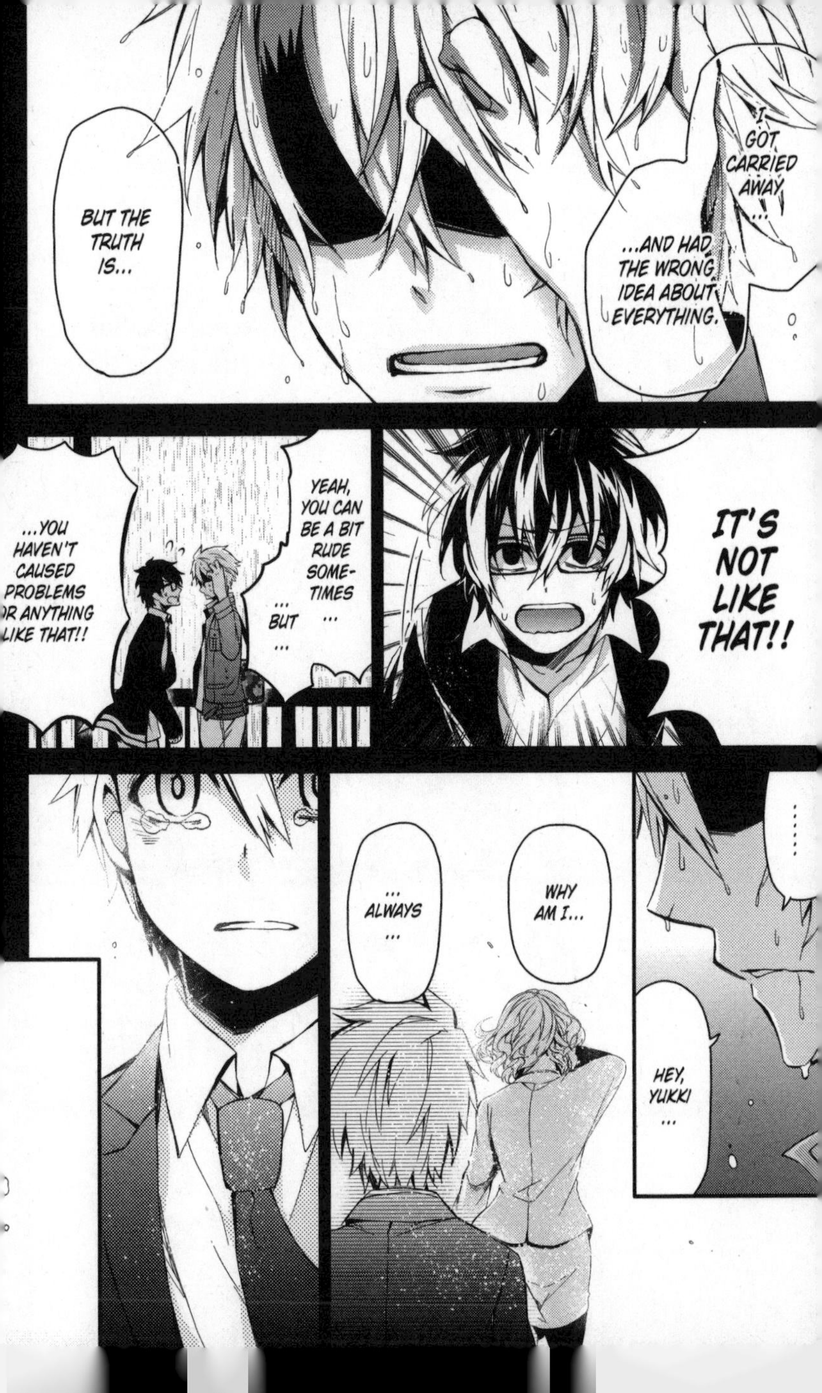
I GOT CARRIED AWAY...
...AND HAD THE WRONG IDEA ABOUT EVERYTHING.
BUT THE TRUTH IS...
IT'S NOT LIKE THAT!!
YEAH, YOU CAN BE A BIT RUDE SOMETIMES... BUT...
...YOU HAVEN'T CAUSED PROBLEMS OR ANYTHING LIKE THAT!!
......
HEY, YUKKI...
WHY AM I...
...ALWAYS...

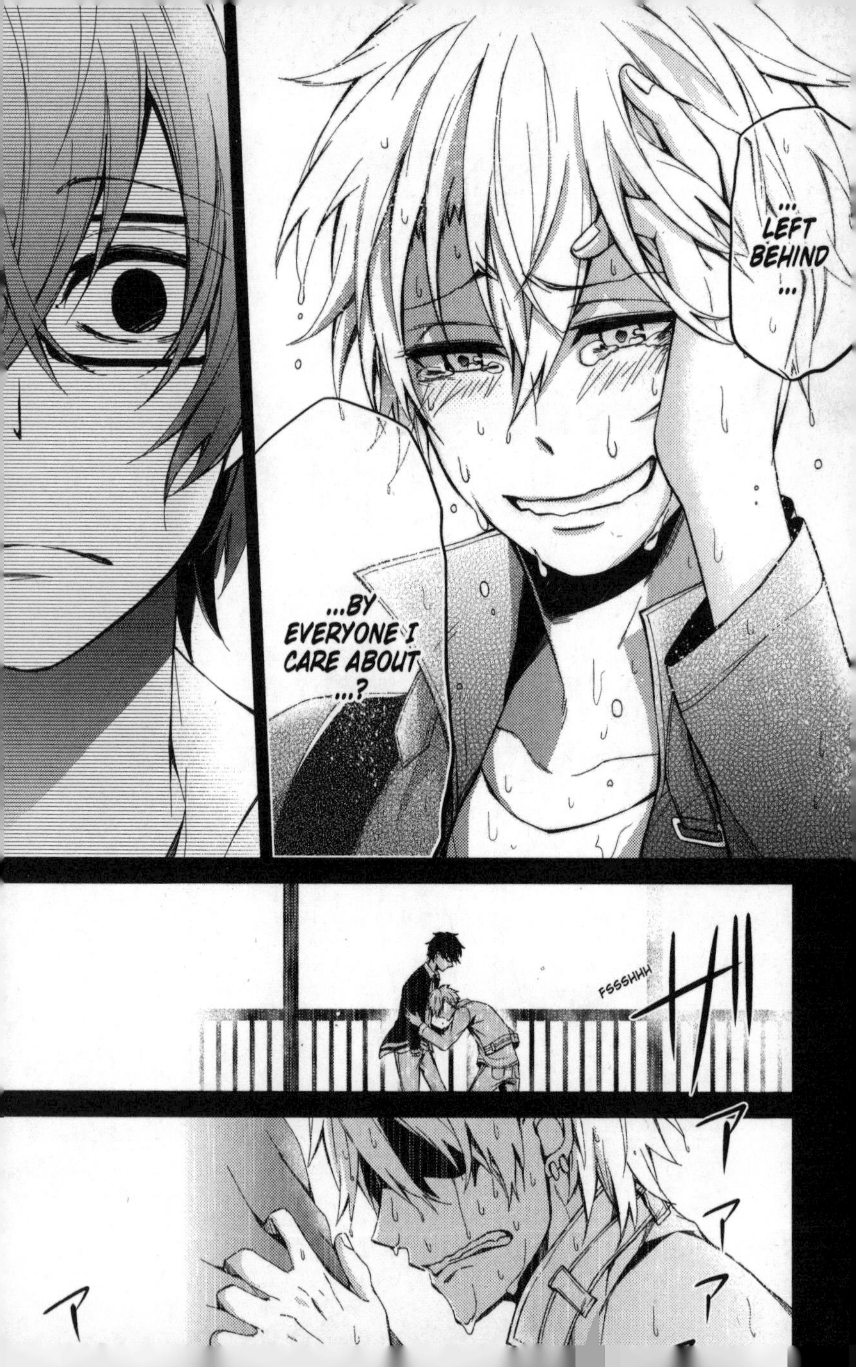
...LEFT BEHIND ...
...BY EVERYONE I CARE ABOUT ...?
FSSSHHH

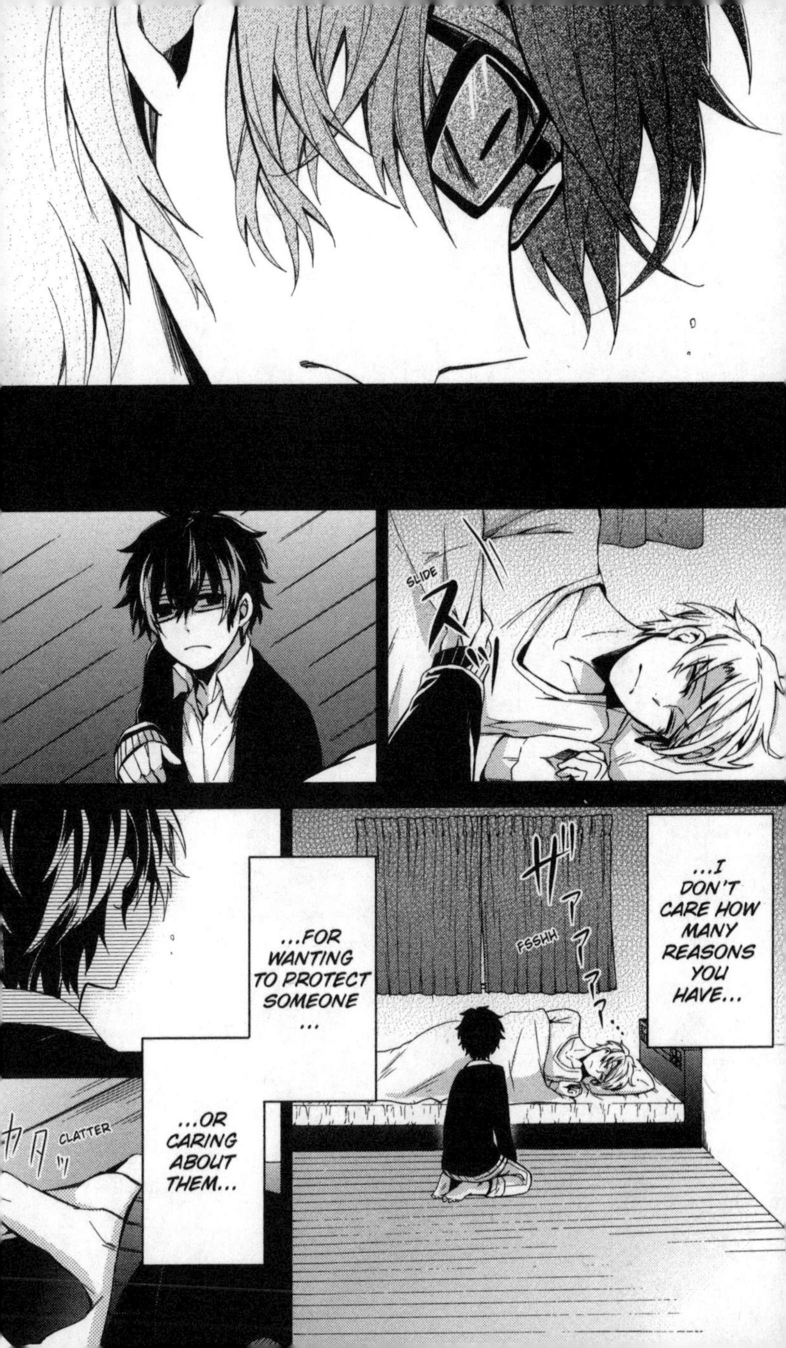
SLIDE
...I DON'T CARE HOW MANY REASONS YOU HAVE...
FSSHH
...FOR WANTING TO PROTECT SOMEONE...
...OR CARING ABOUT THEM...
CLATTER

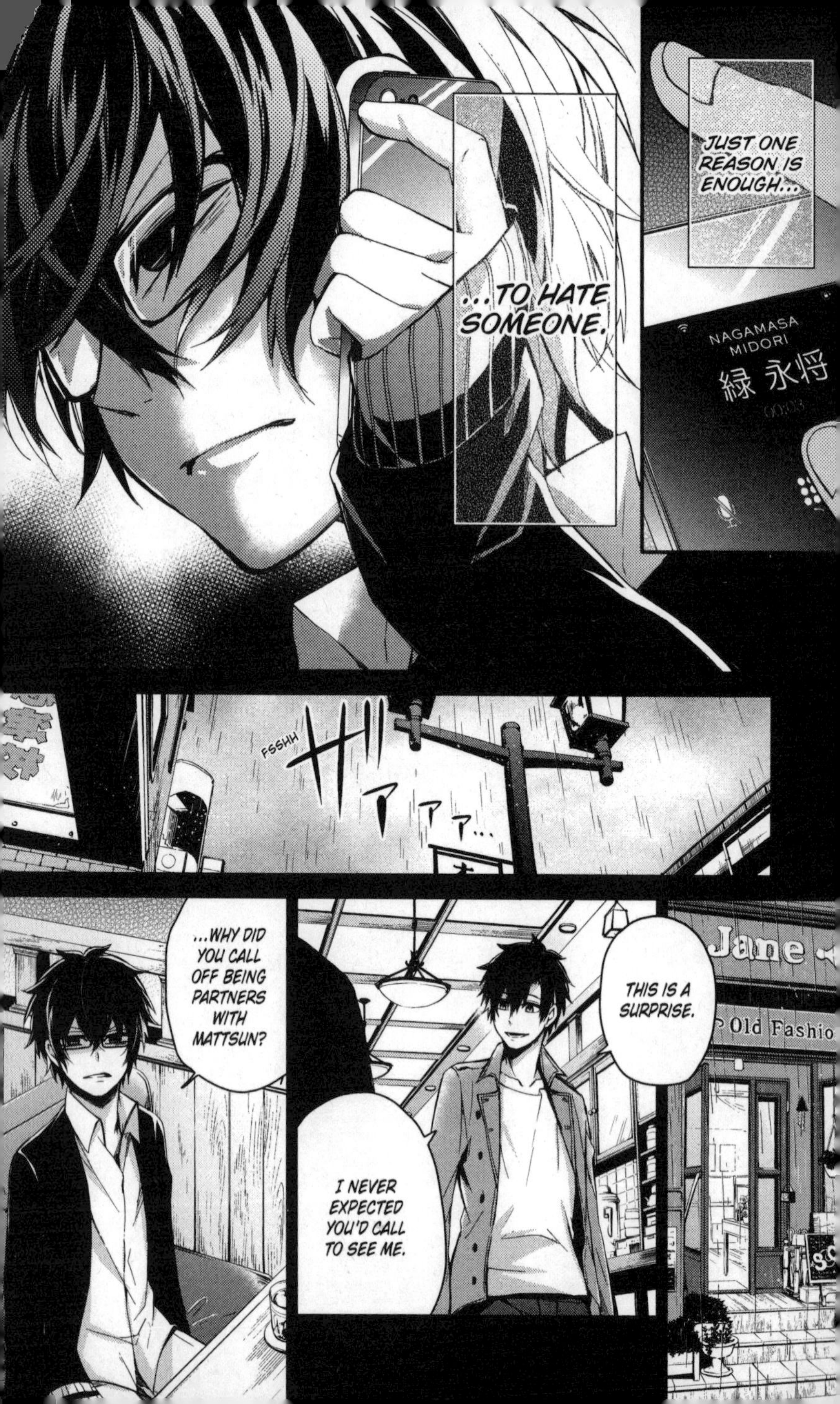
JUST ONE REASON IS ENOUGH...
NAGAMASA MIDORI
緑 永将
00:03
...TO HATE SOMEONE.
FSSHH
Jane
Old Fashio
THIS IS A SURPRISE.
I NEVER EXPECTED YOU'D CALL TO SEE ME.
...WHY DID YOU CALL OFF BEING PARTNERS WITH MATTSUN?

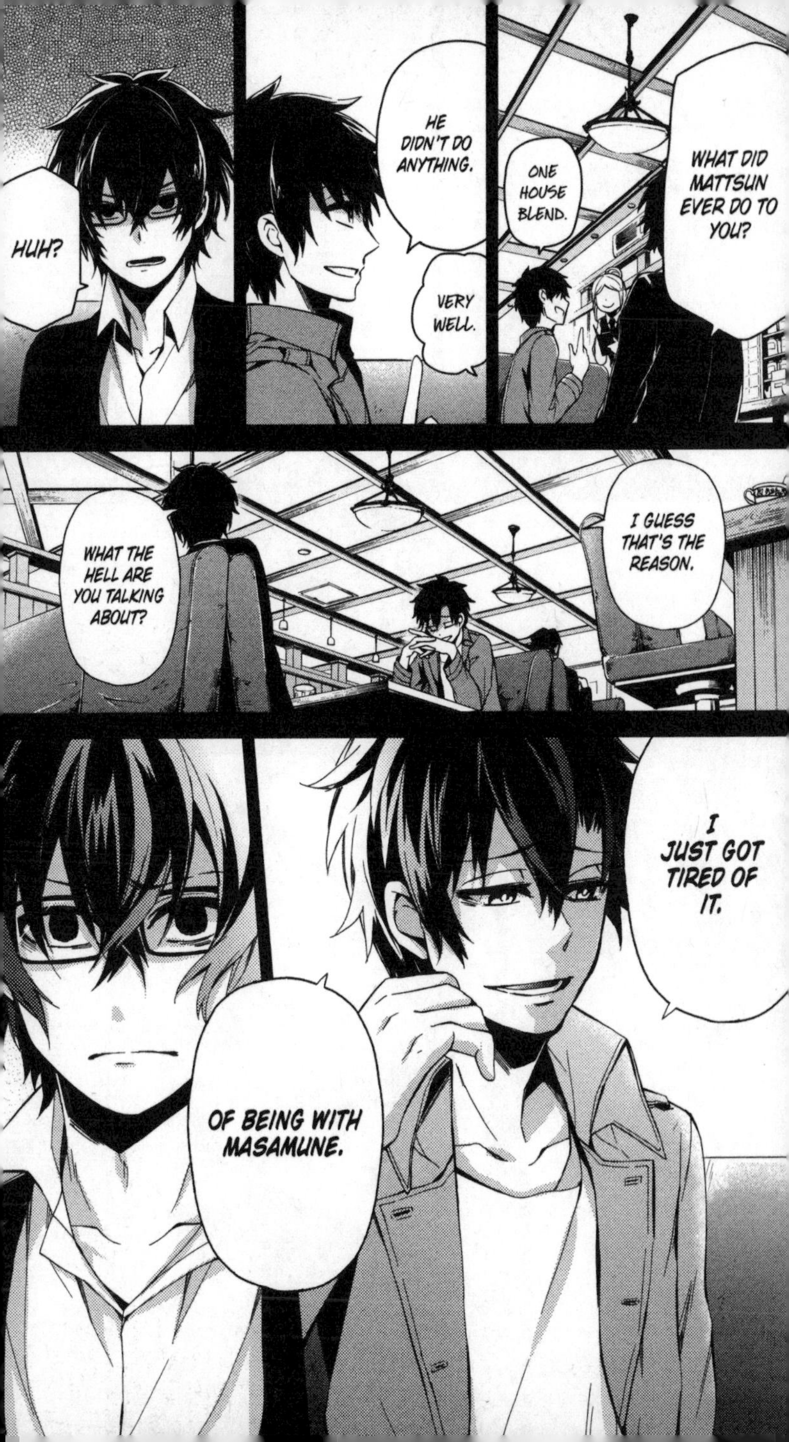
WHAT DID MATTSUN EVER DO TO YOU?
ONE HOUSE BLEND.
HE DIDN'T DO ANYTHING.
VERY WELL.
HUH?
I GUESS THAT'S THE REASON.
WHAT THE HELL ARE YOU TALKING ABOUT?
I JUST GOT TIRED OF IT.
OF BEING WITH MASAMUNE.

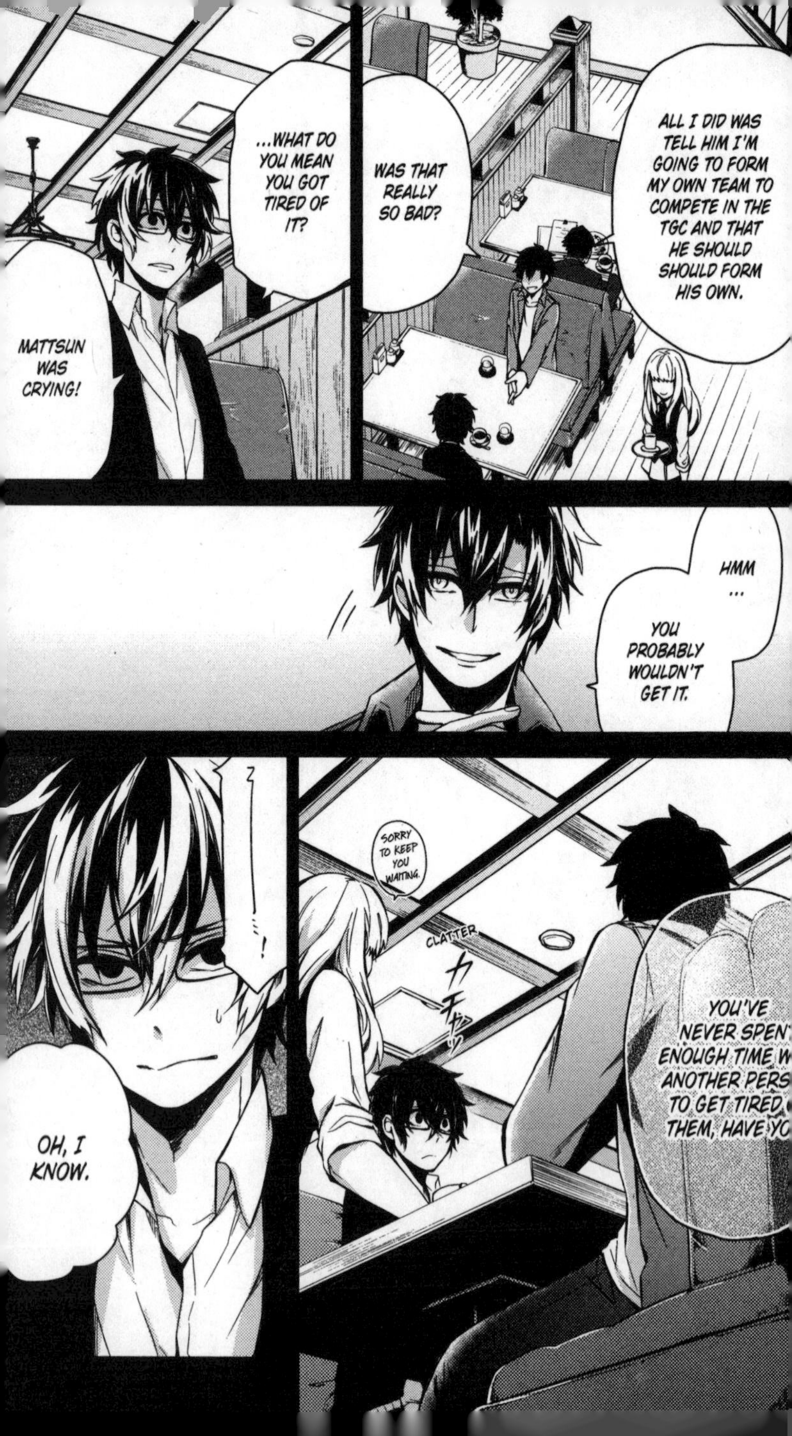
ALL I DID WAS TELL HIM I'M GOING TO FORM MY OWN TEAM TO COMPETE IN THE TGC AND THAT HE SHOULD SHOULD FORM HIS OWN.
WAS THAT REALLY SO BAD?
...WHAT DO YOU MEAN YOU GOT TIRED OF IT?
MATTSUN WAS CRYING!
HMM ...
YOU PROBABLY WOULDN'T GET IT.
YOU'VE NEVER SPENT ENOUGH TIME W ANOTHER PERS TO GET TIRED THEM, HAVE YO
SORRY TO KEEP YOU WAITING.
CLATTER
カチャッ
...!
OH, I KNOW.

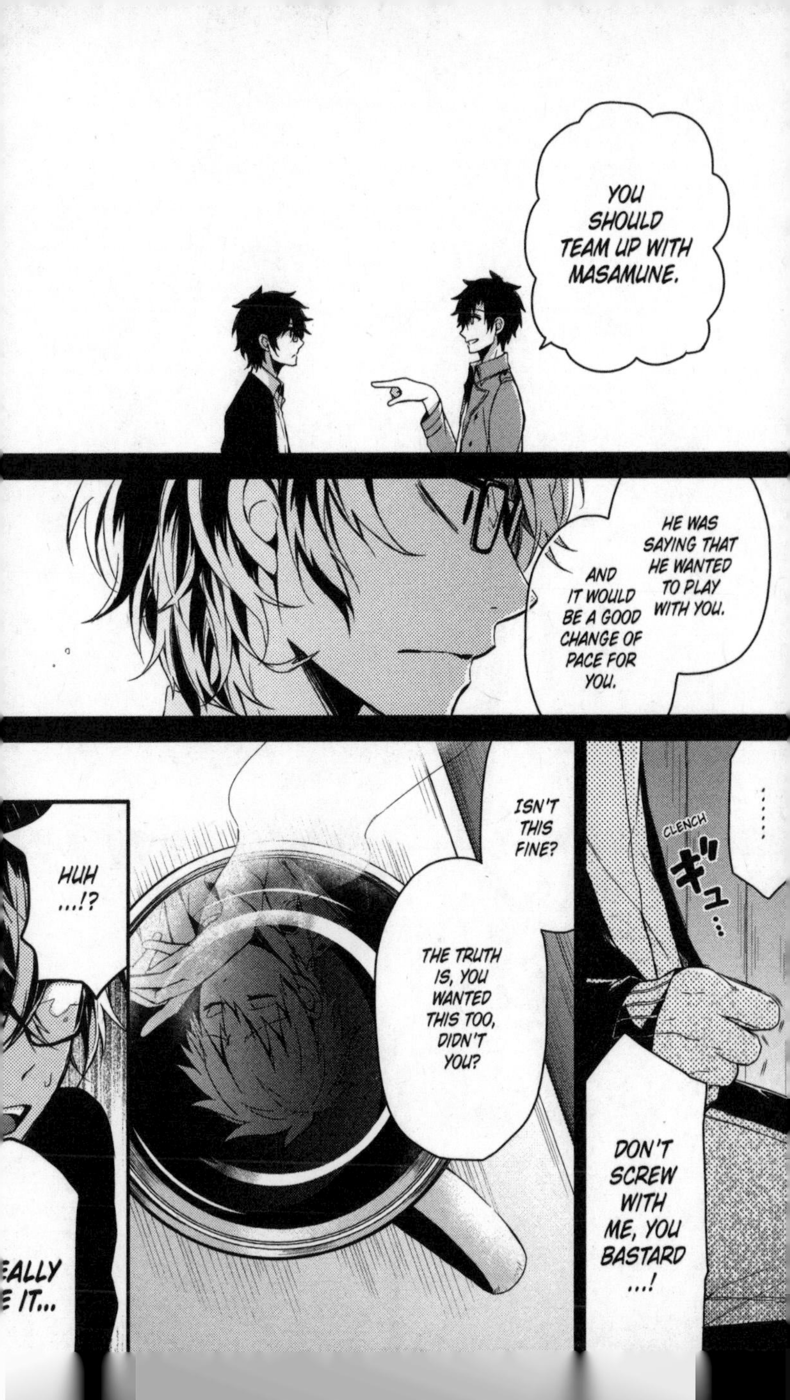
YOU SHOULD TEAM UP WITH MASAMUNE.
HE WAS SAYING THAT HE WANTED TO PLAY WITH YOU.
AND IT WOULD BE A GOOD CHANGE OF PACE FOR YOU.
……
CLENCH
ギュ…
DON'T SCREW WITH ME, YOU BASTARD …!
ISN'T THIS FINE?
THE TRUTH IS, YOU WANTED THIS TOO, DIDN'T YOU?
HUH …!?
EALLY
E IT…

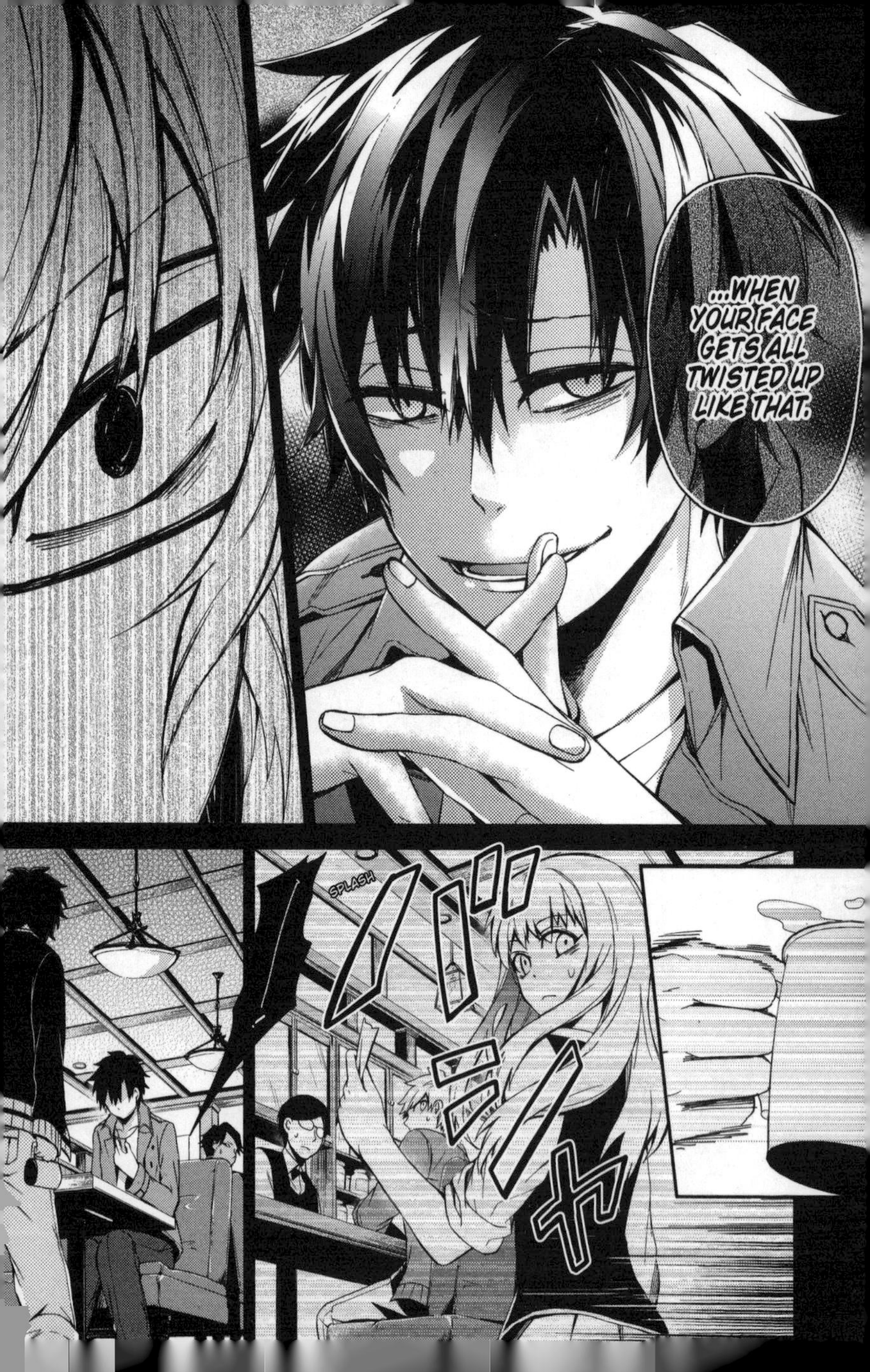
...WHEN YOUR FACE GETS ALL TWISTED UP LIKE THAT.
SPLASH

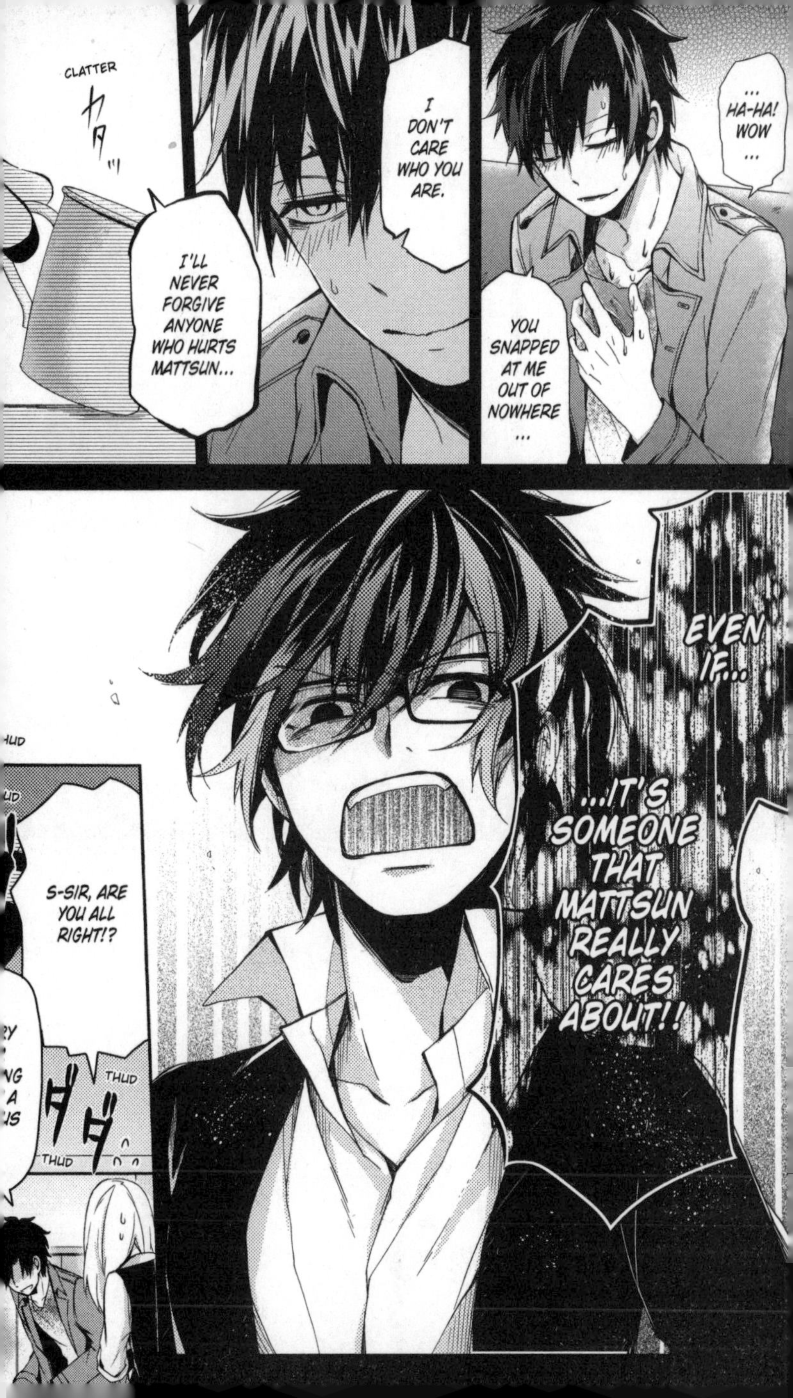
... HA-HA! WOW ...
YOU SNAPPED AT ME OUT OF NOWHERE ...
I DON'T CARE WHO YOU ARE.
CLATTER
I'LL NEVER FORGIVE ANYONE WHO HURTS MATTSUN...
EVEN IF...
...IT'S SOMEONE THAT MATTSUN REALLY CARES ABOUT!!
S-SIR, ARE YOU ALL RIGHT!?
THUD
THUD

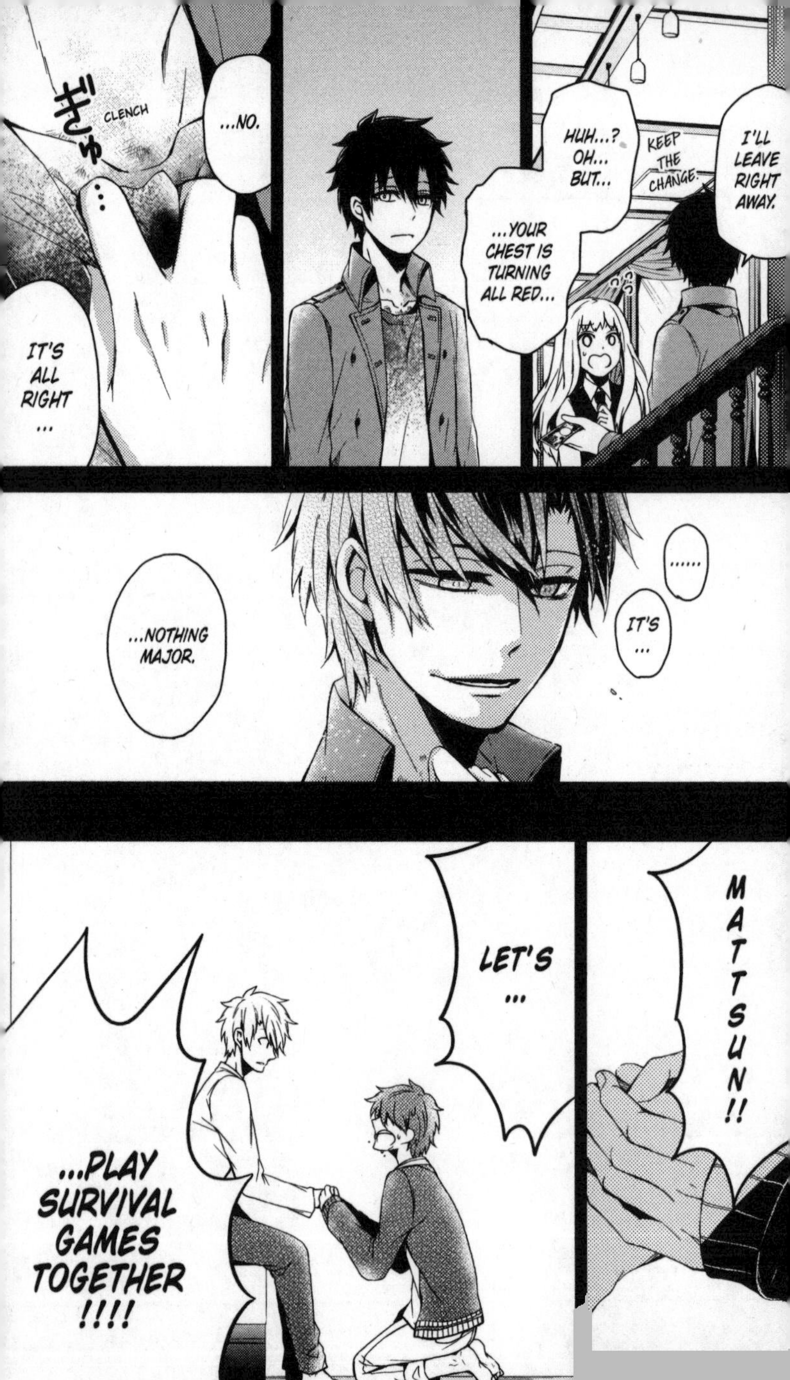
I'LL LEAVE RIGHT AWAY.
KEEP THE CHANGE.
HUH...? OH... BUT...
...YOUR CHEST IS TURNING ALL RED...
...NO.
ぎゅ
CLENCH
IT'S ALL RIGHT ...
......
IT'S ...
...NOTHING MAJOR.
MATTSUN!!
LET'S ...
...PLAY SURVIVAL GAMES TOGETHER !!!!

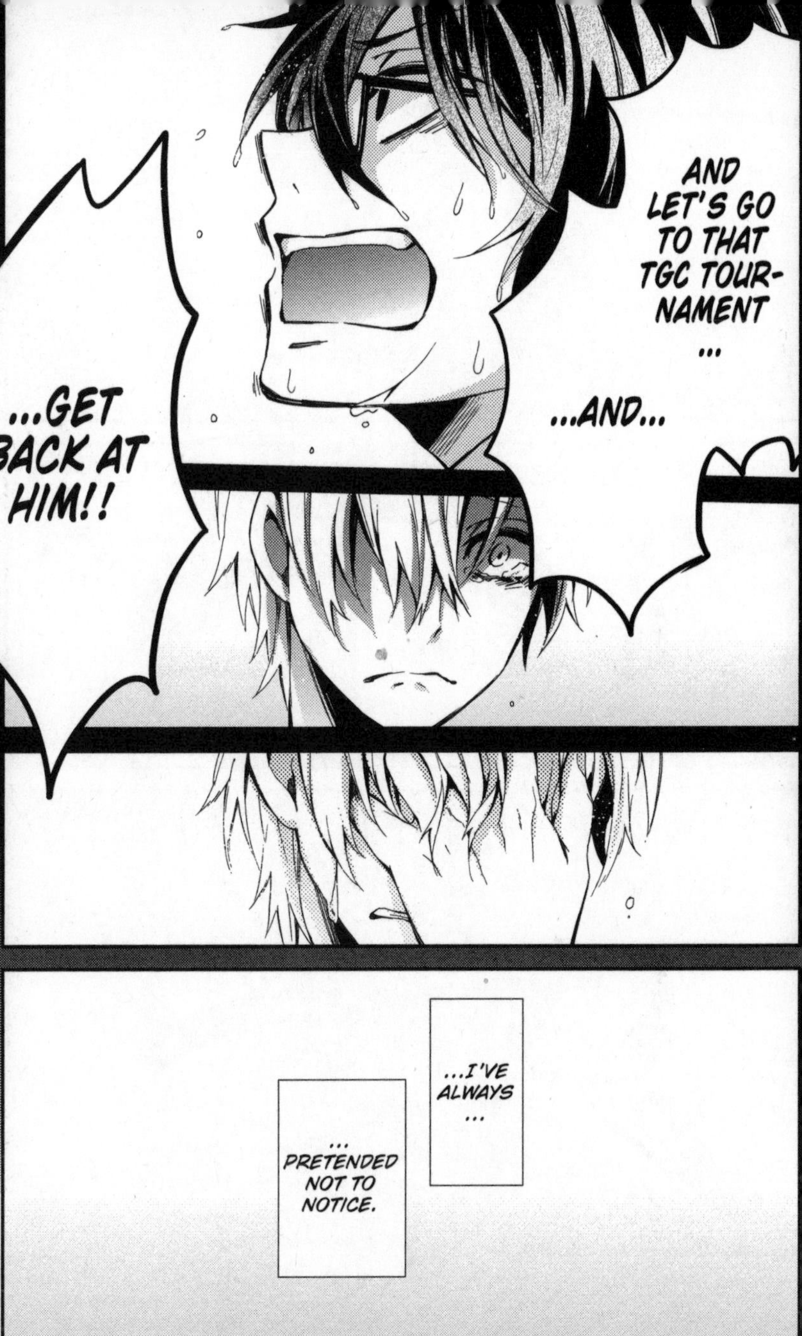
AND LET'S GO TO THAT TGC TOUR-NAMENT...
...AND...
...GET BACK AT HIM!!
...I'VE ALWAYS...
...PRETENDED NOT TO NOTICE.

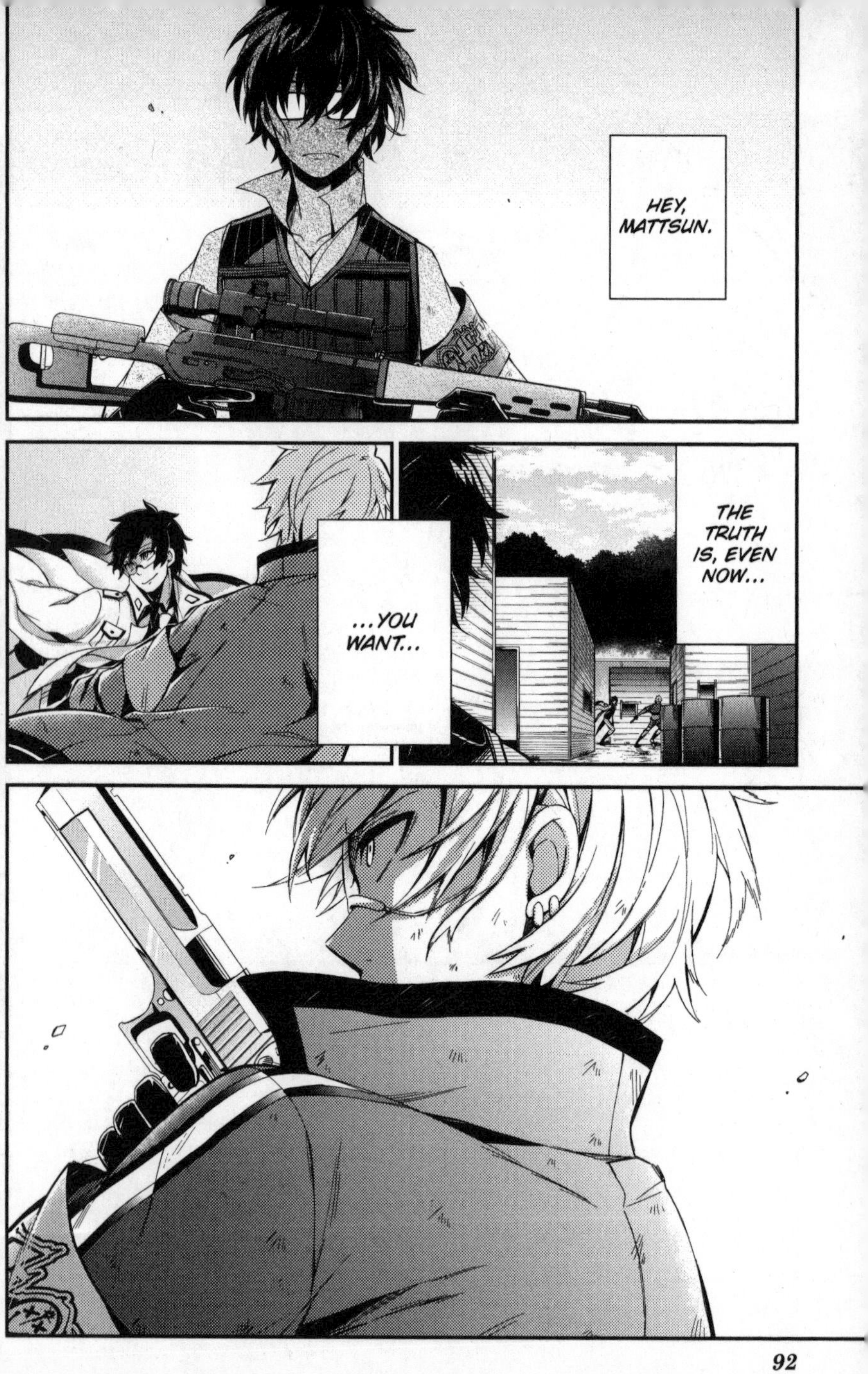
HEY, MATTSUN.
THE TRUTH IS, EVEN NOW...
...YOU WANT...

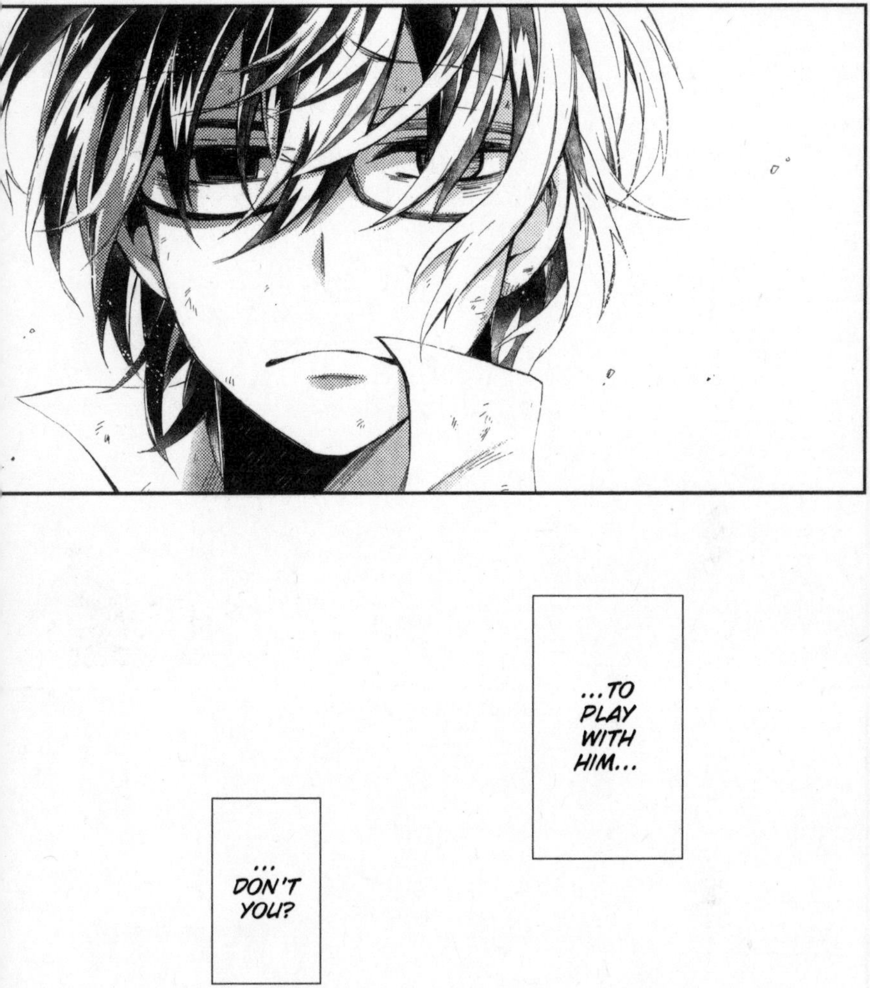
...TO PLAY WITH HIM...
...DON'T YOU?

AOHARU MACHINE GUN

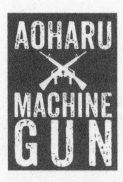

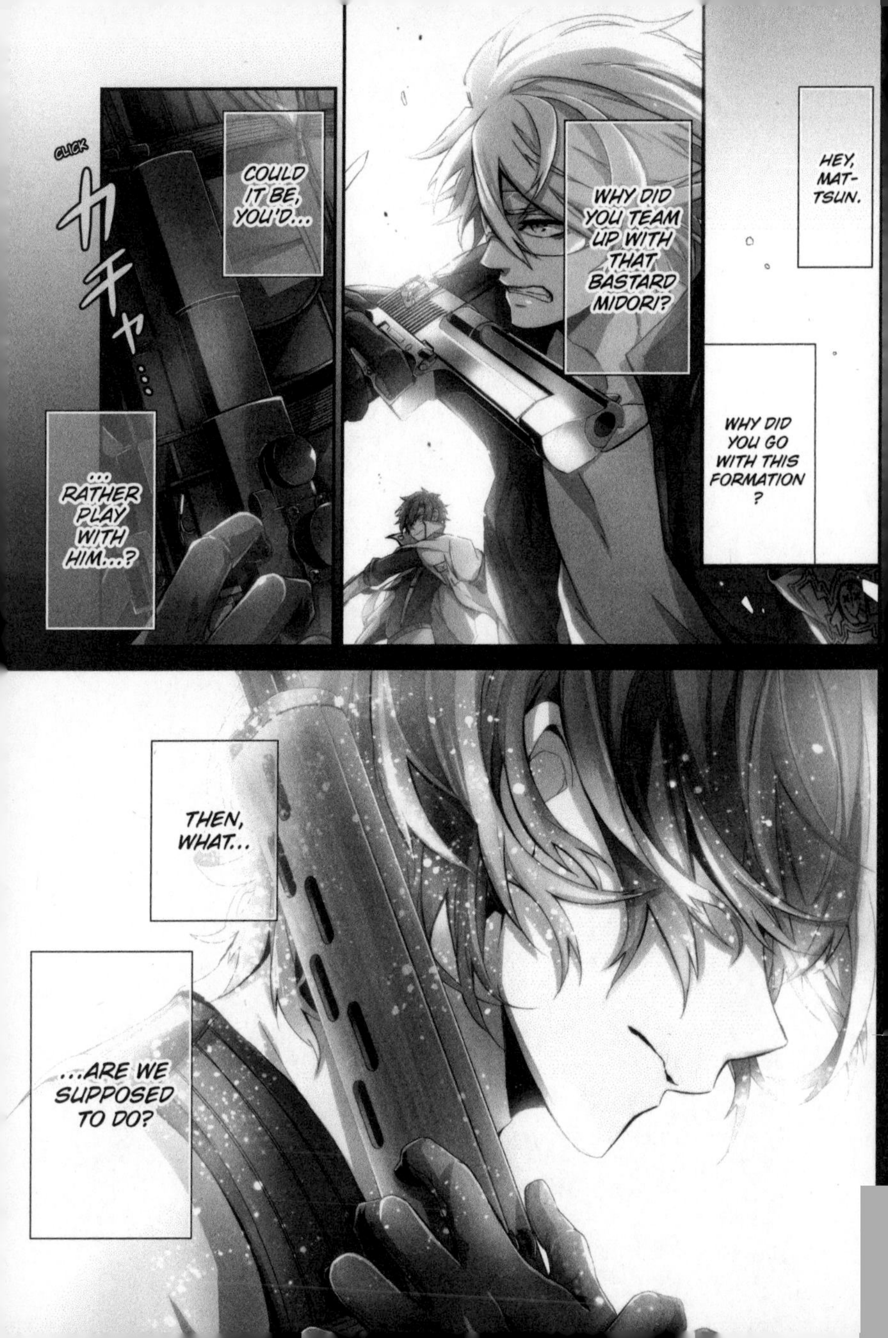
HEY, MAT-TSUN.
WHY DID YOU GO WITH THIS FORMATION?
WHY DID YOU TEAM UP WITH THAT BASTARD MIDORI?
COULD IT BE, YOU'D...
CLICK
カチャ…
...RATHER PLAY WITH HIM...?
THEN, WHAT...
...ARE WE SUPPOSED TO DO?

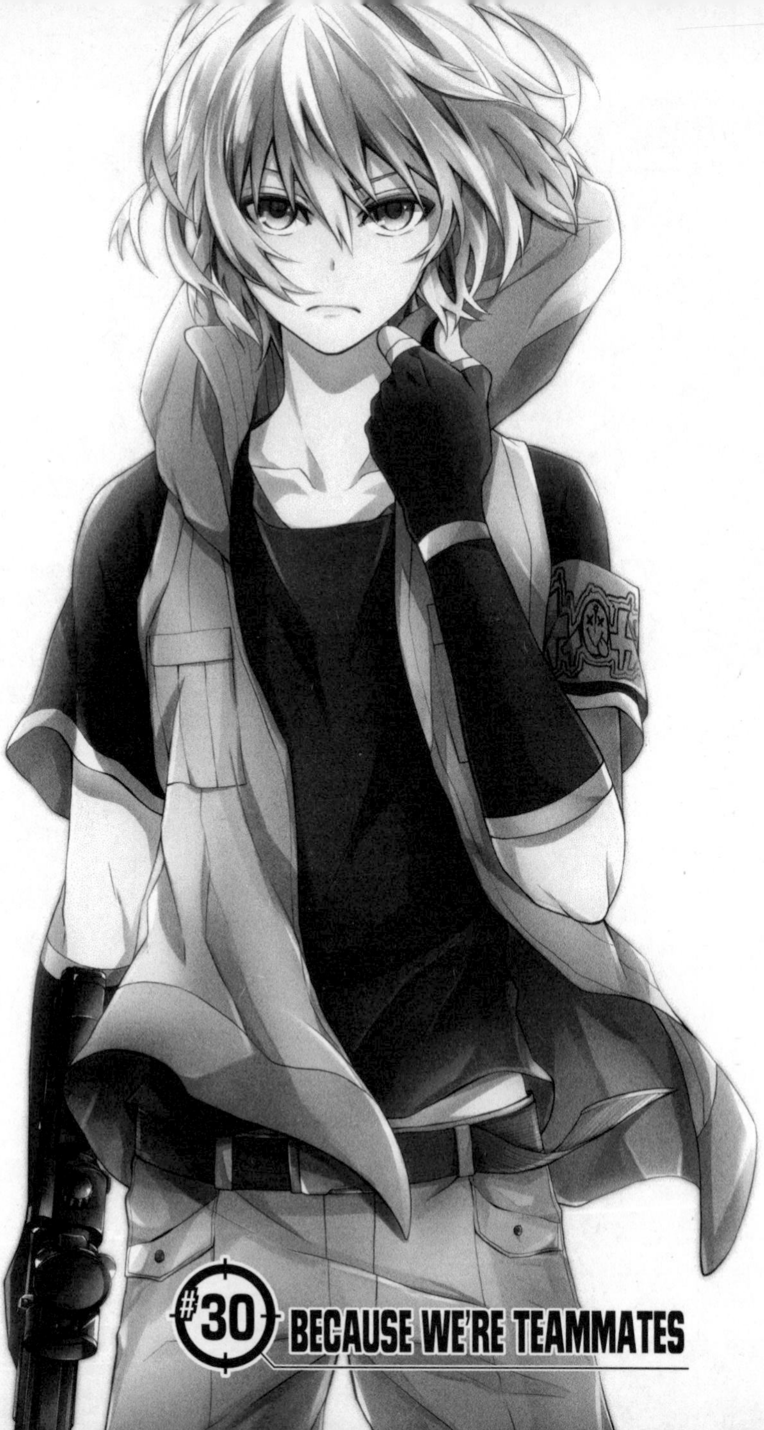

#30 BECAUSE WE'RE TEAMMATES

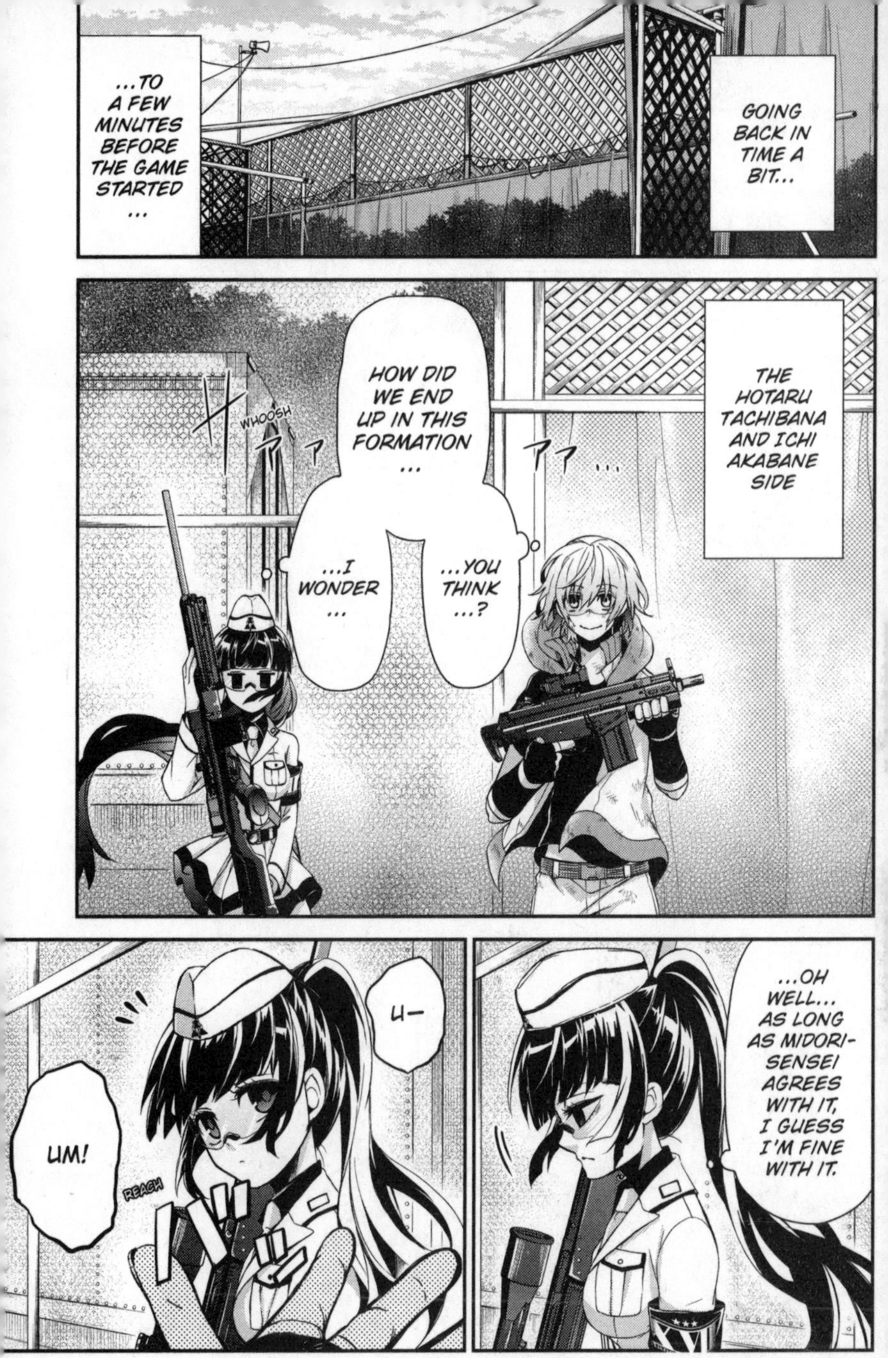
GOING BACK IN TIME A BIT...
...TO A FEW MINUTES BEFORE THE GAME STARTED...
THE HOTARU TACHIBANA AND ICHI AKABANE SIDE
HOW DID WE END UP IN THIS FORMATION...
...YOU THINK...?
...I WONDER...
WHOOSH
...OH WELL... AS LONG AS MIDORI-SENSEI AGREES WITH IT, I GUESS I'M FINE WITH IT.
U-
UM!
REACH

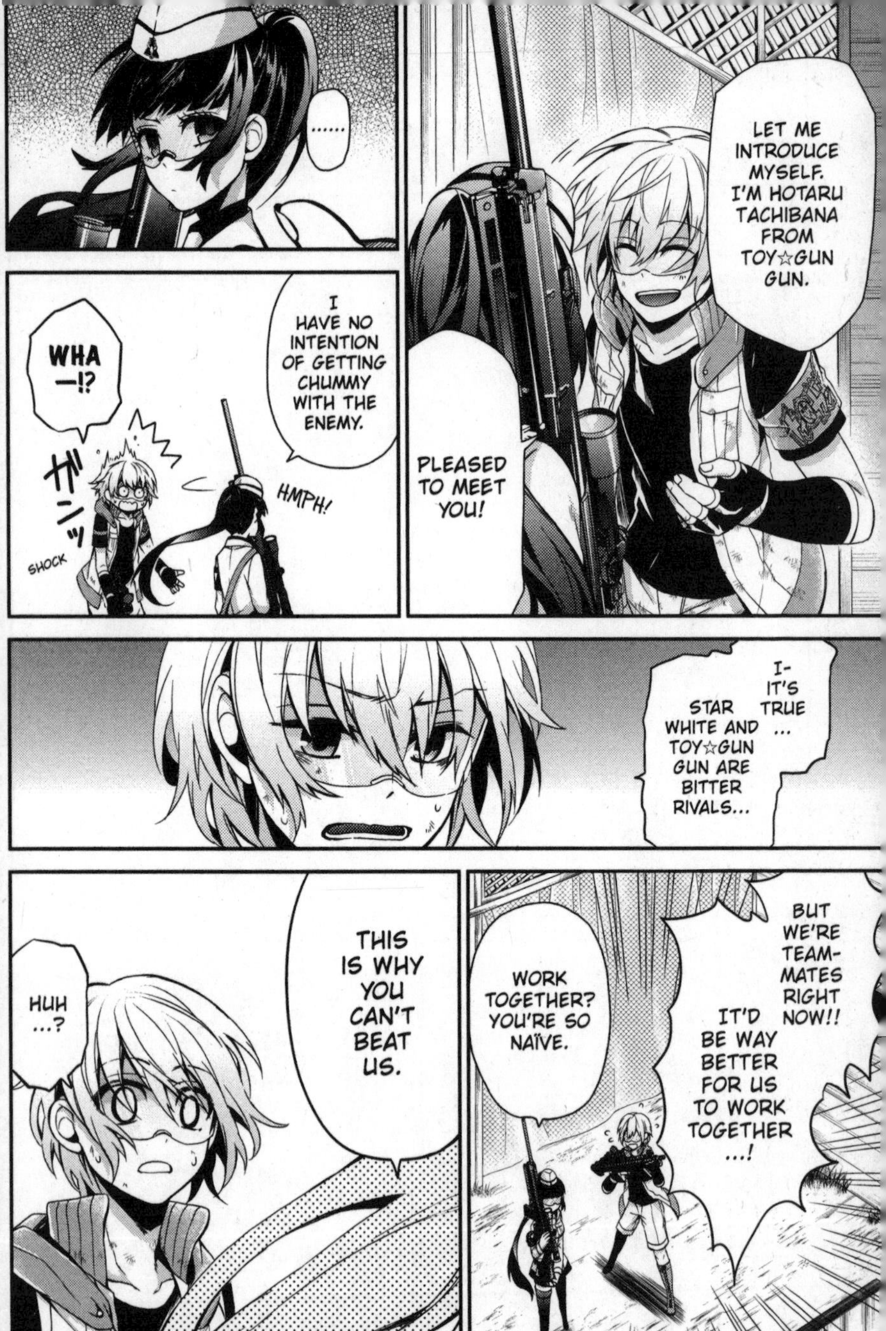
LET ME INTRODUCE MYSELF. I'M HOTARU TACHIBANA FROM TOY☆GUN GUN.
PLEASED TO MEET YOU!
......
I HAVE NO INTENTION OF GETTING CHUMMY WITH THE ENEMY.
HMPH!
WHA—!?
SHOCK
I- IT'S TRUE...
STAR WHITE AND TOY☆GUN GUN ARE BITTER RIVALS...
BUT WE'RE TEAM-MATES RIGHT NOW!!
IT'D BE WAY BETTER FOR US TO WORK TOGETHER...!
WORK TOGETHER? YOU'RE SO NAÏVE.
THIS IS WHY YOU CAN'T BEAT US.
HUH...?

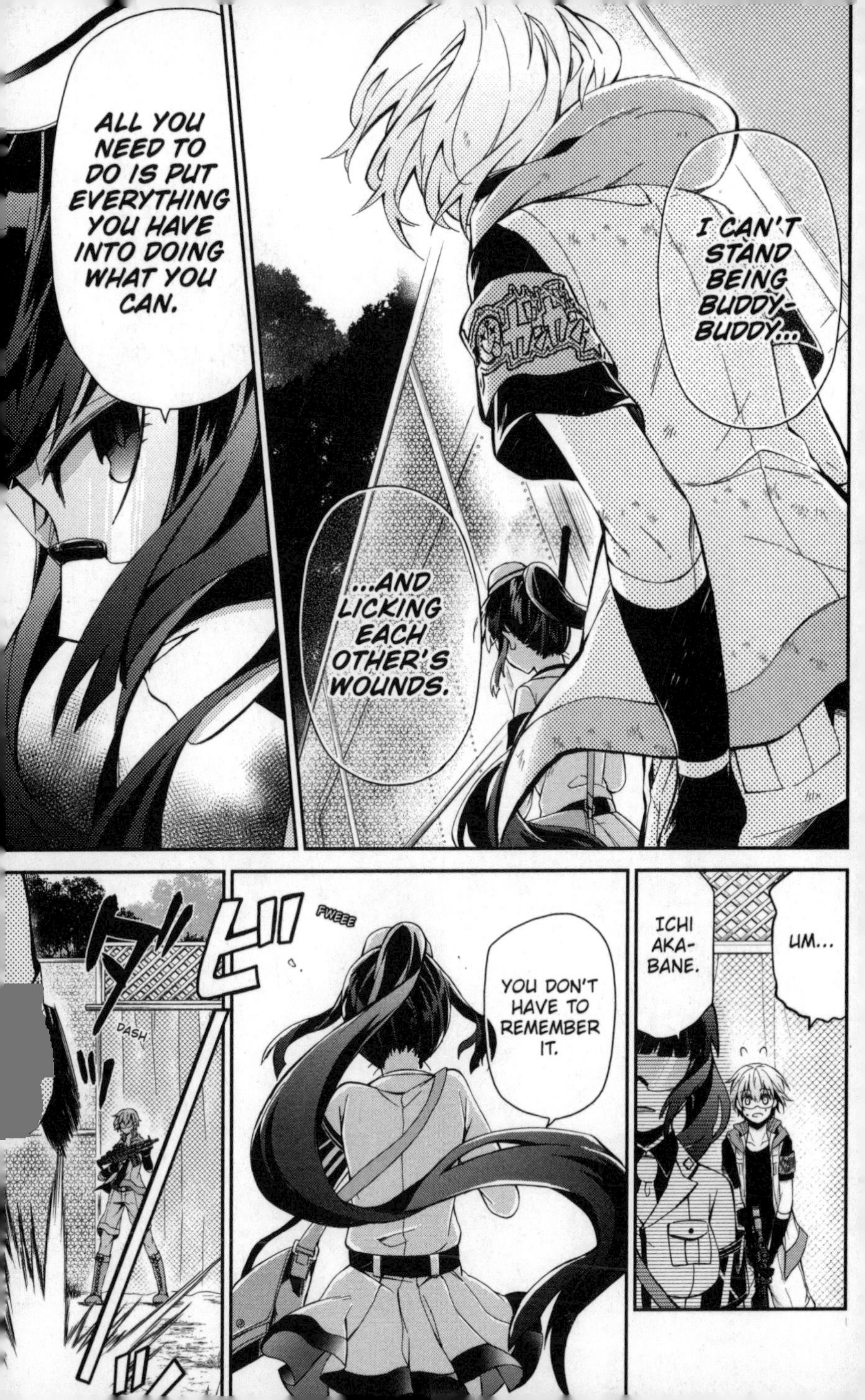
I CAN'T STAND BEING BUDDY-BUDDY...
...AND LICKING EACH OTHER'S WOUNDS.
ALL YOU NEED TO DO IS PUT EVERYTHING YOU HAVE INTO DOING WHAT YOU CAN.
UM...
ICHI AKA-BANE.
FWEEE
YOU DON'T HAVE TO REMEMBER IT.
DASH

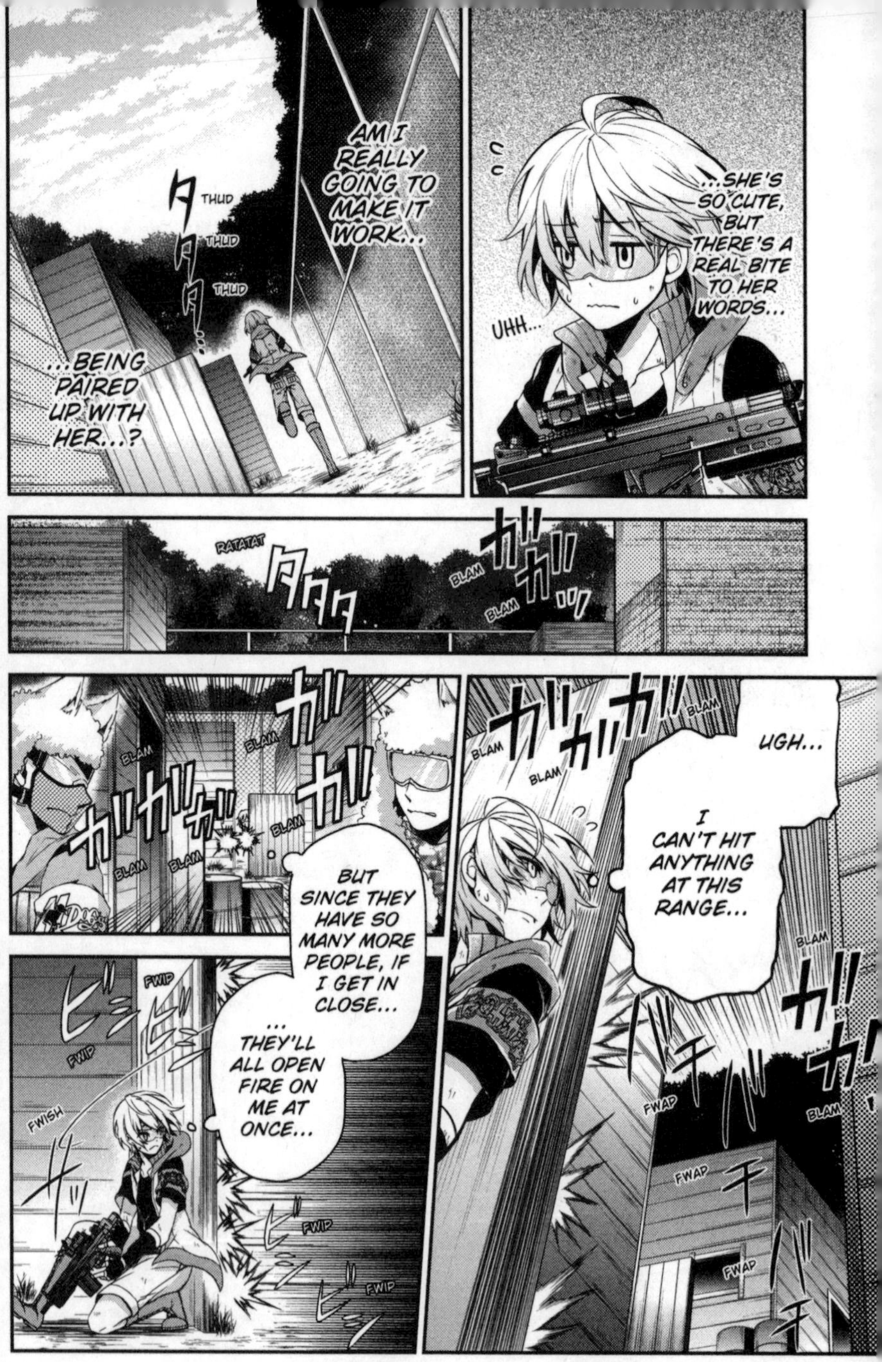
...SHE'S SO CUTE, BUT THERE'S A REAL BITE TO HER WORDS...
UHH...
AM I REALLY GOING TO MAKE IT WORK...
THUD
THUD
THUD
...BEING PAIRED UP WITH HER...?
BLAM
BLAM
RATATAT
BLAM
BLAM
UGH...
I CAN'T HIT ANYTHING AT THIS RANGE...
BLAM
BLAM
BLAM
FWAP
FWAP
FWAP
BLAM
BLAM
BLAM
BLAM
BLAM
BUT SINCE THEY HAVE SO MANY MORE PEOPLE, IF I GET IN CLOSE...
...THEY'LL ALL OPEN FIRE ON ME AT ONCE...
FWIP
FWIP
FWISH
FWIP
FWIP

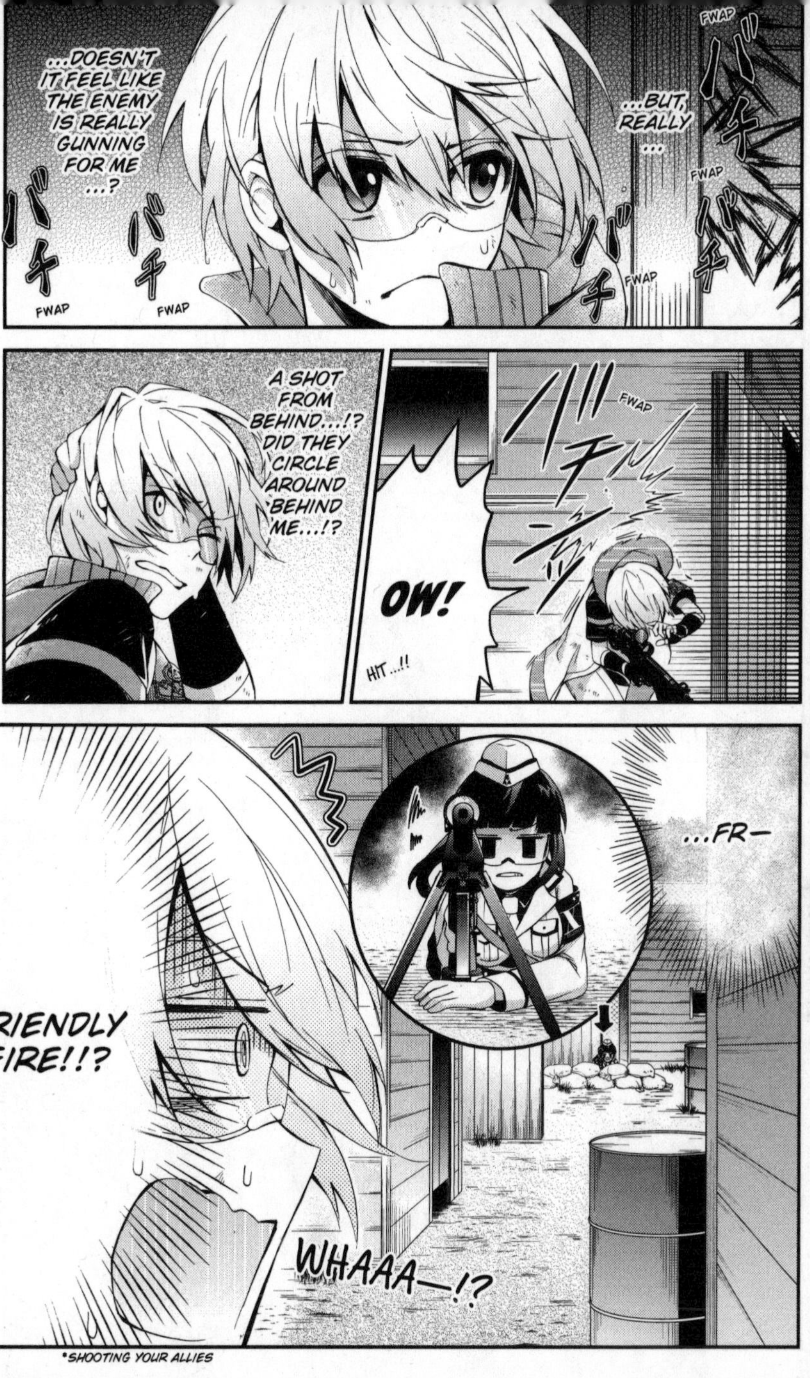
FWAP
FWAP
FWAP
...BUT, REALLY...
...DOESN'T IT FEEL LIKE THE ENEMY IS REALLY GUNNING FOR ME...?
FWAP
FWAP
FWAP
OW!
HIT...!!
A SHOT FROM BEHIND...!? DID THEY CIRCLE AROUND BEHIND ME...!?
...FR—
FRIENDLY FIRE!!?
WHAAA—!?

*SHOOTING YOUR ALLIES

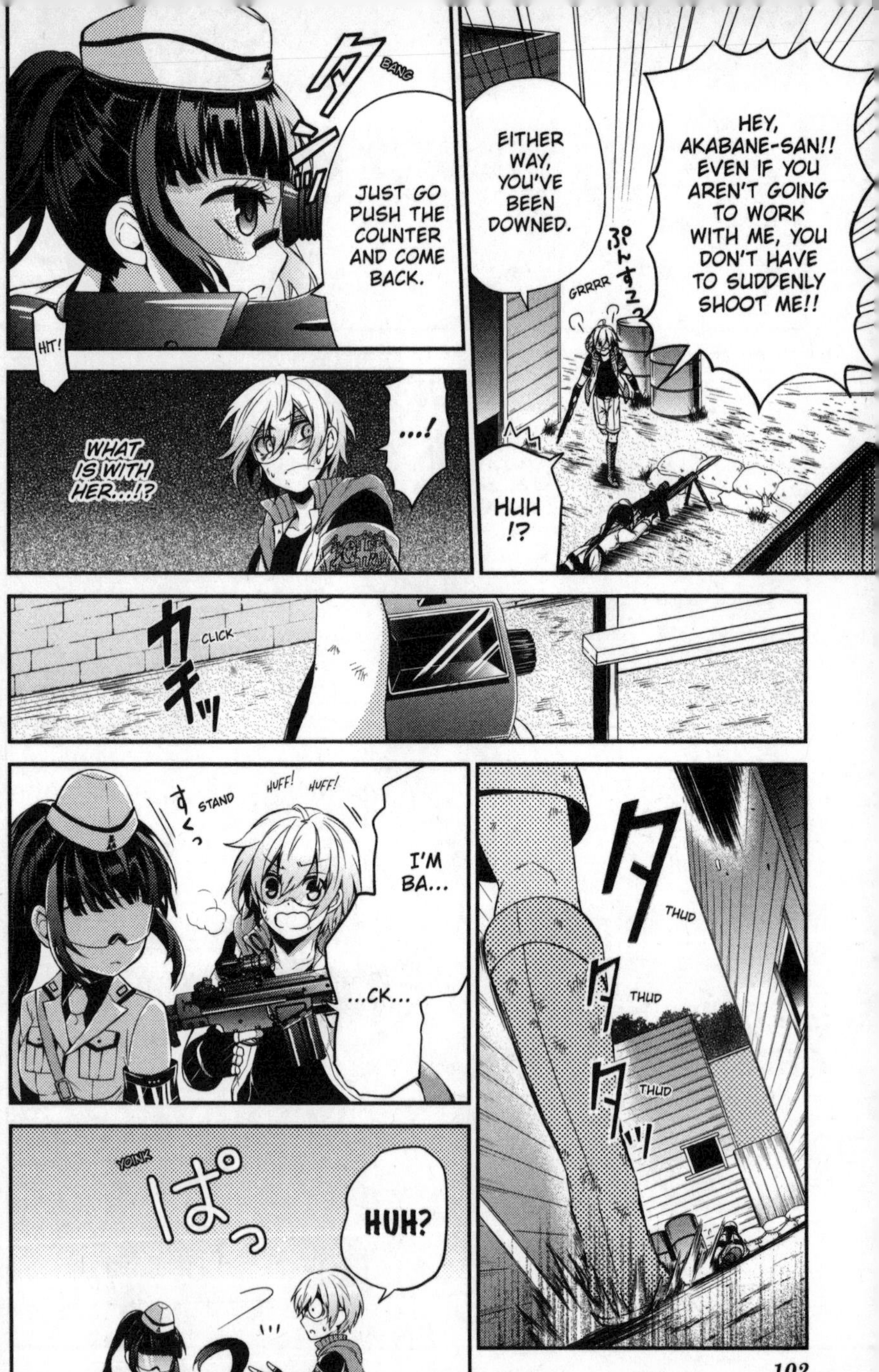
HEY, AKABANE-SAN!! EVEN IF YOU AREN'T GOING TO WORK WITH ME, YOU DON'T HAVE TO SUDDENLY SHOOT ME!!
EITHER WAY, YOU'VE BEEN DOWNED.
ぷんすこ
GRRRR
HUH!?
タ
BANG
JUST GO PUSH THE COUNTER AND COME BACK.
HIT!
...!
WHAT IS WITH HER...!?
カチッ
CLICK
タ
THUD
タ
THUD
タッ
THUD
I'M BA...
...CK...
すくっ
STAND
HUFF! HUFF!
HUH?
ぱっ
YOINK

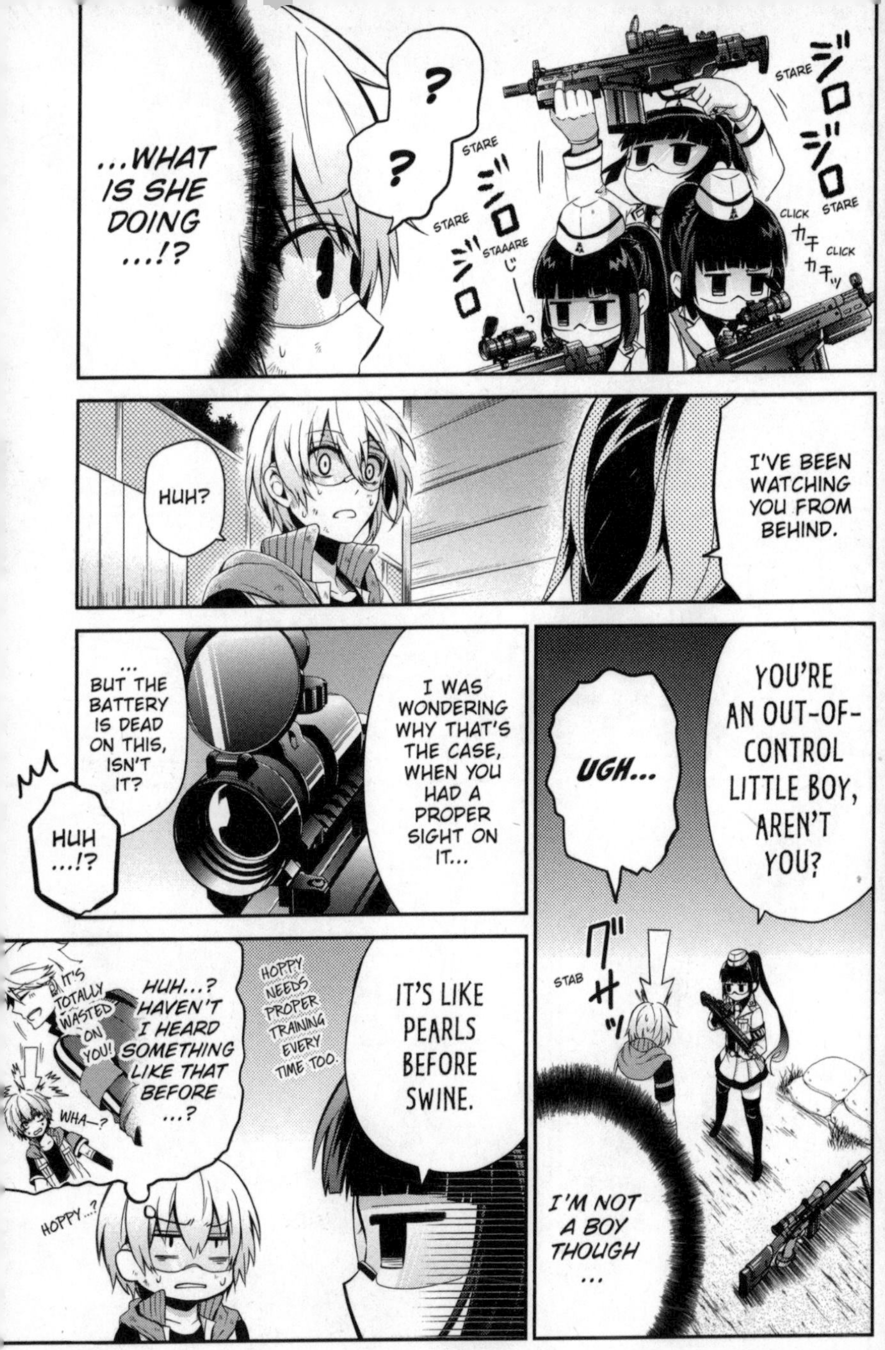
STARE
ジロ
ジロ
STARE
CLICK
カチ
CLICK
カチッ
?
?
STARE
ジロ
STARE
ジロ
STAAARE
じー
...WHAT IS SHE DOING ...!?
I'VE BEEN WATCHING YOU FROM BEHIND.
HUH?
YOU'RE AN OUT-OF-CONTROL LITTLE BOY, AREN'T YOU?
UGH...
STAB
グサッ
I'M NOT A BOY THOUGH ...
I WAS WONDERING WHY THAT'S THE CASE, WHEN YOU HAD A PROPER SIGHT ON IT...
... BUT THE BATTERY IS DEAD ON THIS, ISN'T IT?
HUH ...!?
IT'S LIKE PEARLS BEFORE SWINE.
HOPPY NEEDS PROPER TRAINING EVERY TIME TOO.
HUH...? HAVEN'T I HEARD SOMETHING LIKE THAT BEFORE ...?
IT'S TOTALLY WASTED ON YOU!
WHA—?
HOPPY...?

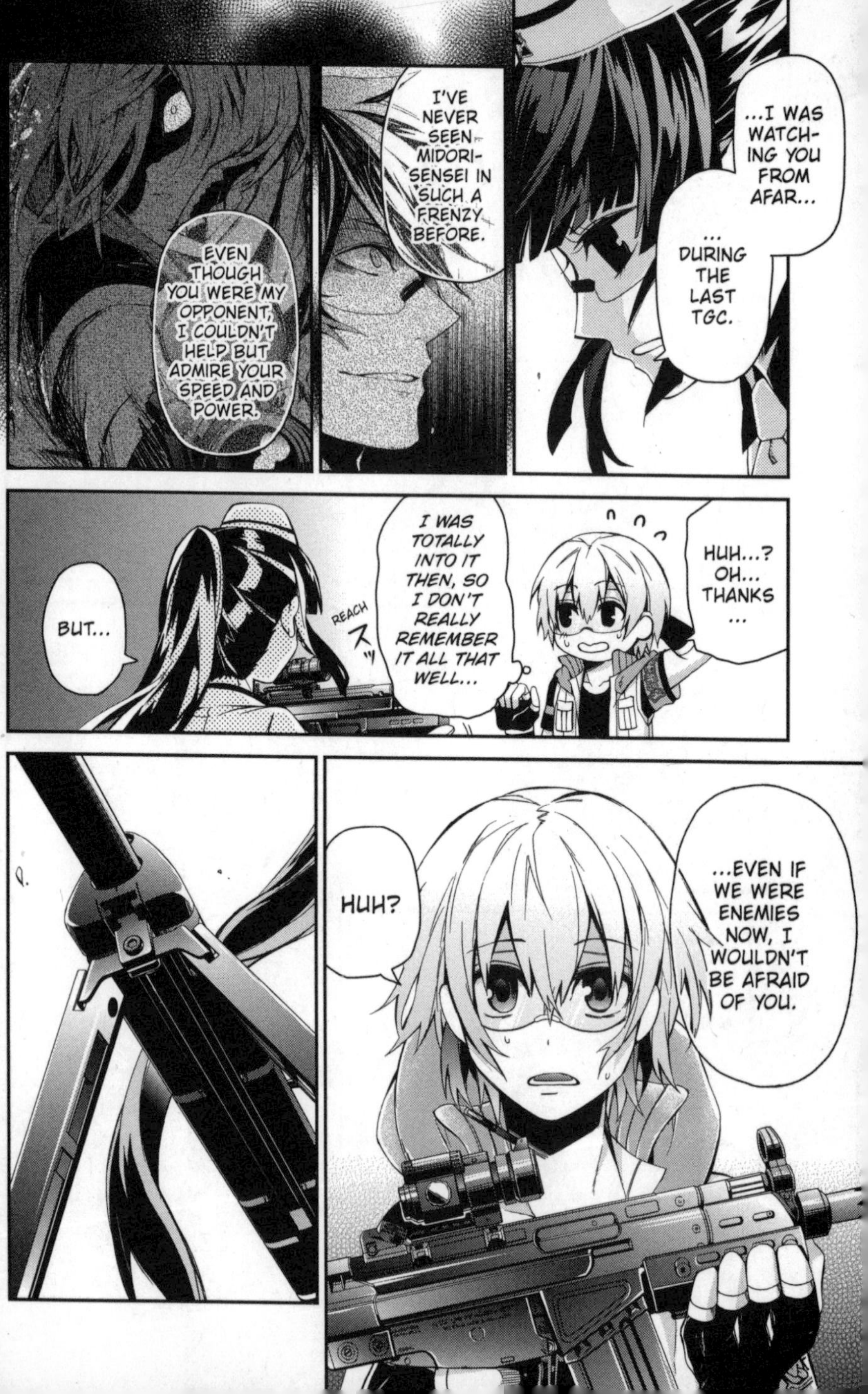
...I WAS WATCHING YOU FROM AFAR...
... DURING THE LAST TGC.
I'VE NEVER SEEN MIDORI-SENSEI IN SUCH A FRENZY BEFORE.
EVEN THOUGH YOU WERE MY OPPONENT, I COULDN'T HELP BUT ADMIRE YOUR SPEED AND POWER.
HUH...? OH... THANKS ...
I WAS TOTALLY INTO IT THEN, SO I DON'T REALLY REMEMBER IT ALL THAT WELL...
REACH
BUT...
...EVEN IF WE WERE ENEMIES NOW, I WOULDN'T BE AFRAID OF YOU.
HUH?

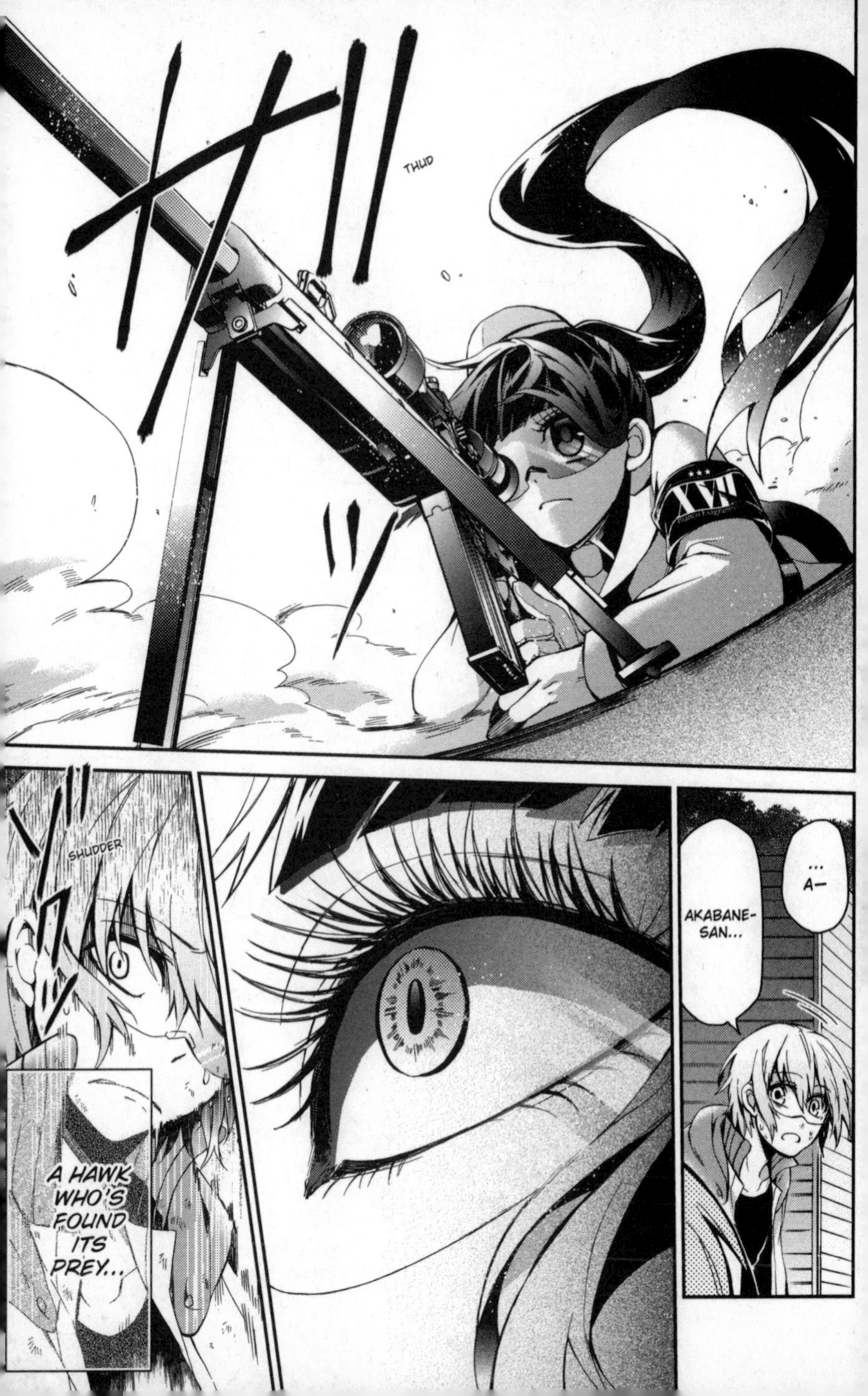
THUD
...A—
AKABANE-SAN...
SHUDDER
A HAWK WHO'S FOUND ITS PREY...

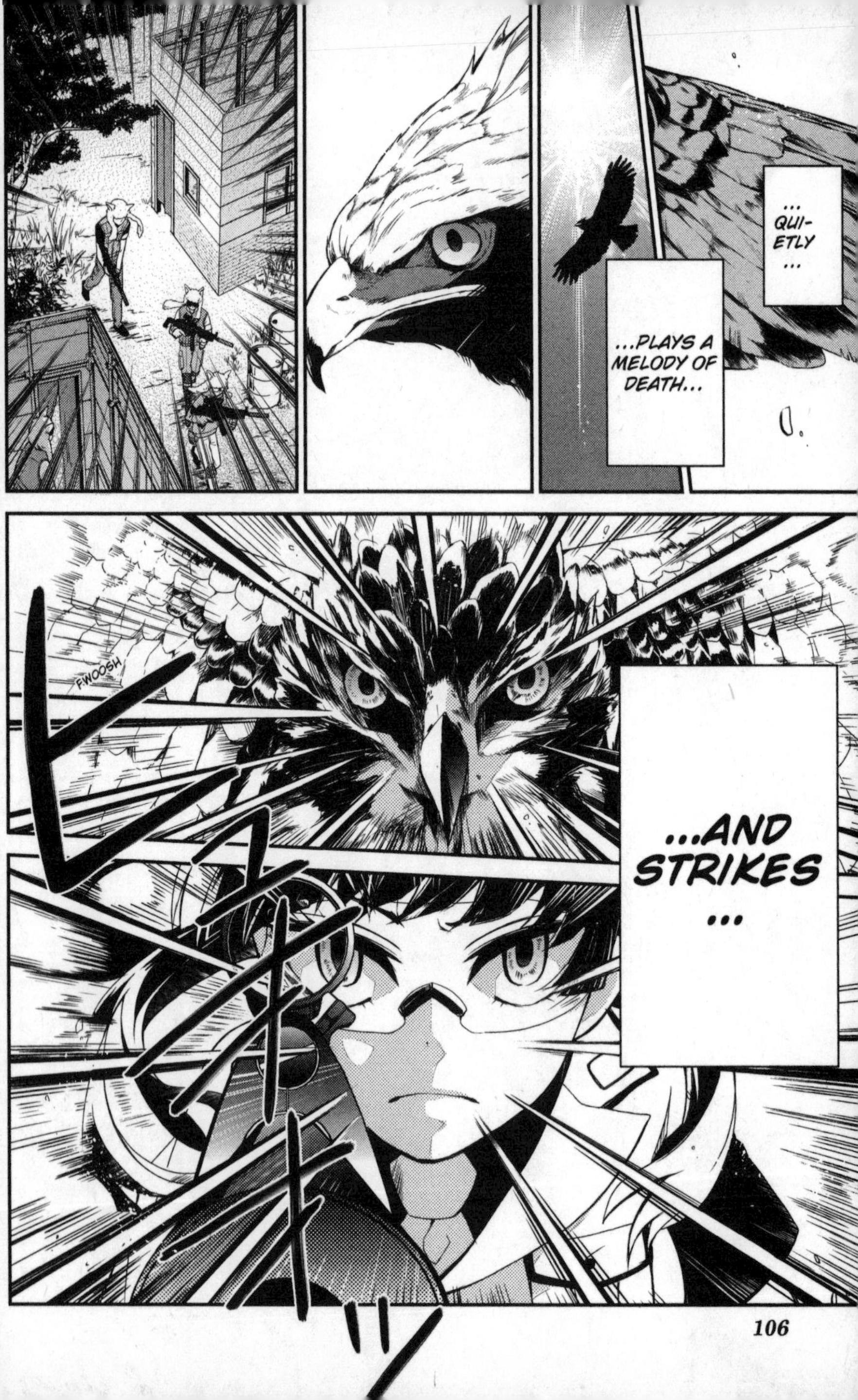
...QUI-ETLY...
...PLAYS A MELODY OF DEATH...
F-WOOSH
...AND STRIKES...

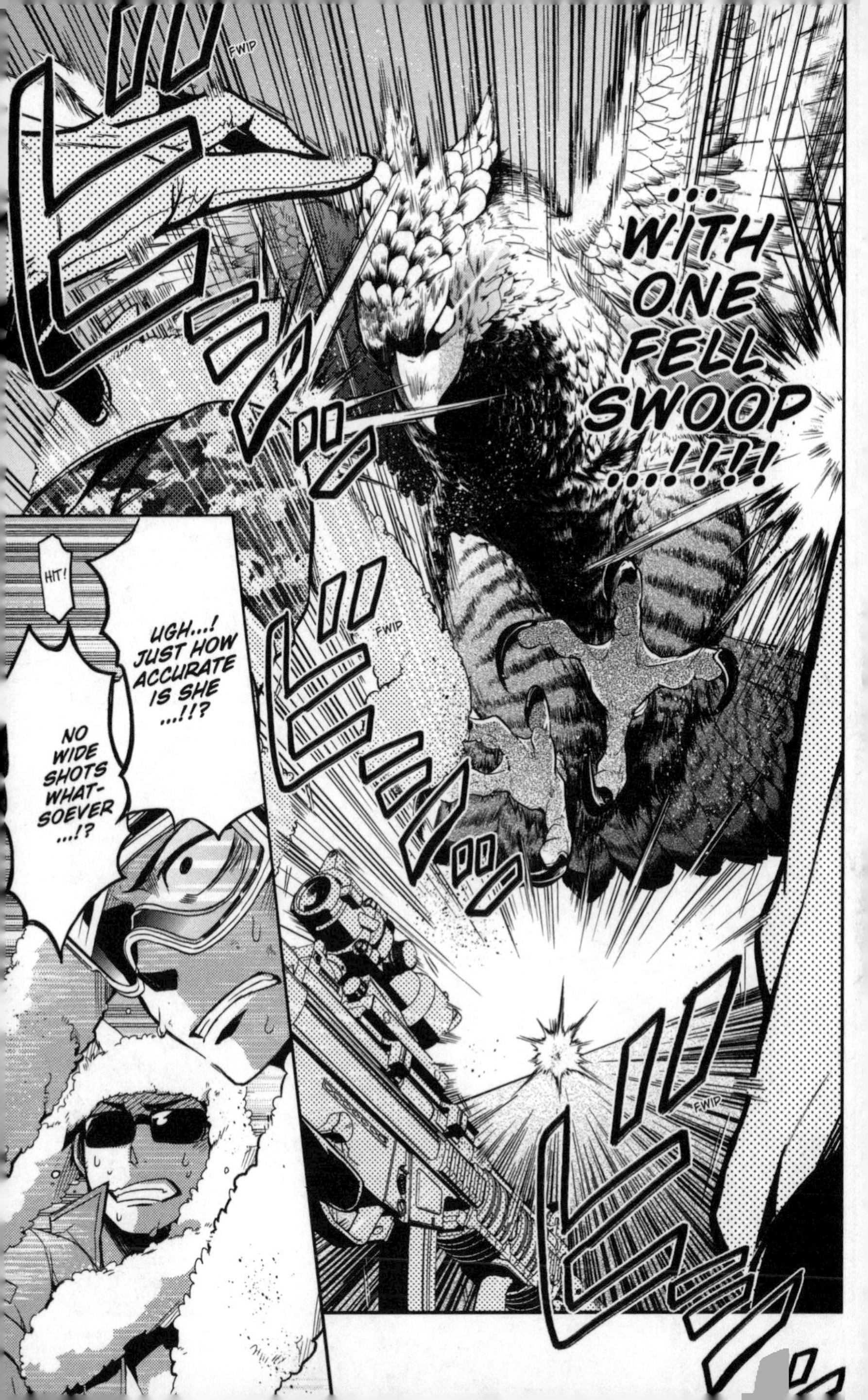
FWIP
...WITH ONE FELL SWOOP...!!!!
FWIP
FWIP
HIT!
UGH...! JUST HOW ACCURATE IS SHE ...!!?
NO WIDE SHOTS WHAT-SOEVER ...!?

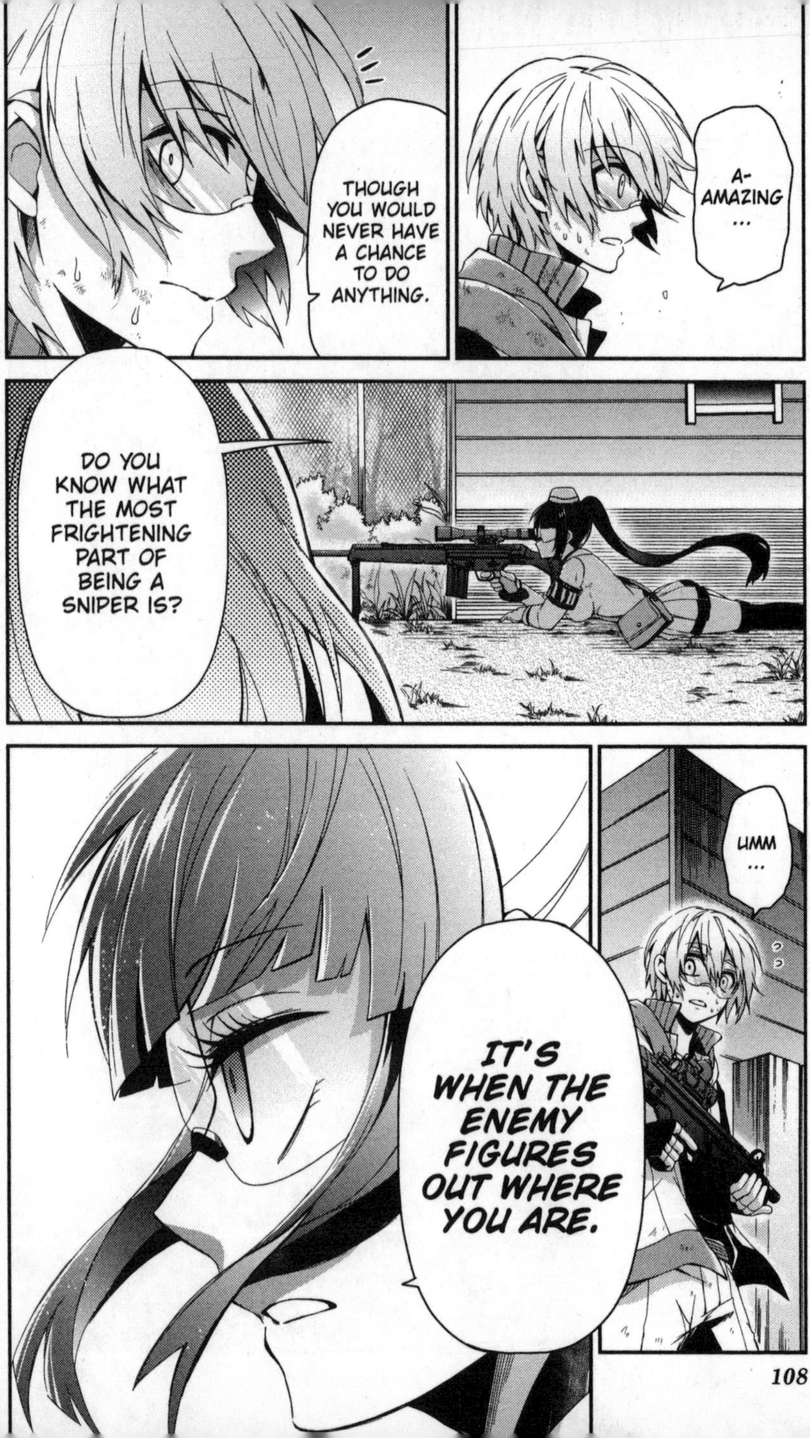
A- AMAZING ...
THOUGH YOU WOULD NEVER HAVE A CHANCE TO DO ANYTHING.
DO YOU KNOW WHAT THE MOST FRIGHTENING PART OF BEING A SNIPER IS?
UMM ...
IT'S WHEN THE ENEMY FIGURES OUT WHERE YOU ARE.

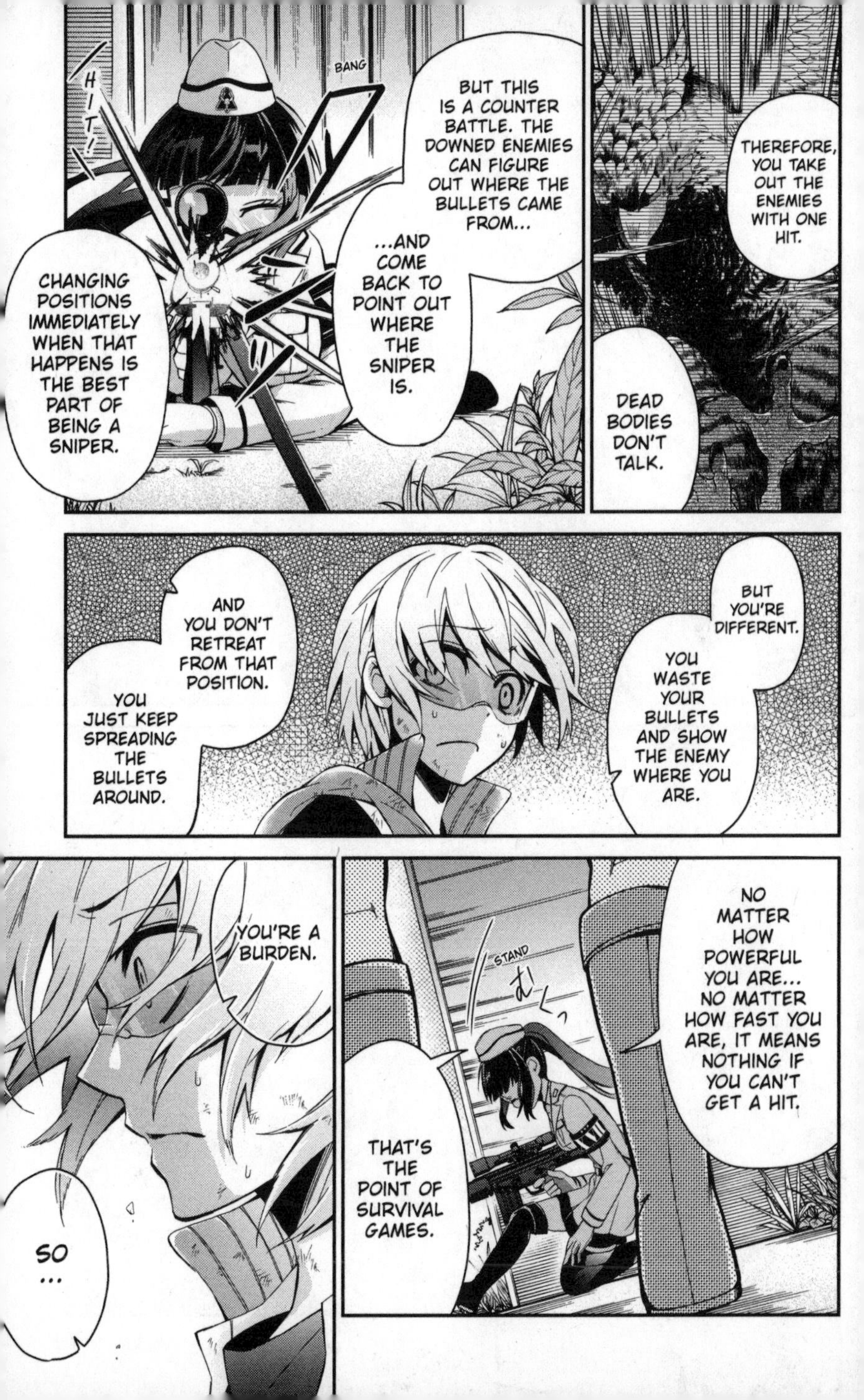
THEREFORE, YOU TAKE OUT THE ENEMIES WITH ONE HIT.
DEAD BODIES DON'T TALK.
BANG
HIT!
BUT THIS IS A COUNTER BATTLE. THE DOWNED ENEMIES CAN FIGURE OUT WHERE THE BULLETS CAME FROM...
...AND COME BACK TO POINT OUT WHERE THE SNIPER IS.
CHANGING POSITIONS IMMEDIATELY WHEN THAT HAPPENS IS THE BEST PART OF BEING A SNIPER.
BUT YOU'RE DIFFERENT.
YOU WASTE YOUR BULLETS AND SHOW THE ENEMY WHERE YOU ARE.
AND YOU DON'T RETREAT FROM THAT POSITION.
YOU JUST KEEP SPREADING THE BULLETS AROUND.
NO MATTER HOW POWERFUL YOU ARE... NO MATTER HOW FAST YOU ARE, IT MEANS NOTHING IF YOU CAN'T GET A HIT.
STAND
THAT'S THE POINT OF SURVIVAL GAMES.
YOU'RE A BURDEN.
SO ...

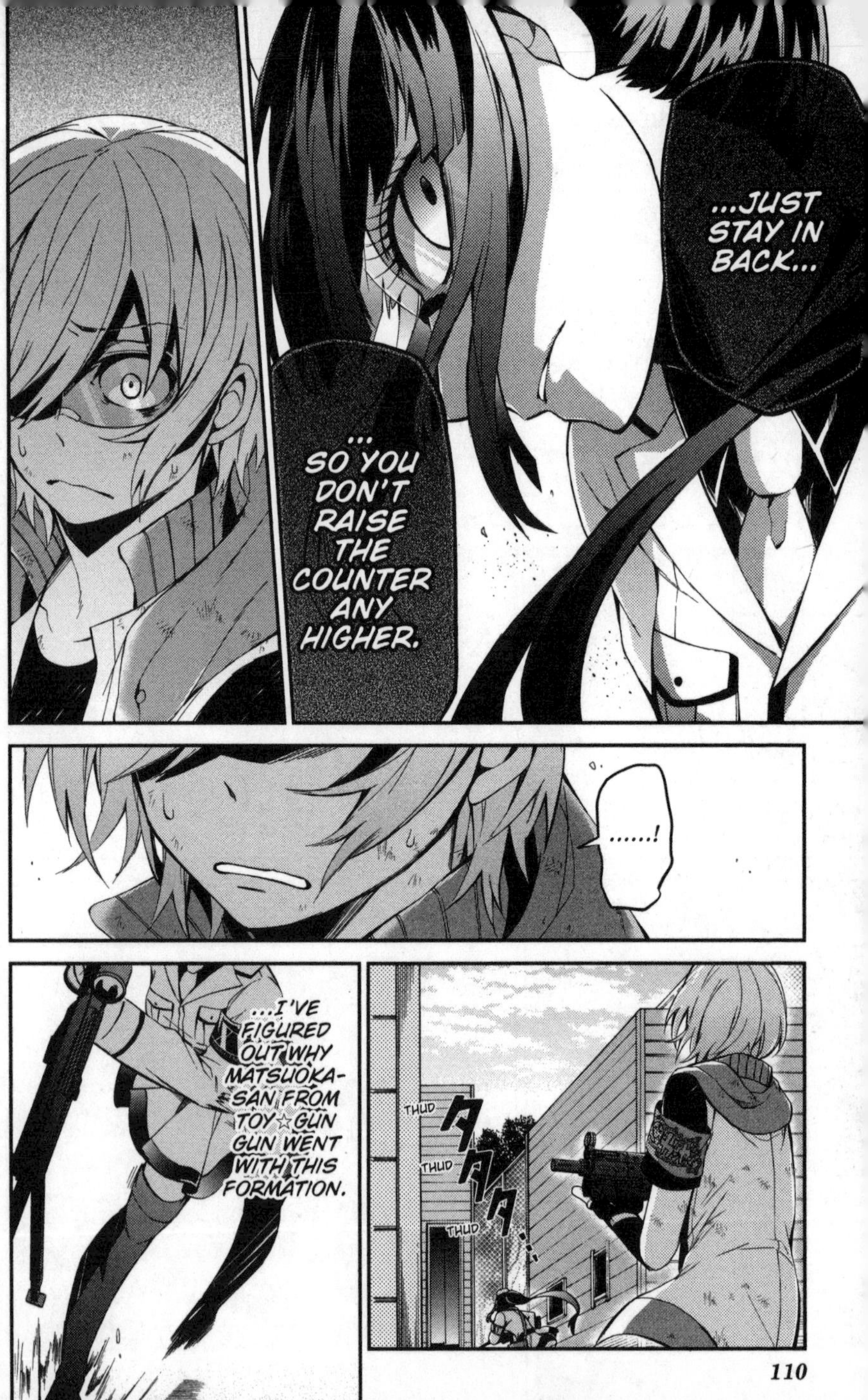
...JUST STAY IN BACK...
... SO YOU DON'T RAISE THE COUNTER ANY HIGHER.
......!
THUD
THUD
THUD
...I'VE FIGURED OUT WHY MATSUOKA-SAN FROM TOY☆GUN GUN WENT WITH THIS FORMATION.

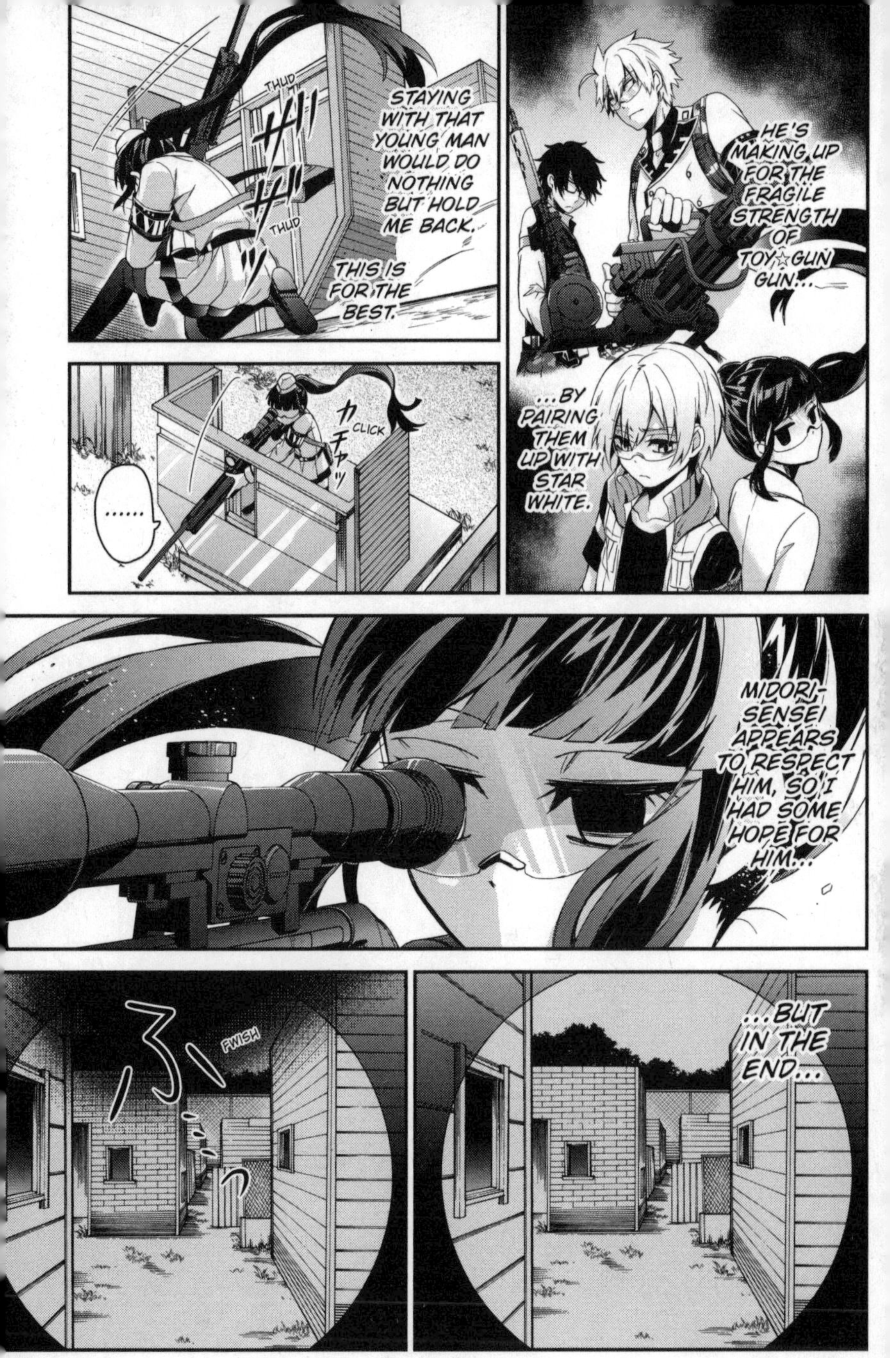
HE'S MAKING UP FOR THE FRAGILE STRENGTH OF TOY☆GUN GUN...
...BY PAIRING THEM UP WITH STAR WHITE.
STAYING WITH THAT YOUNG MAN WOULD DO NOTHING BUT HOLD ME BACK.
THIS IS FOR THE BEST.
THUD
THUD
CLICK
カチャッ
......
MIDORI-SENSEI APPEARS TO RESPECT HIM, SO I HAD SOME HOPE FOR HIM...
...BUT IN THE END...
FWISH

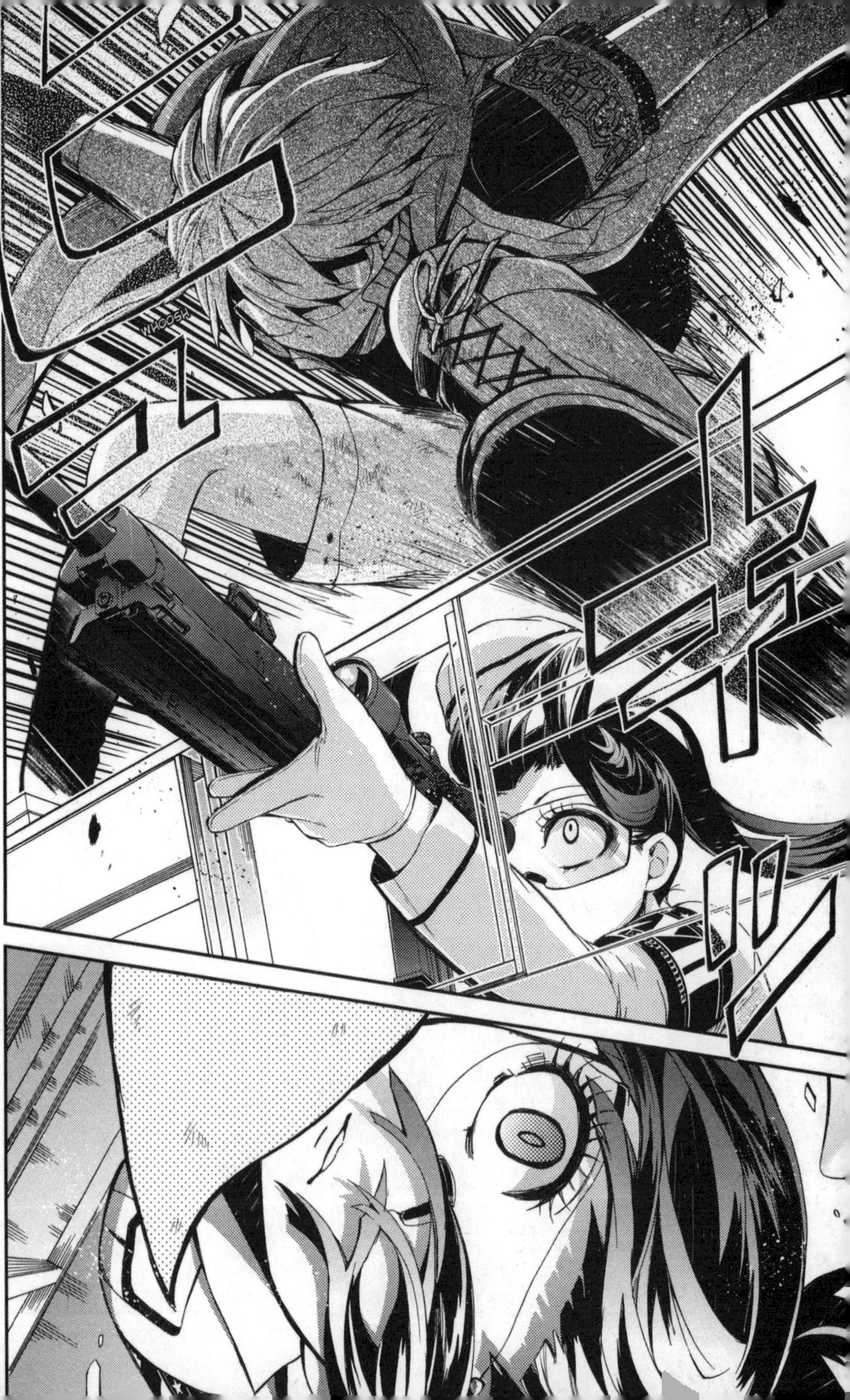
WHOOSH

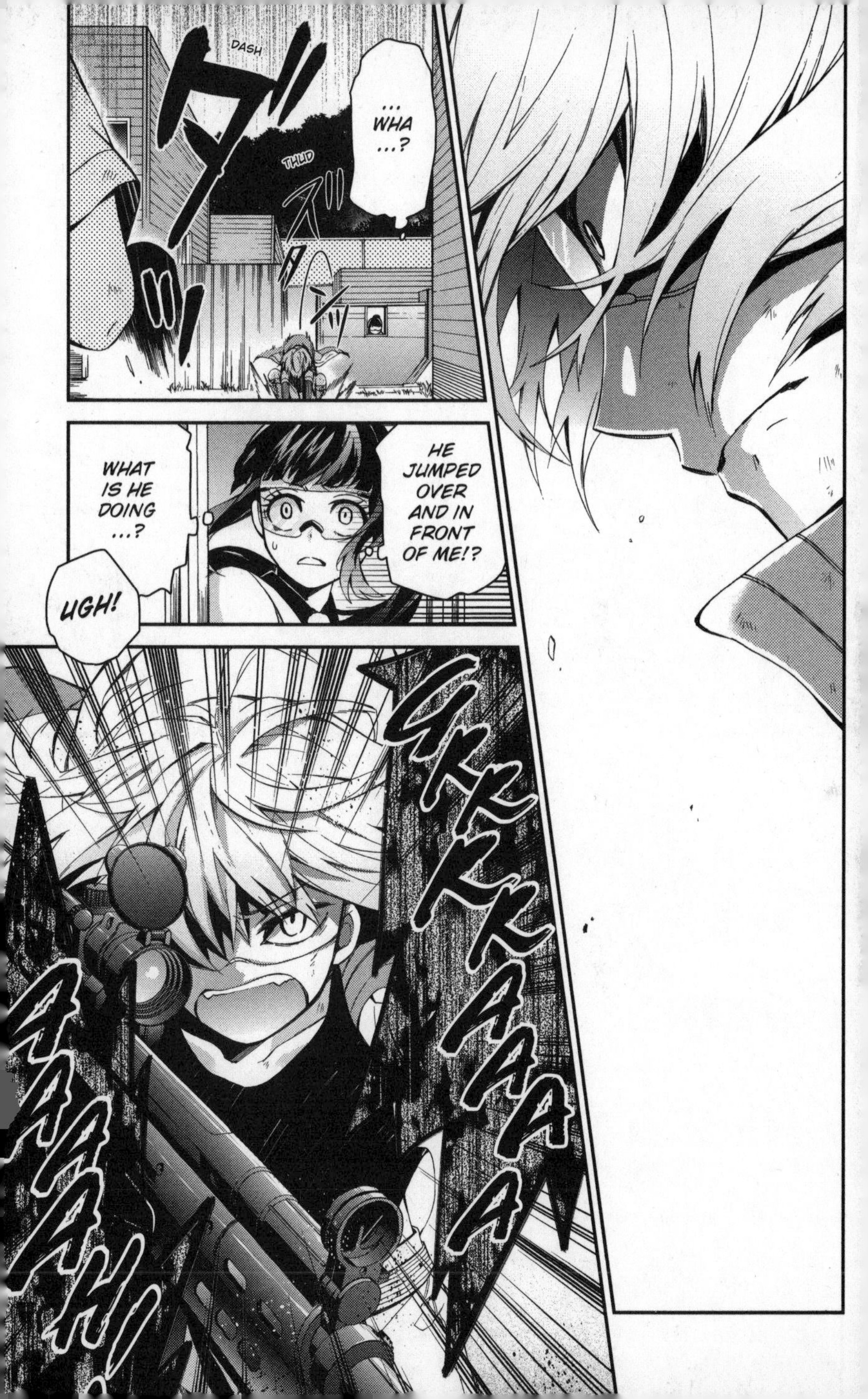
DASH
...WHA...?
THUD
HE JUMPED OVER AND IN FRONT OF ME!?
WHAT IS HE DOING...?
UGH!
URRRKAAAAAAA
AAAAAH!!

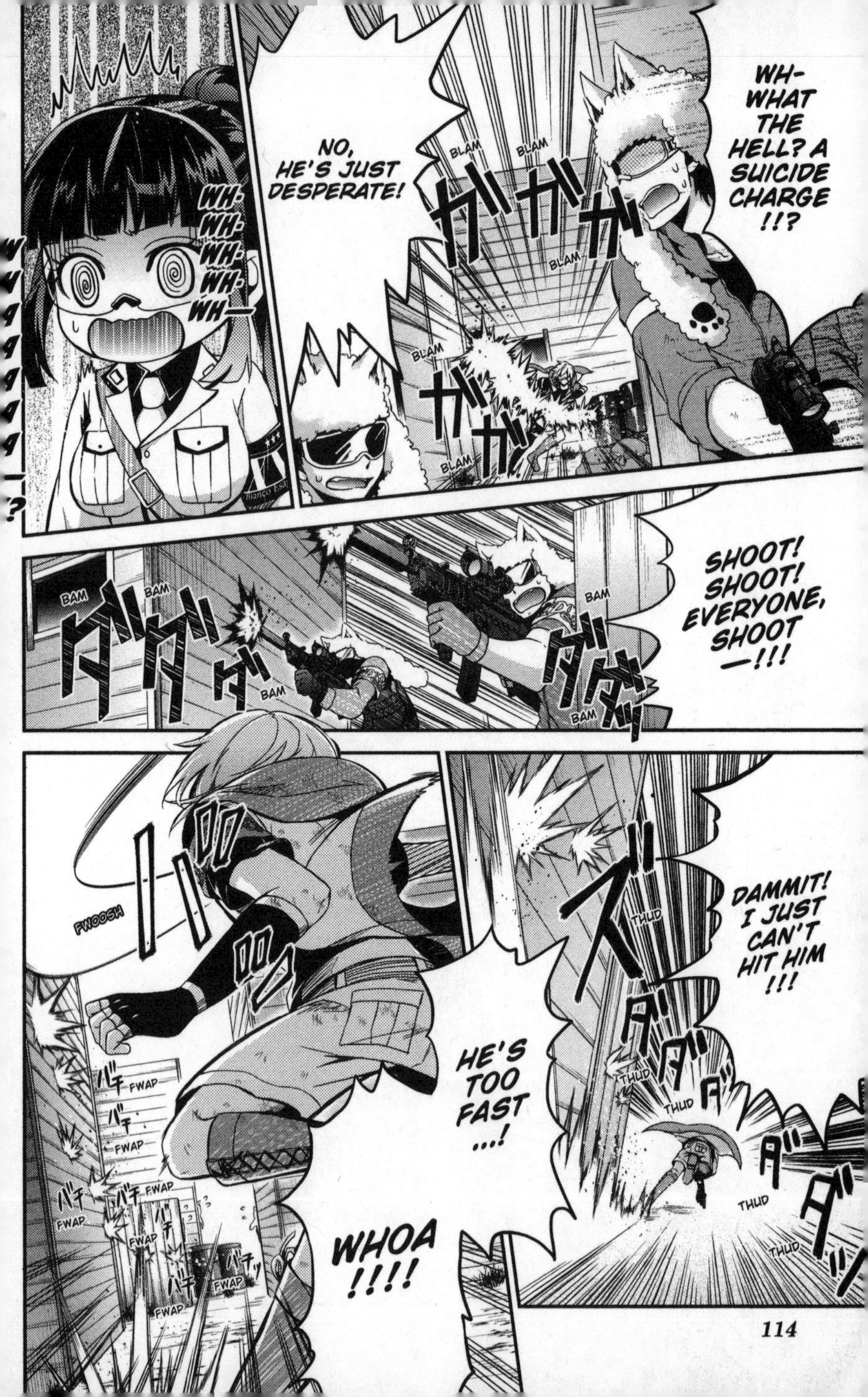
WH-WHAT THE HELL? A SUICIDE CHARGE!!?
BLAM
BLAM
BLAM
BLAM
BLAM
NO, HE'S JUST DESPERATE!
WH-WH-WH-WH-WH—
SHOOT! SHOOT! EVERYONE, SHOOT—!!!
BAM
BAM
BAM
BAM
BAM
DAMMIT! I JUST CAN'T HIT HIM!!!
THUD
THUD
THUD
THUD
THUD
HE'S TOO FAST...!
WHOA!!!!
FWOOSH
FWAP
FWAP
FWAP
FWAP
FWAP
FWAP
FWAP

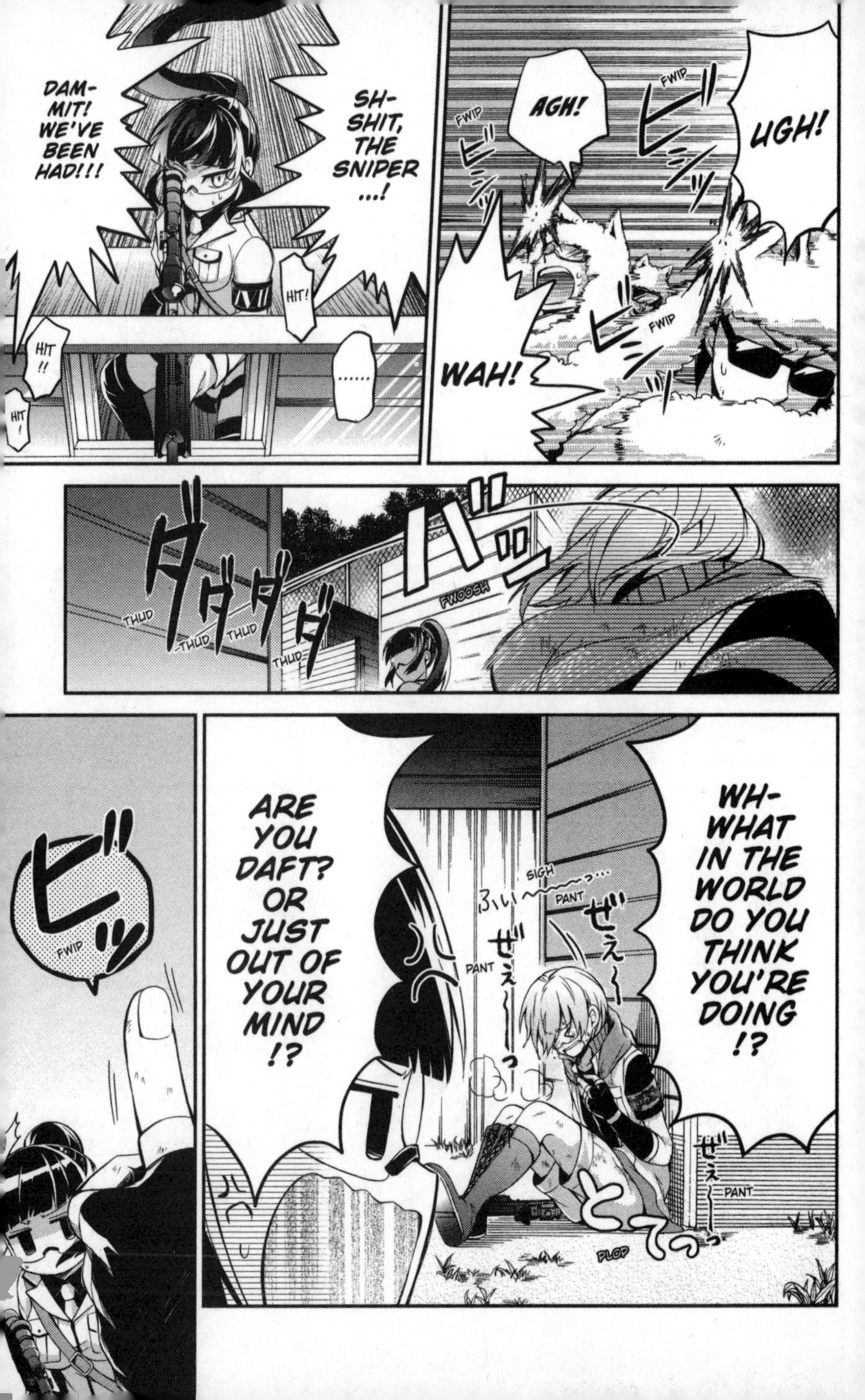
UGH!
FWIP
AGH!
FWIP
FWIP
WAH!
SH-SHIT, THE SNIPER ...!
DAM-MIT! WE'VE BEEN HAD!!!
HIT!
......
HIT !!
HIT !
FWOOSH
THUD
THUD
THUD
THUD
WH-WHAT IN THE WORLD DO YOU THINK YOU'RE DOING !?
SIGH
PANT
ARE YOU DAFT? OR JUST OUT OF YOUR MIND !?
PANT
PANT
PLOP
FWIP

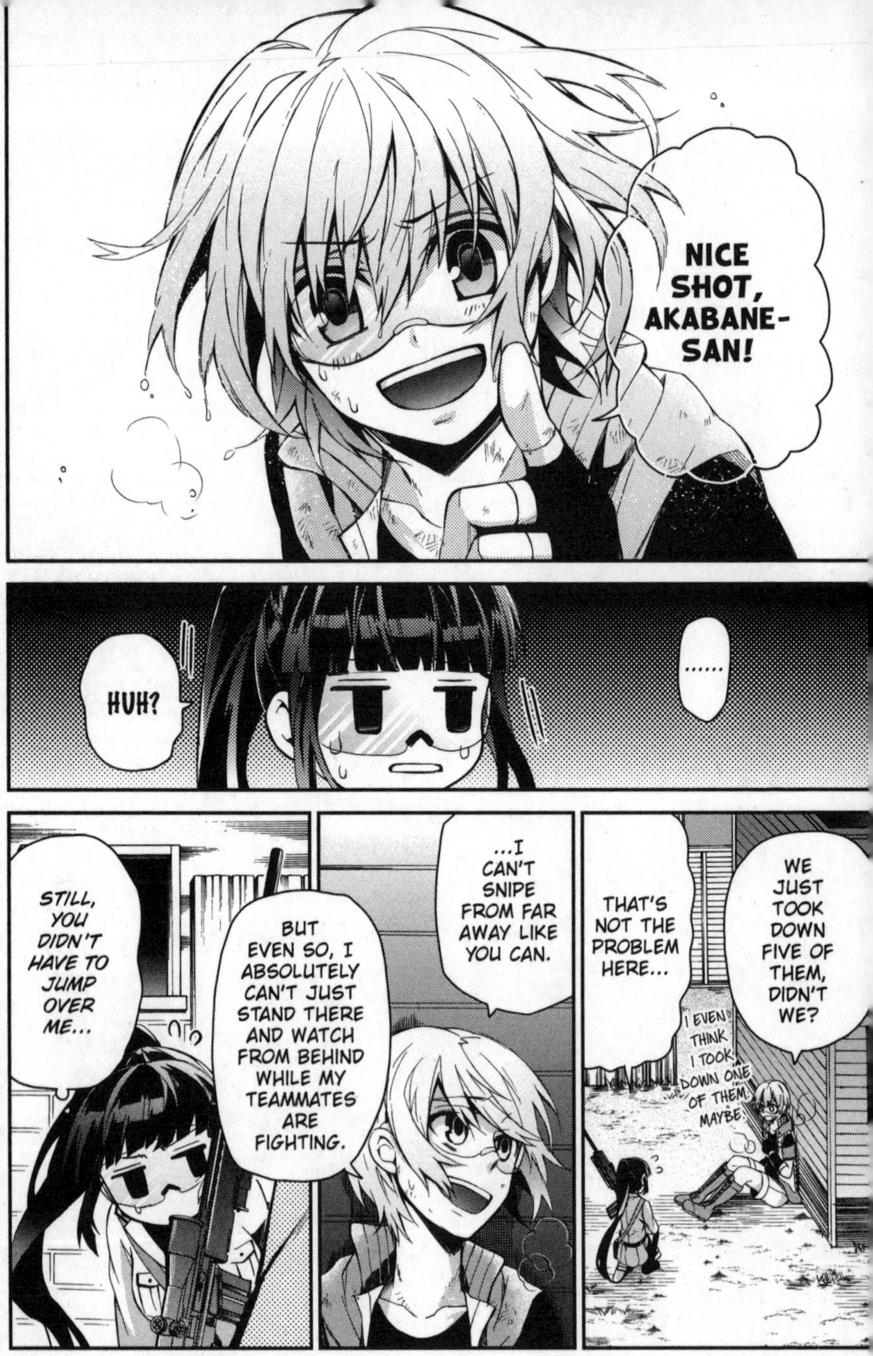
NICE SHOT, AKABANE-SAN!
......
HUH?
WE JUST TOOK DOWN FIVE OF THEM, DIDN'T WE?
I EVEN THINK I TOOK DOWN ONE OF THEM, MAYBE.
THAT'S NOT THE PROBLEM HERE...
...I CAN'T SNIPE FROM FAR AWAY LIKE YOU CAN.
BUT EVEN SO, I ABSOLUTELY CAN'T JUST STAND THERE AND WATCH FROM BEHIND WHILE MY TEAMMATES ARE FIGHTING.
STILL, YOU DIDN'T HAVE TO JUMP OVER ME...

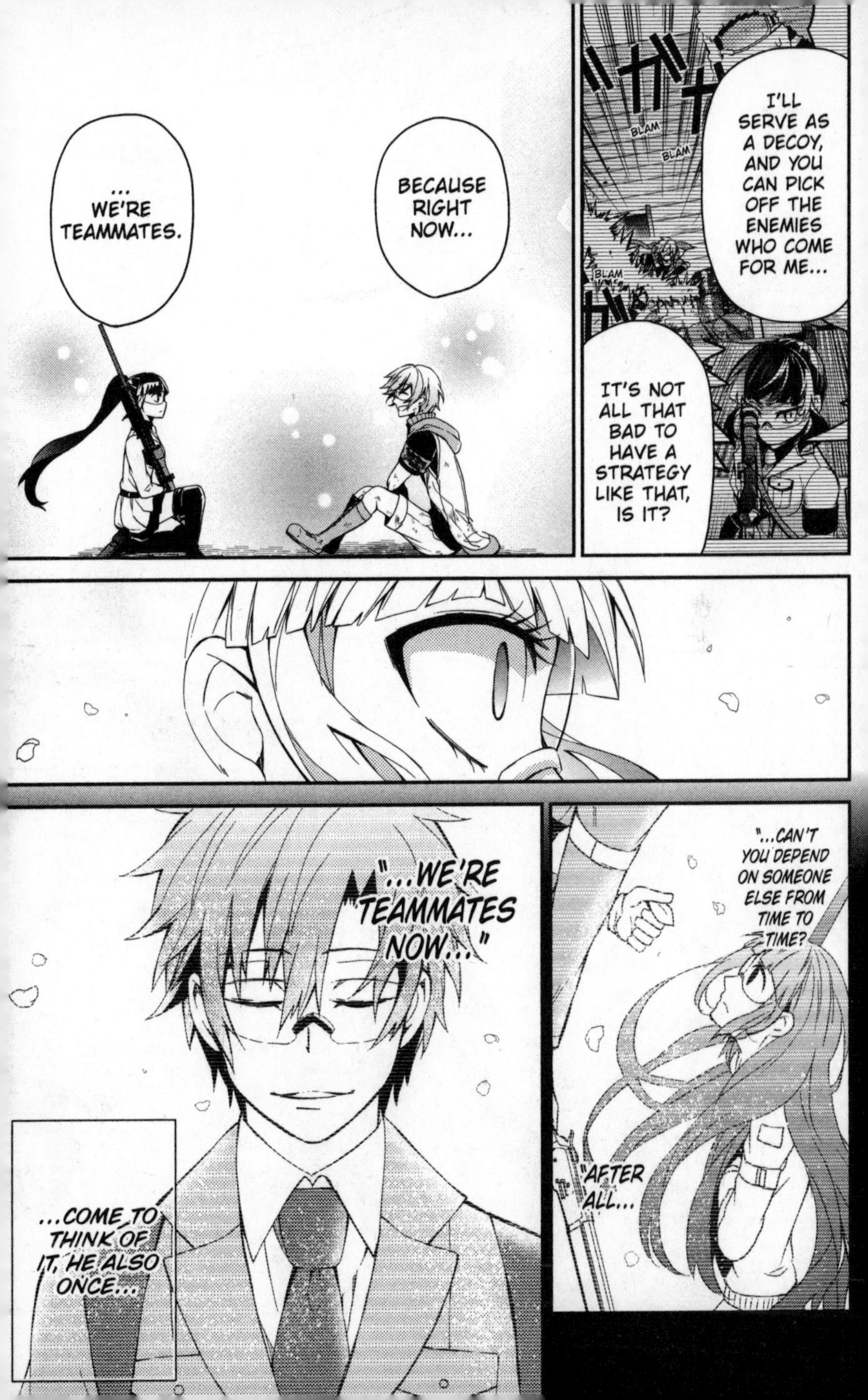
I'LL SERVE AS A DECOY, AND YOU CAN PICK OFF THE ENEMIES WHO COME FOR ME...
BLAM
BLAM
BLAM
IT'S NOT ALL THAT BAD TO HAVE A STRATEGY LIKE THAT, IS IT?
BECAUSE RIGHT NOW...
... WE'RE TEAMMATES.
"...CAN'T YOU DEPEND ON SOMEONE ELSE FROM TIME TO TIME?
"AFTER ALL...
"...WE'RE TEAMMATES NOW..."
...COME TO THINK OF IT, HE ALSO ONCE...

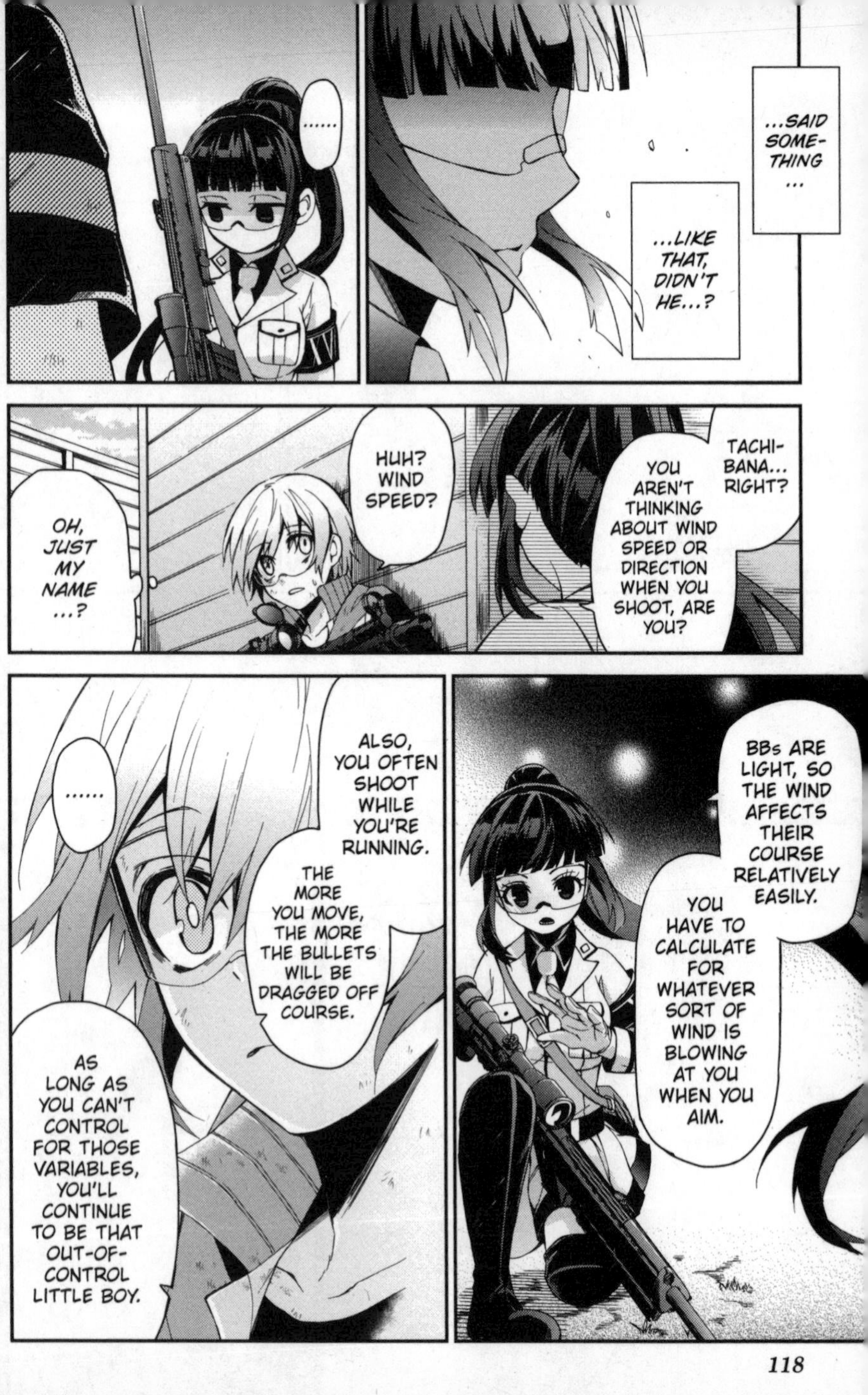
...SAID SOMETHING...
...LIKE THAT, DIDN'T HE...?
......
TACHIBANA... RIGHT?
YOU AREN'T THINKING ABOUT WIND SPEED OR DIRECTION WHEN YOU SHOOT, ARE YOU?
HUH? WIND SPEED?
OH, JUST MY NAME...?
BBs ARE LIGHT, SO THE WIND AFFECTS THEIR COURSE RELATIVELY EASILY.
YOU HAVE TO CALCULATE FOR WHATEVER SORT OF WIND IS BLOWING AT YOU WHEN YOU AIM.
ALSO, YOU OFTEN SHOOT WHILE YOU'RE RUNNING.
THE MORE YOU MOVE, THE MORE THE BULLETS WILL BE DRAGGED OFF COURSE.
......
AS LONG AS YOU CAN'T CONTROL FOR THOSE VARIABLES, YOU'LL CONTINUE TO BE THAT OUT-OF-CONTROL LITTLE BOY.

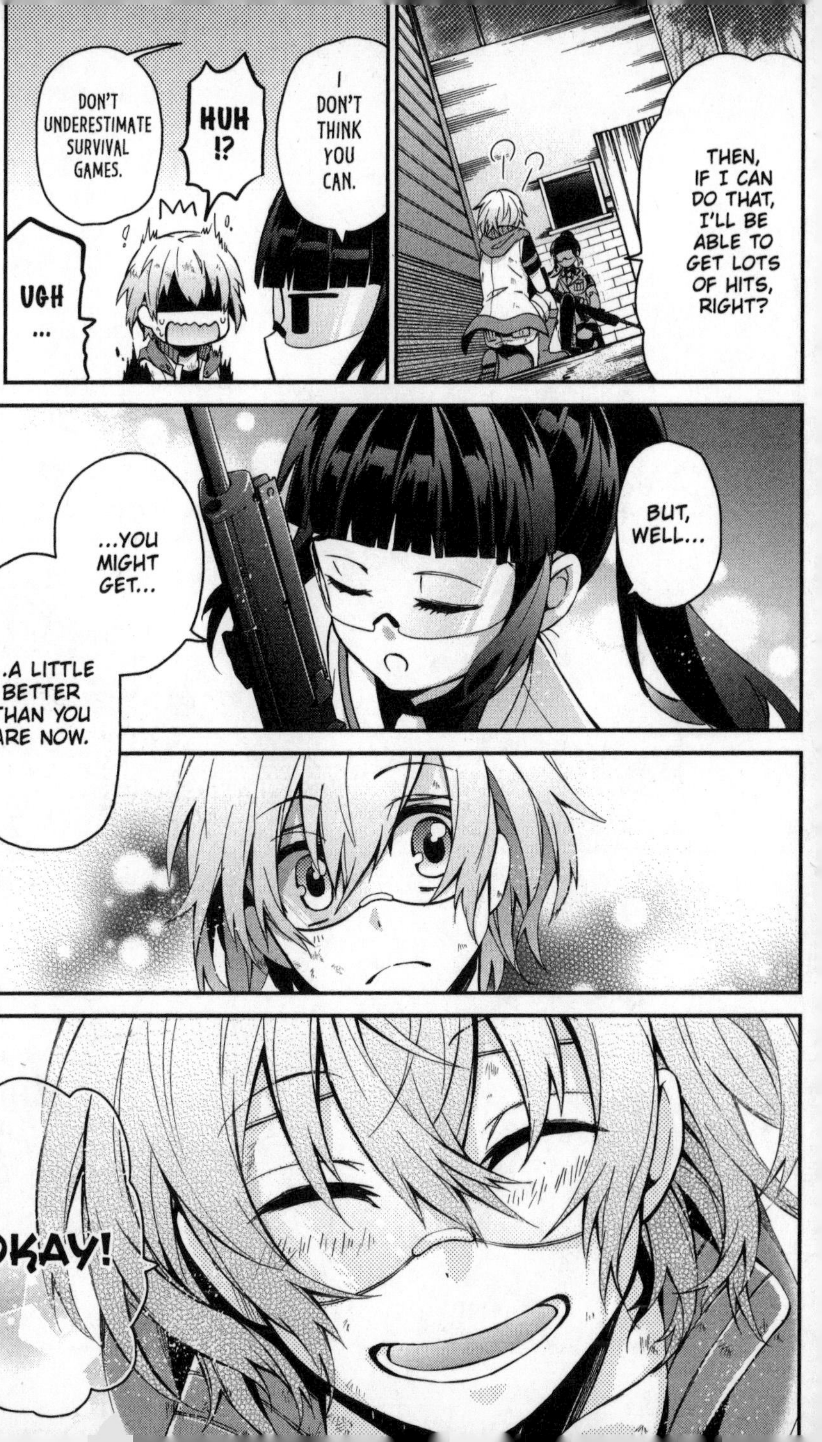
THEN, IF I CAN DO THAT, I'LL BE ABLE TO GET LOTS OF HITS, RIGHT?
I DON'T THINK YOU CAN.
HUH!?
DON'T UNDERESTIMATE SURVIVAL GAMES.
UGH...
BUT, WELL...
...YOU MIGHT GET...
...A LITTLE BETTER THAN YOU ARE NOW.
OKAY!

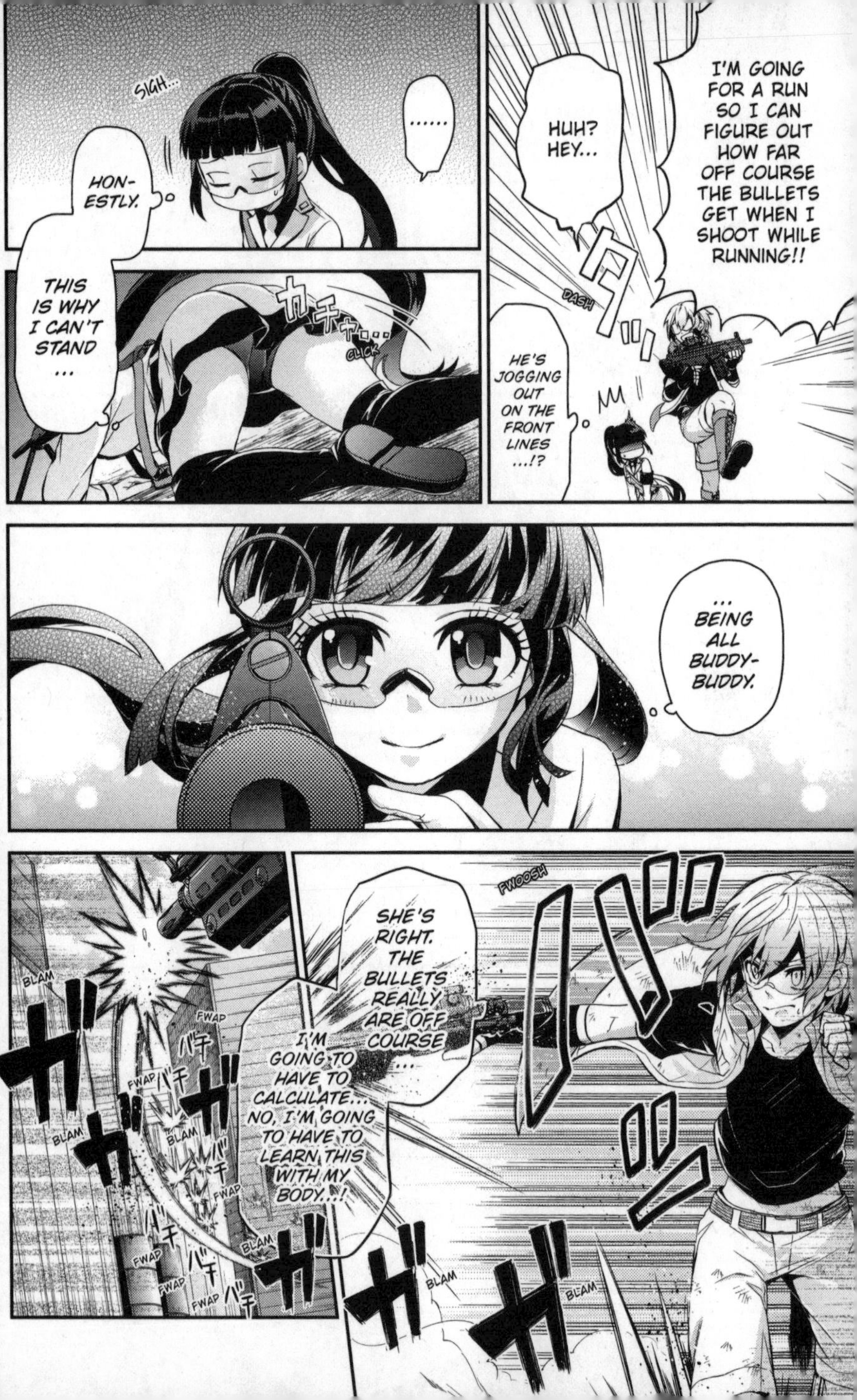
I'M GOING FOR A RUN SO I CAN FIGURE OUT HOW FAR OFF COURSE THE BULLETS GET WHEN I SHOOT WHILE RUNNING!!
HUH? HEY...
DASH
HE'S JOGGING OUT ON THE FRONT LINES ...!?
......
SIGH...
HON-ESTLY.
THIS IS WHY I CAN'T STAND ...
CLICK
... BEING ALL BUDDY-BUDDY.
FWOOSH
SHE'S RIGHT. THE BULLETS REALLY ARE OFF COURSE ...
I'M GOING TO HAVE TO CALCULATE... NO, I'M GOING TO HAVE TO LEARN THIS WITH MY BODY...!
BLAM
BLAM
BLAM
FWAP
FWAP
BLAM
BLAM
FWAP
FWAP
FWAP
FWAP

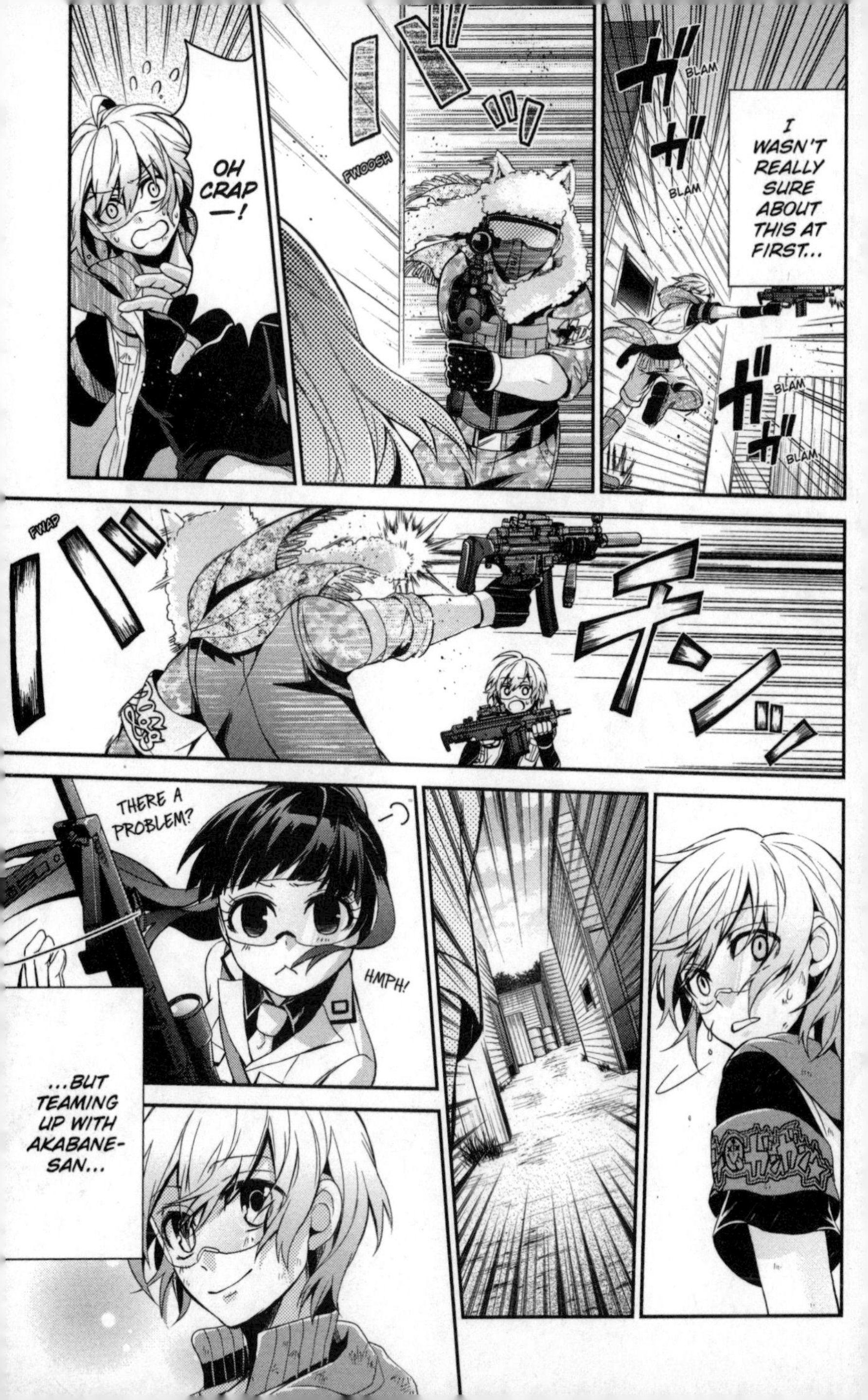
I WASN'T REALLY SURE ABOUT THIS AT FIRST...
BLAM
BLAM
BLAM
BLAM
FWOOSH
OH CRAP—!
FWAP
THERE A PROBLEM?
HMPH!
...BUT TEAMING UP WITH AKABANE-SAN...

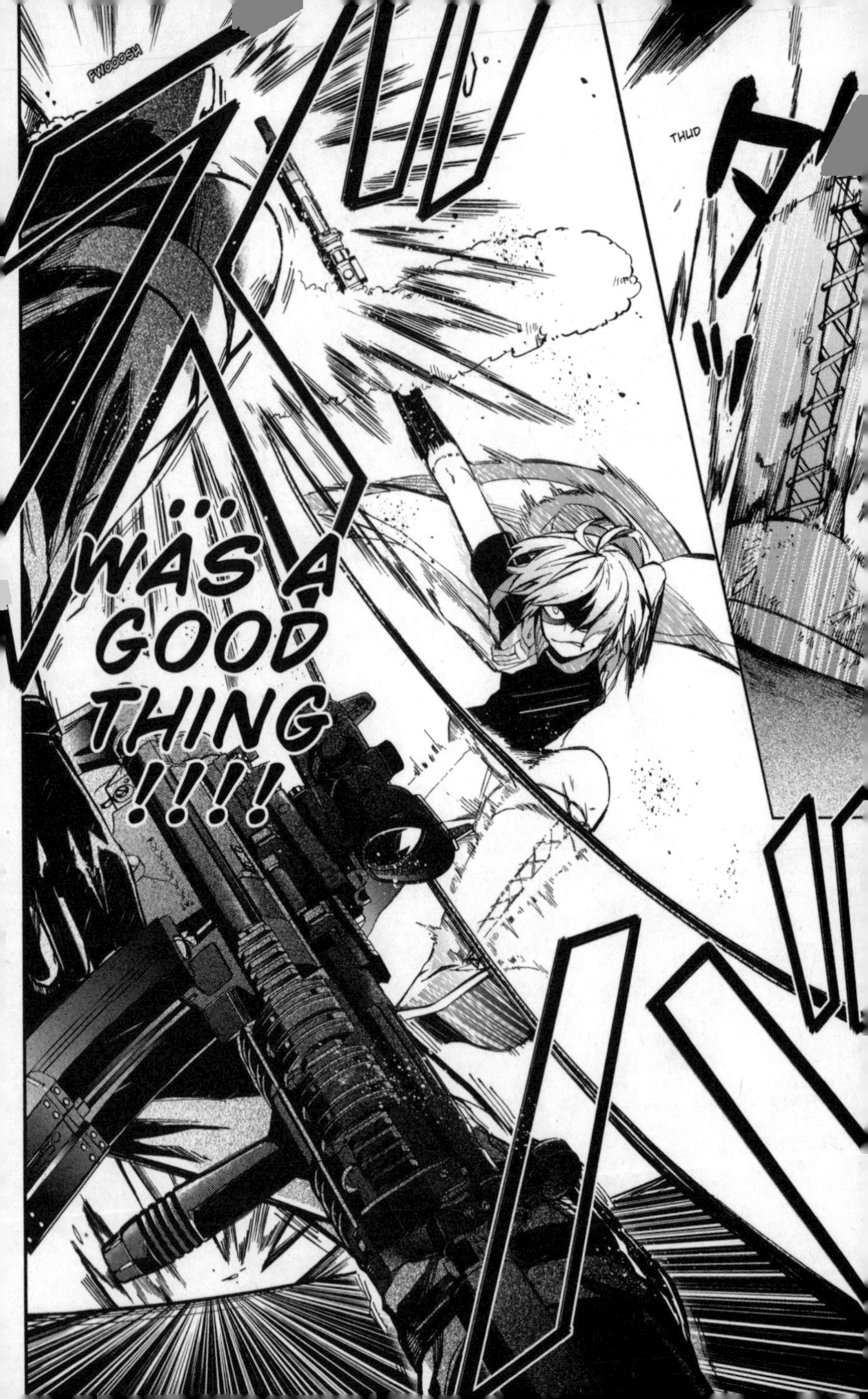
THUD
FWOOOSH
...WAS A GOOD THING!!!!

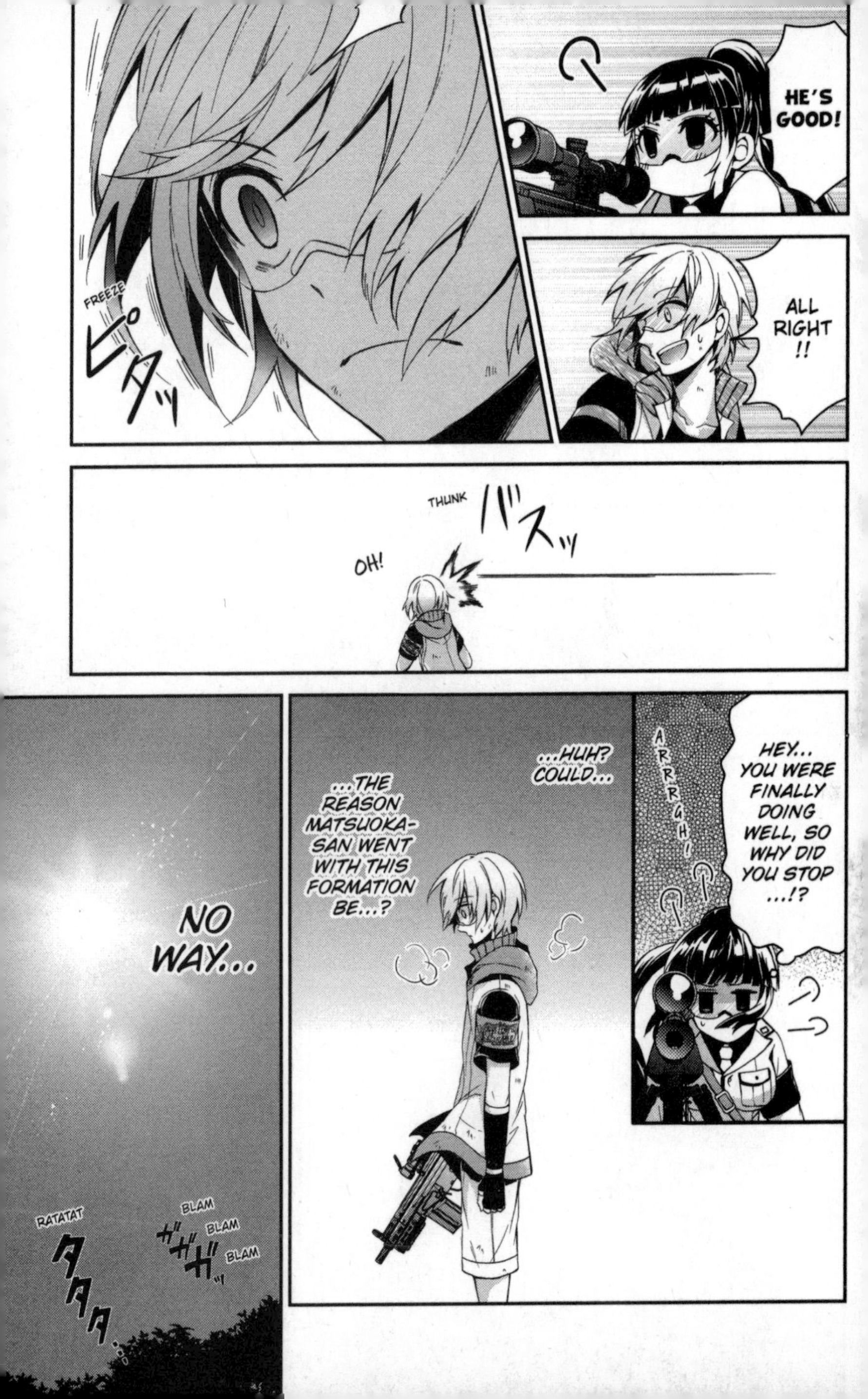
HE'S GOOD!
ALL RIGHT !!
FREEZE
ピタッ
THUNK
バスッ
OH!
ARRRGH!
HEY... YOU WERE FINALLY DOING WELL, SO WHY DID YOU STOP ...!?
...HUH? COULD...
...THE REASON MATSUOKA-SAN WENT WITH THIS FORMATION BE...?
NO WAY...
BLAM
BLAM
BLAM
ガガガッ
RATATAT
タタタ...

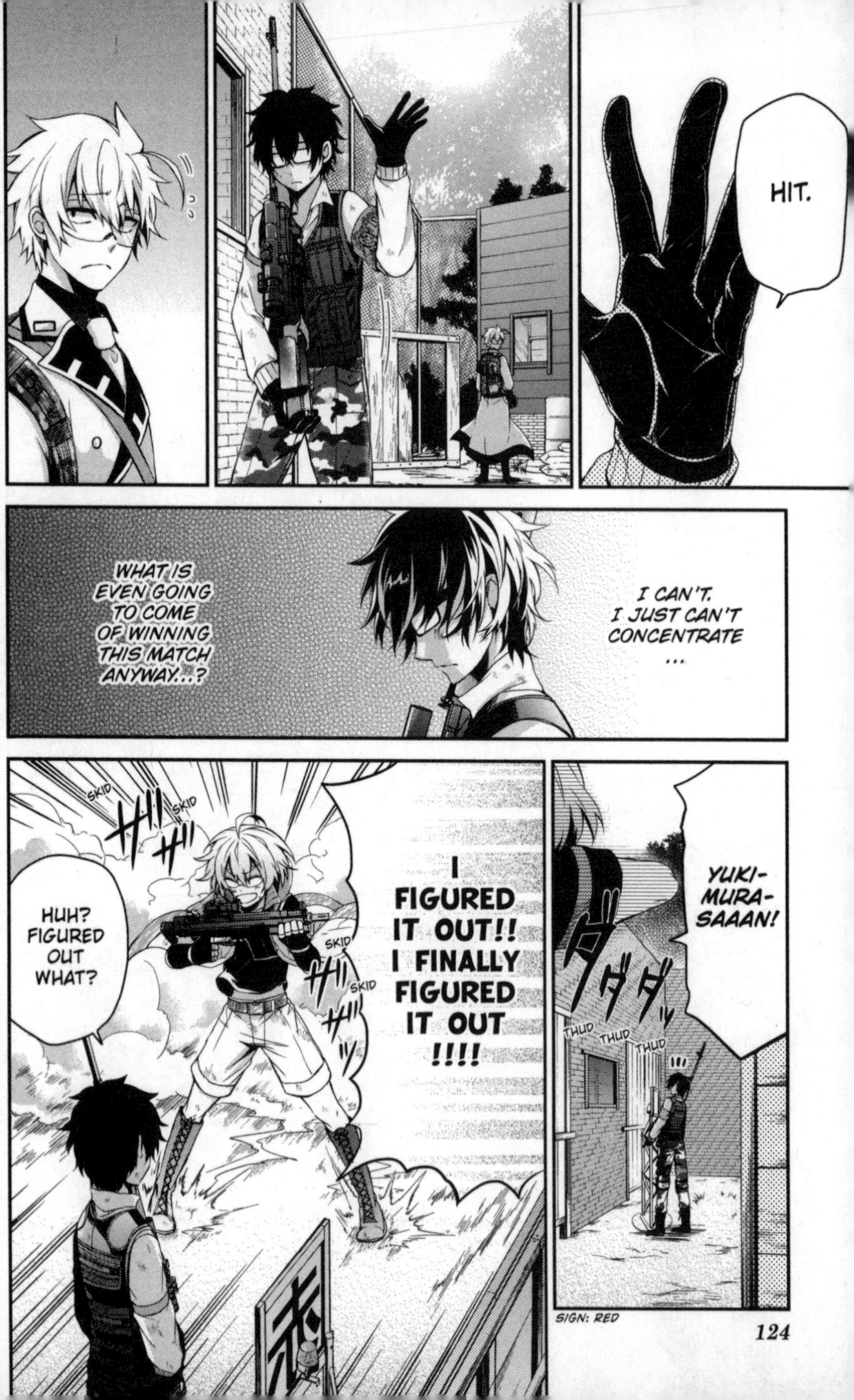
HIT.
I CAN'T. I JUST CAN'T CONCENTRATE ...
WHAT IS EVEN GOING TO COME OF WINNING THIS MATCH ANYWAY...?
YUKI-MURA-SAAAN!
THUD THUD THUD
I FIGURED IT OUT!! I FINALLY FIGURED IT OUT !!!!
SKID SKID
SKID SKID
HUH? FIGURED OUT WHAT?

SIGN: RED

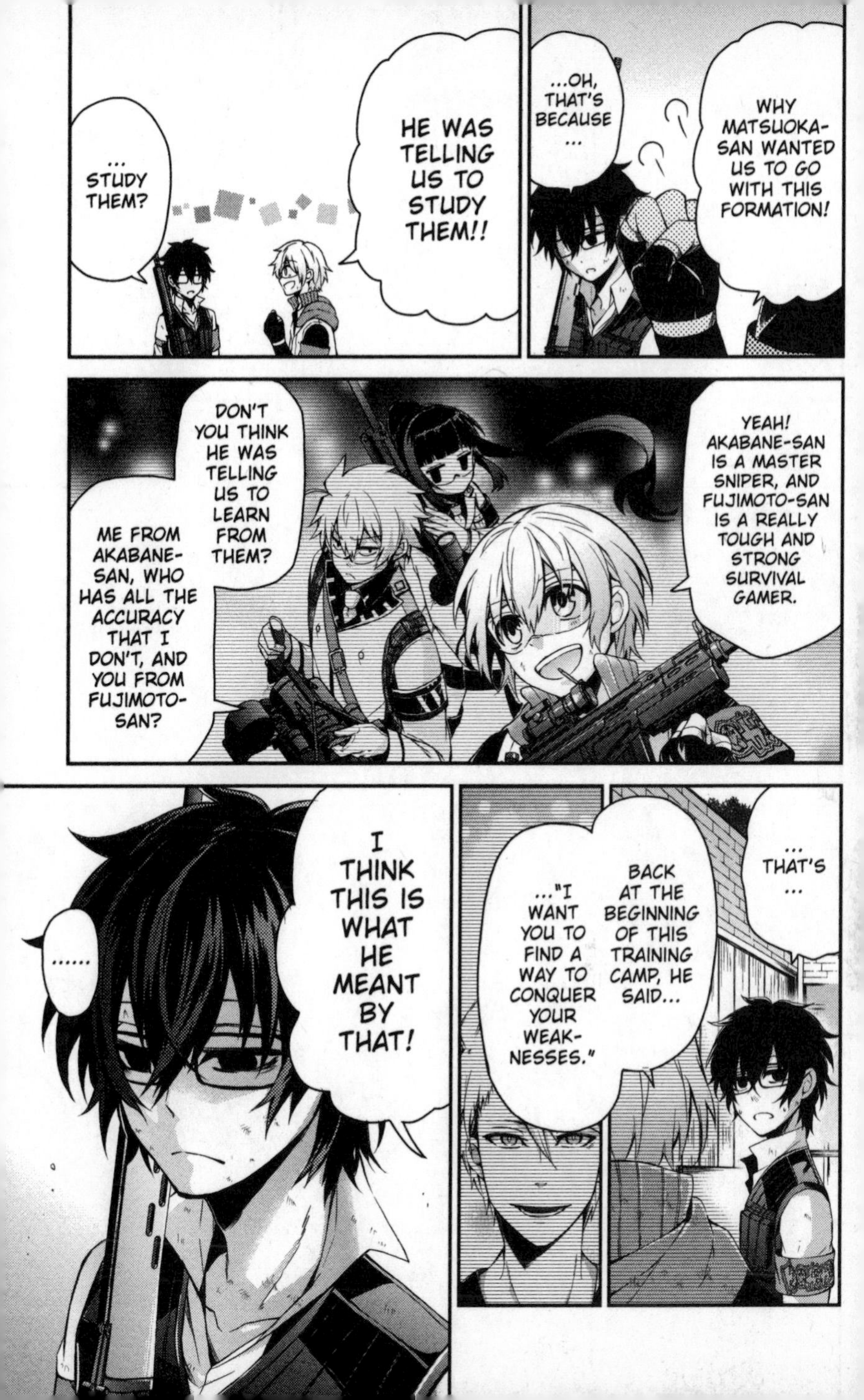
WHY MATSUOKA-SAN WANTED US TO GO WITH THIS FORMATION!
...OH, THAT'S BECAUSE ...
HE WAS TELLING US TO STUDY THEM!!
... STUDY THEM?
YEAH! AKABANE-SAN IS A MASTER SNIPER, AND FUJIMOTO-SAN IS A REALLY TOUGH AND STRONG SURVIVAL GAMER.
DON'T YOU THINK HE WAS TELLING US TO LEARN FROM THEM?
ME FROM AKABANE-SAN, WHO HAS ALL THE ACCURACY THAT I DON'T, AND YOU FROM FUJIMOTO-SAN?
... THAT'S ...
BACK AT THE BEGINNING OF THIS TRAINING CAMP, HE SAID...
..."I WANT YOU TO FIND A WAY TO CONQUER YOUR WEAK-NESSES."
I THINK THIS IS WHAT HE MEANT BY THAT!
......

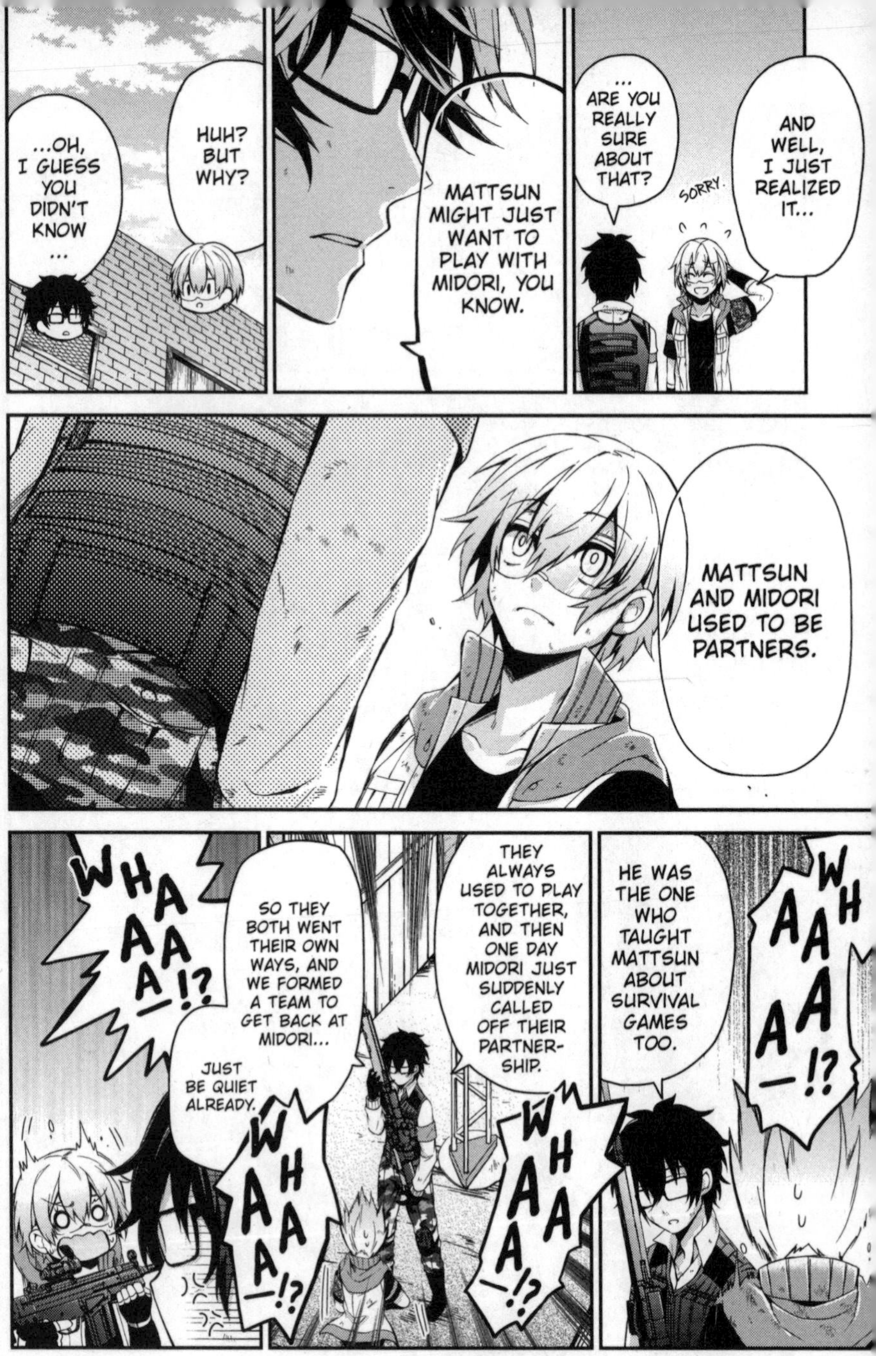
AND WELL, I JUST REALIZED IT...
... ARE YOU REALLY SURE ABOUT THAT?
SORRY.
MATTSUN MIGHT JUST WANT TO PLAY WITH MIDORI, YOU KNOW.
HUH? BUT WHY?
...OH, I GUESS YOU DIDN'T KNOW ...
MATTSUN AND MIDORI USED TO BE PARTNERS.
WHAAAA—!?
HE WAS THE ONE WHO TAUGHT MATTSUN ABOUT SURVIVAL GAMES TOO.
WHAAAA—!?
THEY ALWAYS USED TO PLAY TOGETHER, AND THEN ONE DAY MIDORI JUST SUDDENLY CALLED OFF THEIR PARTNER-SHIP.
SO THEY BOTH WENT THEIR OWN WAYS, AND WE FORMED A TEAM TO GET BACK AT MIDORI...
WHAAAA—!?
JUST BE QUIET ALREADY.
WHAAAA—!?

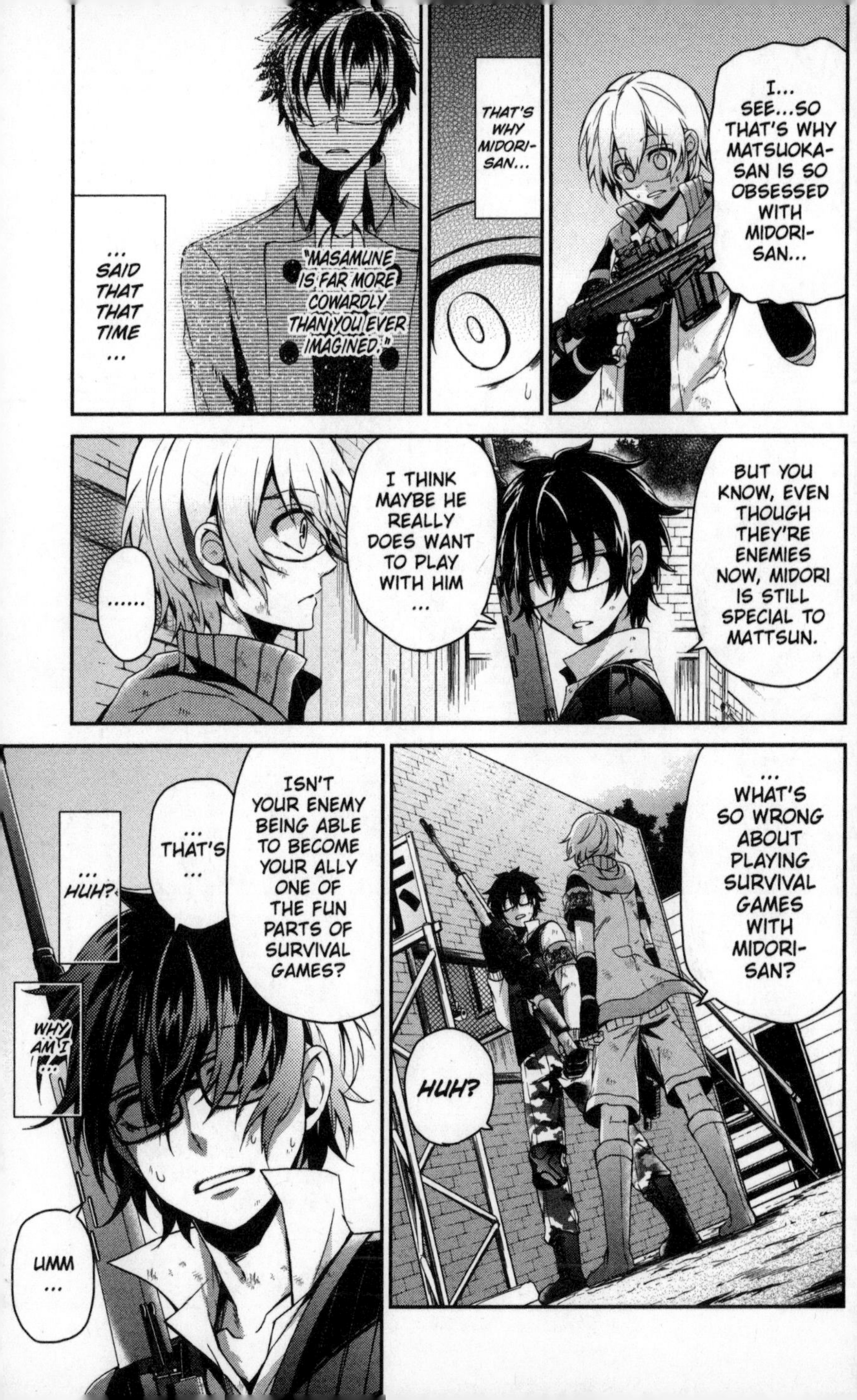
I... SEE...SO THAT'S WHY MATSUOKA-SAN IS SO OBSESSED WITH MIDORI-SAN...
THAT'S WHY MIDORI-SAN...
"MASAMUNE IS FAR MORE COWARDLY THAN YOU EVER IMAGINED."
...SAID THAT THAT TIME...
BUT YOU KNOW, EVEN THOUGH THEY'RE ENEMIES NOW, MIDORI IS STILL SPECIAL TO MATTSUN.
I THINK MAYBE HE REALLY DOES WANT TO PLAY WITH HIM...
......
...WHAT'S SO WRONG ABOUT PLAYING SURVIVAL GAMES WITH MIDORI-SAN?
HUH?
ISN'T YOUR ENEMY BEING ABLE TO BECOME YOUR ALLY ONE OF THE FUN PARTS OF SURVIVAL GAMES?
...THAT'S...
...HUH?
WHY AM I...
UMM...

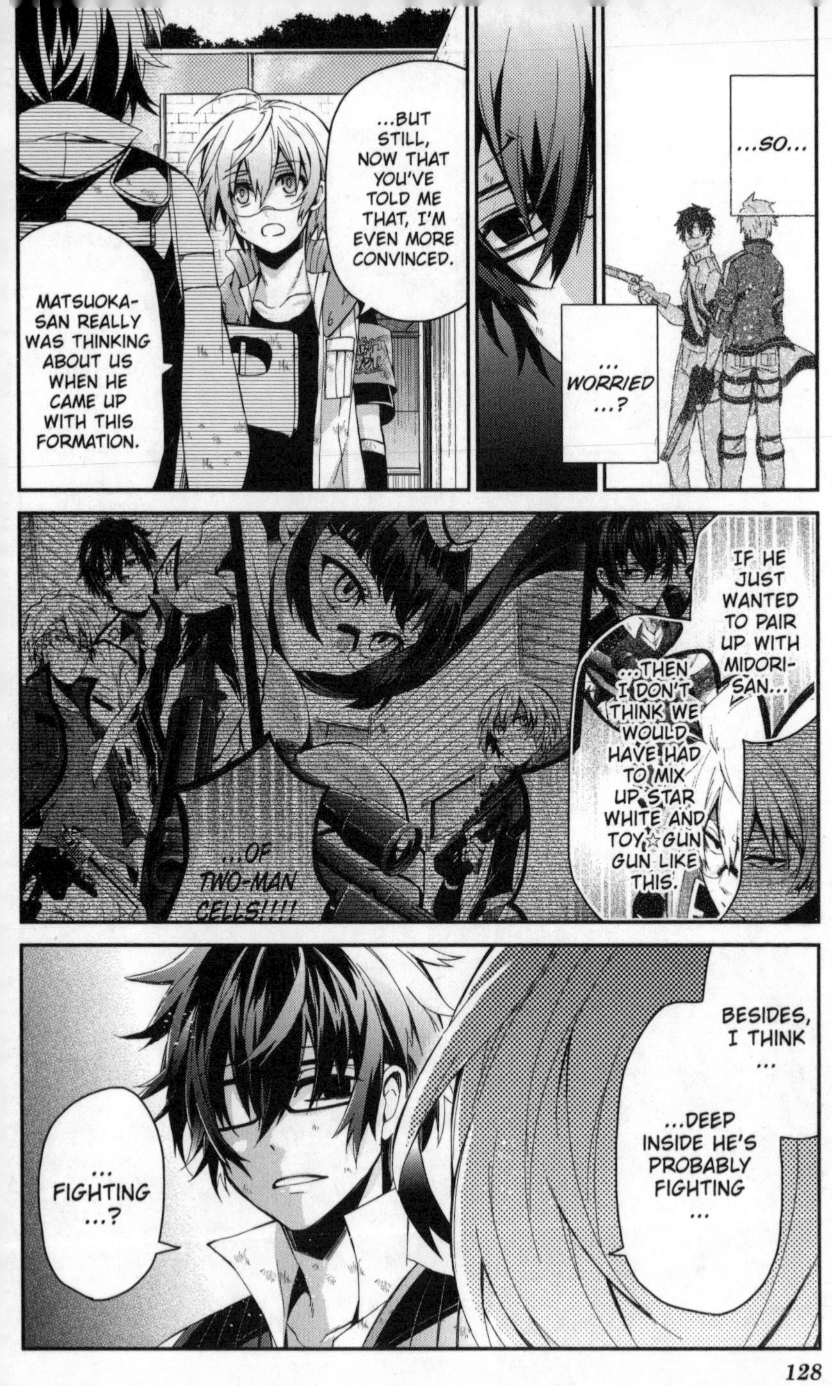
...SO...
...WORRIED...?
...BUT STILL, NOW THAT YOU'VE TOLD ME THAT, I'M EVEN MORE CONVINCED.
MATSUOKA-SAN REALLY WAS THINKING ABOUT US WHEN HE CAME UP WITH THIS FORMATION.
IF HE JUST WANTED TO PAIR UP WITH MIDORI-SAN...
...THEN I DON'T THINK WE WOULD HAVE HAD TO MIX UP STAR WHITE AND TOY☆GUN GUN LIKE THIS.
...OF TWO-MAN CELLS!!!!
BESIDES, I THINK...
...DEEP INSIDE HE'S PROBABLY FIGHTING...
...FIGHTING...?

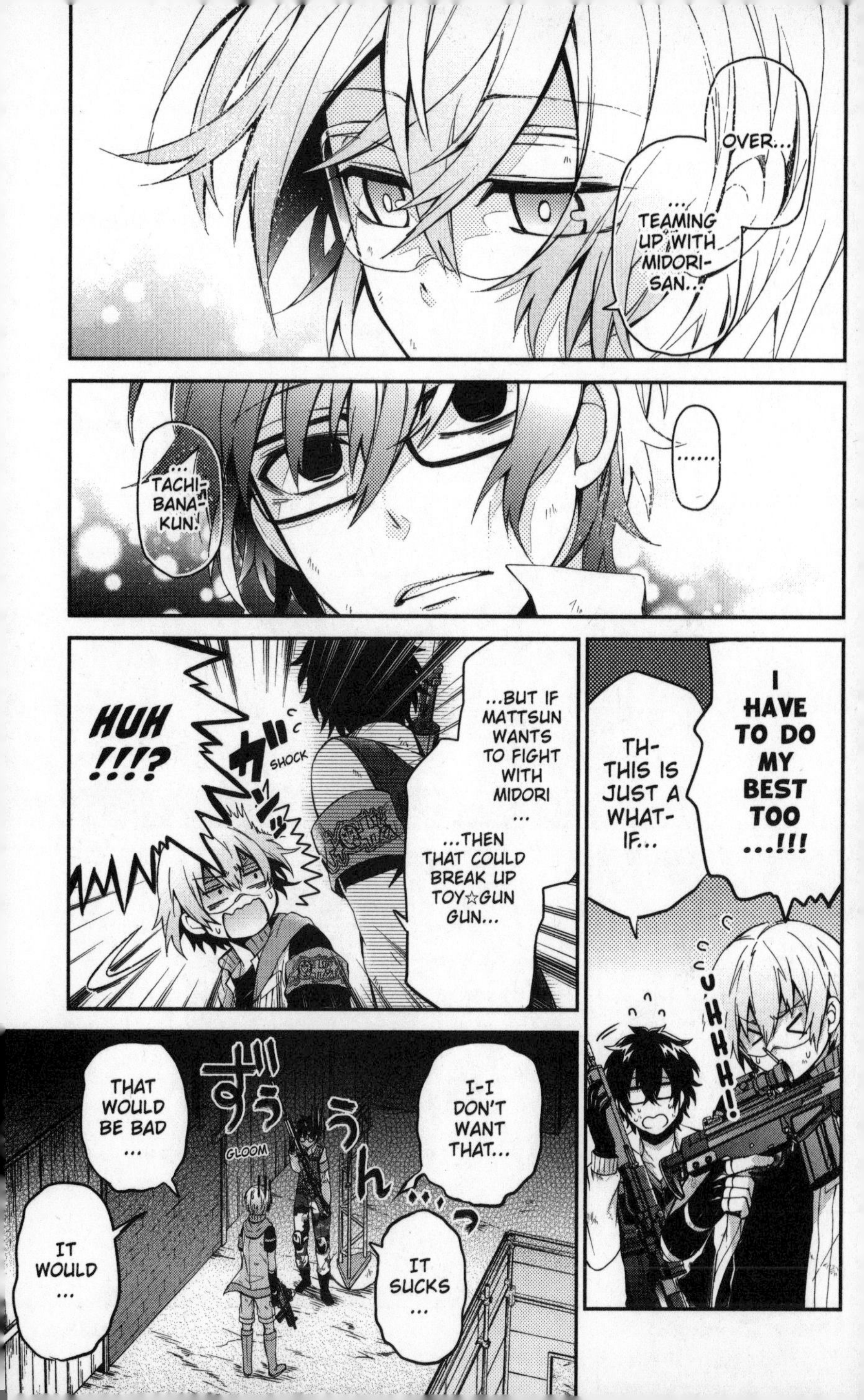
OVER...
...TEAMING UP WITH MIDORI-SAN...
......
...TACHIBANA-KUN.
I HAVE TO DO MY BEST TOO ...!!!
TH-THIS IS JUST A WHAT-IF...
UHHH!
...BUT IF MATTSUN WANTS TO FIGHT WITH MIDORI ...
...THEN THAT COULD BREAK UP TOY☆GUN GUN...
SHOCK
HUH!!!?
I-I DON'T WANT THAT...
THAT WOULD BE BAD ...
GLOOM
IT SUCKS ...
IT WOULD ...

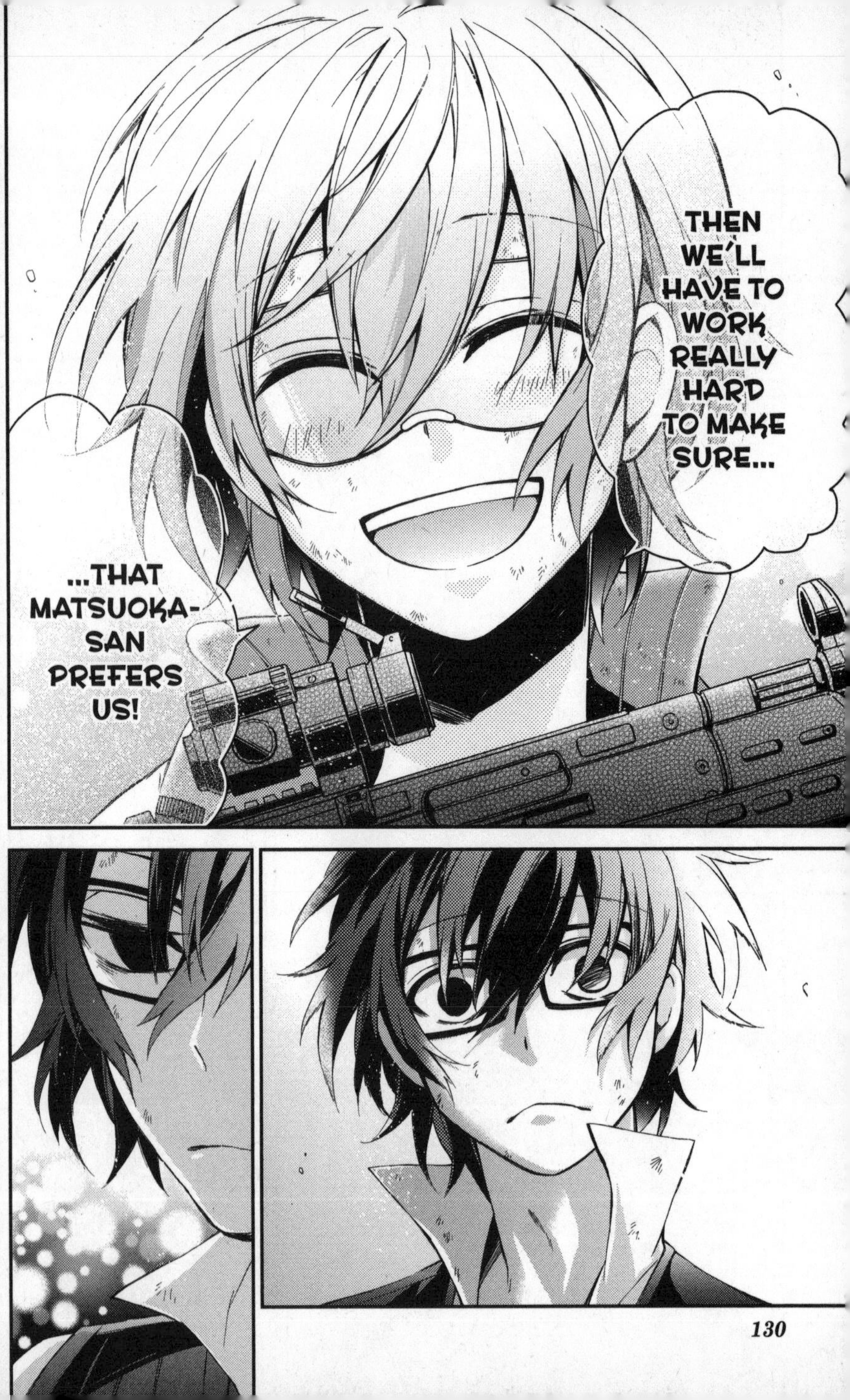
THEN WE'LL HAVE TO WORK REALLY HARD TO MAKE SURE...
...THAT MATSUOKA-SAN PREFERS US!

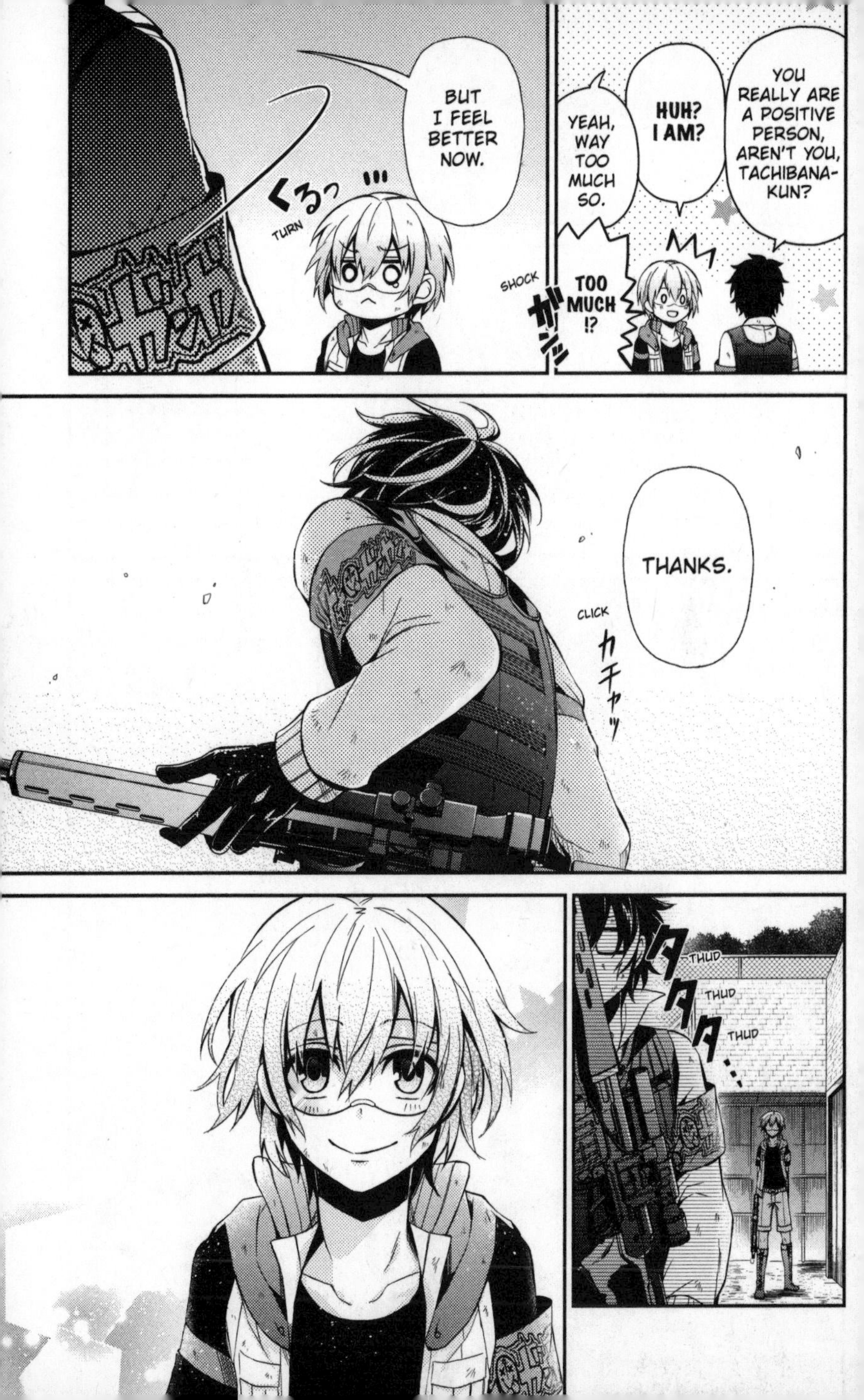
YOU REALLY ARE A POSITIVE PERSON, AREN'T YOU, TACHIBANA-KUN?
HUH? I AM?
YEAH, WAY TOO MUCH SO.
SHOCK
TOO MUCH!?
BUT I FEEL BETTER NOW.
くるっ
TURN
THANKS.
CLICK
カチャッ
タタタ...
THUD
THUD
THUD

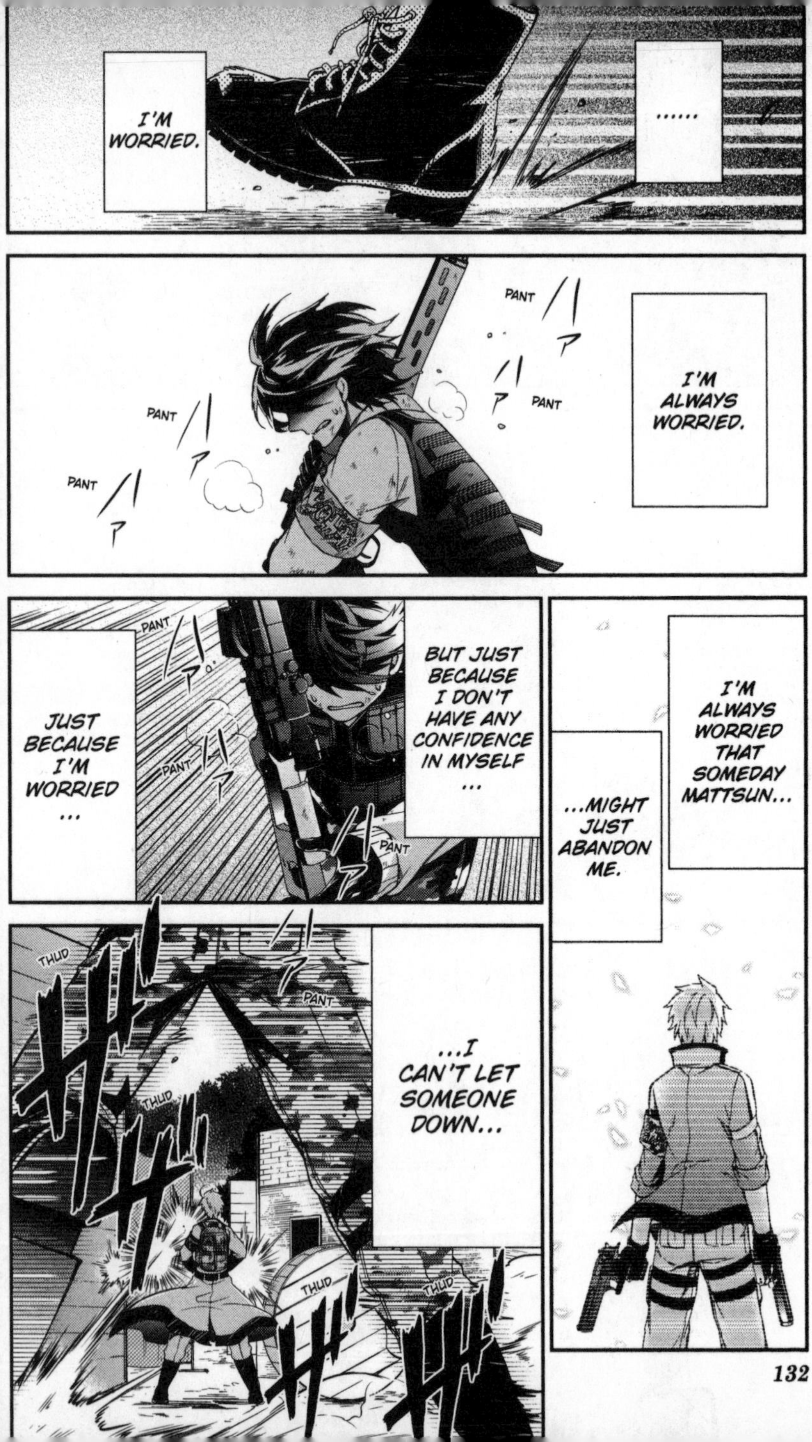
......
I'M WORRIED.
I'M ALWAYS WORRIED.
PANT
PANT
PANT
PANT
I'M ALWAYS WORRIED THAT SOMEDAY MATTSUN...
...MIGHT JUST ABANDON ME.
BUT JUST BECAUSE I DON'T HAVE ANY CONFIDENCE IN MYSELF...
PANT
PANT
PANT
JUST BECAUSE I'M WORRIED...
...I CAN'T LET SOMEONE DOWN...
PANT
THUD
THUD
THUD
THUD

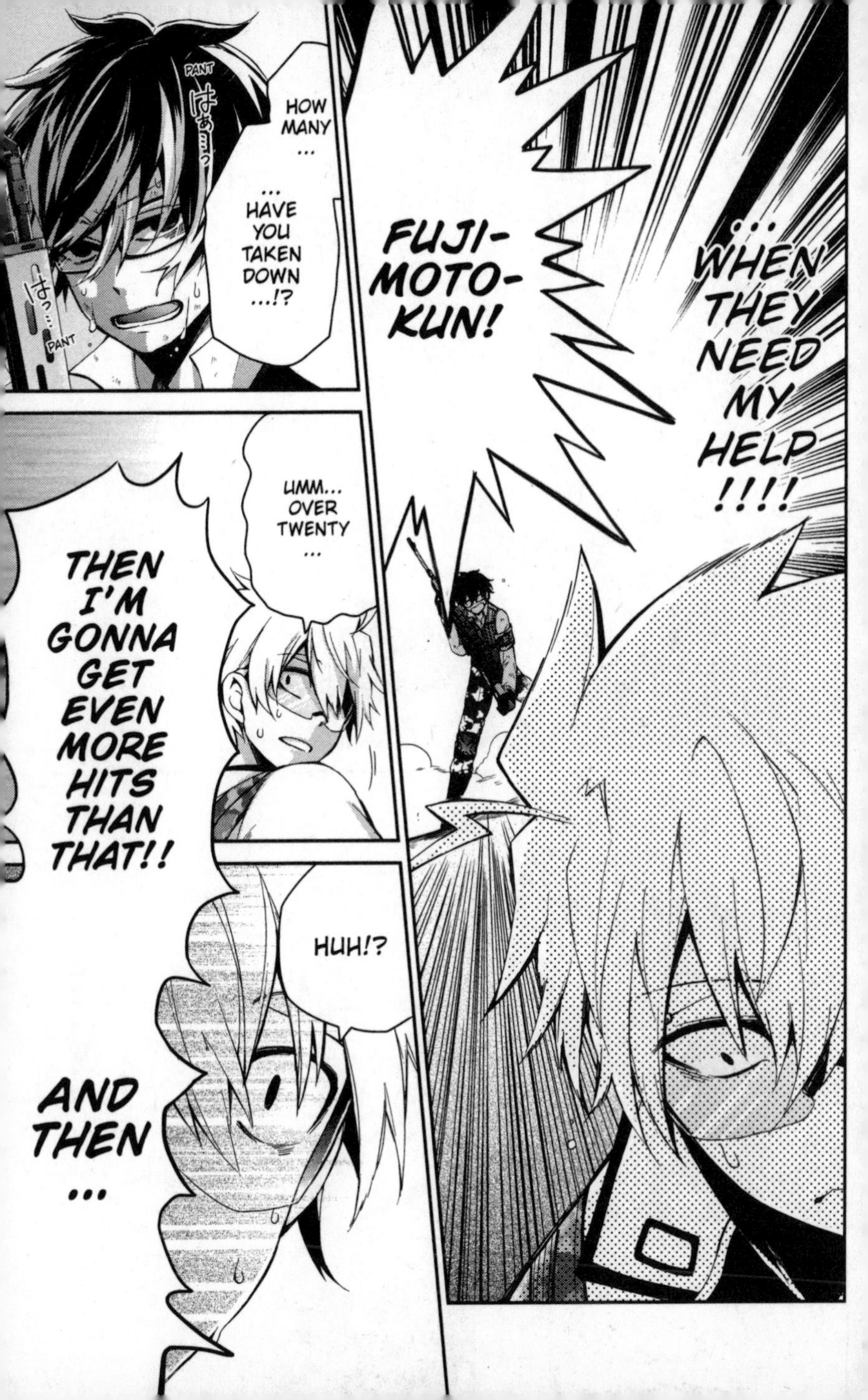
PANT
PANT
HOW MANY … … HAVE YOU TAKEN DOWN …!?
UMM… OVER TWENTY …
THEN I'M GONNA GET EVEN MORE HITS THAN THAT!!
HUH!?
AND THEN …
… WHEN THEY NEED MY HELP !!!!
FUJI-MOTO-KUN!

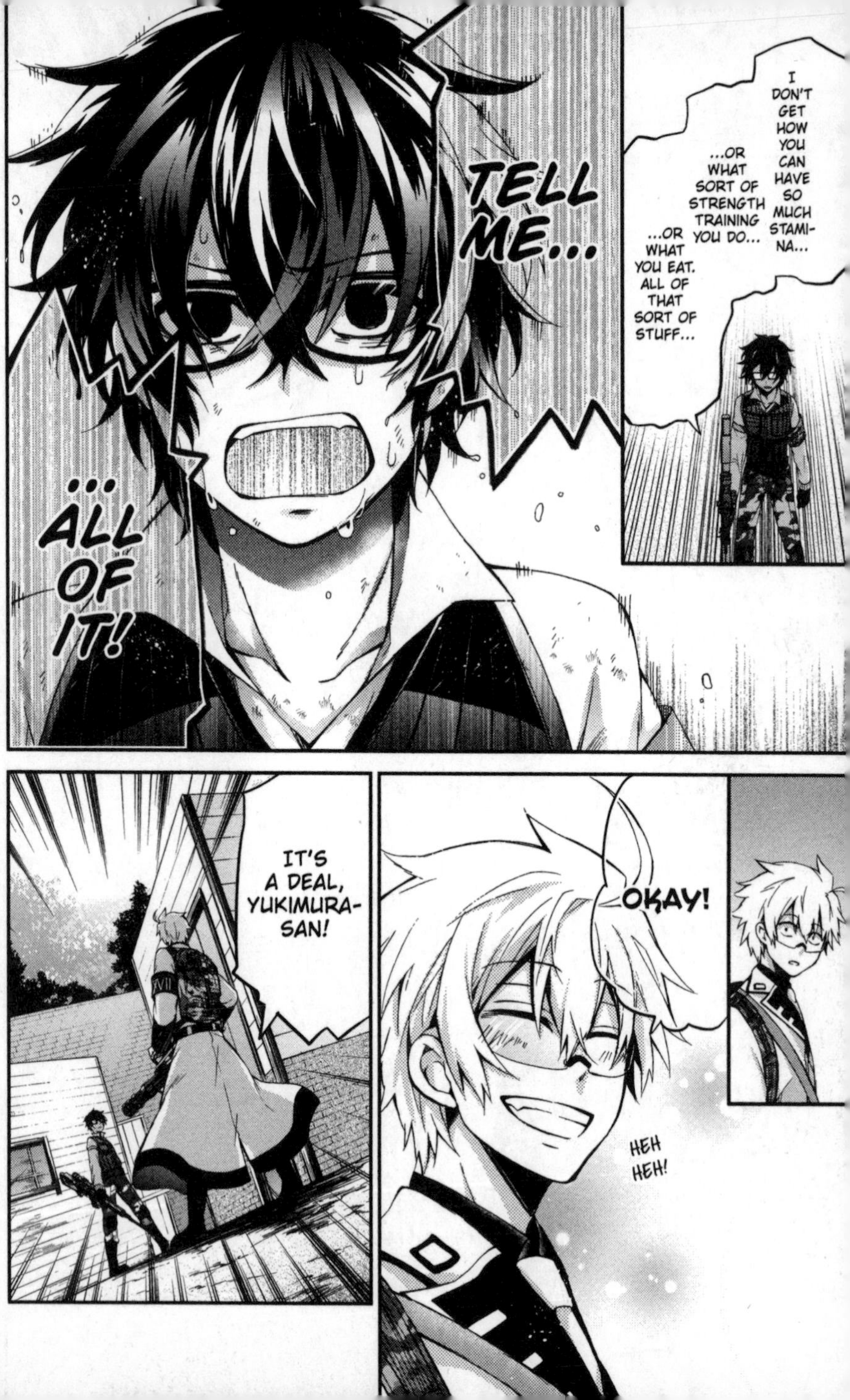
I DON'T GET HOW YOU CAN HAVE SO MUCH STAMINA...
...OR WHAT SORT OF STRENGTH TRAINING YOU DO...
...OR WHAT YOU EAT. ALL OF THAT SORT OF STUFF...
TELL ME...
...ALL OF IT!
OKAY!
HEH HEH!
IT'S A DEAL, YUKIMURA-SAN!

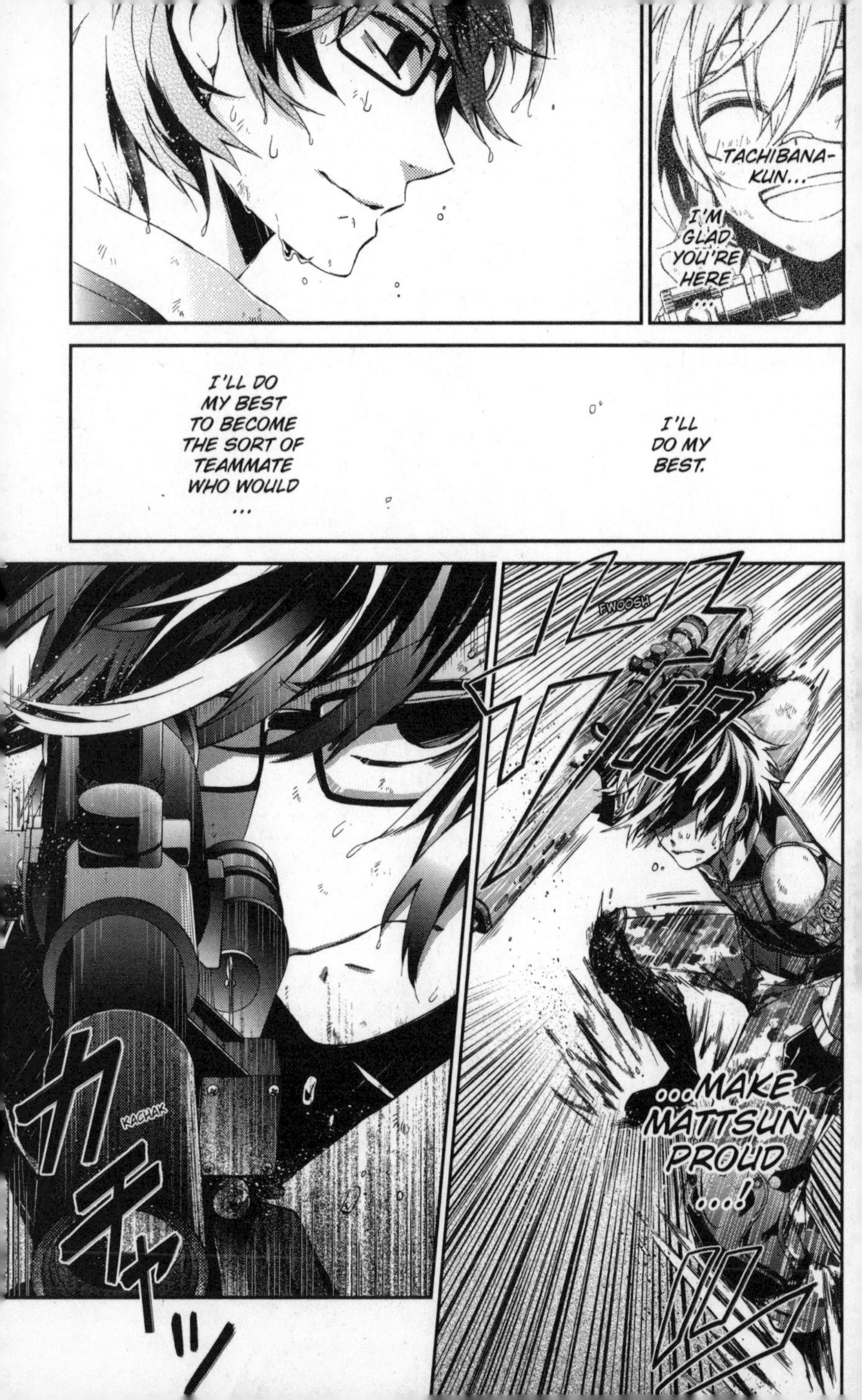
TACHIBANA-KUN...
I'M GLAD YOU'RE HERE...
I'LL DO MY BEST.
I'LL DO MY BEST TO BECOME THE SORT OF TEAMMATE WHO WOULD ...
FWOOSH
...MAKE MATTSUN PROUD ...!
KACHAK
カチャッ

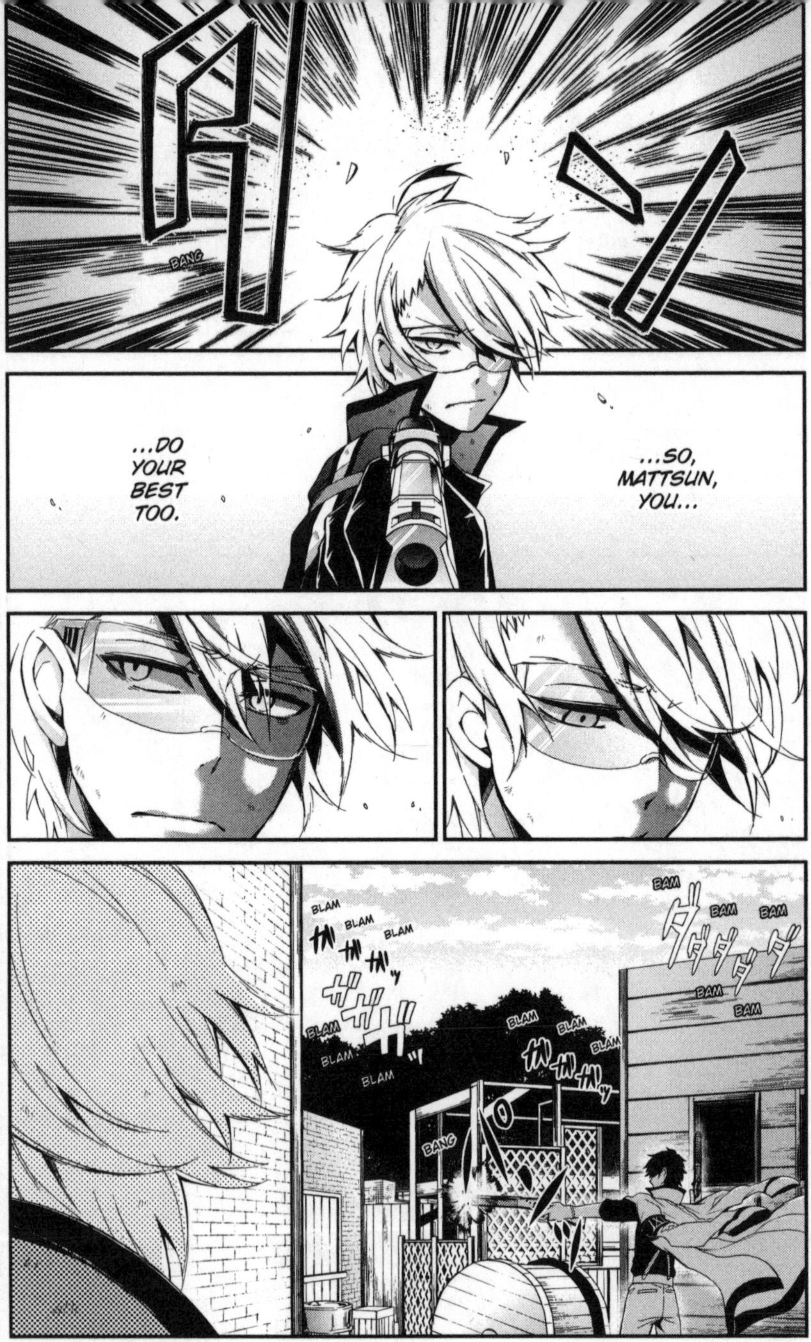
BANG
...SO, MATTSUN, YOU...
...DO YOUR BEST TOO.
BAM BAM BAM BAM BAM BAM
BLAM BLAM BLAM BLAM BLAM BLAM
BLAM BLAM BLAM BLAM
BANG

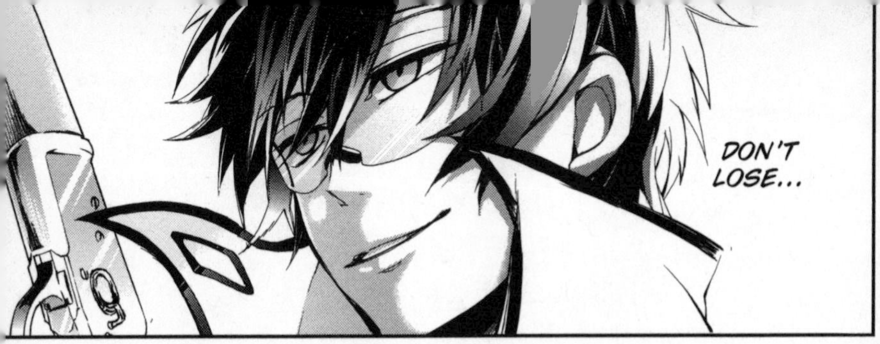
DON'T LOSE...

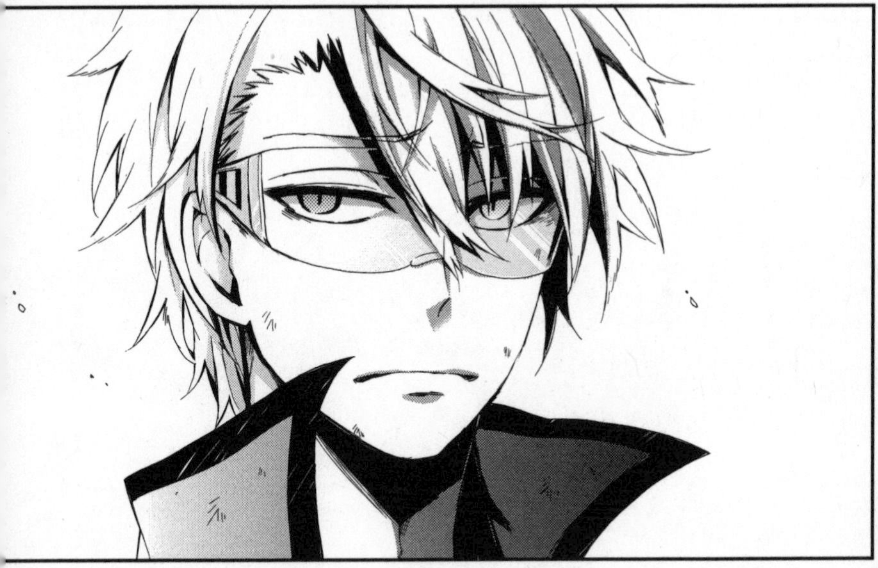

...TO THAT BASTARD MIDORI!

AOHARU
MACHINE
GUN

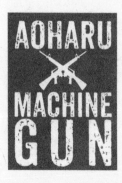

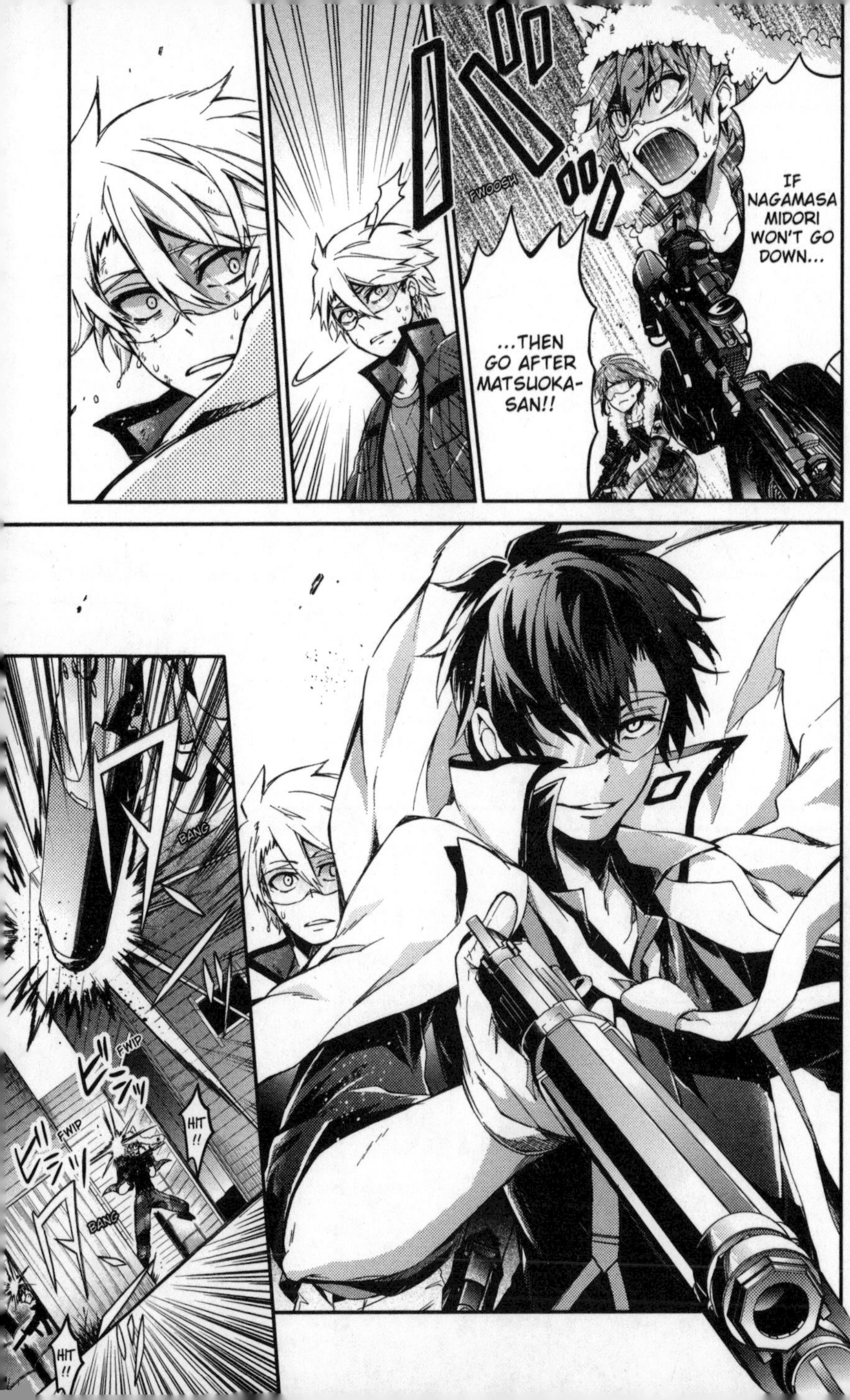
IF NAGAMASA MIDORI WON'T GO DOWN...
FWOOSH
...THEN GO AFTER MATSUOKA-SAN!!
BANG
FWIP
HIT!!
FWIP
BANG
HIT!!

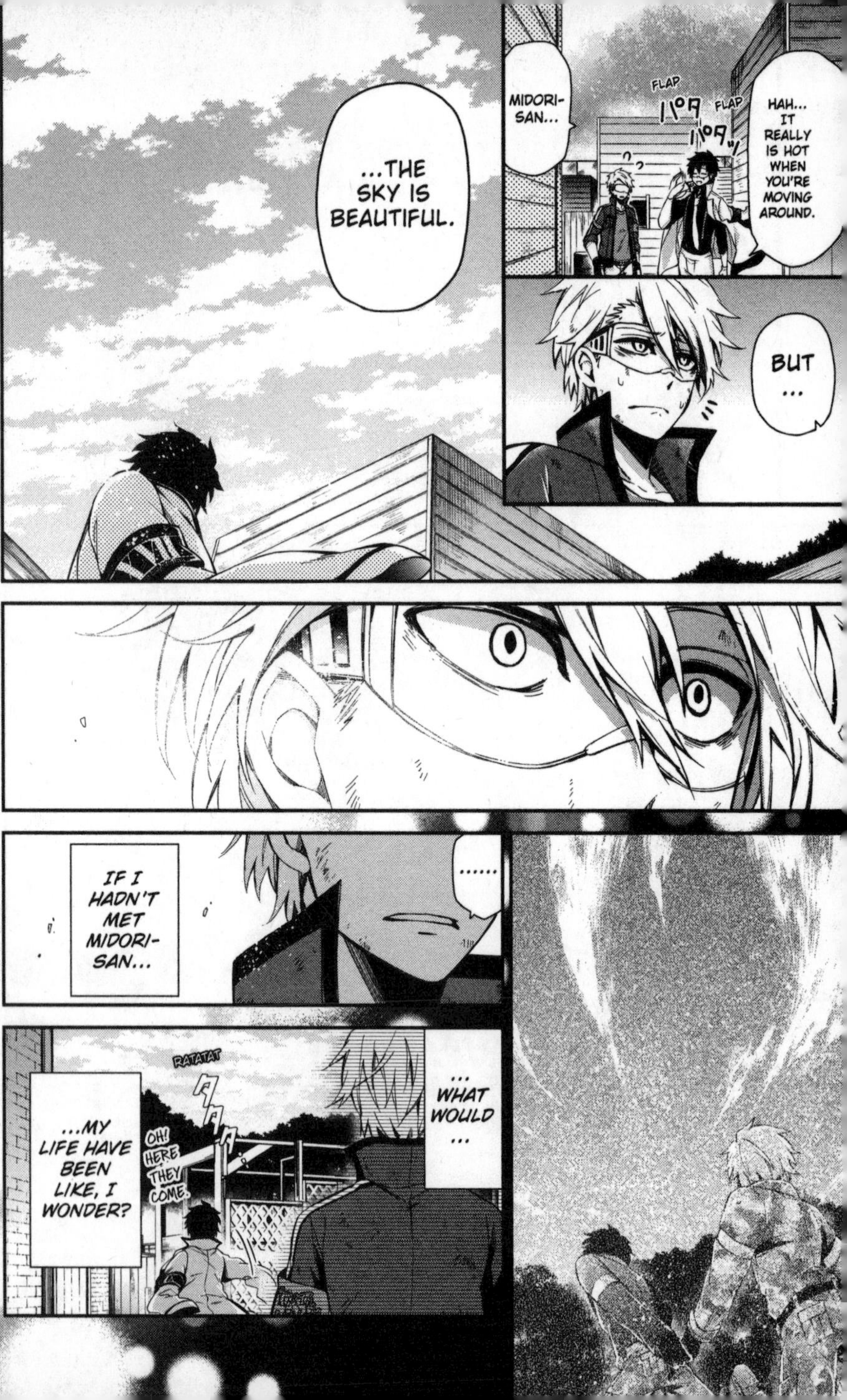
HAH... IT REALLY IS HOT WHEN YOU'RE MOVING AROUND.
FLAP
FLAP
MIDORI-SAN...
BUT ...
...THE SKY IS BEAUTIFUL.
......
IF I HADN'T MET MIDORI-SAN...
... WHAT WOULD ...
RATATAT
OH! HERE THEY COME.
...MY LIFE HAVE BEEN LIKE, I WONDER?

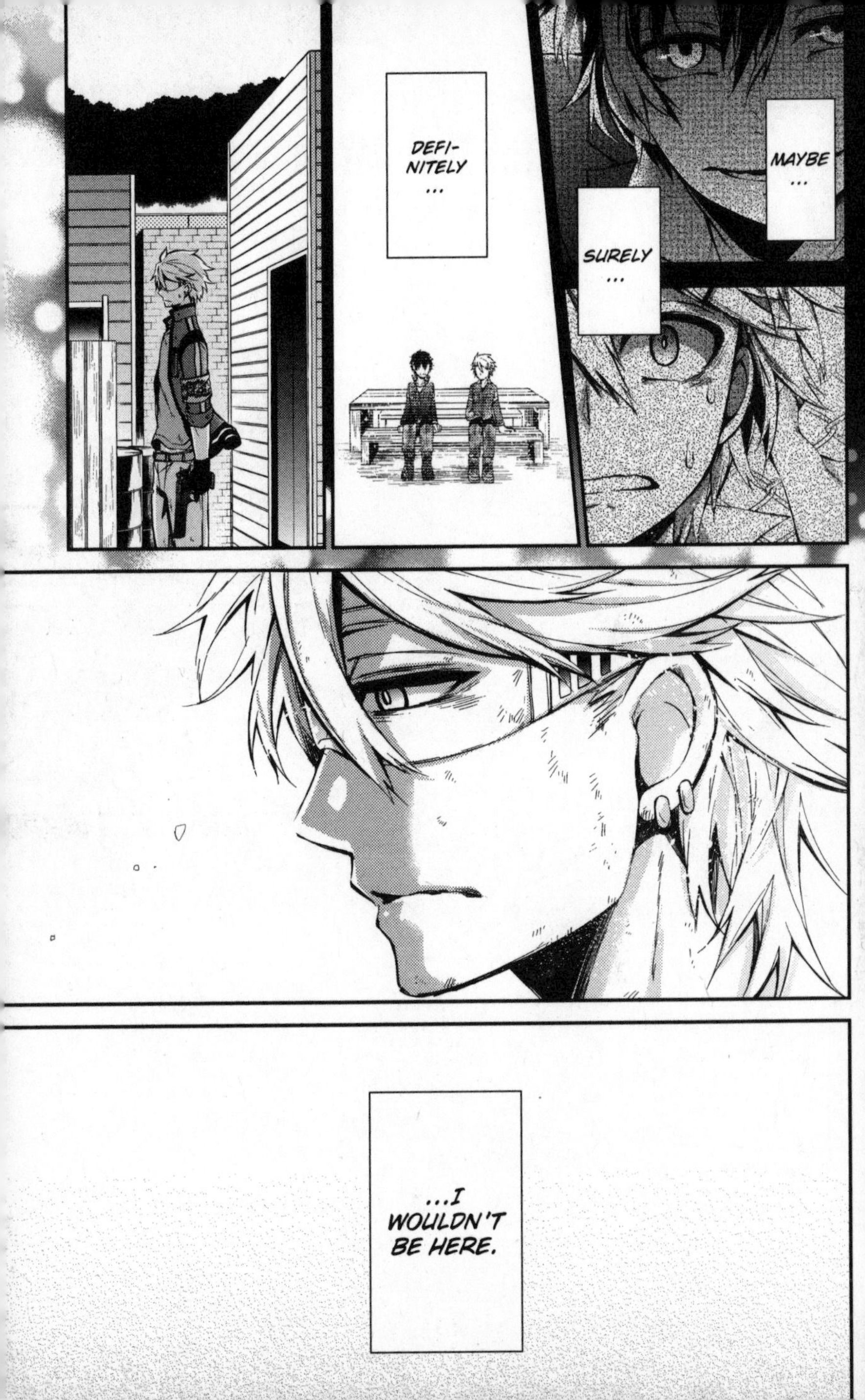

MAYBE ...
SURELY ...
DEFI-NITELY ...
...I WOULDN'T BE HERE.

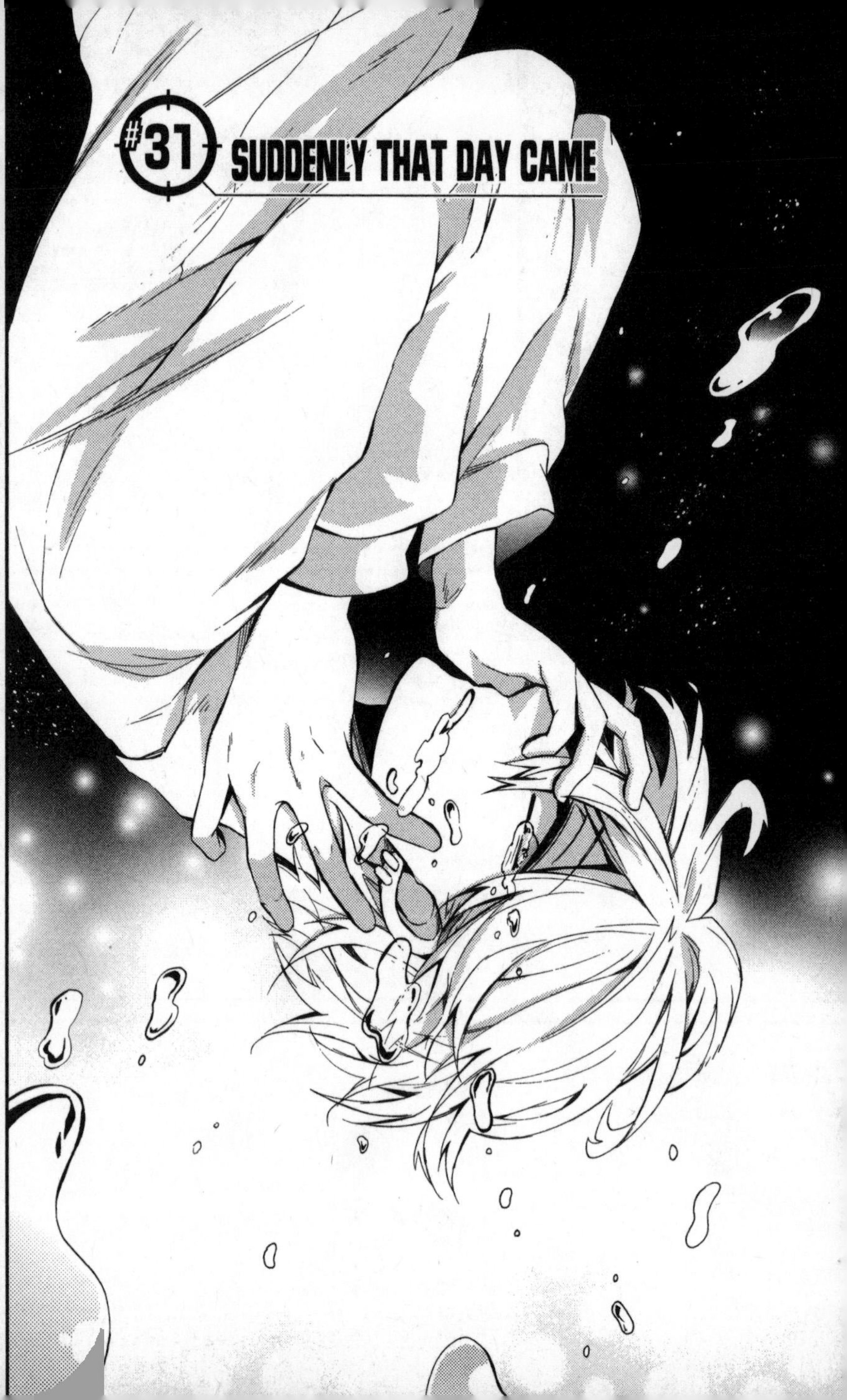
#31
SUDDENLY THAT DAY CAME

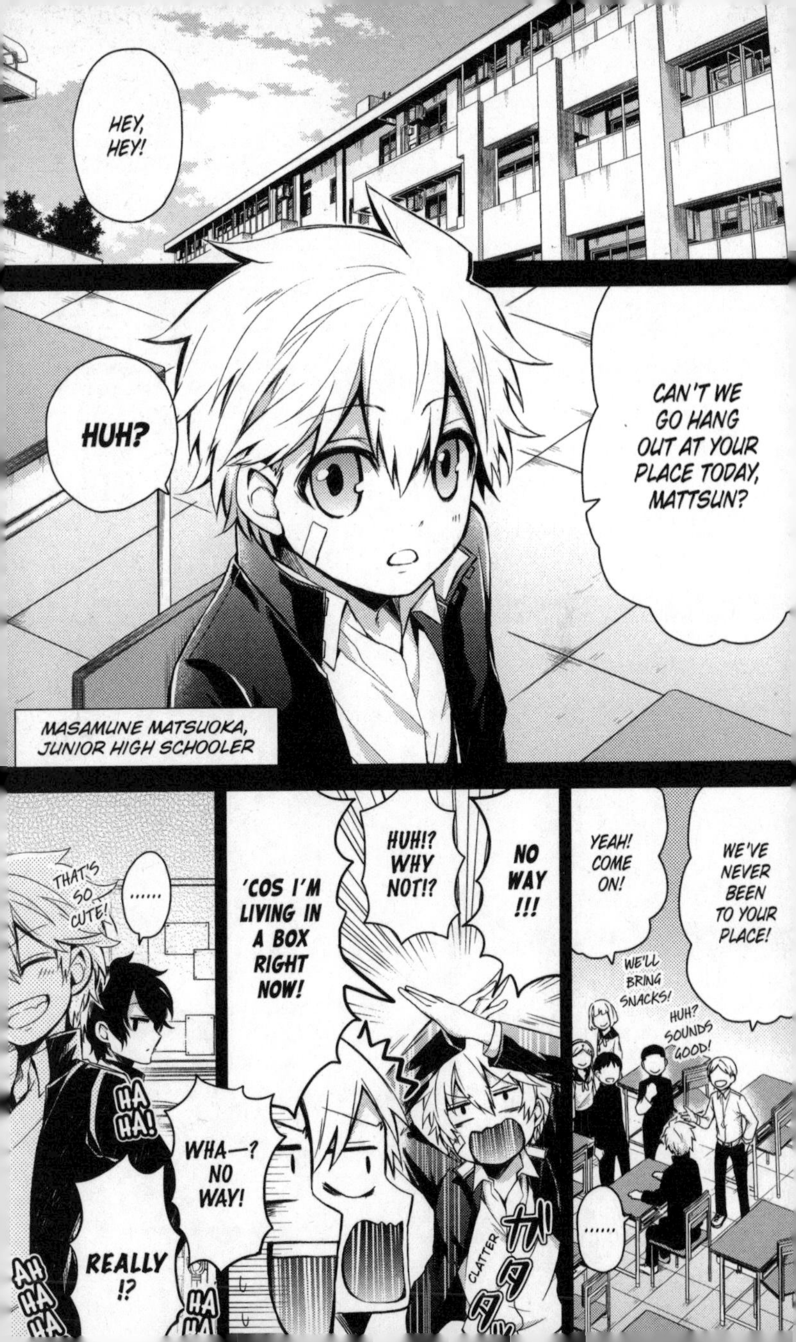
HEY, HEY!
CAN'T WE GO HANG OUT AT YOUR PLACE TODAY, MATTSUN?
HUH?
MASAMUNE MATSUOKA, JUNIOR HIGH SCHOOLER
WE'VE NEVER BEEN TO YOUR PLACE!
YEAH! COME ON!
WE'LL BRING SNACKS!
HUH? SOUNDS GOOD!
......
NO WAY!!!
HUH!? WHY NOT!?
'COS I'M LIVING IN A BOX RIGHT NOW!
CLATTER
......
THAT'S SO CUTE!
HA HA!
WHA—? NO WAY!
REALLY!?
AH HA HA
HA HA

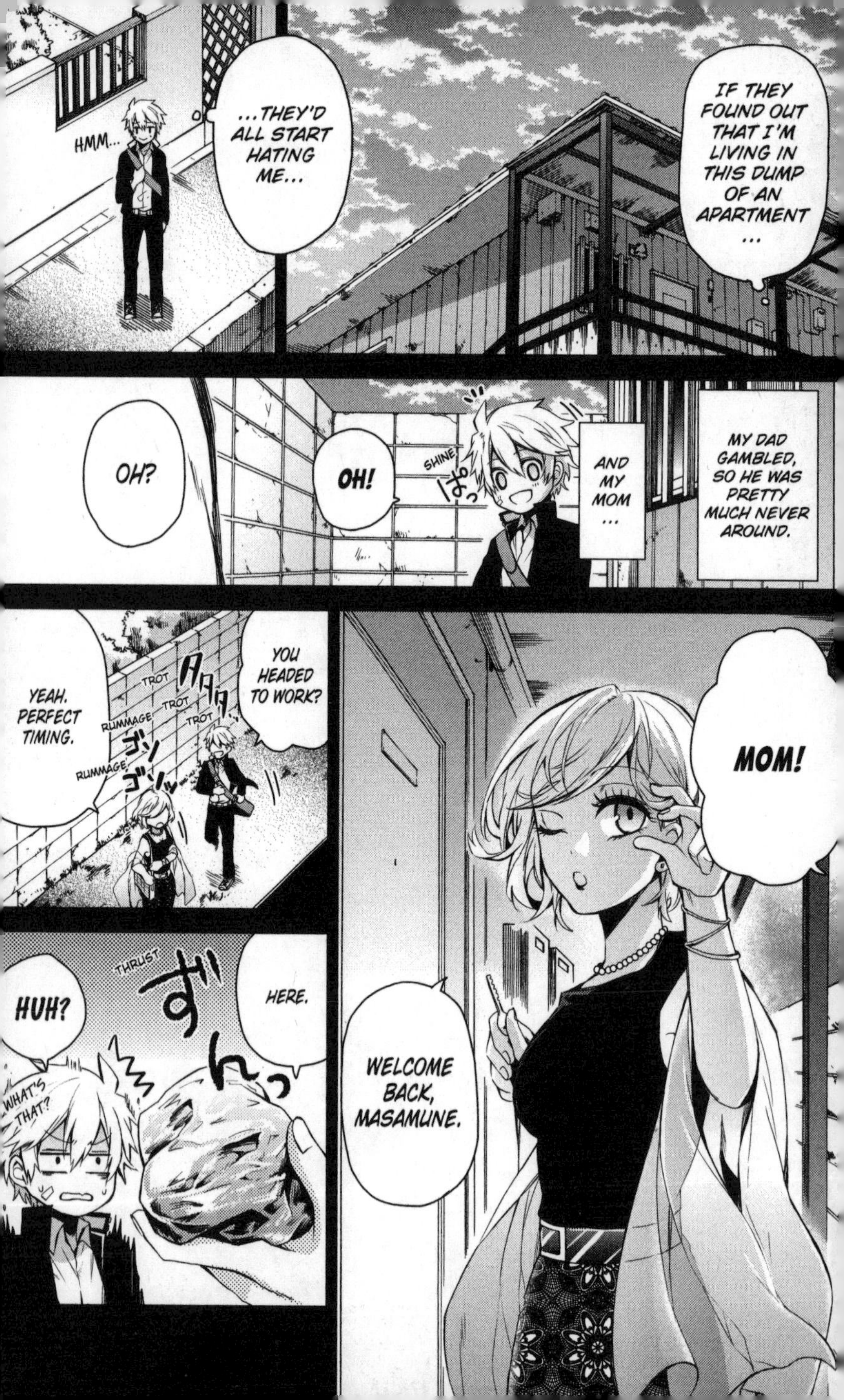
IF THEY FOUND OUT THAT I'M LIVING IN THIS DUMP OF AN APARTMENT...
...THEY'D ALL START HATING ME...
HMM...
MY DAD GAMBLED, SO HE WAS PRETTY MUCH NEVER AROUND.
AND MY MOM...
SHINE
ぱっ
OH!
OH?
MOM!
WELCOME BACK, MASAMUNE.
YOU HEADED TO WORK?
タタタ
TROT TROT TROT
ゴソゴソ
RUMMAGE RUMMAGE
YEAH. PERFECT TIMING.
HERE.
ずんっ
THRUST
HUH?
WHAT'S THAT?

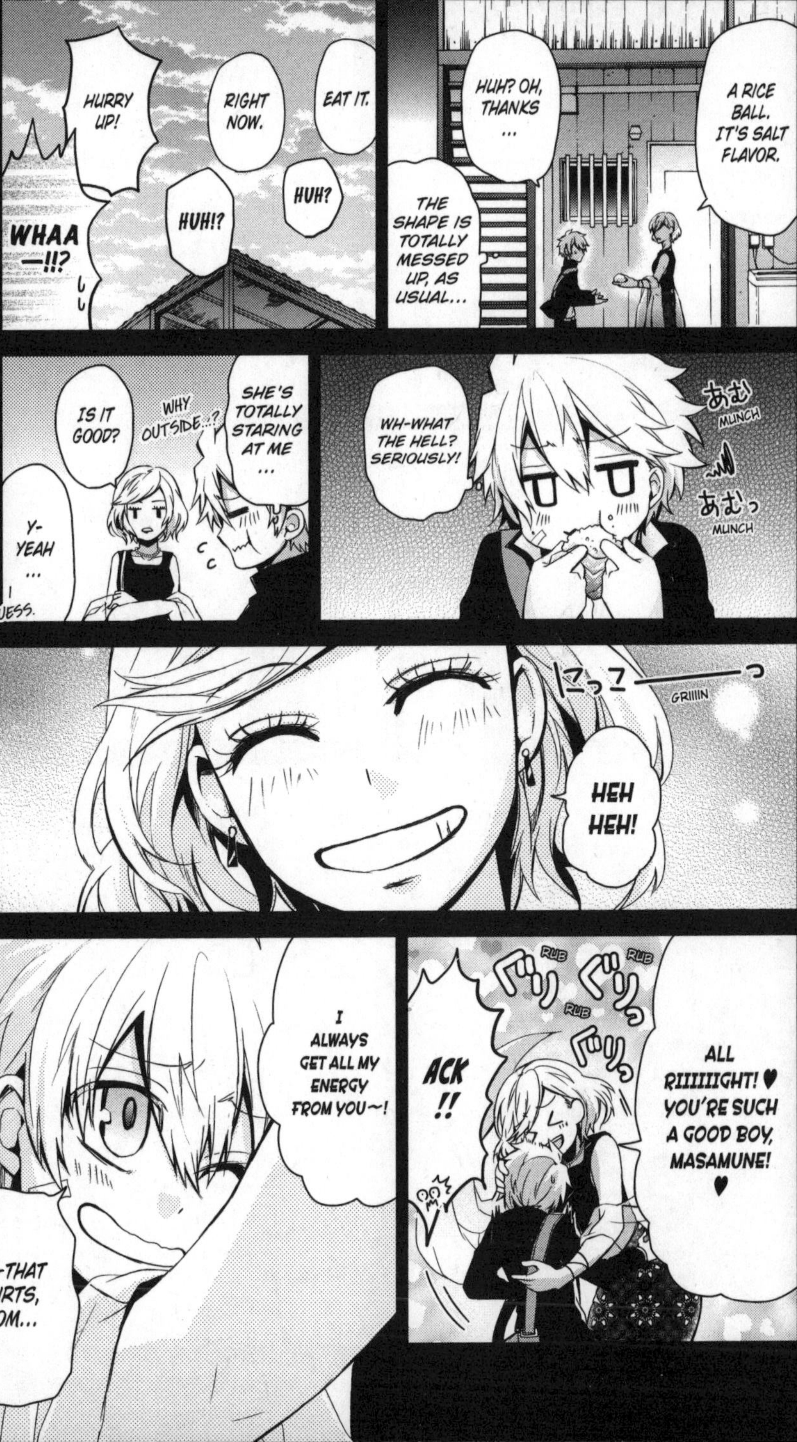
A RICE BALL. IT'S SALT FLAVOR.
HUH? OH, THANKS...
THE SHAPE IS TOTALLY MESSED UP, AS USUAL...
EAT IT.
RIGHT NOW.
HURRY UP!
HUH?
HUH!?
WHAA—!!?
あむ
MUNCH
あむっ
MUNCH
WH-WHAT THE HELL? SERIOUSLY!
SHE'S TOTALLY STARING AT ME...
WHY OUTSIDE...?
IS IT GOOD?
Y-YEAH... I GUESS.
にっこ——っ
GRIIIN
HEH HEH!
ALL RIIIIIIGHT! ♥ YOU'RE SUCH A GOOD BOY, MASAMUNE! ♥
グリ
RUB
グリっ
RUB
グリっ
RUB
ACK!!
I ALWAYS GET ALL MY ENERGY FROM YOU~!
TH-THAT HURTS, MOM...

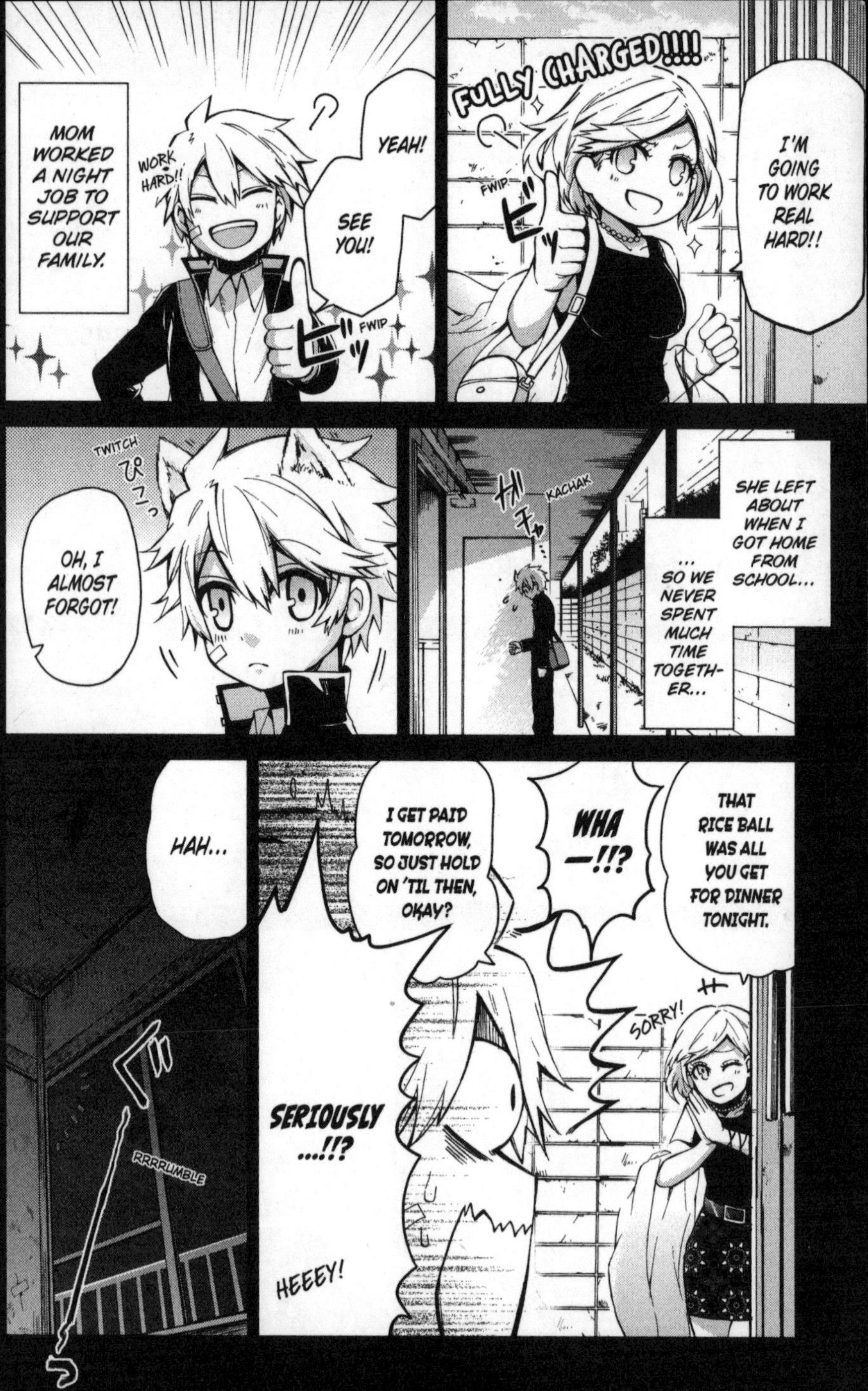
I'M GOING TO WORK REAL HARD!!
FULLY CHARGED!!!!
FWIP
YEAH!
SEE YOU!
MOM WORKED A NIGHT JOB TO SUPPORT OUR FAMILY.
WORK HARD!!
FWIP
SHE LEFT ABOUT WHEN I GOT HOME FROM SCHOOL...
... SO WE NEVER SPENT MUCH TIME TOGETHER...
KACHAK
TWITCH
OH, I ALMOST FORGOT!
THAT RICE BALL WAS ALL YOU GET FOR DINNER TONIGHT.
WHA—!!?
I GET PAID TOMORROW, SO JUST HOLD ON 'TIL THEN, OKAY?
SORRY!
SERIOUSLY ...!!?
HEEEY!
HAH...
RRRRUMBLE

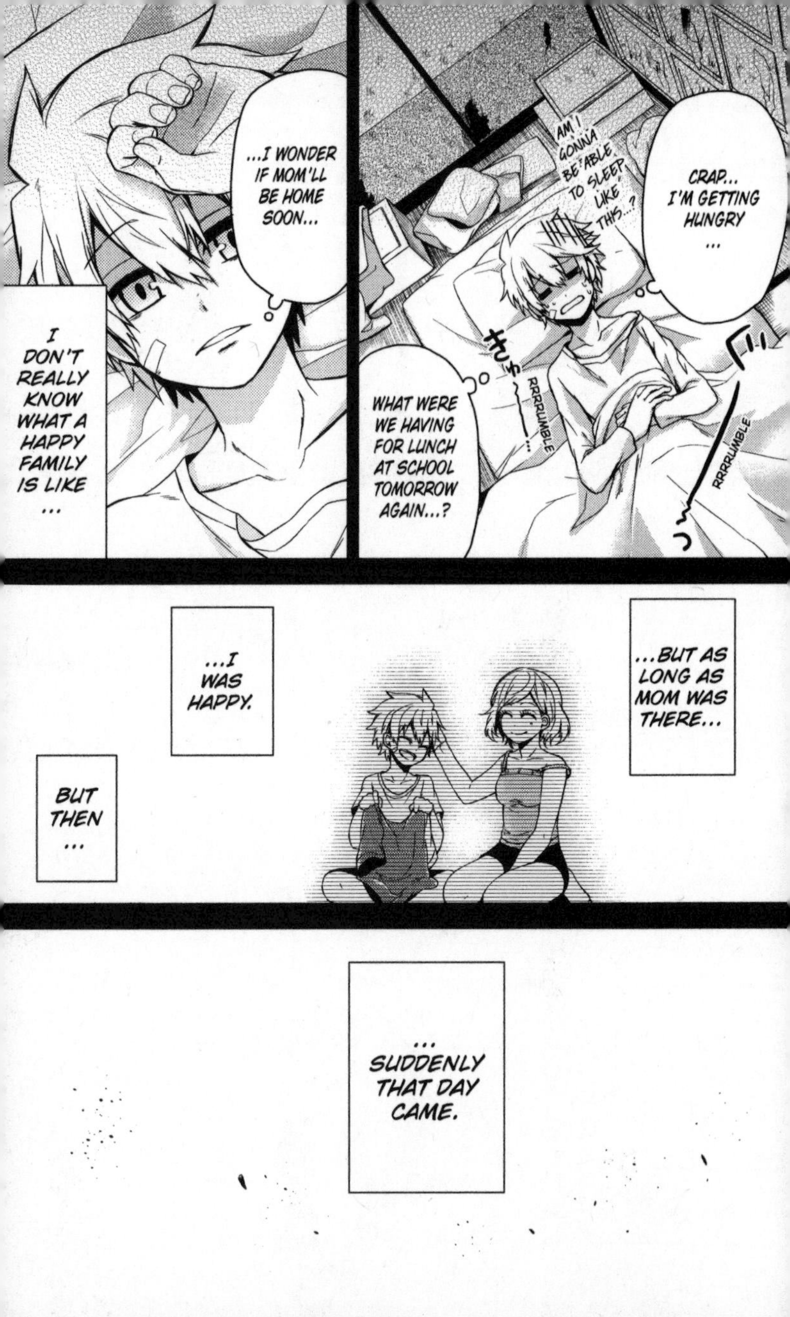
CRAP... I'M GETTING HUNGRY ...
AM I GONNA BE ABLE TO SLEEP LIKE THIS...?
RRRRUMBLE
WHAT WERE WE HAVING FOR LUNCH AT SCHOOL TOMORROW AGAIN...?
RRRRUMBLE...
...I WONDER IF MOM'LL BE HOME SOON...
I DON'T REALLY KNOW WHAT A HAPPY FAMILY IS LIKE ...
...BUT AS LONG AS MOM WAS THERE...
...I WAS HAPPY.
BUT THEN ...
... SUDDENLY THAT DAY CAME.

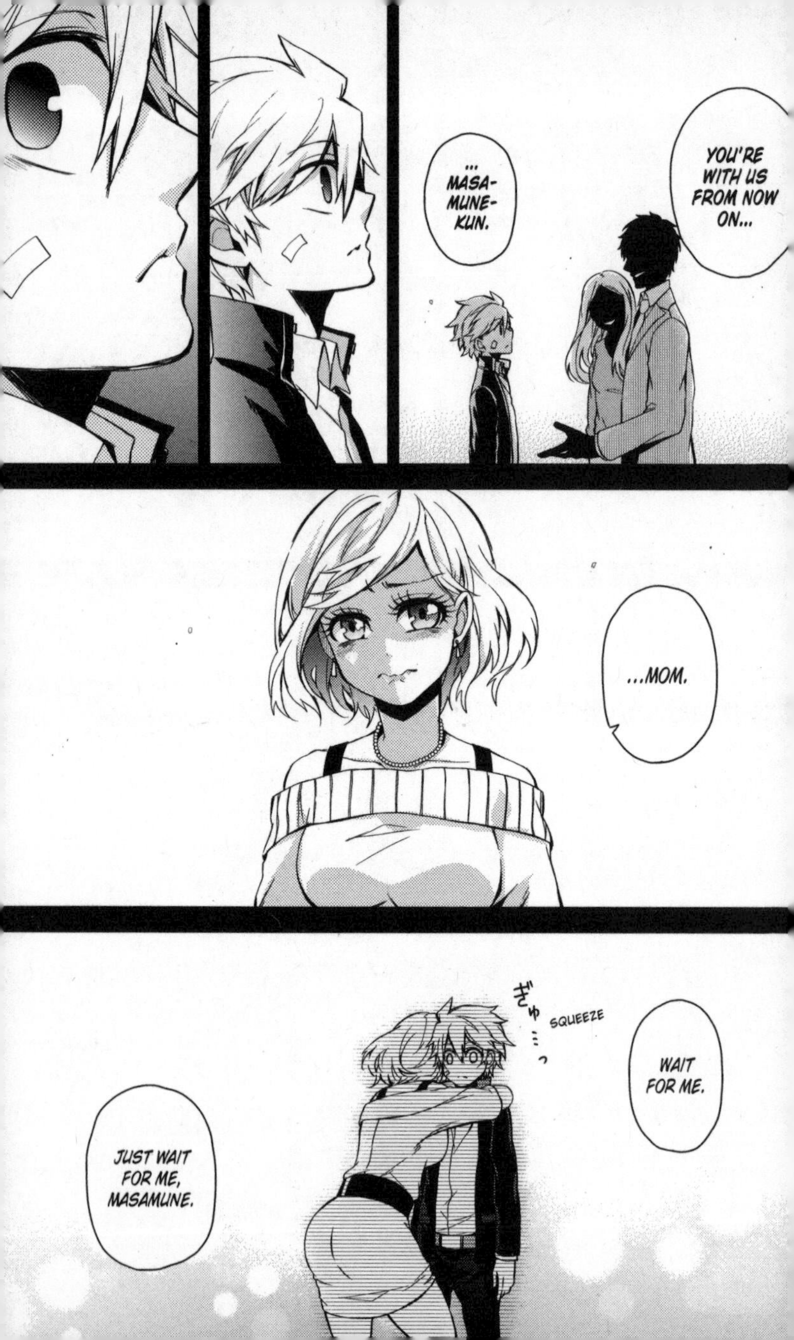
YOU'RE WITH US FROM NOW ON...
...MASA-MUNE-KUN.
...MOM.
WAIT FOR ME.
ぎゅっ
SQUEEZE
JUST WAIT FOR ME, MASAMUNE.

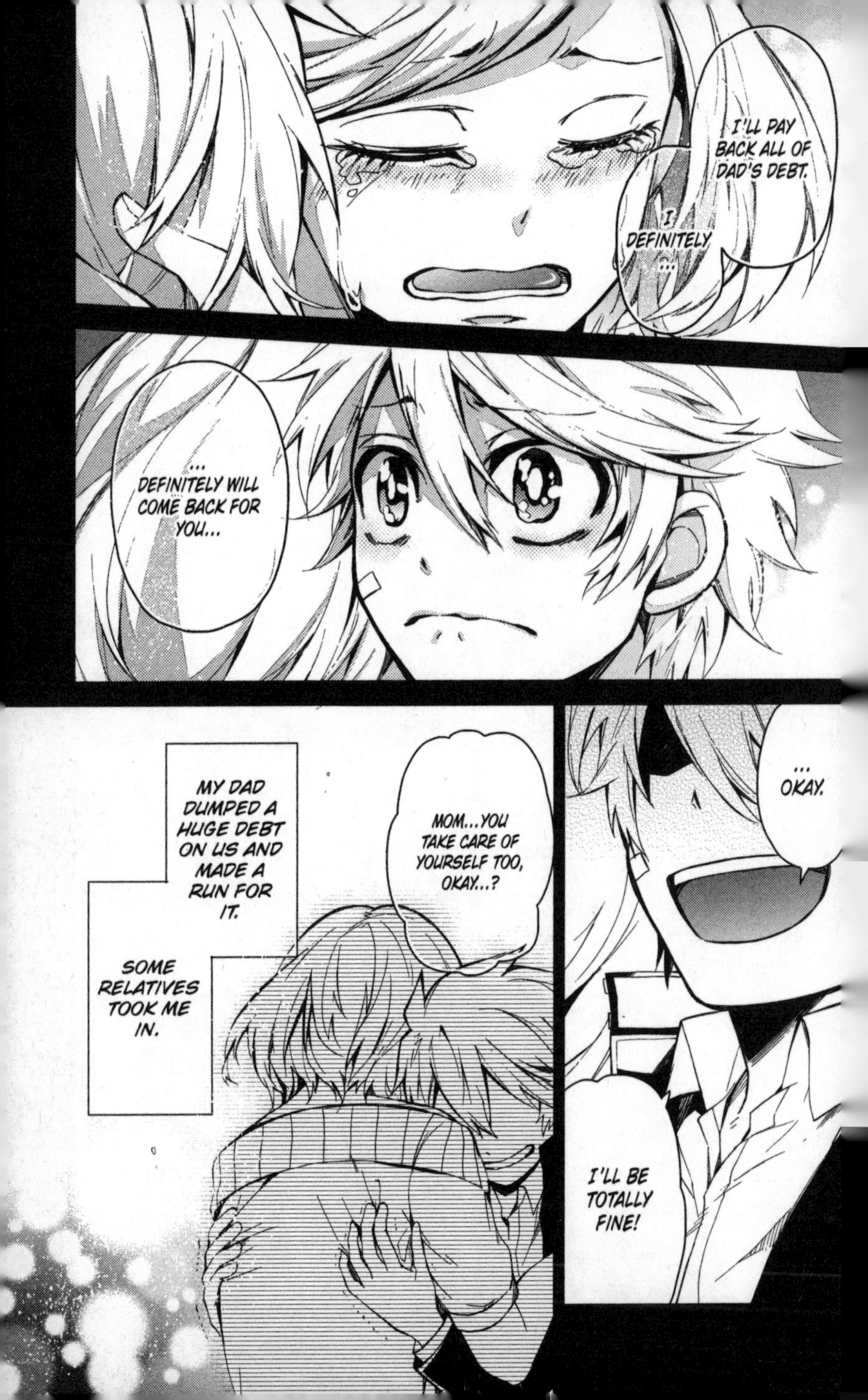
I'LL PAY BACK ALL OF DAD'S DEBT.
I DEFINITELY ...
... DEFINITELY WILL COME BACK FOR YOU...
... OKAY.
I'LL BE TOTALLY FINE!
MOM...YOU TAKE CARE OF YOURSELF TOO, OKAY...?
MY DAD DUMPED A HUGE DEBT ON US AND MADE A RUN FOR IT.
SOME RELATIVES TOOK ME IN.

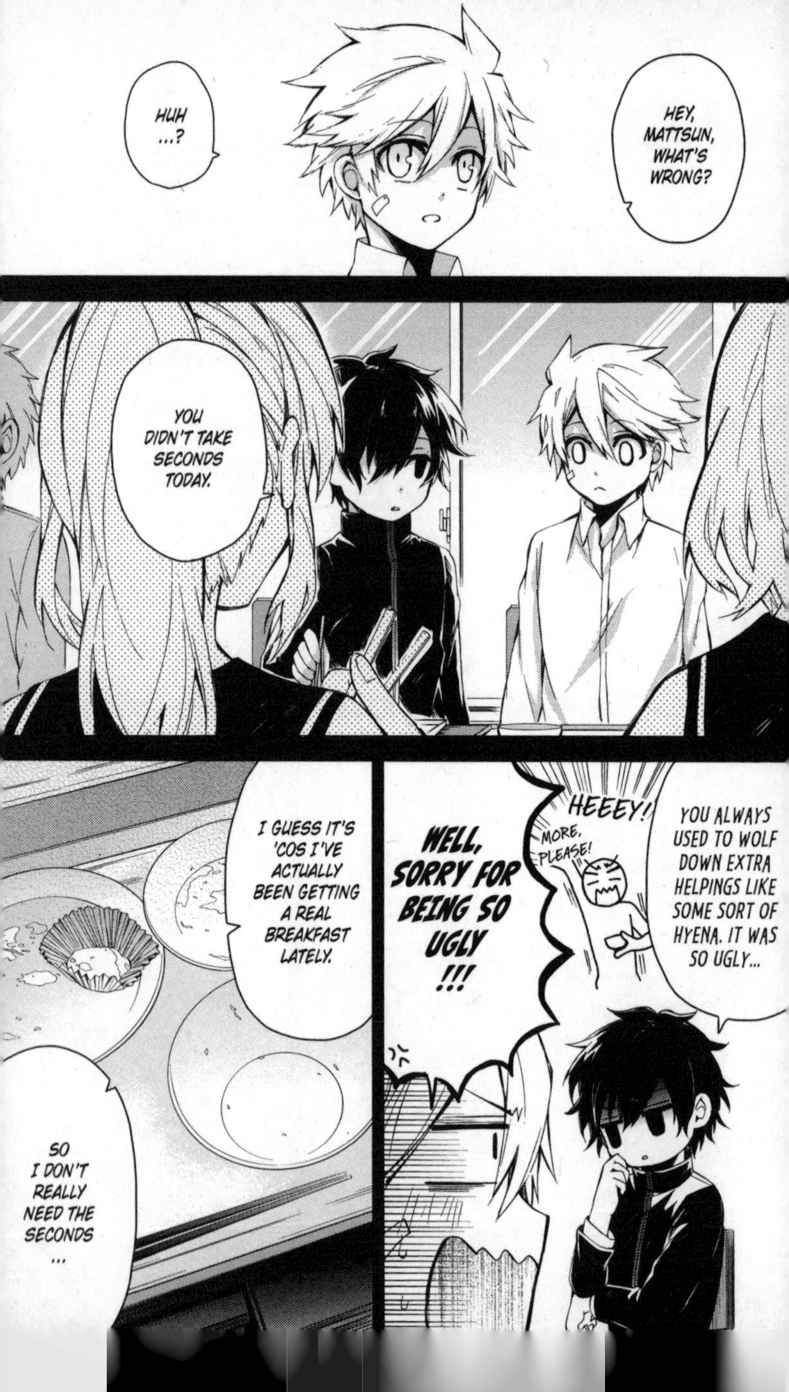
HEY, MATTSUN, WHAT'S WRONG?
HUH ...?
YOU DIDN'T TAKE SECONDS TODAY.
YOU ALWAYS USED TO WOLF DOWN EXTRA HELPINGS LIKE SOME SORT OF HYENA. IT WAS SO UGLY...
HEEEY!
MORE, PLEASE!
WELL, SORRY FOR BEING SO UGLY!!!
I GUESS IT'S 'COS I'VE ACTUALLY BEEN GETTING A REAL BREAKFAST LATELY.
SO I DON'T REALLY NEED THE SECONDS ...

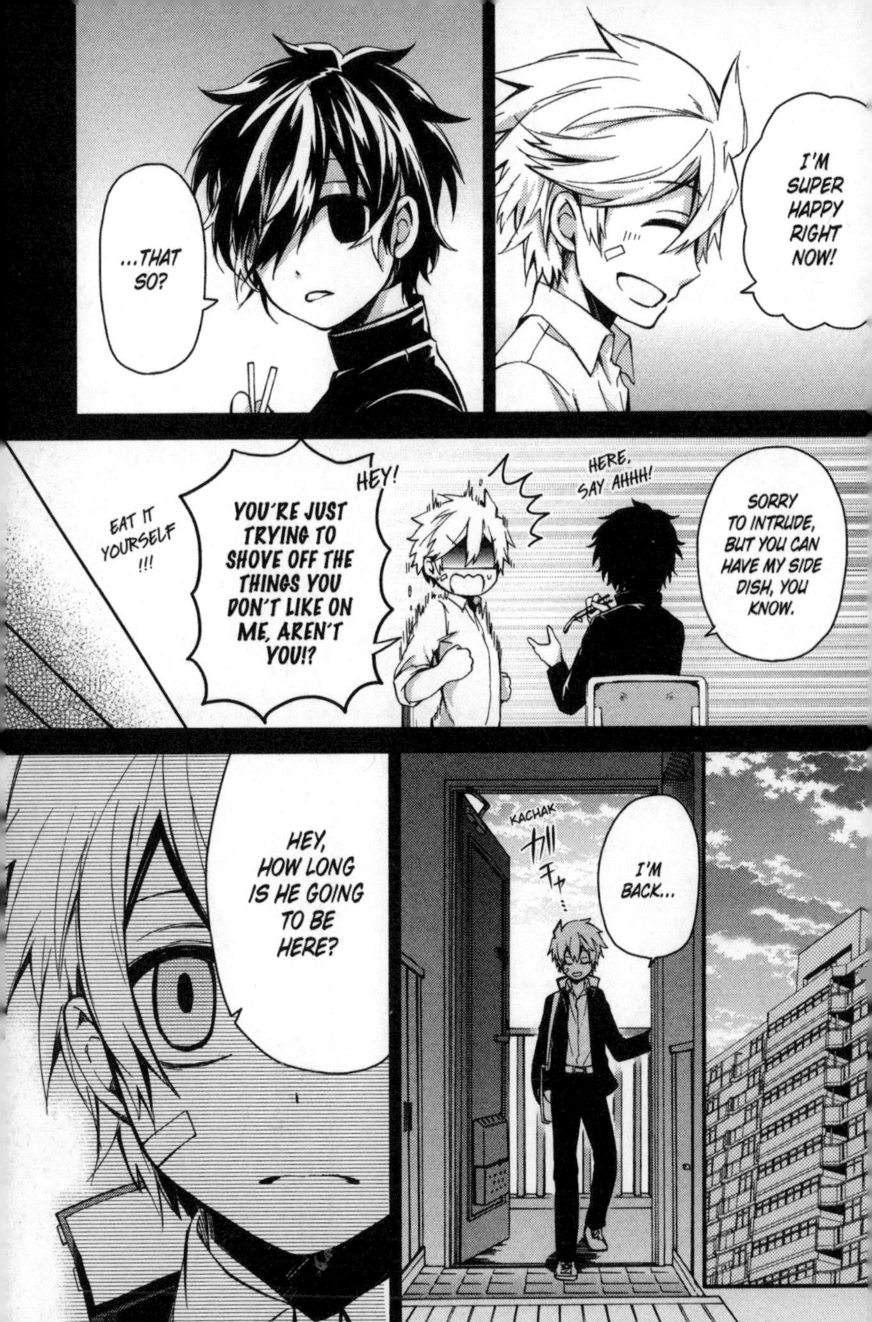
I'M SUPER HAPPY RIGHT NOW!
...THAT SO?
SORRY TO INTRUDE, BUT YOU CAN HAVE MY SIDE DISH, YOU KNOW.
HERE, SAY AHHH!
HEY!
YOU'RE JUST TRYING TO SHOVE OFF THE THINGS YOU DON'T LIKE ON ME, AREN'T YOU!?
EAT IT YOURSELF!!!
KACHAK
I'M BACK...
HEY, HOW LONG IS HE GOING TO BE HERE?

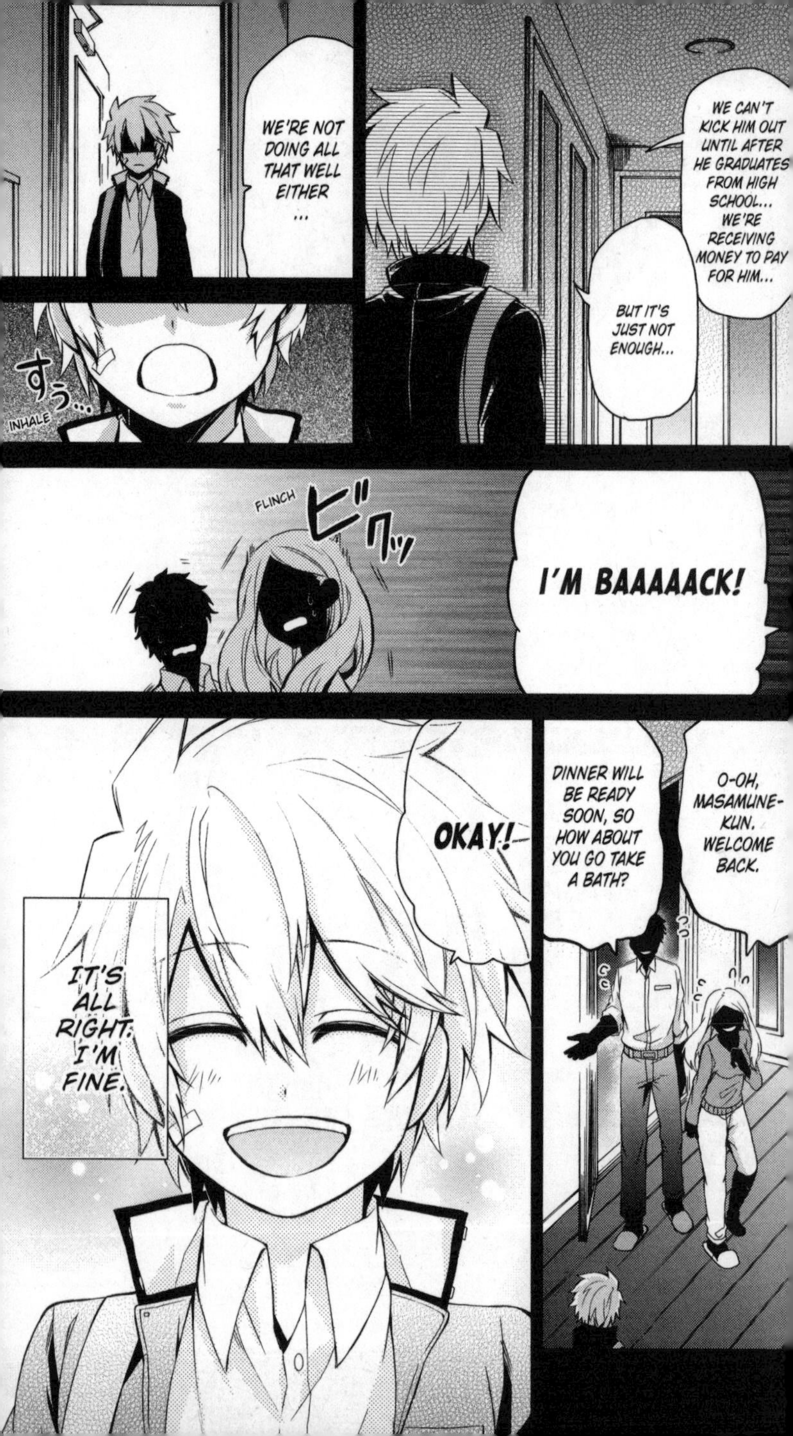
WE CAN'T KICK HIM OUT UNTIL AFTER HE GRADUATES FROM HIGH SCHOOL... WE'RE RECEIVING MONEY TO PAY FOR HIM...
BUT IT'S JUST NOT ENOUGH...
WE'RE NOT DOING ALL THAT WELL EITHER ...
すぅ...
INHALE
I'M BAAAAACK!
ビクッ
FLINCH
O-OH, MASAMUNE-KUN. WELCOME BACK.
DINNER WILL BE READY SOON, SO HOW ABOUT YOU GO TAKE A BATH?
OKAY!
IT'S ALL RIGHT. I'M FINE.

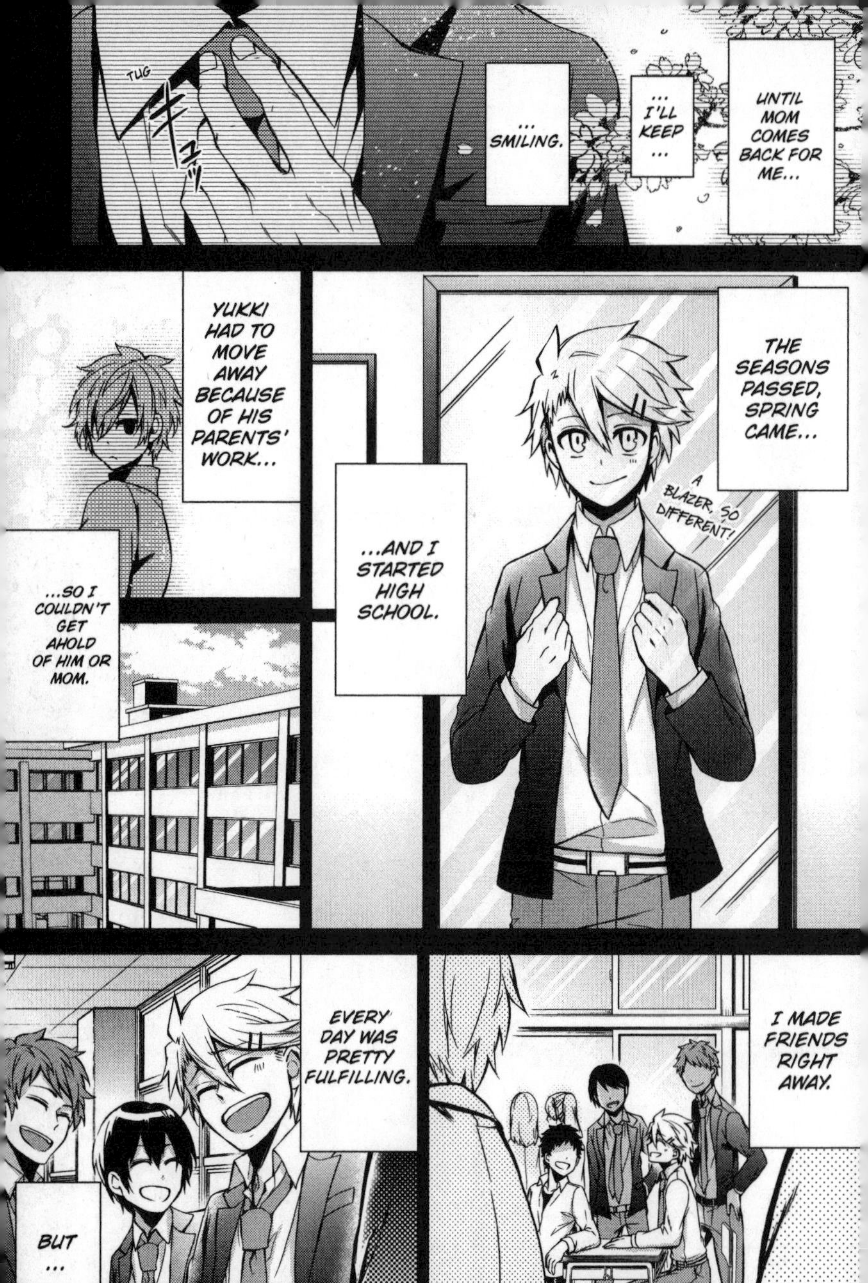
UNTIL MOM COMES BACK FOR ME...
...I'LL KEEP...
...SMILING.
TUG
THE SEASONS PASSED, SPRING CAME...
A BLAZER, SO DIFFERENT!
...AND I STARTED HIGH SCHOOL.
YUKKI HAD TO MOVE AWAY BECAUSE OF HIS PARENTS' WORK...
...SO I COULDN'T GET AHOLD OF HIM OR MOM.
I MADE FRIENDS RIGHT AWAY.
EVERY DAY WAS PRETTY FULFILLING.
BUT...

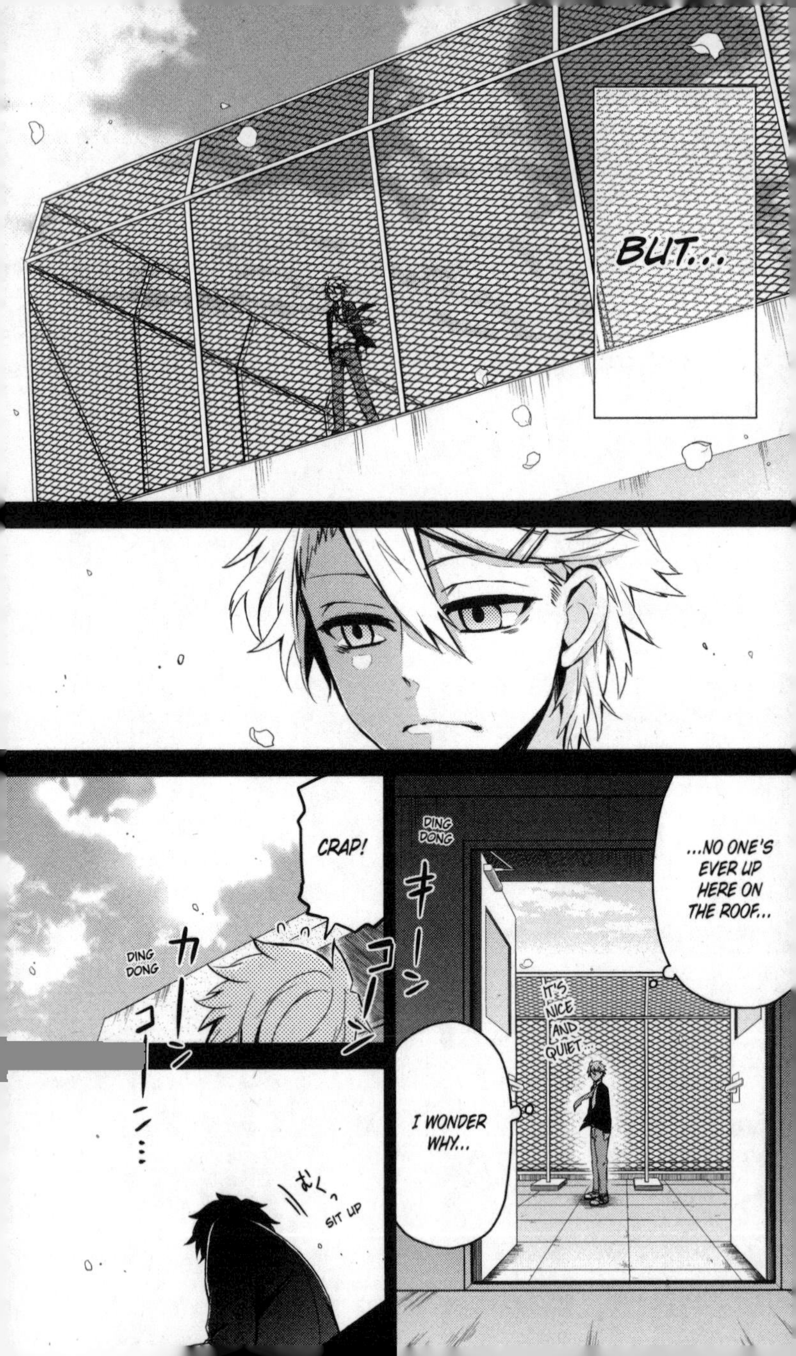
BUT...
...NO ONE'S EVER UP HERE ON THE ROOF...
IT'S NICE AND QUIET...
I WONDER WHY...
DING DONG
CRAP!
DING DONG
むくっ
SIT UP

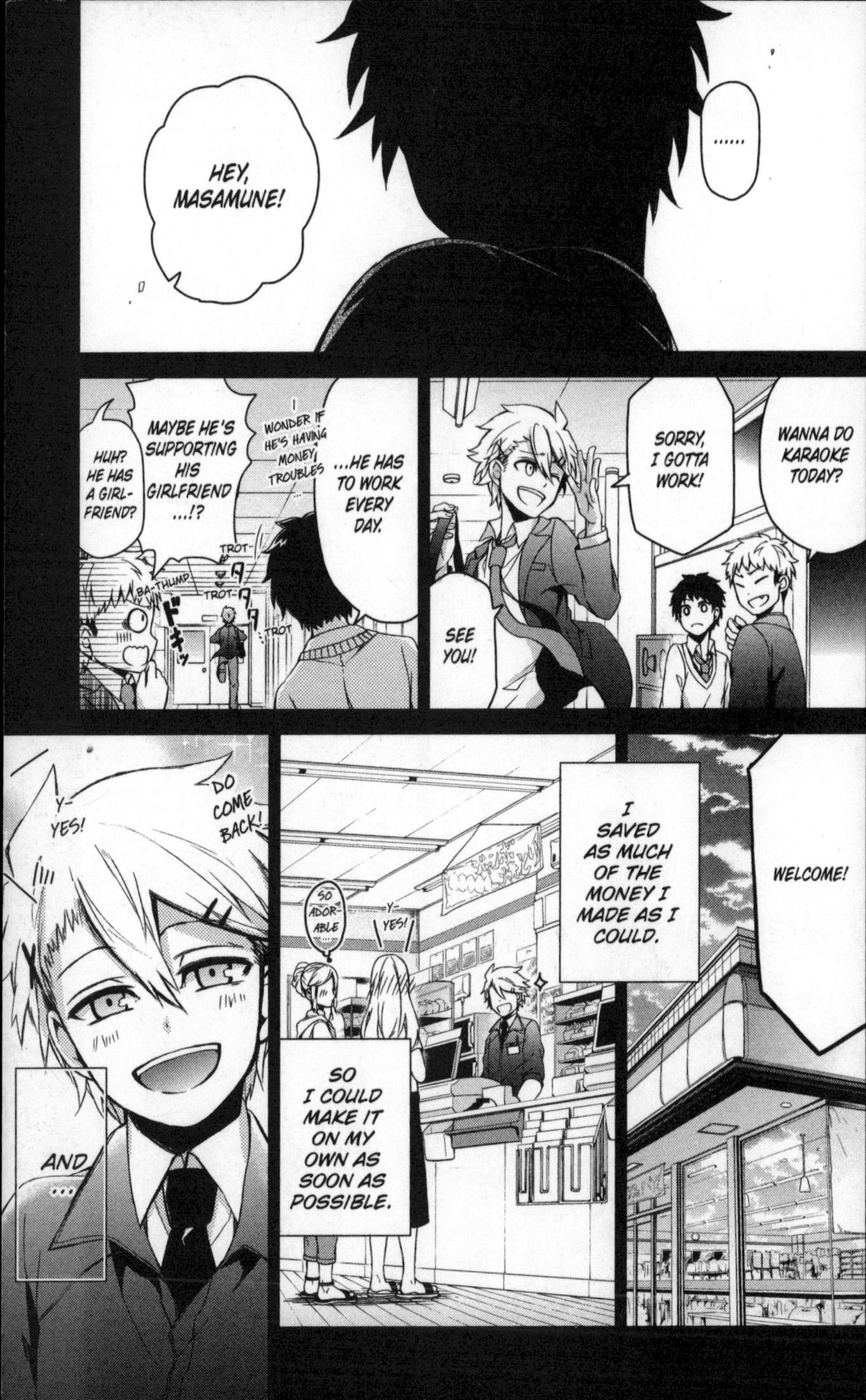
......
HEY, MASAMUNE!
WANNA DO KARAOKE TODAY?
SORRY, I GOTTA WORK!
SEE YOU!
...HE HAS TO WORK EVERY DAY.
I WONDER IF HE'S HAVING MONEY TROUBLES...
MAYBE HE'S SUPPORTING HIS GIRLFRIEND ...!?
HUH? HE HAS A GIRLFRIEND?
TROT- TROT- TROT
BA-THUMP
WELCOME!
I SAVED AS MUCH OF THE MONEY I MADE AS I COULD.
SO ADORABLE...
Y-YES!
SO I COULD MAKE IT ON MY OWN AS SOON AS POSSIBLE.
DO COME BACK!
Y-YES!
AND...

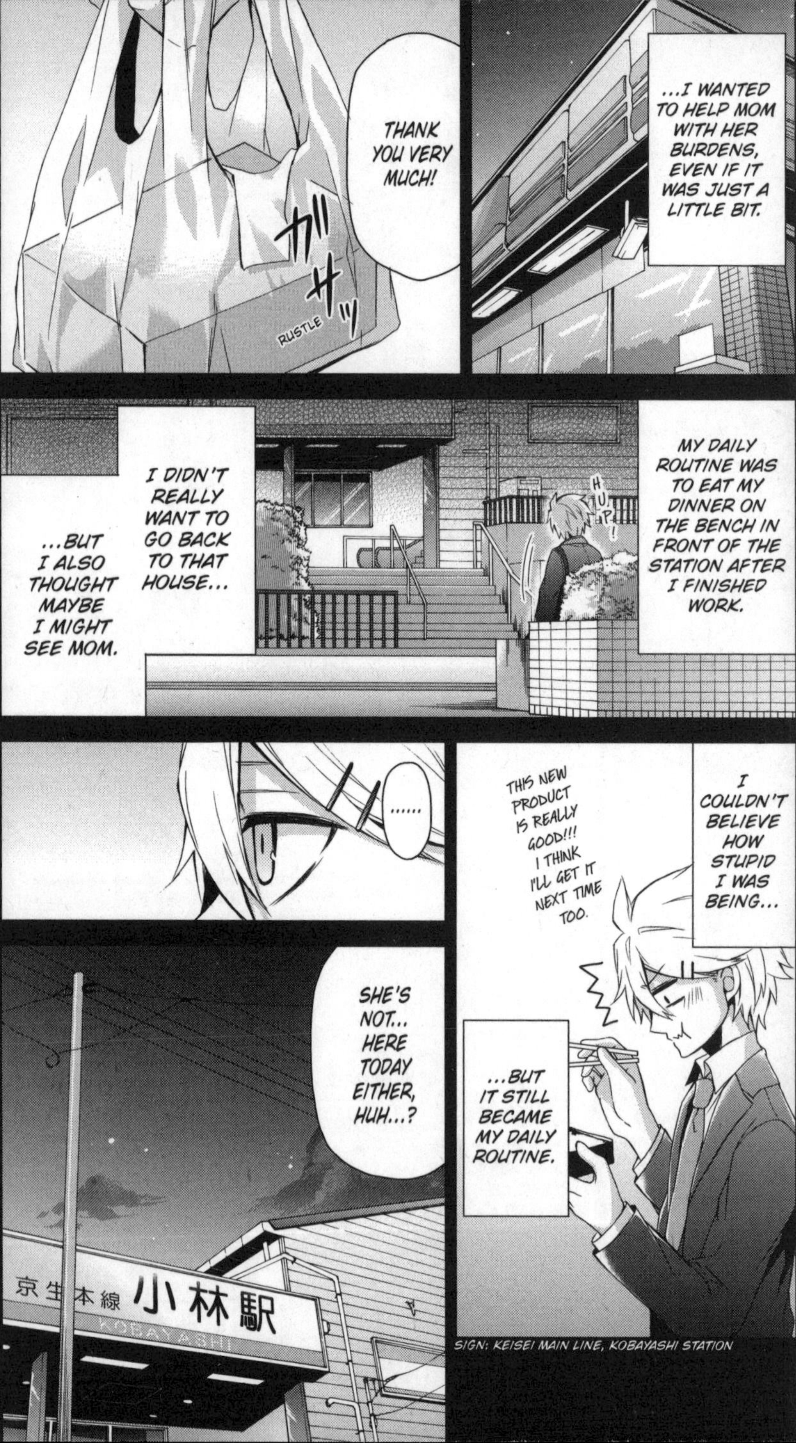
...I WANTED TO HELP MOM WITH HER BURDENS, EVEN IF IT WAS JUST A LITTLE BIT.
THANK YOU VERY MUCH!
RUSTLE
MY DAILY ROUTINE WAS TO EAT MY DINNER ON THE BENCH IN FRONT OF THE STATION AFTER I FINISHED WORK.
HUP!
I DIDN'T REALLY WANT TO GO BACK TO THAT HOUSE...
...BUT I ALSO THOUGHT MAYBE I MIGHT SEE MOM.
I COULDN'T BELIEVE HOW STUPID I WAS BEING...
THIS NEW PRODUCT IS REALLY GOOD!!! I THINK I'LL GET IT NEXT TIME TOO.
...BUT IT STILL BECAME MY DAILY ROUTINE.
......
SHE'S NOT... HERE TODAY EITHER, HUH...?
京生本線 小林駅
KOBAYASHI
SIGN: KEISEI MAIN LINE, KOBAYASHI STATION

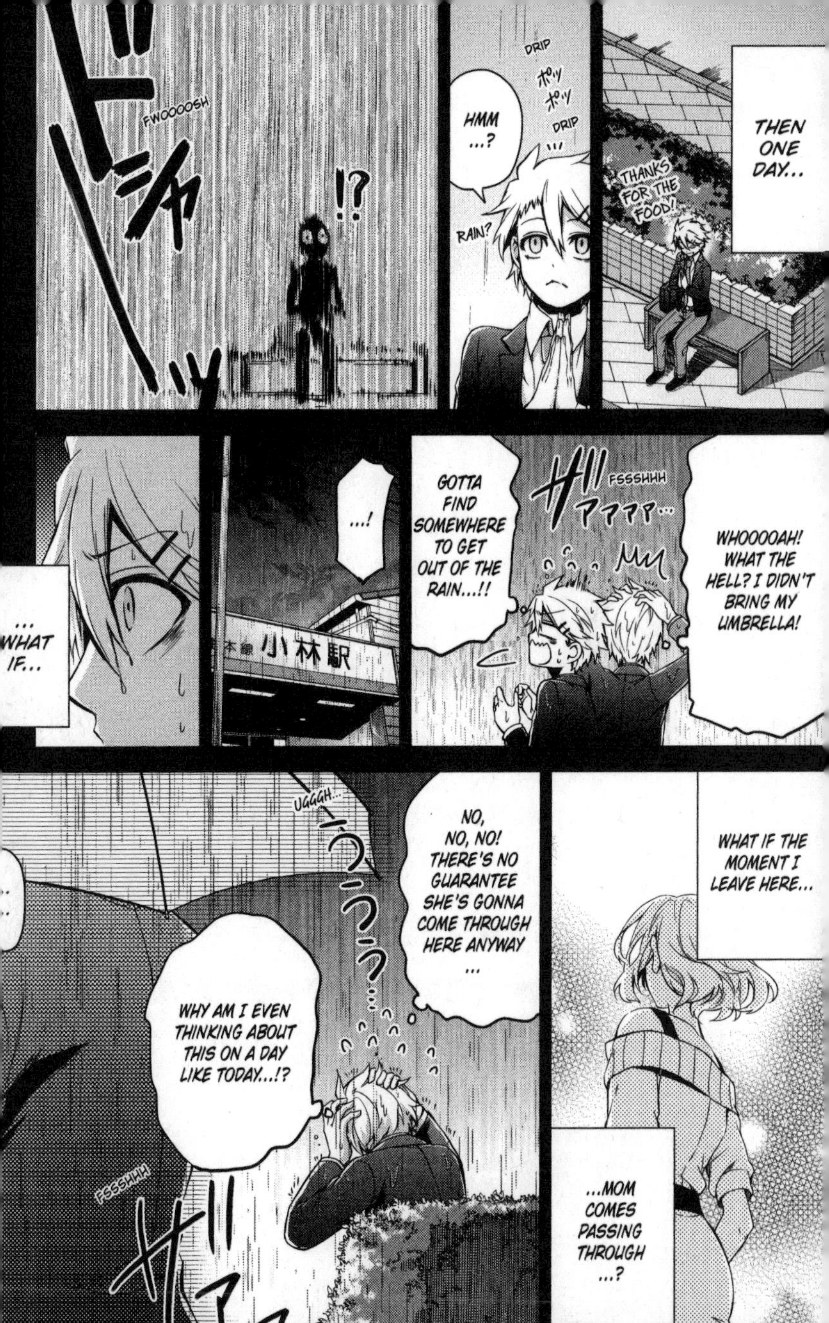
THEN ONE DAY...
THANKS FOR THE FOOD!
DRIP
ポツ
ポツ
DRIP
HMM ...?
RAIN?
ドシャッ
FWOOOOSH
!?
WHOOOOAH! WHAT THE HELL? I DIDN'T BRING MY UMBRELLA!
ザァァァァ…
FSSSHHH
GOTTA FIND SOMEWHERE TO GET OUT OF THE RAIN...!!
...!
小林駅
...WHAT IF...
WHAT IF THE MOMENT I LEAVE HERE...
...MOM COMES PASSING THROUGH ...?
NO, NO, NO! THERE'S NO GUARANTEE SHE'S GONNA COME THROUGH HERE ANYWAY ...
UGGGH...
うううう…
WHY AM I EVEN THINKING ABOUT THIS ON A DAY LIKE TODAY...!?
FSSSHHH
ザァァ

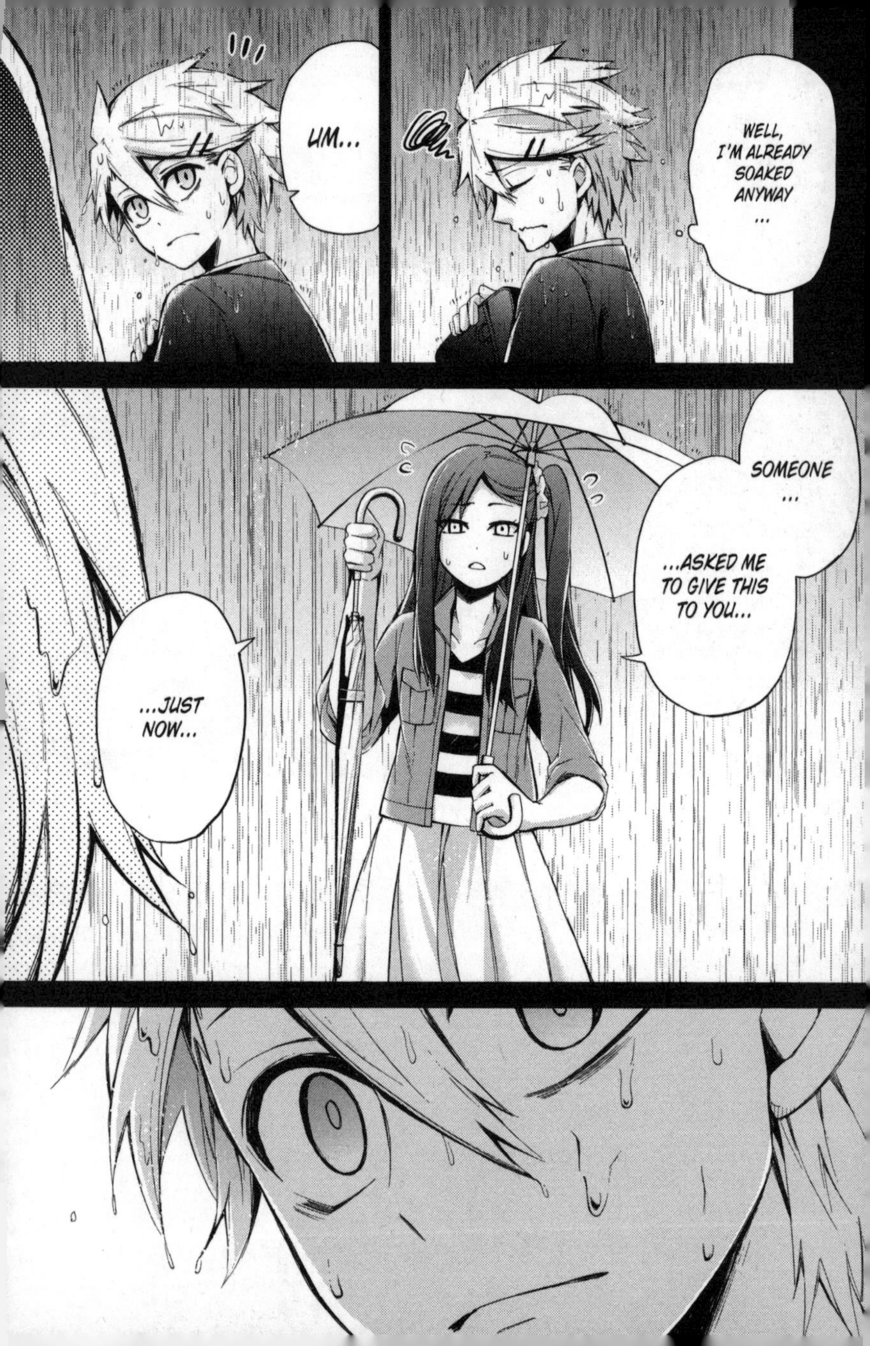
WELL, I'M ALREADY SOAKED ANYWAY ...
UM...
SOMEONE ...
...ASKED ME TO GIVE THIS TO YOU...
...JUST NOW...

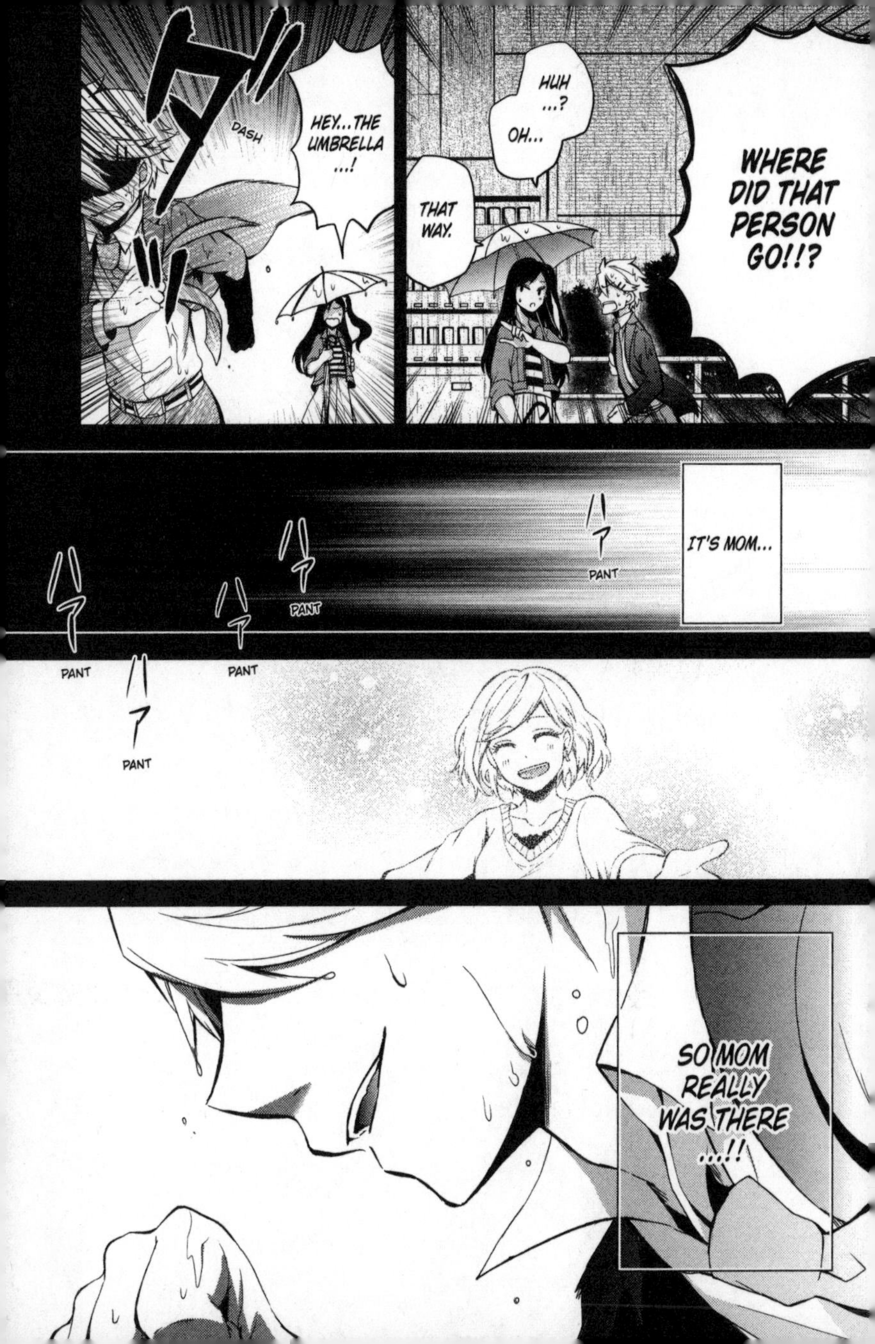
WHERE DID THAT PERSON GO!!?
HUH...? OH...
THAT WAY.
HEY...THE UMBRELLA...!
DASH
IT'S MOM...
PANT
PANT
PANT
PANT
PANT
SO MOM REALLY WAS THERE...!!

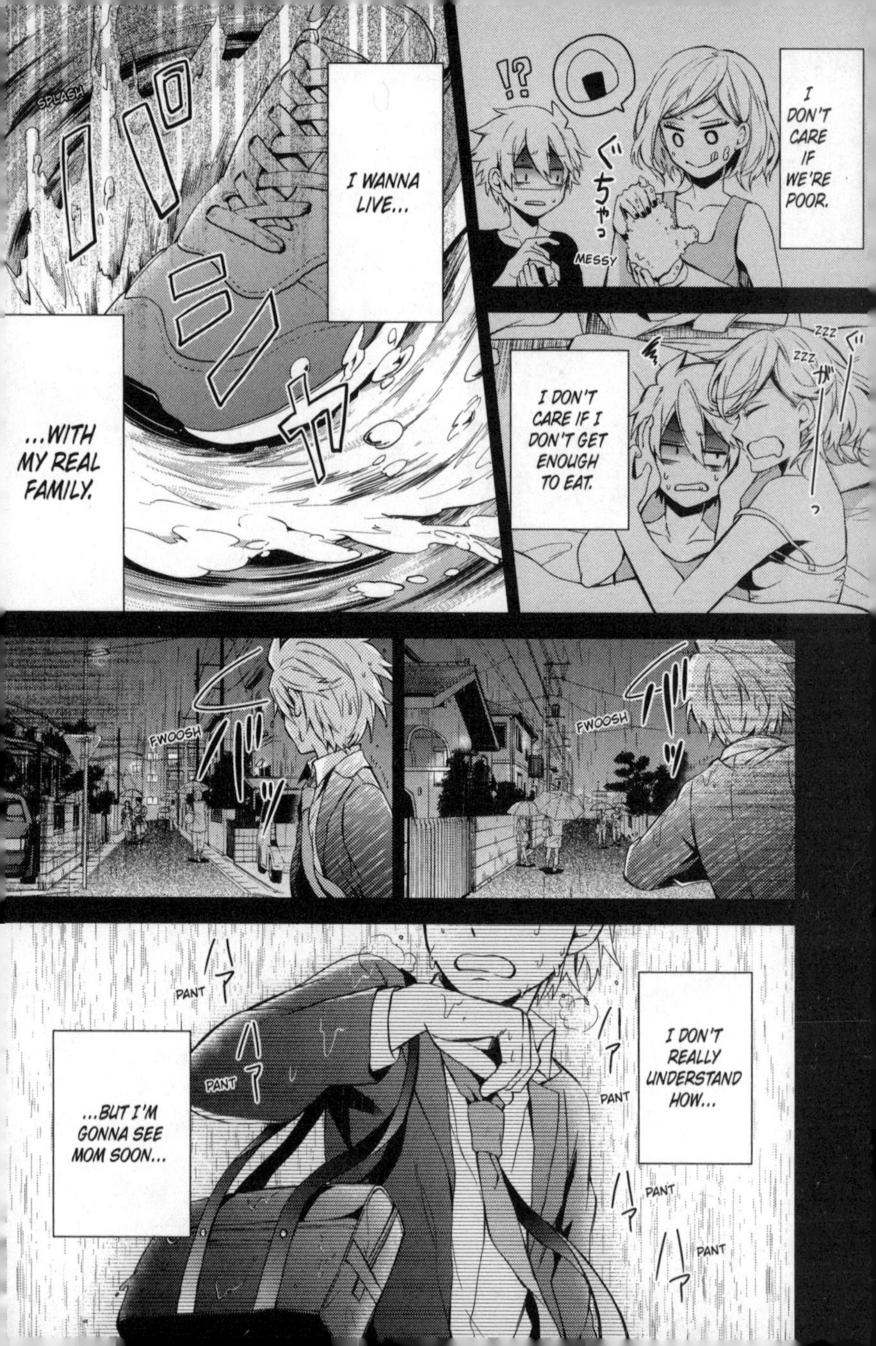

I DON'T CARE IF WE'RE POOR.
!?
ぐちゃっ
MESSY
ZZZ
ZZZ
I DON'T CARE IF I DON'T GET ENOUGH TO EAT.
SPLASH
I WANNA LIVE...
...WITH MY REAL FAMILY.
FWOOSH
FWOOSH
I DON'T REALLY UNDERSTAND HOW...
PANT
PANT
PANT
PANT
PANT
...BUT I'M GONNA SEE MOM SOON...

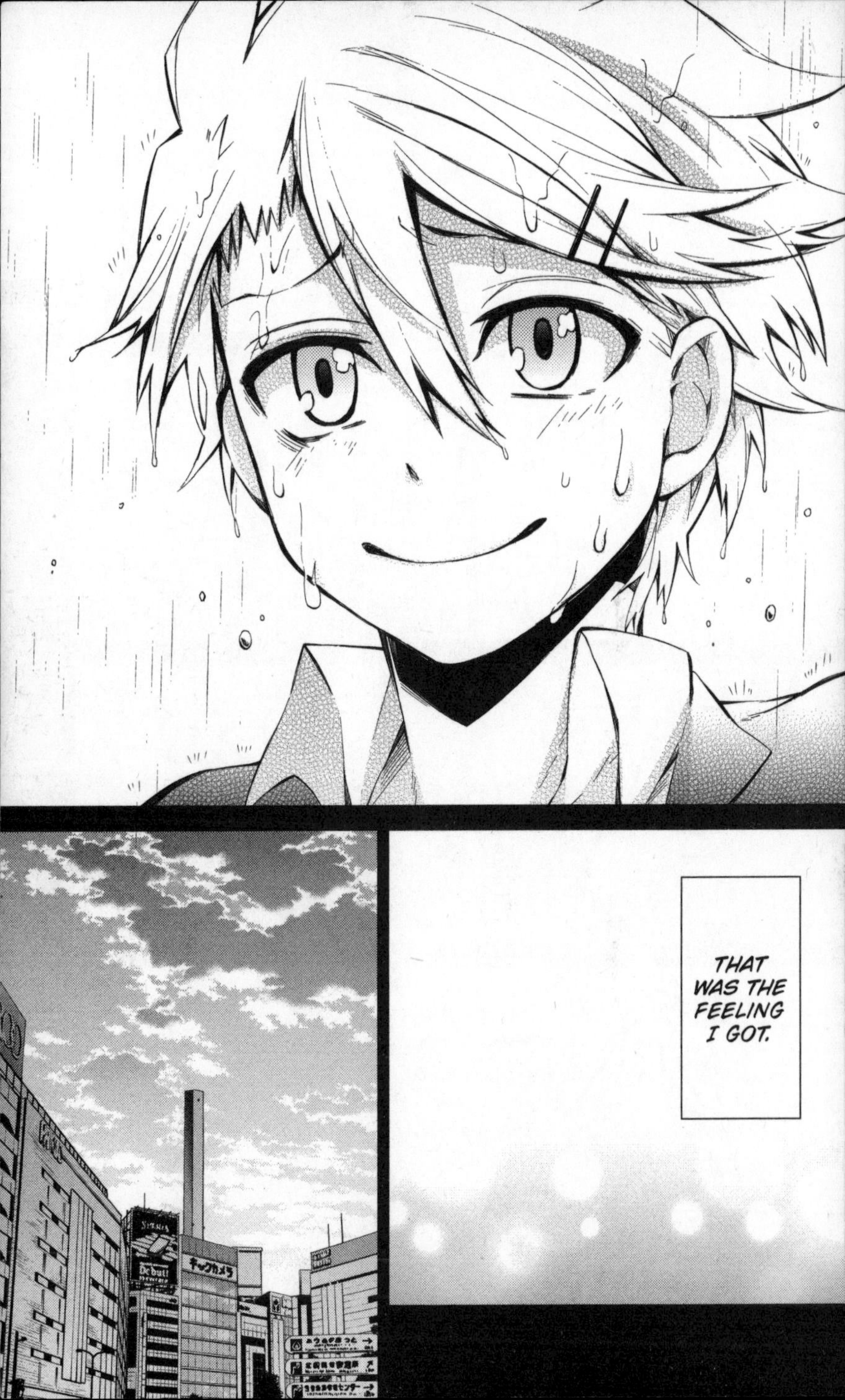
THAT WAS THE FEELING I GOT.

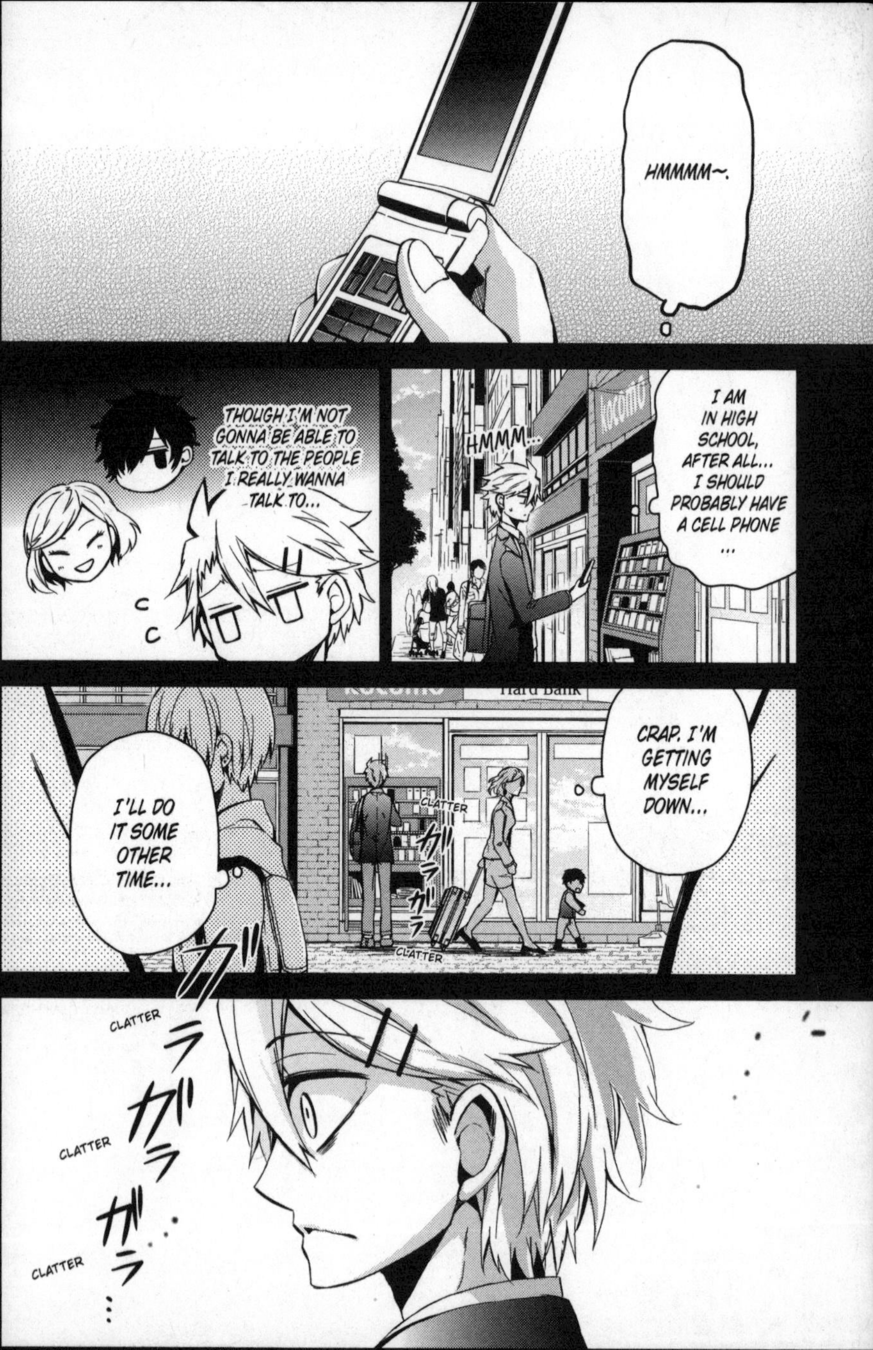
HMMMM~.
I AM IN HIGH SCHOOL, AFTER ALL... I SHOULD PROBABLY HAVE A CELL PHONE ...
HMMM...
THOUGH I'M NOT GONNA BE ABLE TO TALK TO THE PEOPLE I REALLY WANNA TALK TO...
CRAP. I'M GETTING MYSELF DOWN...
CLATTER
ガラガラ
CLATTER
I'LL DO IT SOME OTHER TIME...
CLATTER
ガラガラ
CLATTER
CLATTER
...

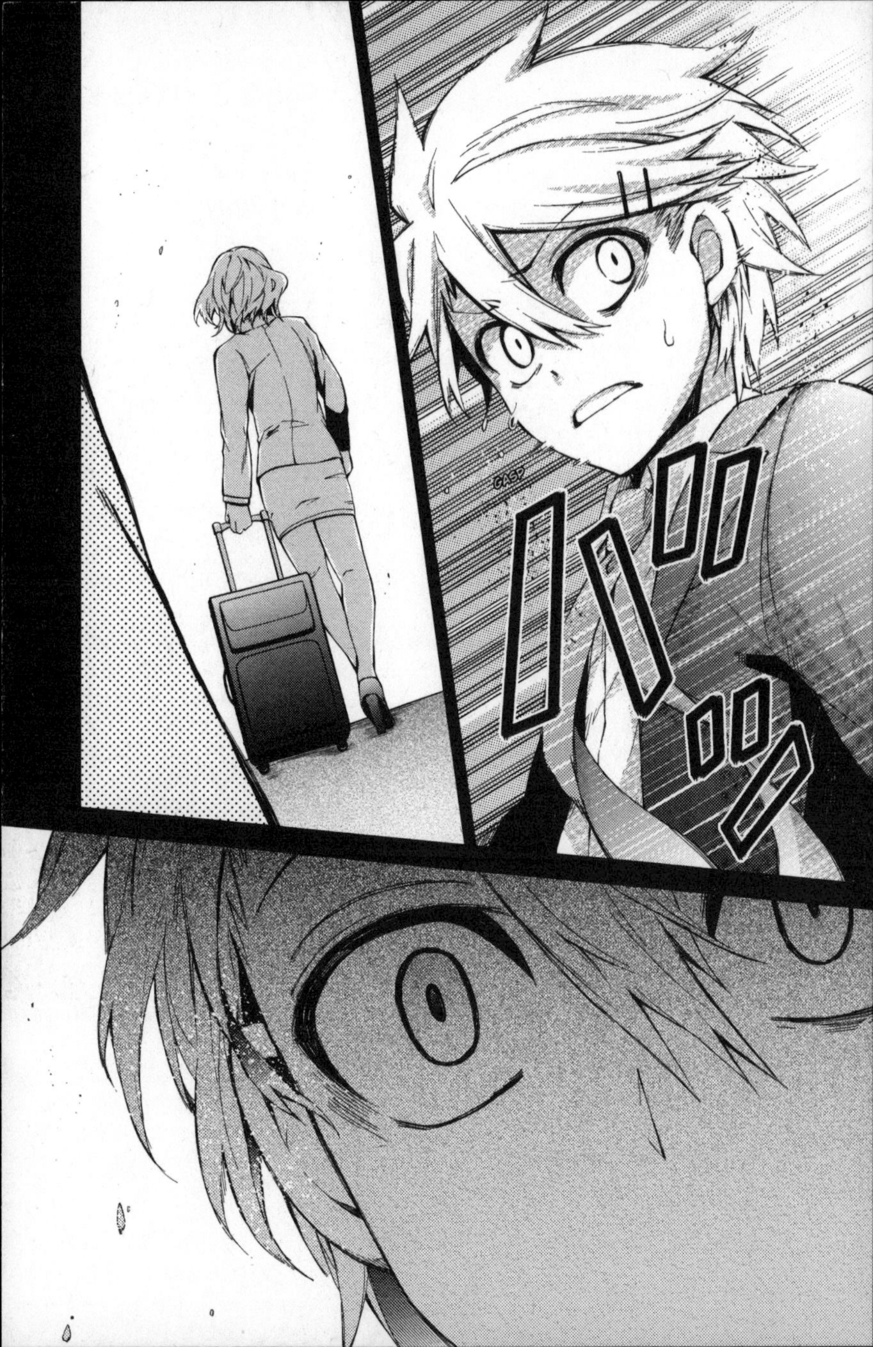
ハッ
GASP

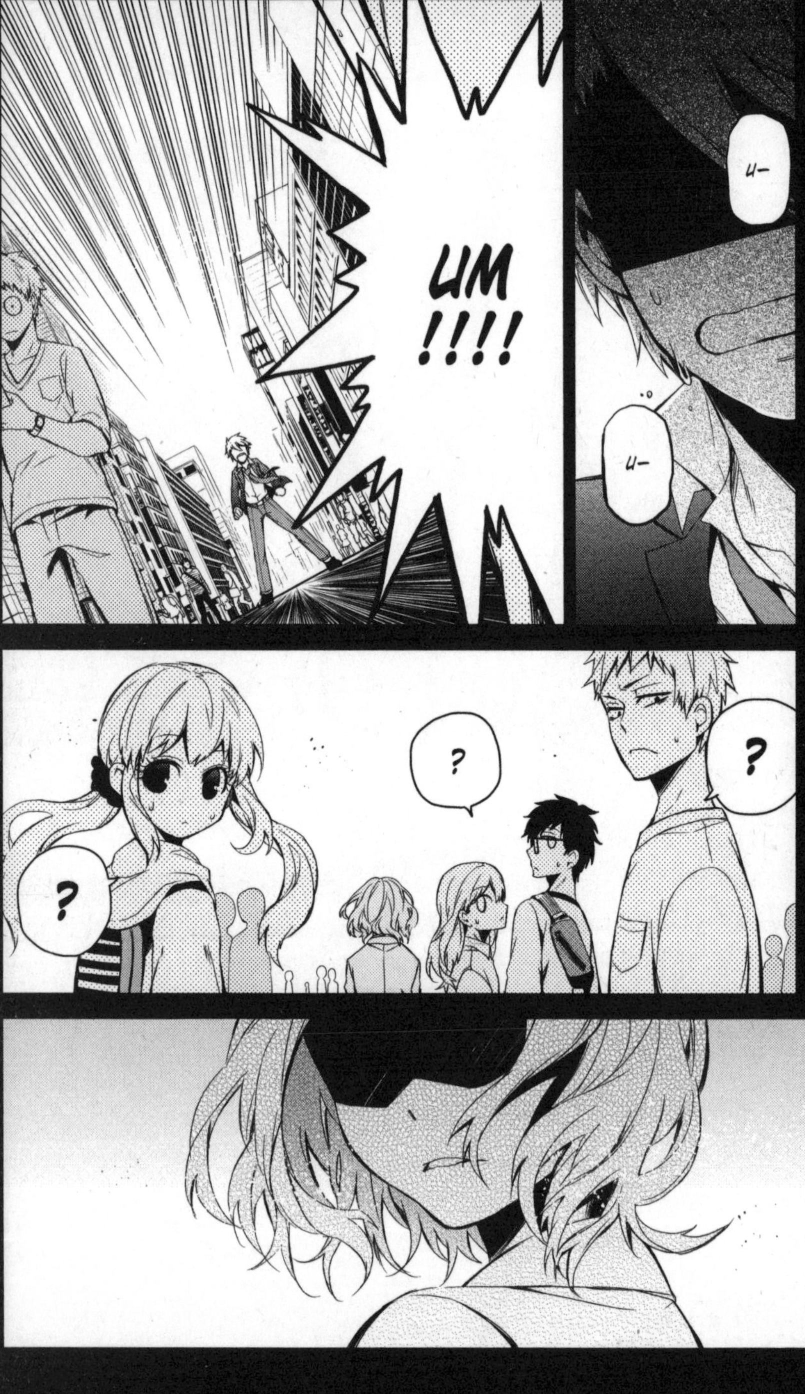
U–
U–
UM !!!!
?
?
?

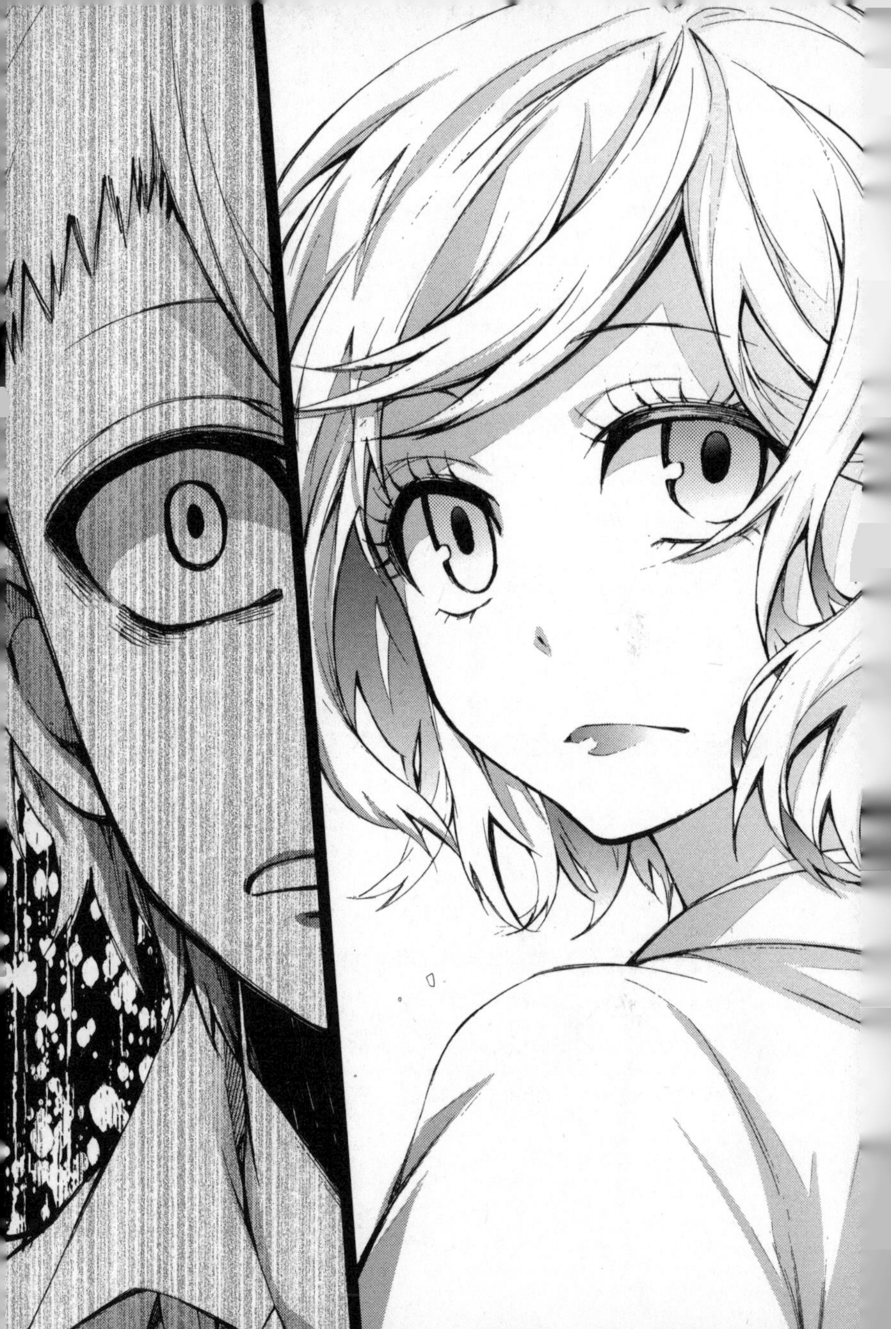

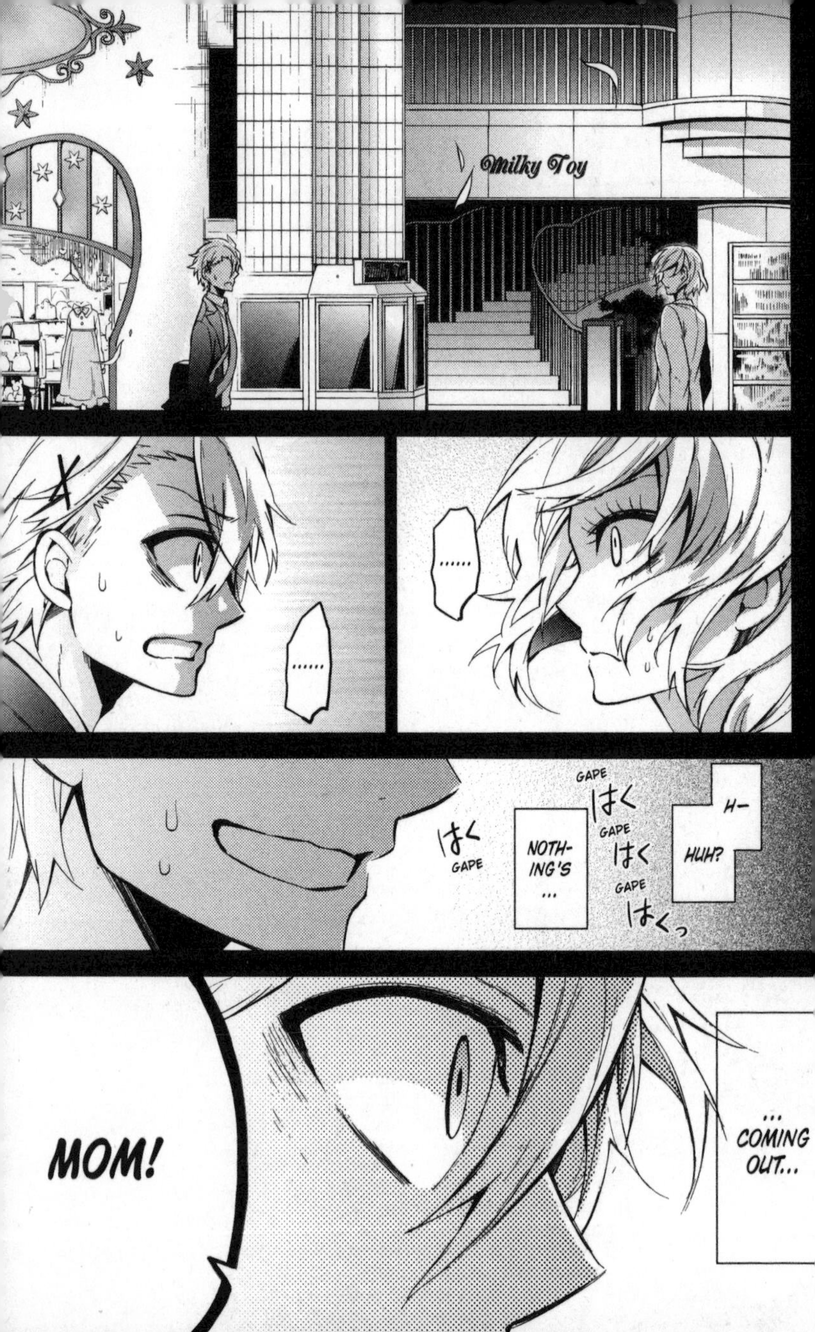
Milky Toy
......
......
H- HUH?
GAPE
はく
GAPE
はく
GAPE
はくっ
NOTH-ING'S ...
はく
GAPE
... COMING OUT...
MOM!

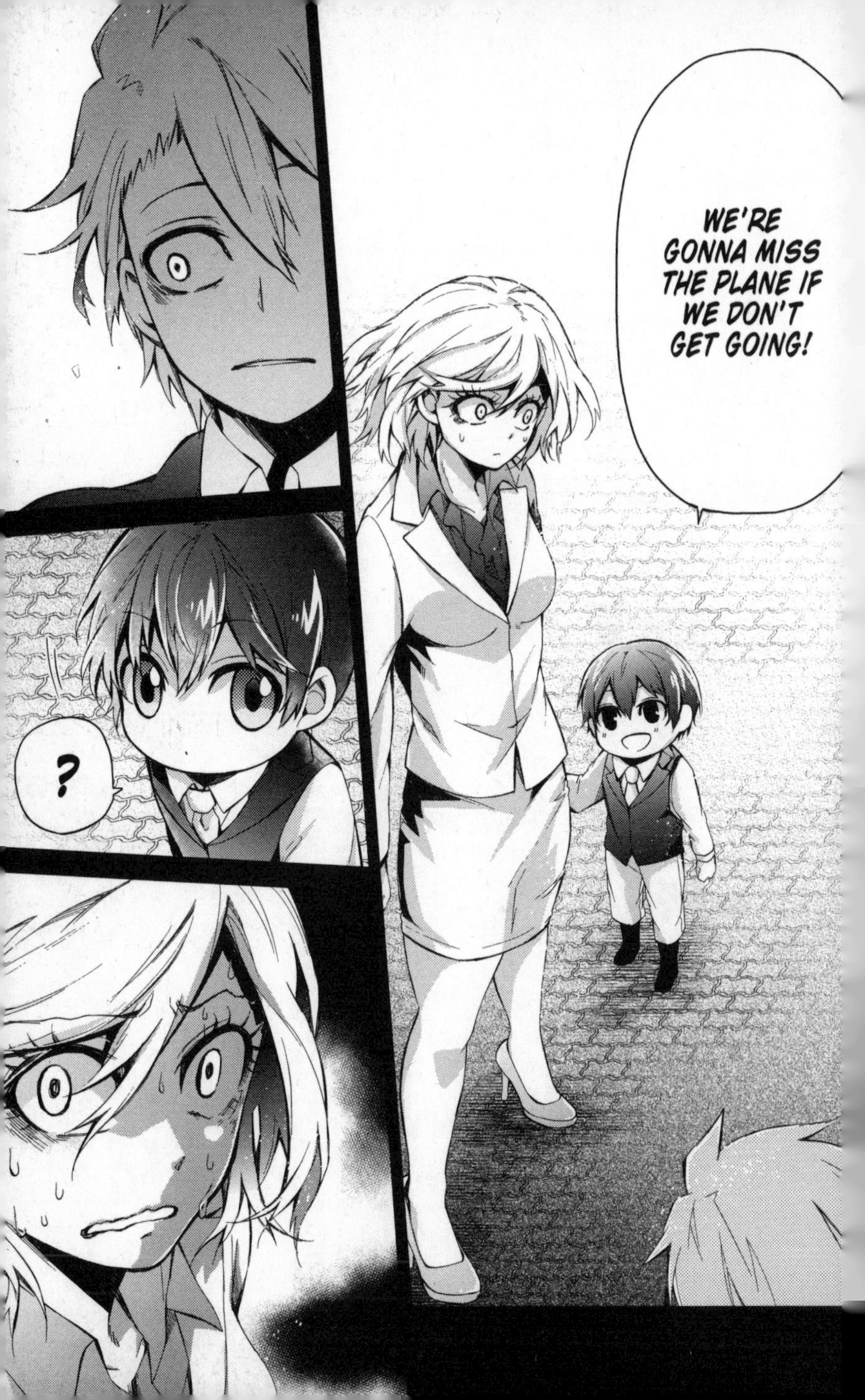
WE'RE GONNA MISS THE PLANE IF WE DON'T GET GOING!
?

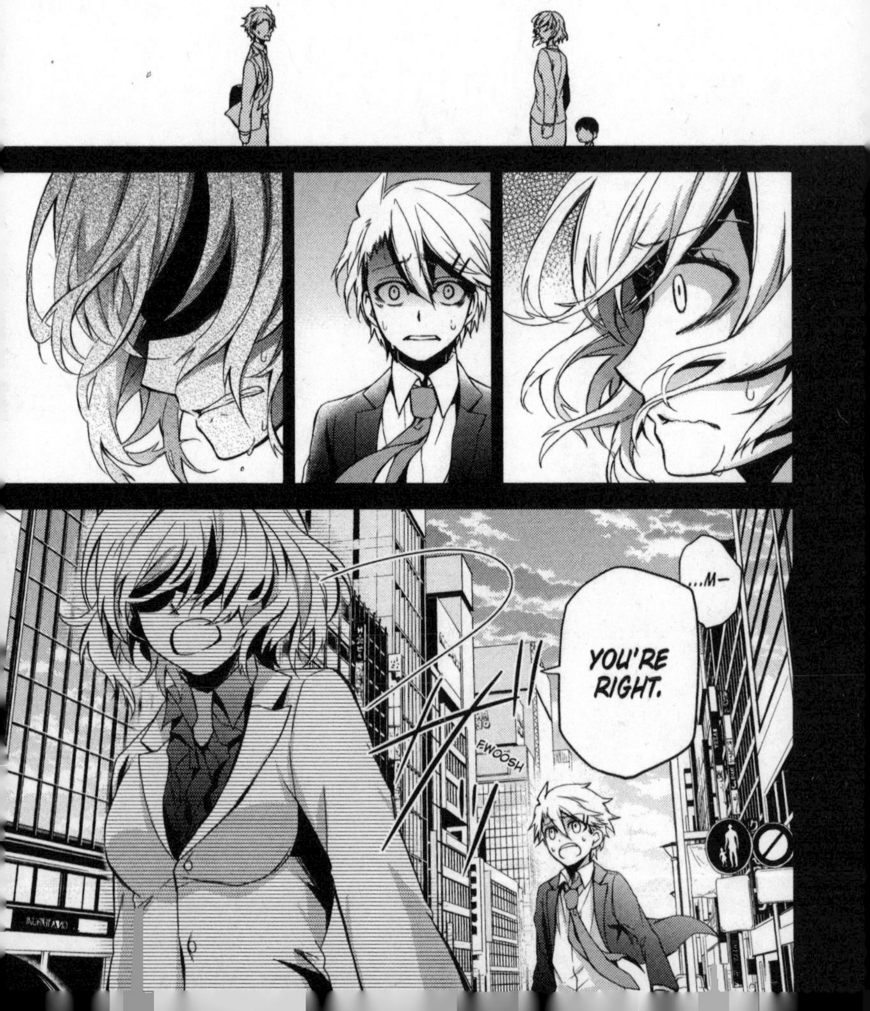
...M—
YOU'RE RIGHT.
FWOOSH

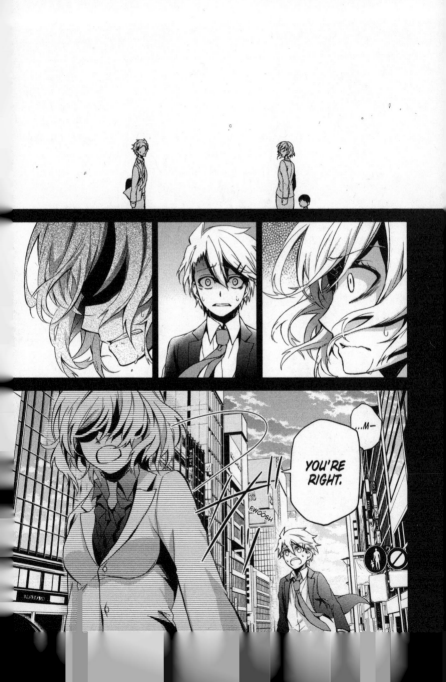

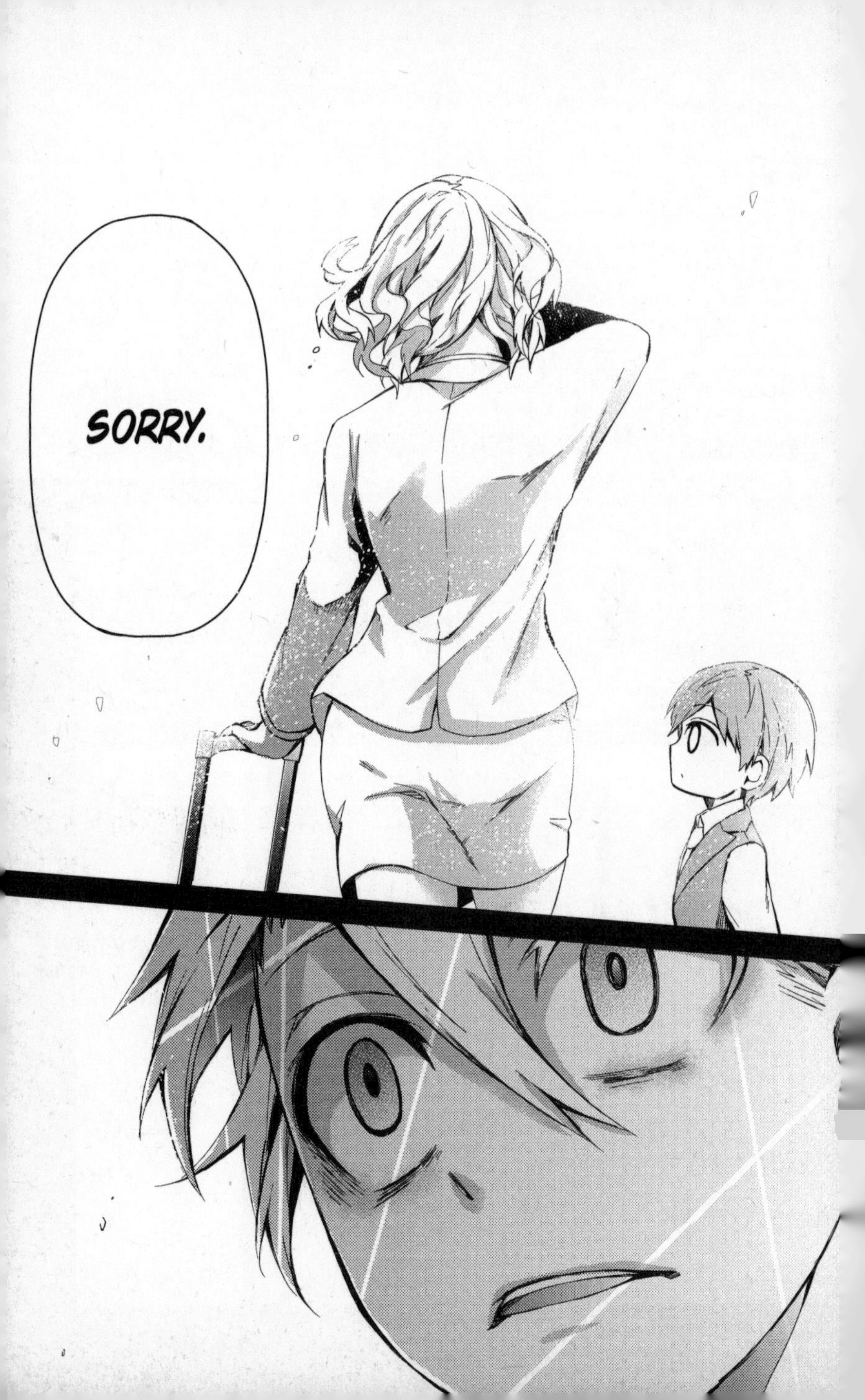
SORRY.

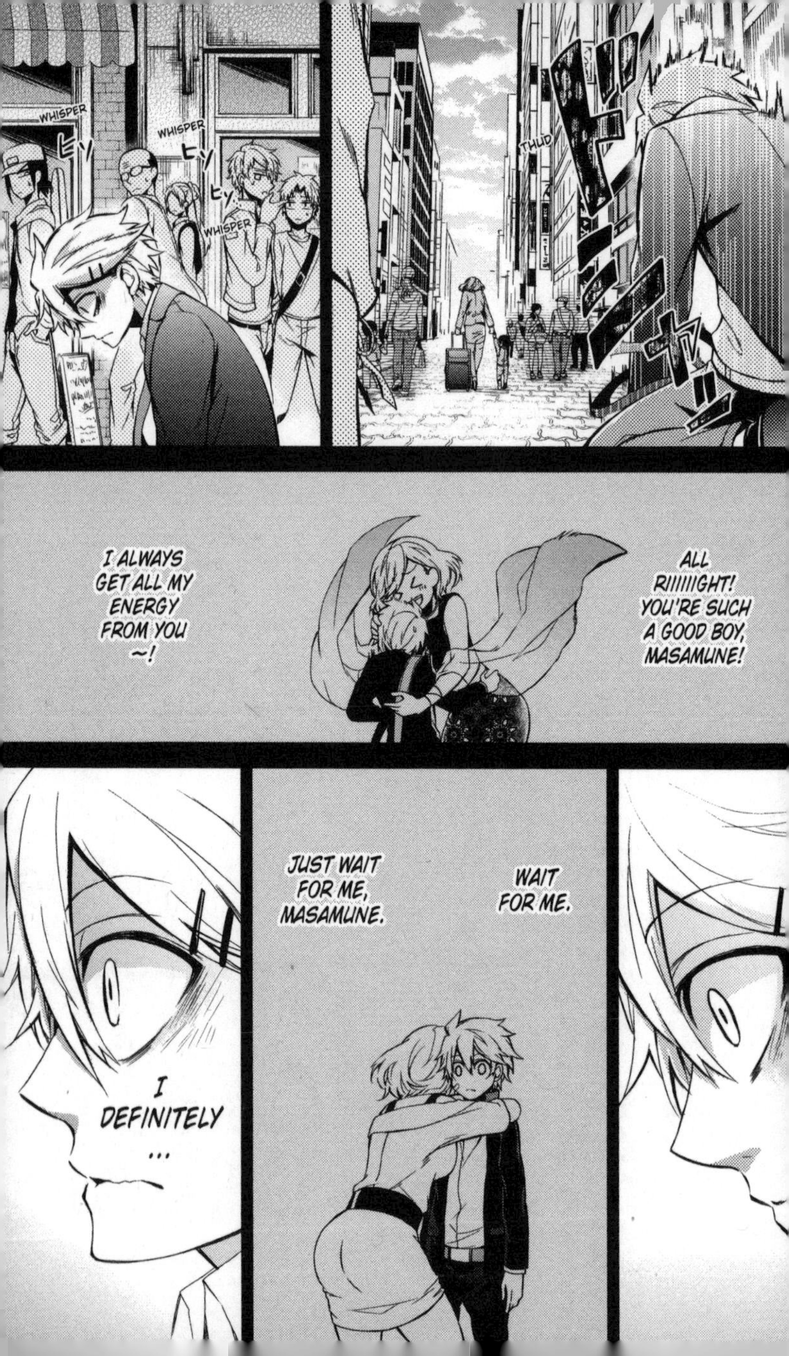
THUD
WHISPER
ヒソ
WHISPER
ヒソ
WHISPER
ヒソ
ALL RIIIIIIGHT! YOU'RE SUCH A GOOD BOY, MASAMUNE!
I ALWAYS GET ALL MY ENERGY FROM YOU ~!
WAIT FOR ME.
JUST WAIT FOR ME, MASAMUNE.
I DEFINITELY ...

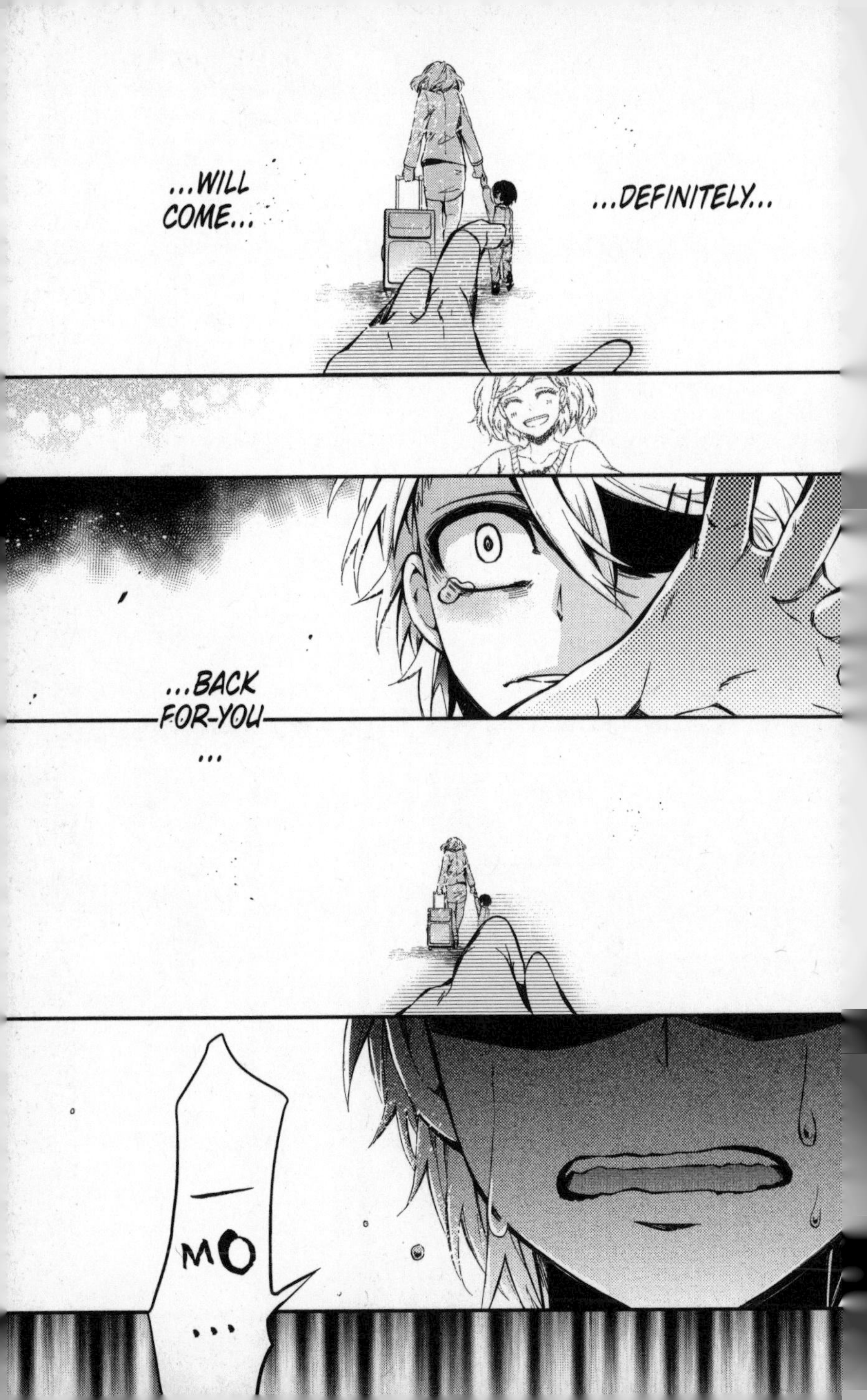
...DEFINITELY...
...WILL COME...
...BACK FOR YOU...
MO...

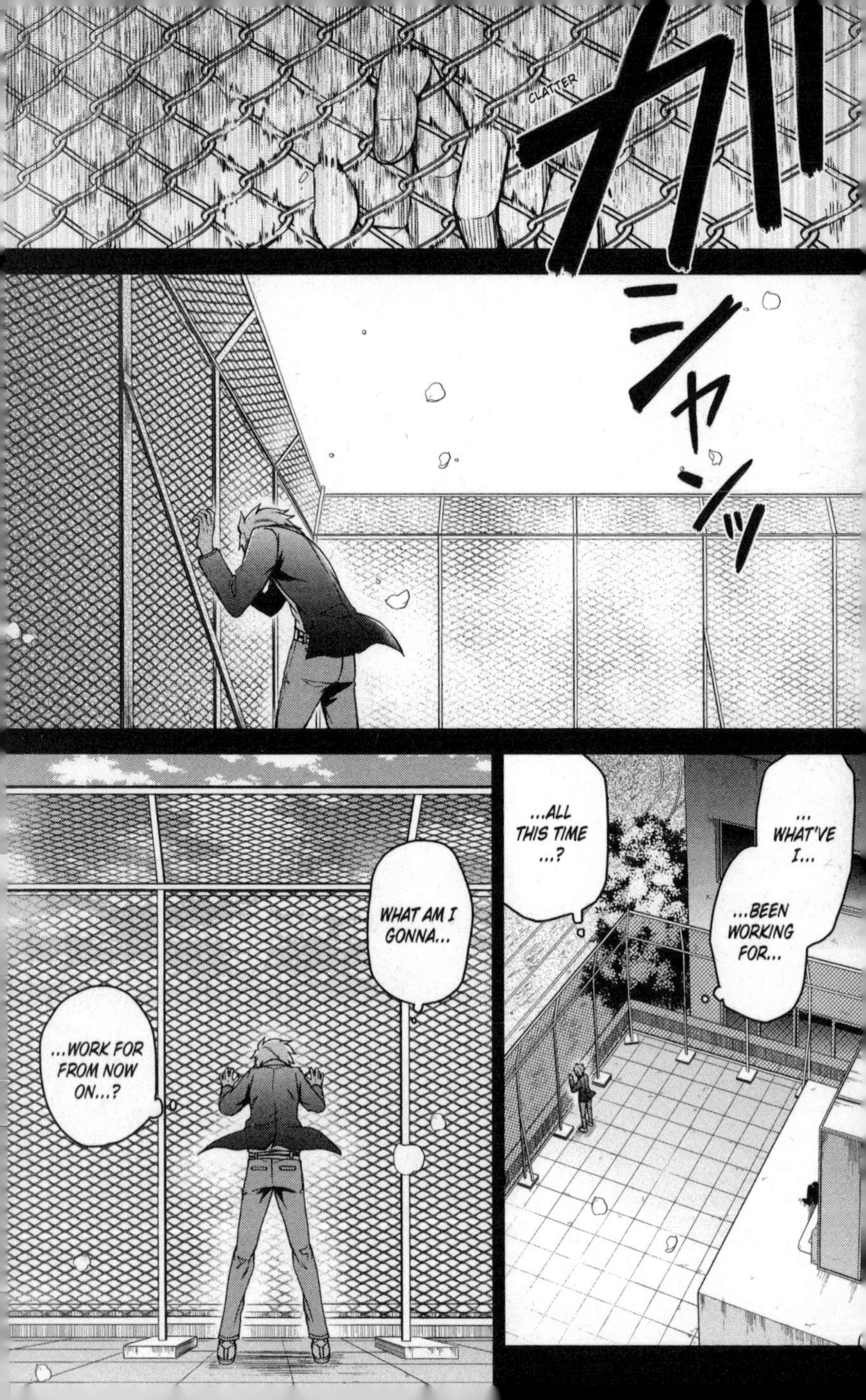
CLATTER
カシャンッ
...WHAT'VE I...
...BEEN WORKING FOR...
...ALL THIS TIME ...?
WHAT AM I GONNA...
...WORK FOR FROM NOW ON...?

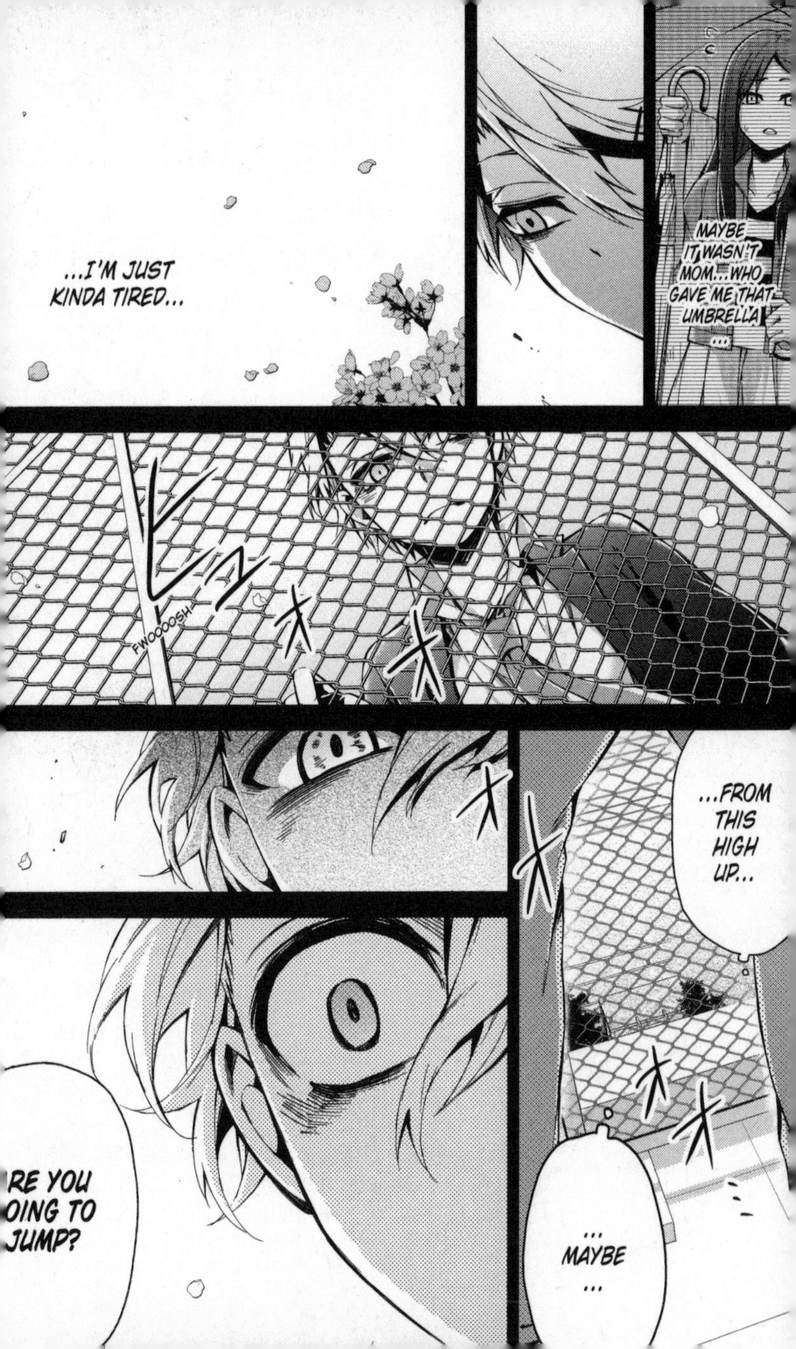
MAYBE IT WASN'T MOM...WHO GAVE ME THAT UMBRELLA ...
...I'M JUST KINDA TIRED...
FWOOOOSH
...FROM THIS HIGH UP...
... MAYBE ...
RE YOU OING TO JUMP?

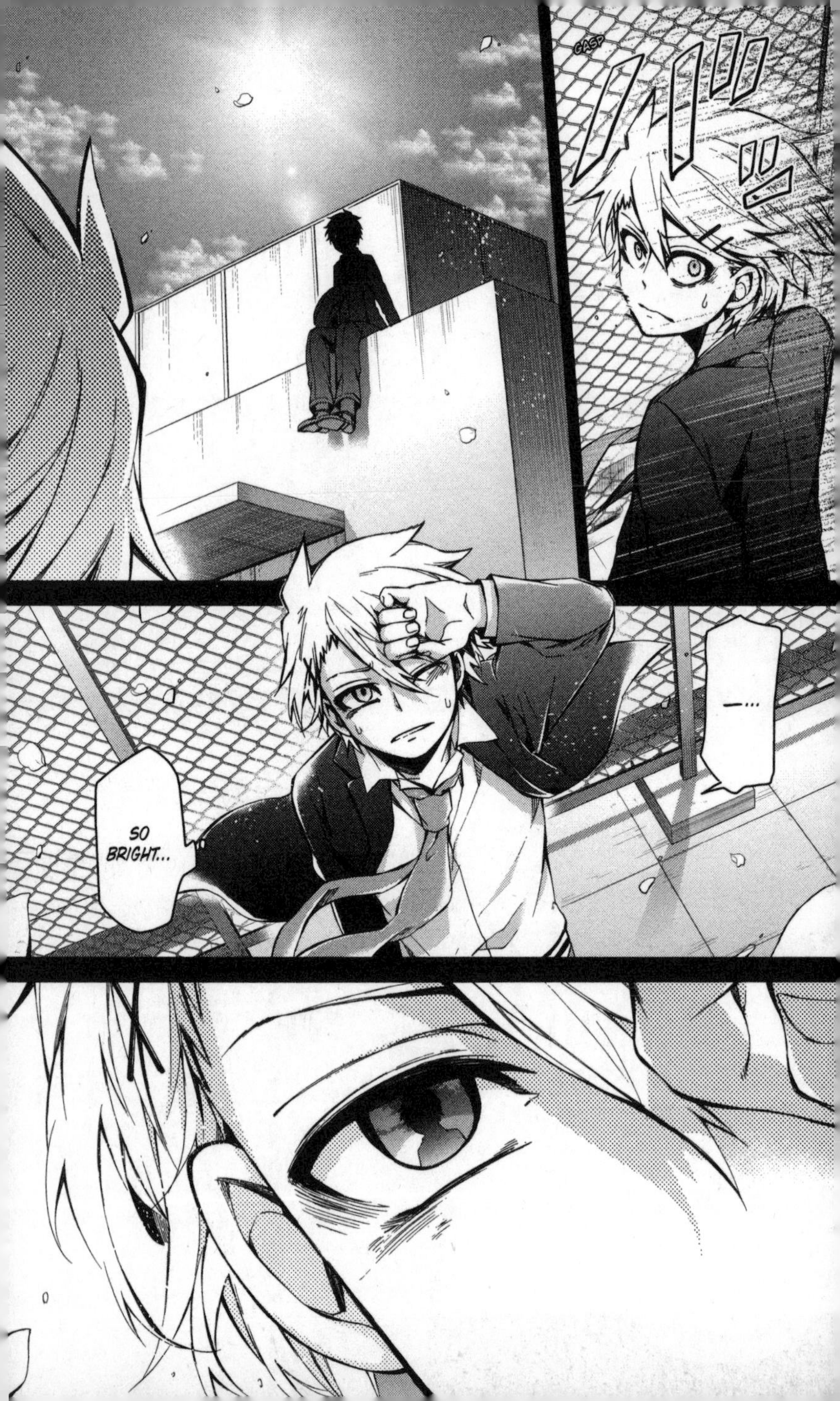
GASP
—...
SO BRIGHT...

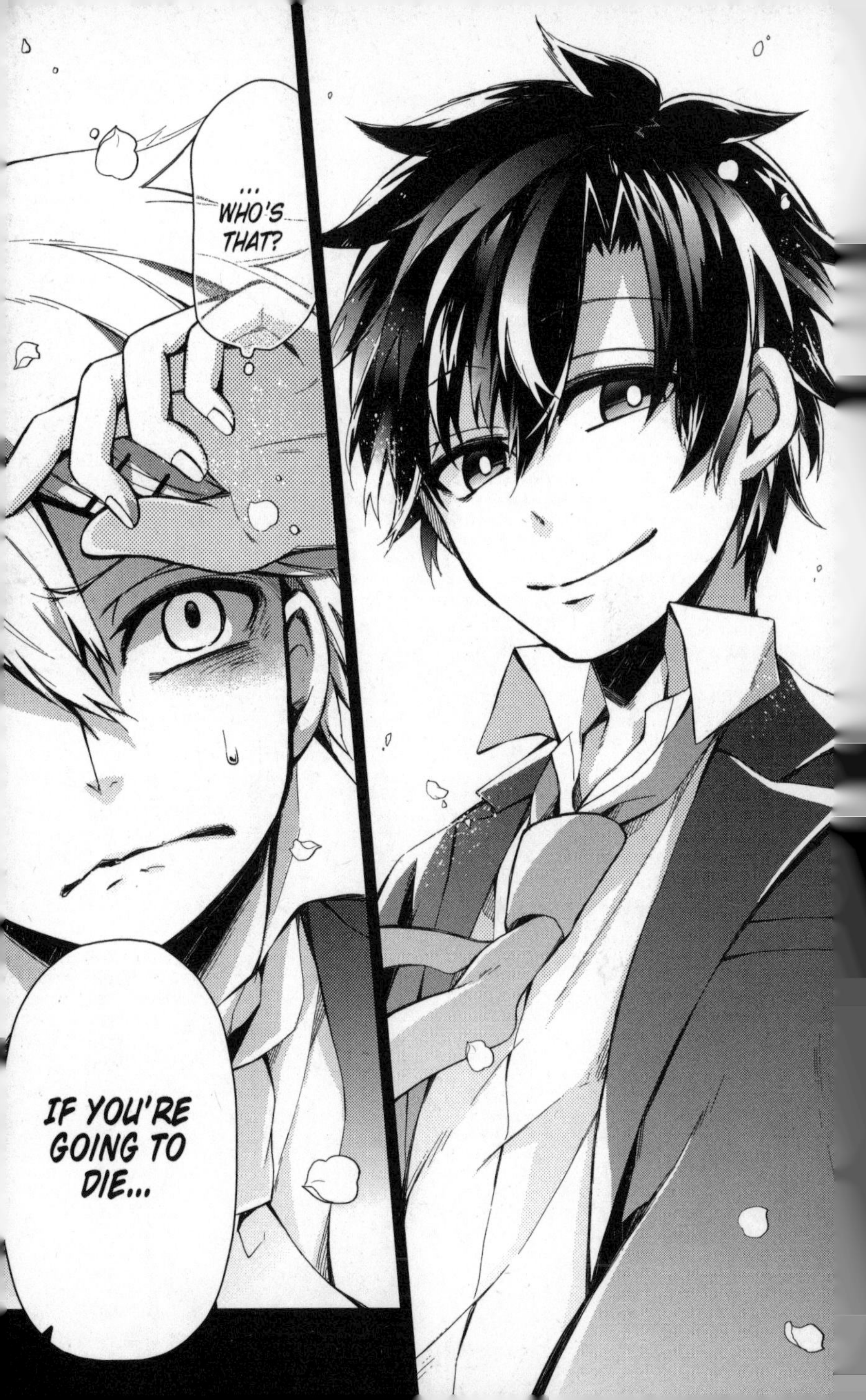
...WHO'S THAT?
IF YOU'RE GOING TO DIE...

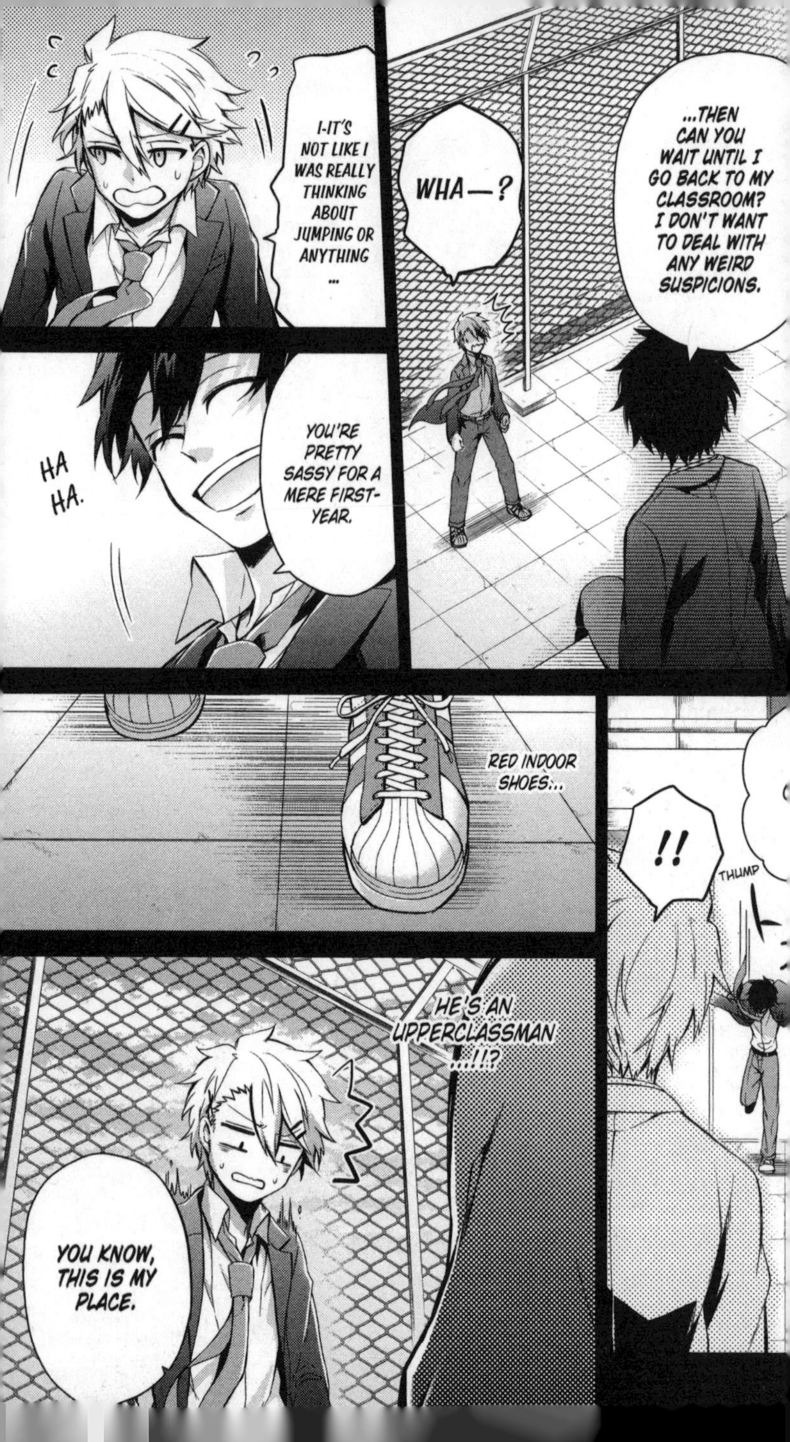

...THEN CAN YOU WAIT UNTIL I GO BACK TO MY CLASSROOM? I DON'T WANT TO DEAL WITH ANY WEIRD SUSPICIONS.
WHA—?
I-IT'S NOT LIKE I WAS REALLY THINKING ABOUT JUMPING OR ANYTHING ...
YOU'RE PRETTY SASSY FOR A MERE FIRST-YEAR.
HA HA.
!!
THUMP
RED INDOOR SHOES...
HE'S AN UPPERCLASSMAN ...!!?
YOU KNOW, THIS IS MY PLACE.

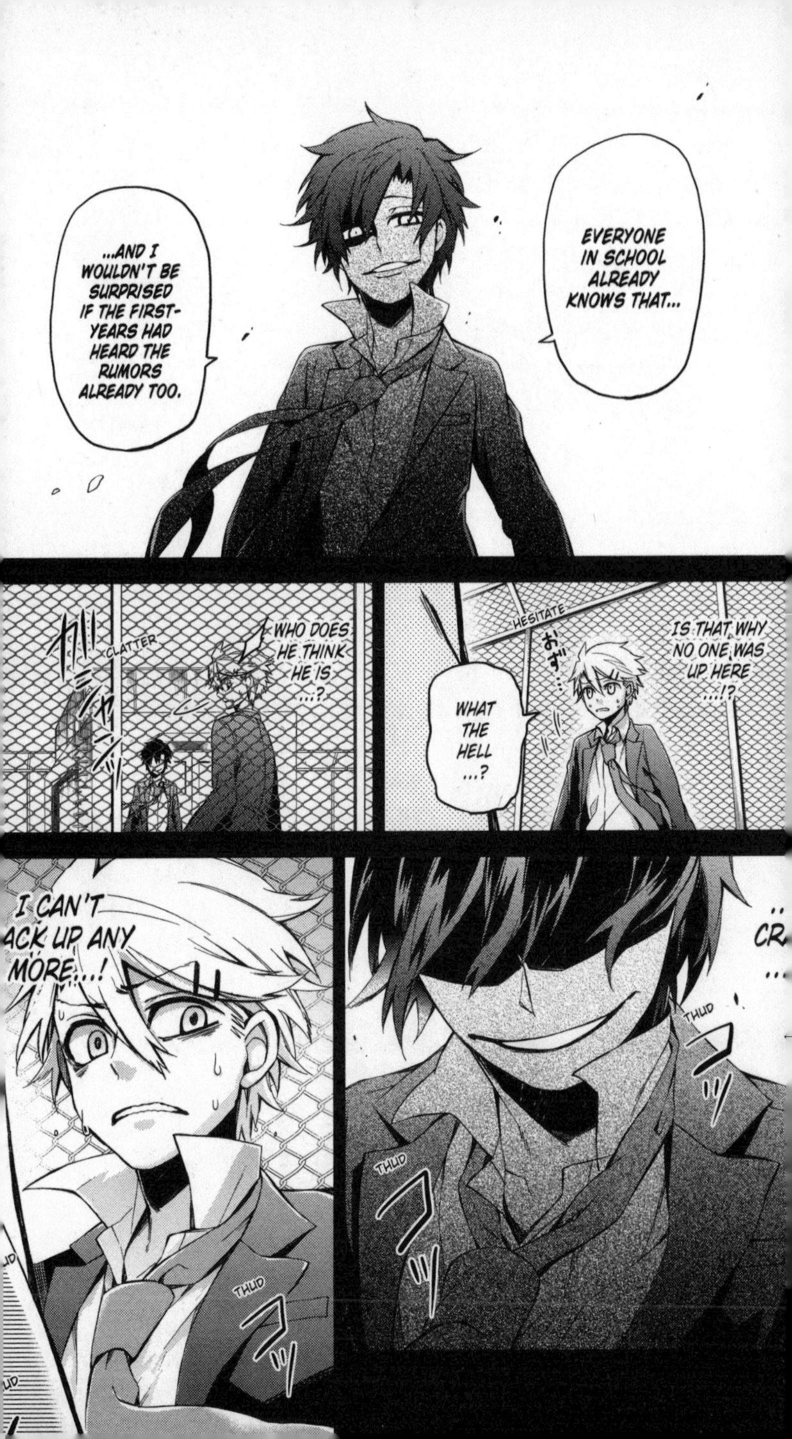
EVERYONE IN SCHOOL ALREADY KNOWS THAT...
...AND I WOULDN'T BE SURPRISED IF THE FIRST-YEARS HAD HEARD THE RUMORS ALREADY TOO.
IS THAT WHY NO ONE WAS UP HERE ...!?
HESITATE
おず
WHAT THE HELL ...?
WHO DOES HE THINK HE IS ...?
CLATTER
THUD
THUD
I CAN'T
ACK UP ANY
MORE...!
THUD

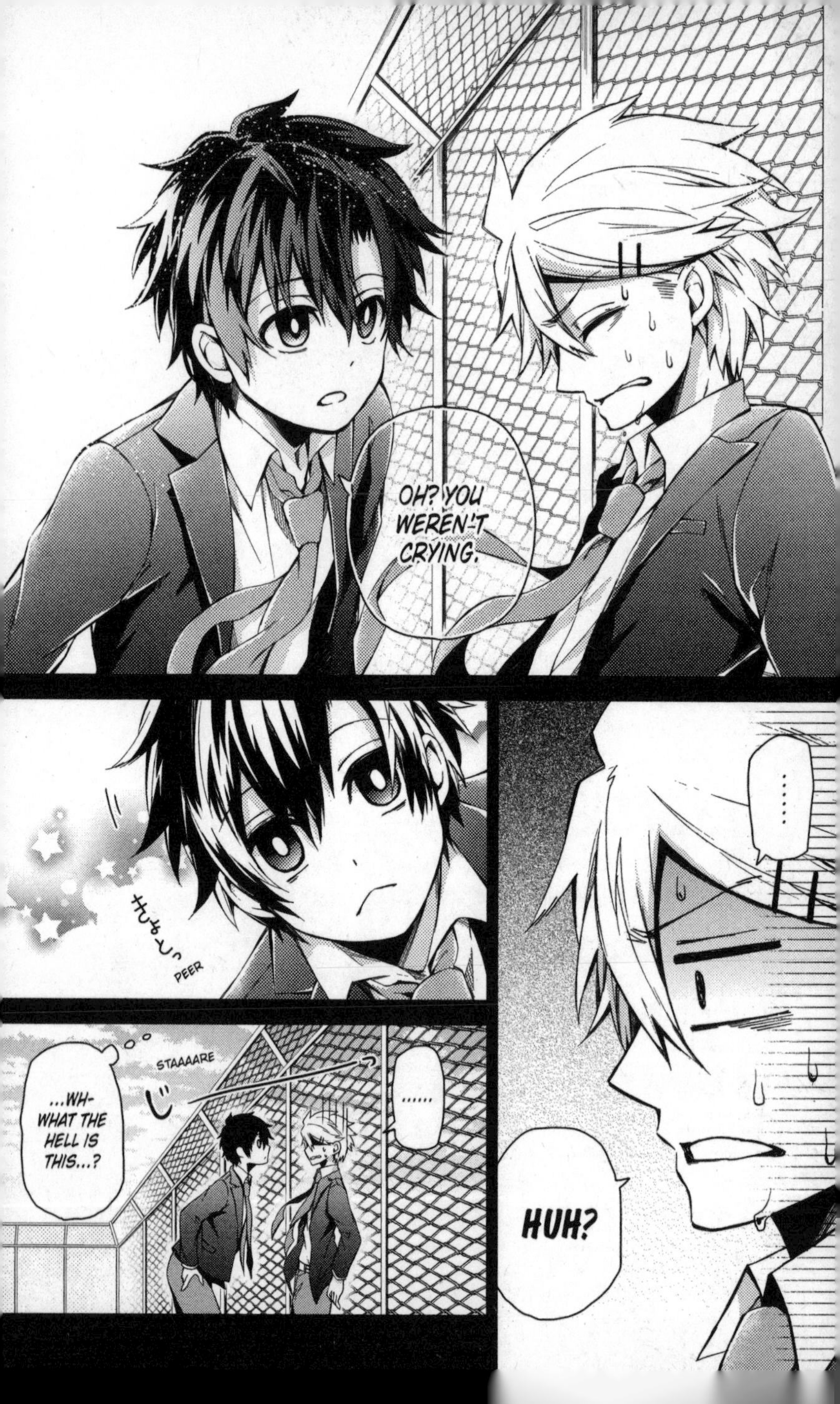
OH? YOU WEREN'T CRYING.
......
HUH?
きょとっ
PEER
......
じ
STAAAARE
...WH-WHAT THE HELL IS THIS...?

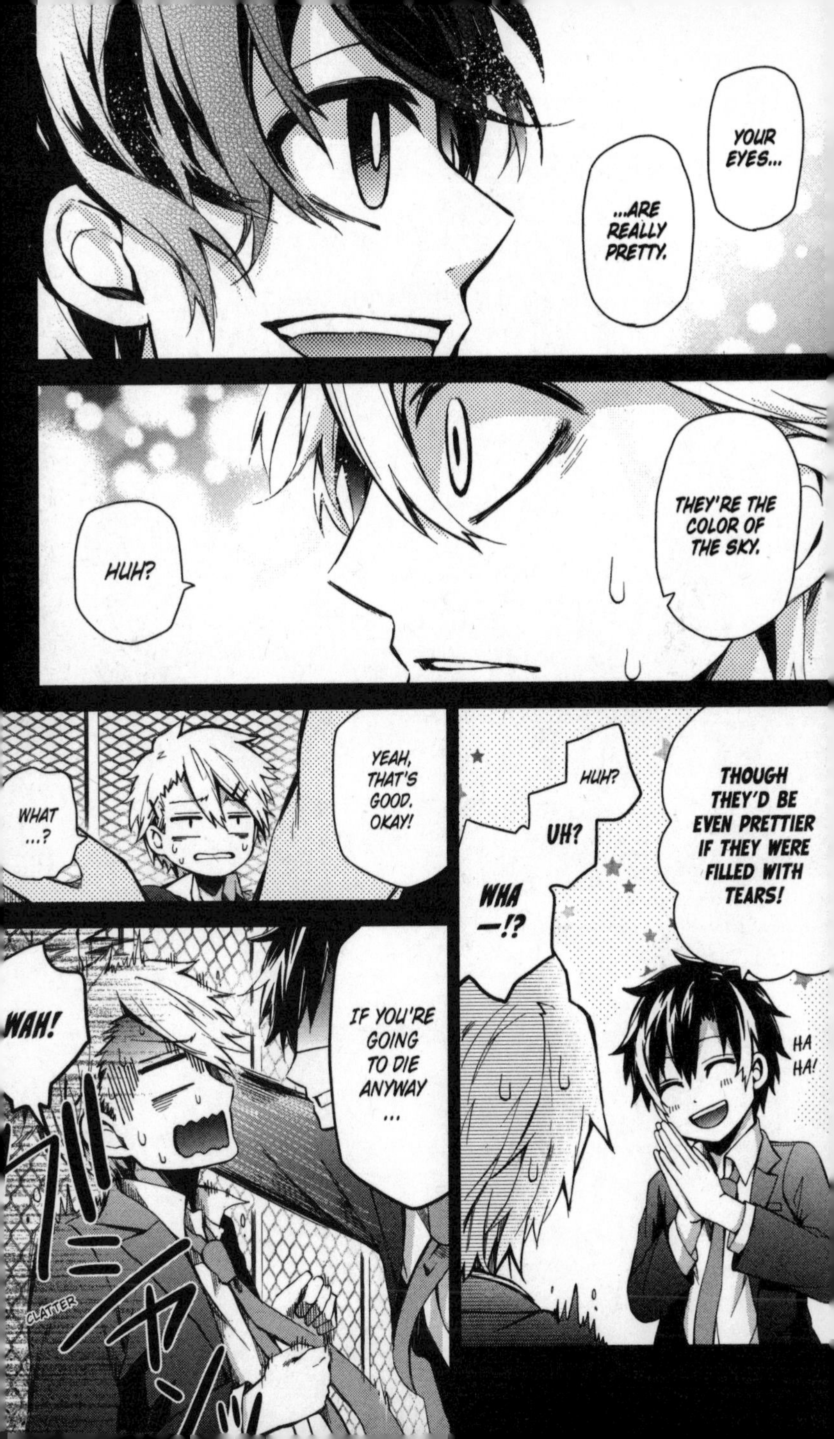
YOUR EYES...
...ARE REALLY PRETTY.
THEY'RE THE COLOR OF THE SKY.
HUH?
THOUGH THEY'D BE EVEN PRETTIER IF THEY WERE FILLED WITH TEARS!
HA HA!
HUH?
UH?
WHA—!?
YEAH, THAT'S GOOD. OKAY!
WHAT ...?
IF YOU'RE GOING TO DIE ANYWAY ...
WAH!
CLATTER

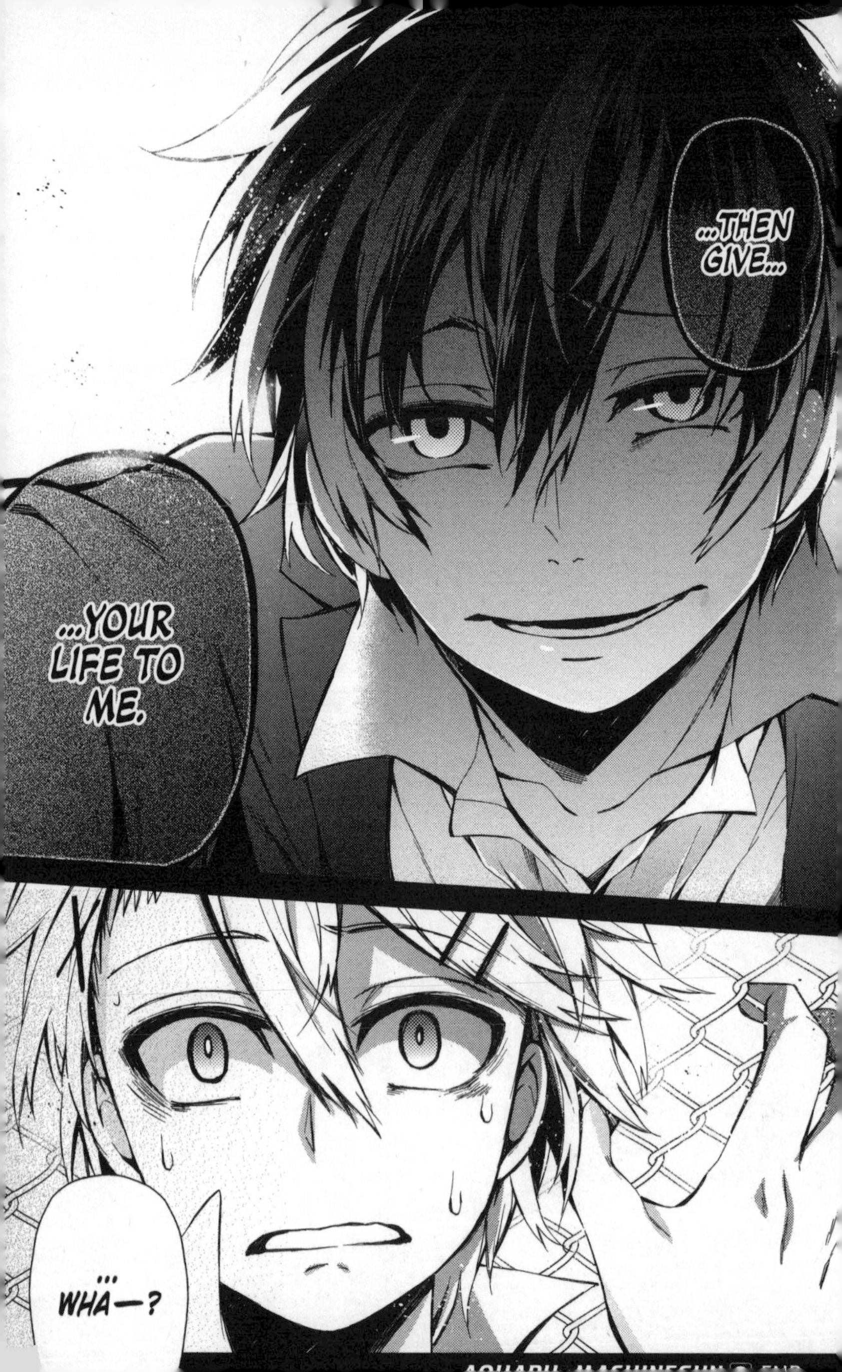
...THEN GIVE...
...YOUR LIFE TO ME.
... WHÄ—?

AOHARU

MACHINE
GUN

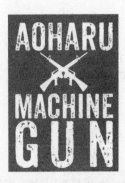

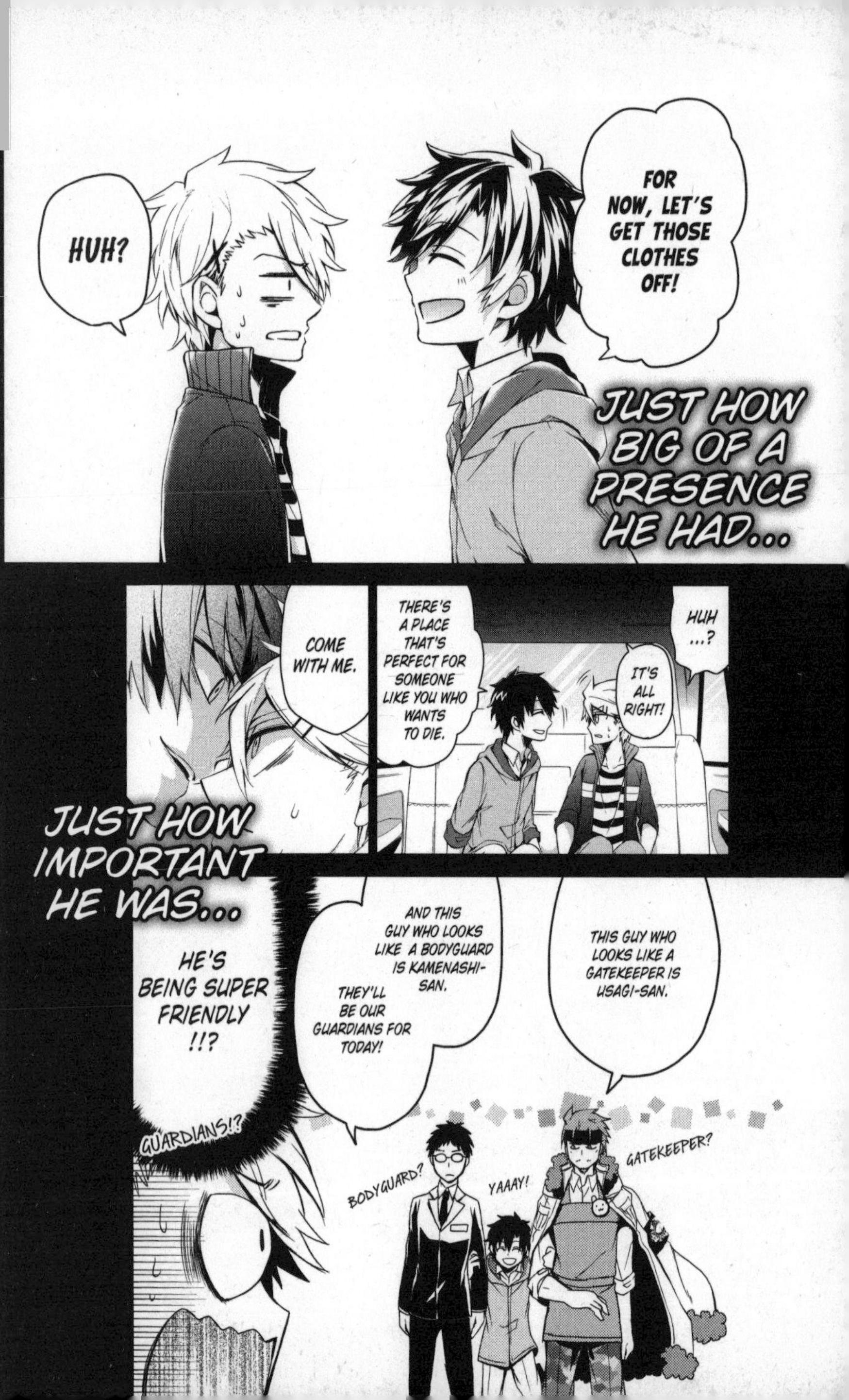
FOR NOW, LET'S GET THOSE CLOTHES OFF!
HUH?
JUST HOW BIG OF A PRESENCE HE HAD...
HUH ...?
IT'S ALL RIGHT!
THERE'S A PLACE THAT'S PERFECT FOR SOMEONE LIKE YOU WHO WANTS TO DIE.
COME WITH ME.
JUST HOW IMPORTANT HE WAS...
THIS GUY WHO LOOKS LIKE A GATEKEEPER IS USAGI-SAN.
AND THIS GUY WHO LOOKS LIKE A BODYGUARD IS KAMENASHI-SAN.
THEY'LL BE OUR GUARDIANS FOR TODAY!
GATEKEEPER?
YAAAY!
BODYGUARD?
HE'S BEING SUPER FRIENDLY !!?
GUARDIANS!?

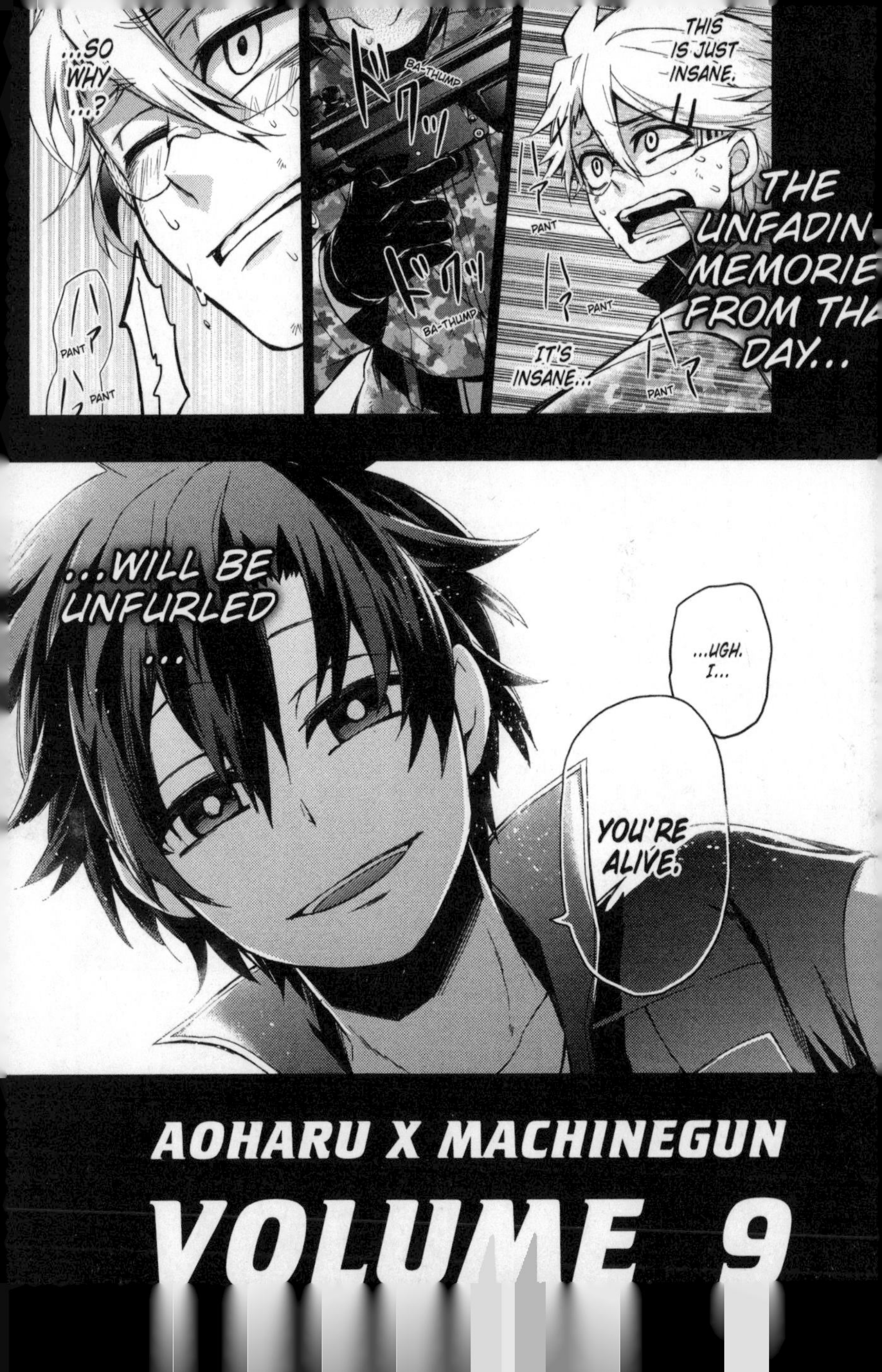

THIS IS JUST INSANE.
THE UNFADIN MEMORIE FROM THA DAY...
PANT
PANT
IT'S INSANE...
PANT
ドクッ
BA-THUMP
ドクッ
BA-THUMP
...SO WHY...?
PANT
PANT
...WILL BE UNFURLED...
...UGH. I...
YOU'RE ALIVE.

AOHARU X MACHINEGUN

VOLUME 9

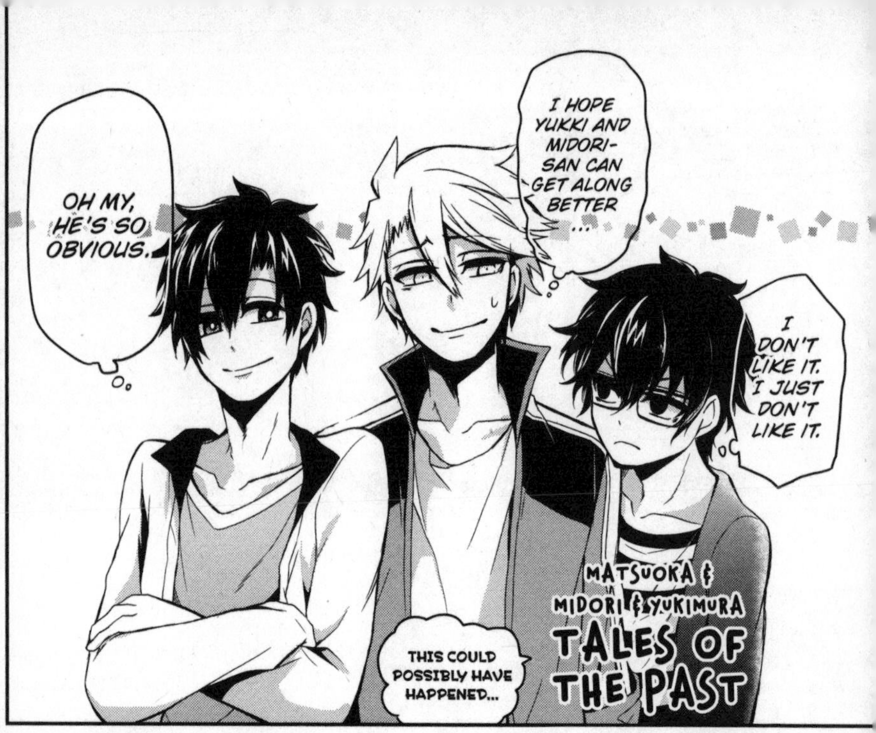
I HOPE YUKKI AND MIDORI-SAN CAN GET ALONG BETTER ...
I DON'T LIKE IT. I JUST DON'T LIKE IT.
OH MY, HE'S SO OBVIOUS.
MATSUOKA & MIDORI & YUKIMURA
TALES OF THE PAST
THIS COULD POSSIBLY HAVE HAPPENED...

AT THE BAR (WHEN THEY WERE STILL HANGING OUT TOGETHER)

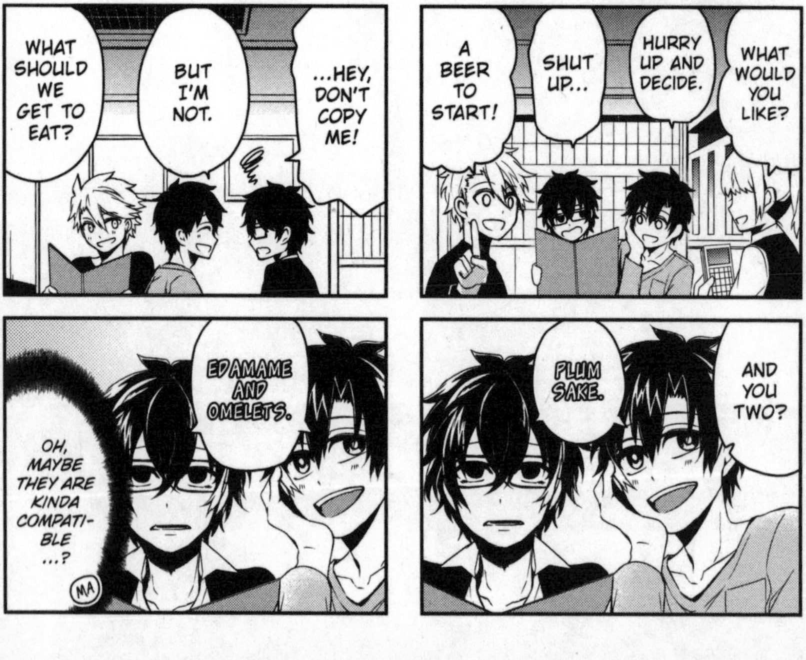
WHAT WOULD YOU LIKE?
HURRY UP AND DECIDE.
SHUT UP...
A BEER TO START!
...HEY, DON'T COPY ME!
BUT I'M NOT.
WHAT SHOULD WE GET TO EAT?
AND YOU TWO?
PLUM SAKE.
EDAMAME AND OMELETS.
OH, MAYBE THEY ARE KINDA COMPATI-BLE ...?
MA

THEY WENT TO THE ZOO. (WHAT WERE THEY GOING TO DO AS A GROUP OF THREE GUYS?)

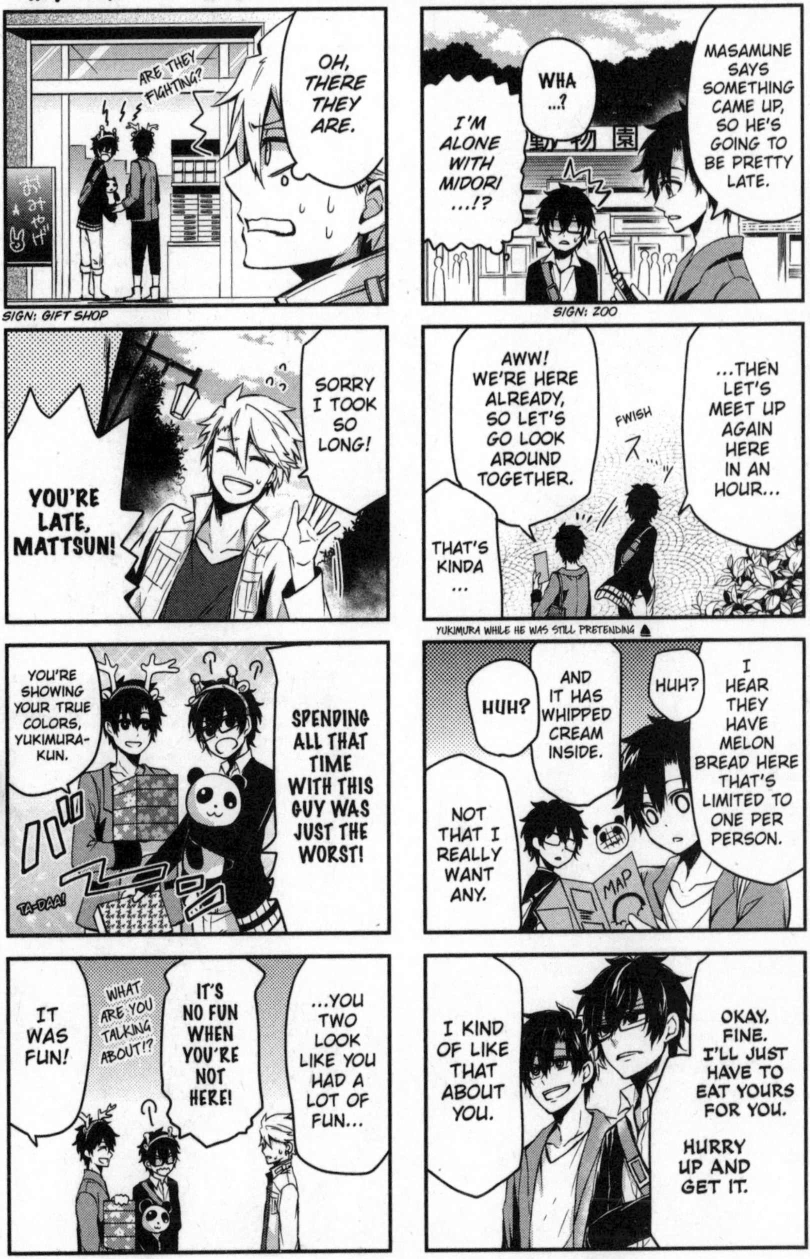

MASAMUNE SAYS SOMETHING CAME UP, SO HE'S GOING TO BE PRETTY LATE.
WHA...?
I'M ALONE WITH MIDORI...!?
SIGN: ZOO
...THEN LET'S MEET UP AGAIN HERE IN AN HOUR...
FWISH
AWW! WE'RE HERE ALREADY, SO LET'S GO LOOK AROUND TOGETHER.
THAT'S KINDA...
YUKIMURA WHILE HE WAS STILL PRETENDING
I HEAR THEY HAVE MELON BREAD HERE THAT'S LIMITED TO ONE PER PERSON.
HUH?
AND IT HAS WHIPPED CREAM INSIDE.
HUH?
NOT THAT I REALLY WANT ANY.
MAP
OKAY, FINE. I'LL JUST HAVE TO EAT YOURS FOR YOU.
HURRY UP AND GET IT.
I KIND OF LIKE THAT ABOUT YOU.
OH, THERE THEY ARE.
ARE THEY FIGHTING?
SIGN: GIFT SHOP
SORRY I TOOK SO LONG!
YOU'RE LATE, MATTSUN!
SPENDING ALL THAT TIME WITH THIS GUY WAS JUST THE WORST!
YOU'RE SHOWING YOUR TRUE COLORS, YUKIMURA-KUN.
TA-DAA!
GROWN MEN LETTING LOOSE
...YOU TWO LOOK LIKE YOU HAD A LOT OF FUN...
IT'S NO FUN WHEN YOU'RE NOT HERE!
WHAT ARE YOU TALKING ABOUT!?
IT WAS FUN!

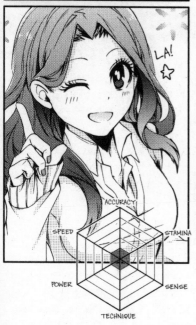

KANAE YAJIMA (♀) OCCUPATION: HIGH SCHOOL STUDENT

LA! ☆
ACCURACY
SPEED
STAMINA
POWER
SENSE
TECHNIQUE

- BIRTHDAY: 11/29
- HEIGHT/WEIGHT: 5' 1"/IT'S A SECRET! ☆
- BLOOD TYPE: B
- CLASS: SAME AS HOTARU

- FAVORITE THINGS: THINGS TO UP HER FEMININITY, PEOPLE WHO ARE COOL BOTH INSIDE AND OUT
- LEAST FAVORITE THINGS: BUGS, ONIONS, ALL SPORTS, TALKING ABOUT JUNIOR HIGH
- HOBBY: STUDYING HOW TO DO NAILS AND GROWN-UP MAKEUP
- SKILLS: DIETING
- FAMILY: FATHER, MOTHER, BROTHER (THREE YEARS YOUNGER)
- BEST DISH: ANYTHING LIKE MEAT AND POTATO STEW
- HER IDEAL MAN: SOMEONE KIND, COOL, GORGEOUS, MANLY, AND LIKE HOTARU

HANAKO SAGARA (♀) OCCUPATION: OFFICE WORKER

- BIRTHDAY: 9/7
- HEIGHT/WEIGHT: 5' 3"/106 LBS.
- BLOOD TYPE: A
- GUN USED: PS90 HC P90TR P90
- PLAYSTYLE: REAR GUARD ↑MAIN
- TEAM: NONE RIGHT NOW

- FAVORITE THINGS: ORDERING THINGS, ROMANCE GAMES
- LEAST FAVORITE THINGS: PEOPLE WHO DON'T TRY AT WORK
- HOBBY: WORKING OUT
- GOAL: SHE WANTS TO PARTICIPATE IN THE TGC.
- BEST DISH: PASTA
- HER IDEAL MAN: SOMEONE WHO WILL MAKE FIRM DECISIONS, LIKE A GUY FROM A ROMANCE GAME

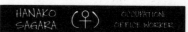

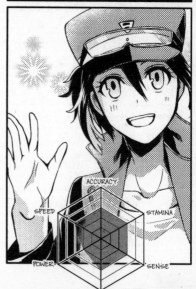

ACCURACY
SPEED
STAMINA
POWER
SENSE
TECHNIQUE

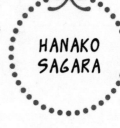

KANAE YAJIMA

SHE'S A CHARACTER WHO OFTEN SHOWS UP WHEN TACHIBANA GOES BACK TO HER EVERYDAY LIFE. SHE'S A SORT OF SYMBOL OF WHAT A HIGH SCHOOL GIRL IS LIKE OR WHAT A NORMAL PERSON IS LIKE, SO SHE'S VERY IMPORTANT AS A CONTRAST TO TACHIBANA. HER LOOKS ARE ALSO THE OPPOSITE OF TACHIBANA'S, SO I DELIBERATELY GAVE HER LONG HAIR, FULL EYELASHES, A SHORT SKIRT, AND LARGE BREASTS.

SINCE I WAS MAKING HER TACHIBANA'S OPPOSITE, MAYBE SOME PEOPLE THINK I SHOULD HAVE MADE HER SHY, BUT I THINK IT'S MORE CHARMING TO HAVE TACHIBANA GET DRAGGED AROUND BY HER PARTICULAR FEMININE SORT OF SELFISHNESS, AND I FIGURED HAVING THAT IN TACHIBANA'S EVERYDAY LIFE WOULD MAKE A GOOD CONTRAST...

IT'S PRETTY MUCH EXACTLY LIKE A BOYFRIEND GETTING DRAGGED AROUND BY HIS GIRLFRIEND, YEAH.
(*THOUGH TACHIBANA'S A GIRL.)

HER NAME IS FROM HIDEYUKI YAJIMA'S DAUGHTER, THE SECOND WIFE OF MUNESHIGE TACHIBANA.

HANAKO SAGARA

ONE OF THE FEMALE SURVIVAL GAMERS WHO MADE AN APPEARANCE AT THE SERIES' FIRST REGULAR TOURNEY—I GAVE HER A BOTH SPORTY AND FEMININE LOOK TO TRY TO SHOW THAT WOMEN DO THIS TOO. (THOUGH RATHER THAN HAVING FEMININITY, IT'S MORE LIKE SHE JUST HAS BREASTS.) THERE ARE FEMALE SURVIVAL GAMERS WHO ARE ALSO SUPER CHATTY AND STUFF, BUT SAGARA IS THE SORT OF CHIVALROUS ADULT WOMAN WHO EVEN THE MEN CALL "CAPTAIN." (ALMOST LIKE YOU'D WANT TO CALL HER ONEE-SAN.)

ON ONE HAND, HER TWO TGC COMPETITOR COWORKERS WHO SHOWED UP IN VOLUME FIVE, YUKAWA AND MIKISABUROU, HAVE FEELINGS FOR HER, WHICH SHE DOESN'T NOTICE AT ALL, BUT SHE ALSO HAS A GIRLY SIDE THAT WANTS A LOVE LIFE LIKE THE ONES IN ROMANCE GAMES (OTOME GAMES). SOMEDAY I WANT TO DRAW HER AS AN OFFICE WORKER!

HER NAME COMES FROM SOUZOU SAGARA, THE CAPTAIN OF THE SEKIHOUTAI.

Thank yOu♡

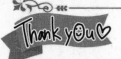

MY EDITOR, THE EDITOR-IN-CHIEF,
THE SALES STAFF, THE DESIGNERS

TOKYO MARUI, DEKA SHIMAMURA-SAMA, THE AKIHABARA BRANCH OF WILLYPEET, HIRANO-SAMA

[HELP RESEARCHING]
AUTO-CAMP UNION-SAMA
SURVIVAL FIELD UNION—UNION BASE-SAMA

[LAYER SEPARATION] KOMINA-SAMA

[EMBLEM DESIGN] SHISHIHIME-SAMA

[BACKGROUNDS AND FINISHING ASSISTANTS]
BUNJI-SAMA
WAKA SANADA (DOKUGANRYUU)-SAMA
SHIRASE (HITLER)-SAMA

MY FATHER, MY MOTHER, MY BROTHER, AND YOU!

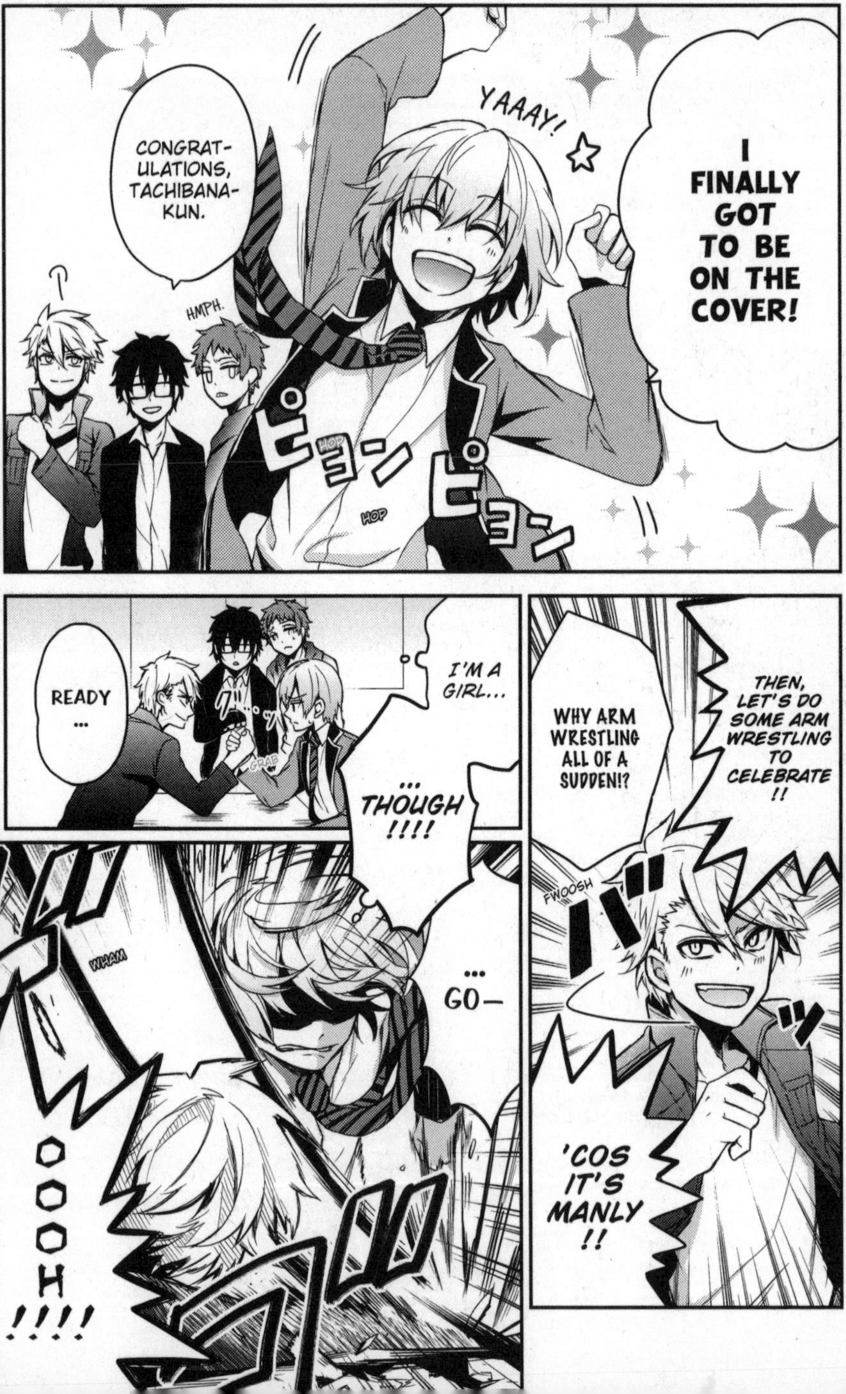
I FINALLY GOT TO BE ON THE COVER!
YAAAY! ☆
ピョン
HOP
ピョン
HOP
HMPH.
CONGRAT-ULATIONS, TACHIBANA-KUN.
THEN, LET'S DO SOME ARM WRESTLING TO CELEBRATE!!
WHY ARM WRESTLING ALL OF A SUDDEN!?
FWOOSH
'COS IT'S MANLY!!
I'M A GIRL...
...THOUGH!!!!
GRAB
READY ...
... GO—
WHAM
OOOOH!!!!

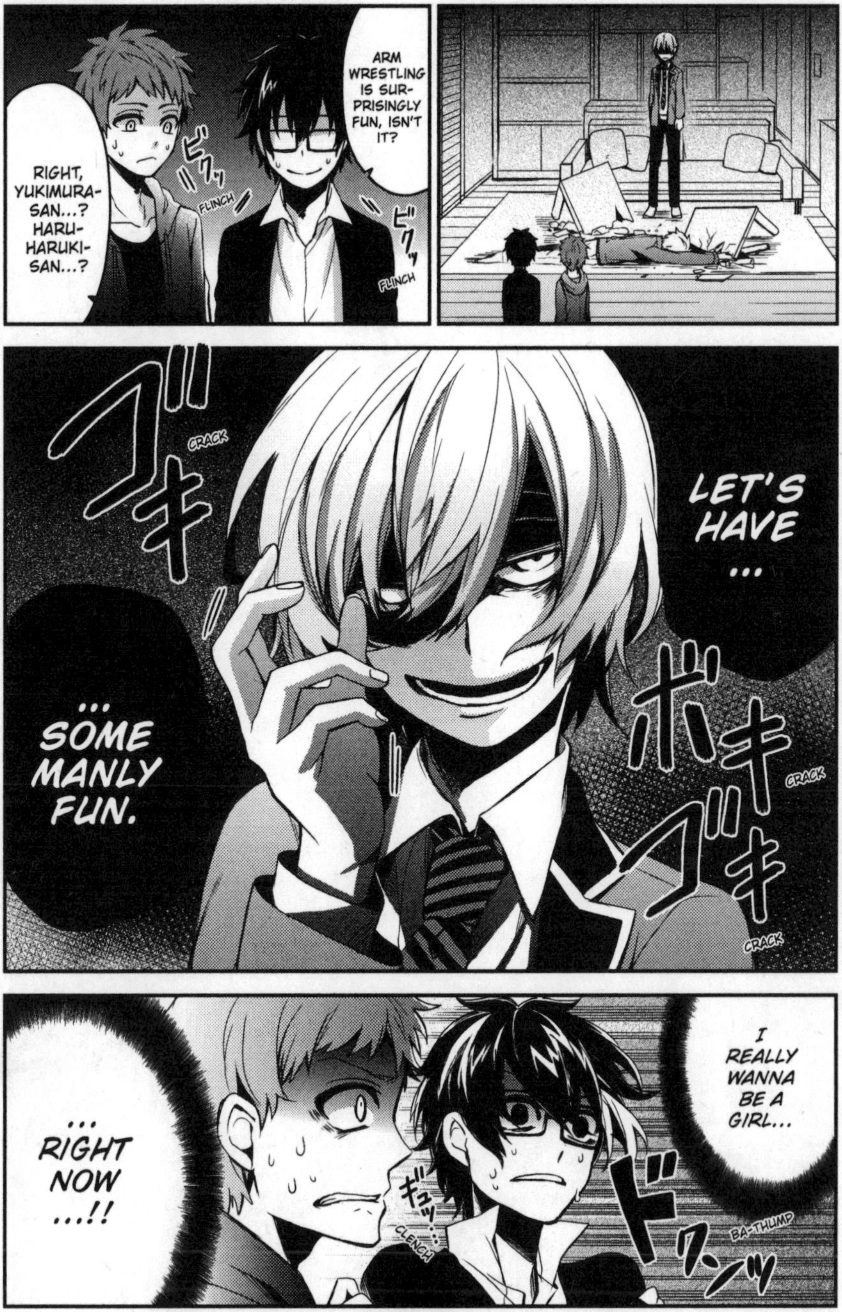
ARM WRESTLING IS SURPRISINGLY FUN, ISN'T IT?
ビクッ
FLINCH
ビクッ
FLINCH
RIGHT, YUKIMURA-SAN...? HARU-HARUKI-SAN...?
LET'S HAVE...
ボキ
CRACK
ゴキ
CRACK
ゴキ
CRACK
...SOME MANLY FUN.
I REALLY WANNA BE A GIRL...
ドクンッ
BA-THUMP
ギュッ...
CLENCH
...RIGHT NOW...!!

IS THEIR TIME FINALLY UP...!!? TO BE...PROBABLY NOT CONTINUED.

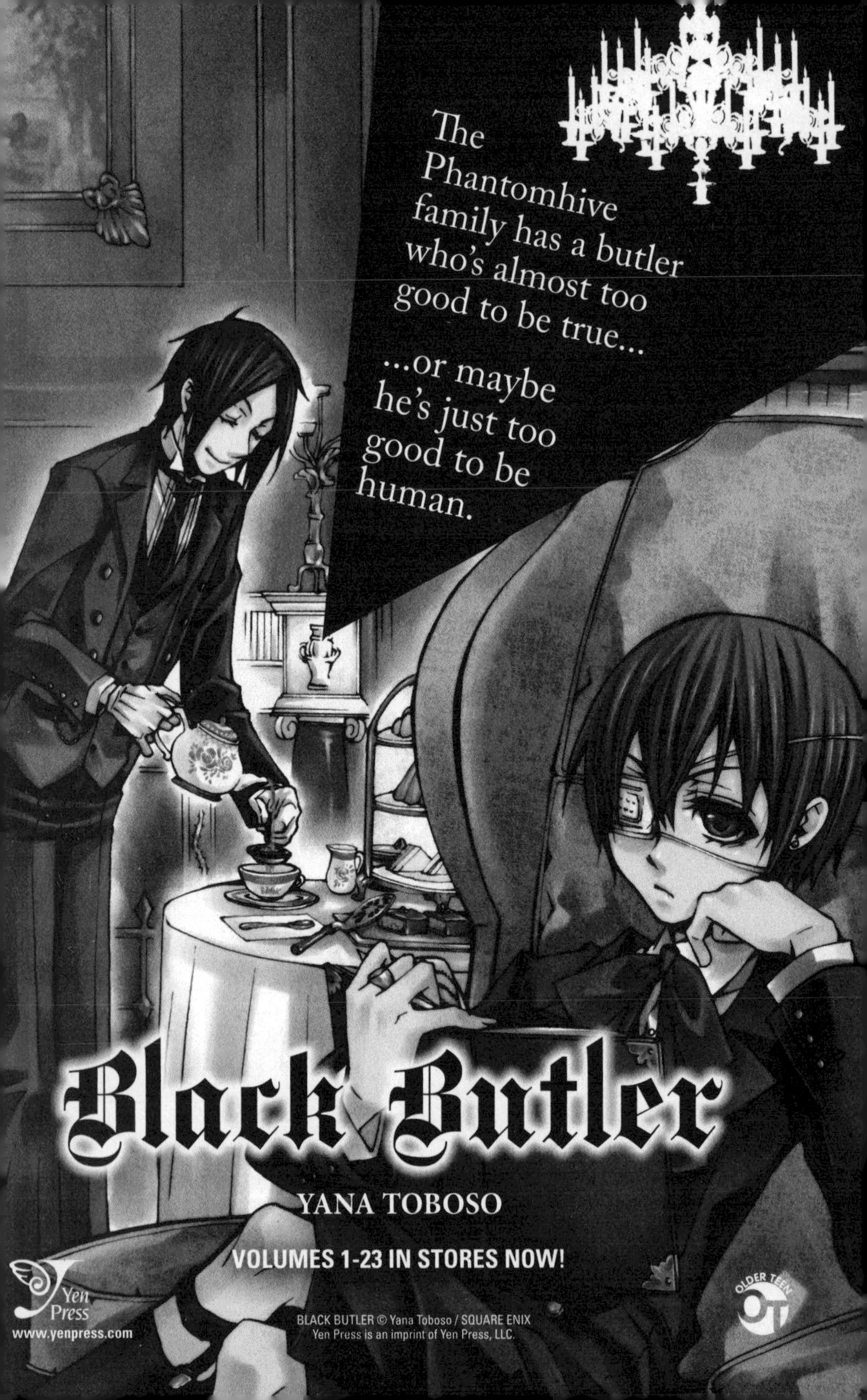
The Phantomhive family has a butler who's almost too good to be true...
...or maybe he's just too good to be human.
Black Butler
YANA TOBOSO
VOLUMES 1-23 IN STORES NOW!
Yen Press
www.yenpress.com
BLACK BUTLER © Yana Toboso / SQUARE ENIX
Yen Press is an imprint of Yen Press, LLC.
OLDER TEEN
OT

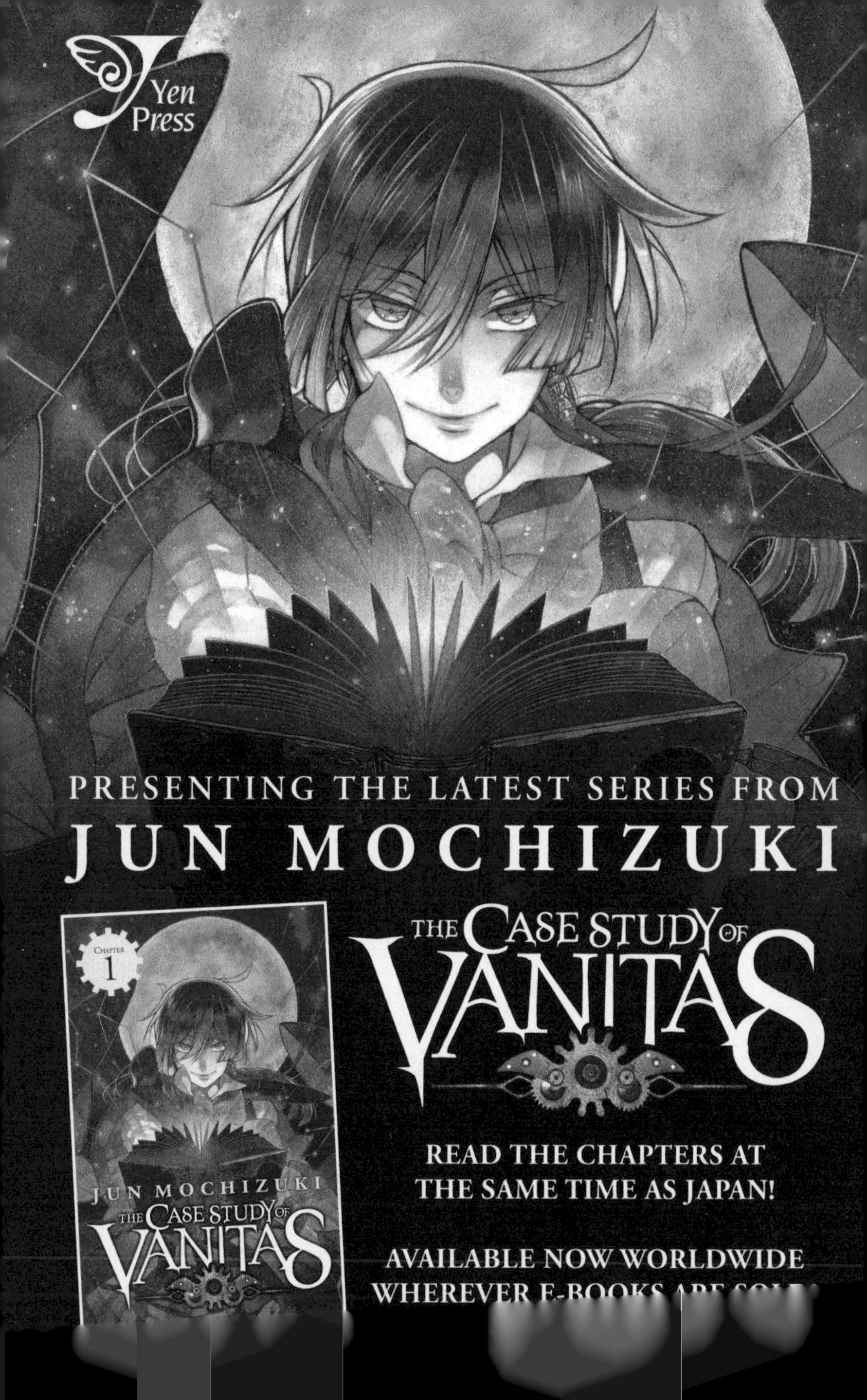
Yen Press
PRESENTING THE LATEST SERIES FROM
JUN MOCHIZUKI
CHAPTER 1
JUN MOCHIZUKI
THE CASE STUDY OF VANITAS
THE CASE STUDY OF VANITAS
READ THE CHAPTERS AT THE SAME TIME AS JAPAN!
AVAILABLE NOW WORLDWIDE
WHEREVER E-BOOKS

by NAOE

Translation: Leighann Harvey
Lettering: Bianca Pistillo

AOHARU×KIKANJU Volume 8 ©2015 NAOE/ SQUARE ENIX CO., LTD. First published in Japan in 2015 by SQUARE ENIX CO., LTD. English translation rights arranged with SQUARE ENIX CO., LTD. and Yen Press, LLC through Tuttle-Mori Agency, Inc., Tokyo.

English Translation ©2017 by SQUARE ENIX CO., LTD.

Yen Press
1290 Avenue of the Americas
New York, NY 10104

Visit us at yenpress.com
facebook.com/yenpress
twitter.com/yenpress
yenpress.tumblr.com
instagram.com/yenpress

First Yen Press Print Edition: December 2017
Originally published as an ebook in February 2017 by Yen Press.

Yen Press is an imprint of Yen Press, LLC.
The Yen Press name and logo are trademarks of Yen Press, LLC.

The publisher is not responsible for websites (or their content) that are not owned by the publisher.

Library of Congress Control Number: 2016946057

ISBN: 978-0-316-43571-0 (paperback)

10 9 8 7 6 5 4 3 2 1

BVG

Printed in the United States of America